INTERDISCIPLINARY ANALYSIS AND RESEARCH

Theory and Practice of Problem-Focused

Research and Development

Daryl E. Chubin
Alan L. Porter
Frederick A. Rossini
Terry Connolly
editors

1986

LOMOND

Library of Congress Catalog Number: 85-082057

ISBN: 0-912338-53-9 (Clothbound)
0-912338-54-7 (Microfiche)

Printed in the United States of America

Published by
Lomond Publications, Inc.
P.O. Box 88
Mt. Airy, Maryland 21771

*To those who coaxed us to go
beyond discipline. . .*

TABLE OF CONTENTS*

---

* Authors' identification is as of the time of original publication.

PART I

STATE OF THE ART
AND ITS APPLICATION

1

INTERDISCIPLINARY RESEARCH: THE WHY AND THE HOW

Daryl E. Chubin
Alan L. Porter
Frederick A. Rossini

About Research Processes

Anybody who does research wonders occasionally, usually not aloud, about the process itself. In the course of collaboration, we began to share our private curiosity about research processes, and wondered why nobody had assembled the literature on "interdisciplinary research" (IDR). After all, such collaboration had long become common, though not dominant, in science and engineering. Surely there should be an introduction written primarily for the researcher, manager, and student, and, secondarily, for the layperson, to explain the "nuts and bolts" of IDR—what it is, how it is done, and why it produces important scientific knowledge.

Convinced of the "why" for a book on IDR, our thoughts turned to "how." The components we envisioned included an elementary introduction to the subject, more sophisticated than a primer but less intimidating than a monograph. Given the scope of the literature to encompass, we also decided to compile and excerpt a selection of primary materials written by respected professionals in academic, industrial, and public settings. To complement these sections, a bibliography of sources annotated to reveal content and provide guidance seemed essential. Thus, in the spirit of demonstrating IDR as a valuable alternative to disciplinary approaches in the solution of research problems, we crafted a book of original ideas, our synthesis of others' ideas, and a comprehensive listing of publications for readers to consult and evaluate for their own purposes.

Utility will be the ultimate measure of this book's success. It must motivate its readers to convert "private curiosity" into shared, and therefore, public forms of study, debate, and sustained communication with peers as well as with future generations of researchers. For IDR to flourish, this book cannot be left on a library shelf. No, the craft must be practiced, refined, applied again and again to the problems that torment researchers regardless of their discipline, methodology, or purpose. IDR is a resource which must be nurtured like any other; it needs traditions and adherents. But most of all, IDR needs PRACTITIONERS—in schools of business/management and of medicine, in departments of social science and of engineering, in corporate offices of strategic planning and government R&D laboratories, wherever multi-skill, problem-focused research is done.

Four researchers wondering about research processes now issue an invitation to learning about how IDR gets done. In the remainder of this introduction, we outline one framework for understanding IDR and the processes it entails. Several other frameworks will be encountered elsewhere. All create research dreams, and all merit serious consideration.

Definitions and Difficulties*

Research dreams, of course, are built empirically. As studies of research processes have multiplied, so too have the number predicated on the belief that IDR is the appropriate mode to attack many challenging research problems. Interest in the study of IDR grew as many saw problems of great intellectual and societal interest cut across scholarly and professional disciplines. In those instances, disciplines appear dull and useless. But while "discipline" is a convenient scapegoat, it is, after all, intrinsic to "interdisciplinarity."

Most definitions of IDR stress the interactions among component disciplines. Intellectually, however, disciplines represent historical, evolutionary aggregates of shared scholarly interests. These aggregates gain legitimacy in the university as "departments." As organizational niches, departments bureaucratize knowledge by subject matter and

---

* This section and the one that follows are based on A. L. Porter and F. A. Rossini, "Interdisciplinary Research Redefined: Multi-skill, Problem-focussed Research in the STRAP Framework."*R&D Management* 14 (1984): 105-111. Illustrations and hypotheses derived from the authors' recent empirical study of NSF-supported IDR projects are omitted here. The reader is encouraged to consult the original article for details.

stake a claim to research and train students in it. But abstract knowledge cannot be so readily pigeon-holed. And so individuals with disciplinary degrees occasionally develop, as their careers unfold, "impure" or "hybrid" backgrounds and interests. One of the authors of this book has a PhD in physics, an academic appointment in philosophy, and a primary research commitment to various facets of technology and science policy. Were he collaborating with a sociologist (as he is), would that constitute interdisciplinarity? What if his coworker were a physicist?

If our labels sometimes prevent conceptualization, then consider IDR in another way. Must IDR always involve more than one person? In a paper reproduced here, Taylor argues that the individual interdisciplinarian, the "ideal polymath," is only a construct. Such a person, he insists, cannot exist. Perhaps this is academic hubris again. If we look beyond the academy to the industrial and government laboratory, we may find that confounded intellectual and organizational arrangements are not atypical. The fit among credentialed individual, organizational setting, and research problem is far more complicated than even the student of IDR has been willing to admit.

The willingness to admit ignorance and formulate alternative approaches are just two characteristics of IDR collaboration. These can be strengths or impediments, but making them explicit is key. In that vein, we offer at the outset a reconceptualization of IDR, the STRAP Framework.

The STRAP Framework

Our central assumption is the problem dominance of research. By this we mean that every research project is designed to solve a problem that is bounded, to some degree, by disciplinary concerns, societal interests, etc. Our emphasis is on problems that require complex intellectual and/or organizational solutions.

We have considered several alternatives to the notion of discipline. The one we favor is "intellectual skills." We distinguish between two types of skills: substantive knowledge and techniques. Substantive knowledge is about something (e.g., molecules containing carbon, bees, the Politburo), while techniques are systematic approaches to the generation and production of knowledge (e.g., regression analysis, particle acceleration, neural recording). Many techniques can be used to study the same substantive area, while many substantive areas can be illuminated by the same technique. To utilize these concepts they must be operationalized to replace the unwieldy "discipline."

Briefly, substantive area can be operationally described by identifying a subject of knowledge to which a research community can relate. The area can be broad or narrow, but it must be sufficiently limited that an individual can maintain in-depth competence. While this description leaves gray areas, it is a first approximation. A technique, on the other hand, can be operationalized as a physical and/or cognitive procedure that may result in the generation or transformation of knowledge. A technique must also allow for individual expertise as well as being demonstrably useful in the solution of at least some class of research problems.

The relation between intellectual skills and disciplines appears to be complex. The substantive areas and techniques encompassed by disciplines have changed markedly over time. Certain substantive areas and techniques may be involved in several disciplines, whereas any particular discipline typically incorporates a range of substantive areas and techniques into its ongoing research programs.

In our own work, we have distinguished between high and low levels of expertise in substantive areas and techniques. A high level of expertise qualifies as "state of the art," the ability to make original contributions to develop the intellectual skill, e.g., in the literature. The low level of expertise represents comprehension and the ability to use and communicate the basic features of the intellectual skill in question; this is "textbook" or technician-level expertise.

Table 1 presents a typology of research problem dimensions constructed to illustrate the complex requirements we have attached to IDR. We begin with the identification of substantive areas, S, and techniques, T, involved in the project. The depth of knowledge required is denoted for each by capitalization for high level and lower case for low.

In addition, we have selected three other fundamental variables that emerge from our studies of IDR. The first variable is the range, R, of the intellectual skills required for the problem. R is partitioned into three categories: (1) all skills are found in a single established research area; (2) skills are only found in more than one research area, but represent the same broad intellectual area (e.g., physical sciences, life

Table 1 Multiskill, problem-focused research dimensions

S	*Substantive Knowledge* Elements Needed	
	—'Frontier professional' Understanding Required	S_1
	—'Journeyman, textbook' Understanding Sufficient	s_1
T	*Technique* Needed	
	—'Expert' Level Needed	T_1
	—'Technician' Level Sufficient	t_1
R	*Range*	
	where subscripts to S and T:	
	i = A, B, C implies these routinely reside within an established research area;	R_1^1
	i = D, E, F (as well as A, B, or C) implies these draw from research areas other than A, B, C, but within the same broad intellectual area	R_2
	i = X, Y, Z (as well as A, B, or C) implies these are associated with research areas notably different from A, B, C.	R_3
A	*Administrative Unit Complexity*	
	—Single unit	A_1
	—multiple, linked units (report to the same higher administrator)	A_2
	—multiple, dispersed units	A_3
P	*Personnel*	
	—Single individual	P_1^-
	—Quasi-Permanent Team (e.g., a lab)	P_2
	—Ad Hoc Project Team	P_3

Source: Porter and Rossini, 1984: 107

sciences, or social sciences); and (3) skills are from diverse research areas that cross the boundaries of broad intellectual areas (e.g., engineering and law, humanistic and behavioral psychology). The final two variables are administrative complexity, A, and personnel, P. These variables are straightforward both conceptually and operationally.

A research project can be described by the STRAP variables with an enumeration of S and T, and values for R, A, and P. As the subscripts of the RAP variables in Table 1 increase, the project which is described moves from relative simplicity to complexity. The STRAP framework, we believe, provides promise as an alternative to most work that takes as its point of departure the interaction among disciplines. The multi-skill emphasis directs attention to the project as a unit of analysis and more explicitly to the "ingredients" of successful research. Furthermore, it opens a broad range of personnel configurations to be considered in the management of such research, especially the single investigator model that is no longer precluded a priori. By deemphasizing disciplinarity, we can accommodate an impressive array of intellectual and organizational factors. At the very least, this should make the STRAP framework more relevant to industrial and governmental research.

Underlying the development of STRAP is our realization that many intellectual areas impinge on our understanding of multi-skill, problem-focused research (including R&D management), research on interdisciplinary research processes, the study of complex problem-solving, the sociology of knowledge, and the organizational behavior of scientific institutions. We have structured the contents of this book to trigger other "realizations," alternative formulations, and claims to knowledge. To enhance the effort, we now showcase, through a sample of diverse literatures, accounts of the performance, evaluation, and interpretation of IDR.

Organization of the Book

The excerpted papers that we have selected for reproduction here are organized into five sections. Each corresponds to a question which researchers are likely to ask: why, who, where, what, and how?

We seek to tell you first WHY IDR should be done. Six authors give their rationales. The message strikes at a common theme despite some disparate emphases: Disciplines may be necessary; they are not sufficient for solving "undisciplined problems" (Rose). Disciplines "differentiate" as knowledge demands (Hagstrom). They also become self-perpetuating and therefore "ethnocentric" (Campbell), and somewhat obsolete if not "arbitrary" (Birnbaum). In all, interdisciplinarity is a "dialectical" process with its own rhetoric (Klein) and organizational challenges (Hattery).

Then we must examine WHO performs IDR. Since teams are composed of individuals, there is need for recruitment. "Team-building" (Taylor) is a process whereby special researchers (Anbar), or those with special needs are brought together, e.g., to see the world in a particular way (Petrie) or to communicate with the unlike-minded (Wilbanks). If they mesh, then IDR may be the appropriate label; if they do not, then vintage adjectives such as "multidisciplinary" (Blackwell) apply.

No examination of process is complete without a comparable view of its context. WHERE IDR is performed is a multifaceted question. Some teams span nations (Wilpert), while most span divisions with a single cultural unit (Long). The most popular, and most nettlesome, is the university. Orientations there rigidify to frustrate administrators (Saxberg, et al.), transform departments (Rossini, et al.), and threaten the status quo of organizational form (Teich). Accommodating these modifications to research definition, practice, and rewards (Williams, et al.) is never easy and often unsatisfactory to all concerned. Context can clearly affect the quality or perception of content.

Among the many case examples of IDR, the content of the problems researched is diverse and far-reaching. The WHAT of IDR illustrates that its domain is the natural as well as the social sciences, engineering and the humanities. Its aliases range from "impact assessment" (Burdge and Opryzek) to "applied sociology" (Berk). Its foci include pharmaceuticals (Stucki), integrated circuits (Jones), forestry (Barmark and Wallen), agricultural economics (Swanson), and climate (Chen). In all these narrative accounts, the authors report self-consciously about their experiences in a project supposedly facilitated by an IDR team.

Finally, the lessons of IDR are summarized by those who have studied it as well as those who have lived it. Pedagogical styles vary from down-to-earth "HOW-to's" (Cassell) to literature reviews (MacDonald) and lectures on essential elements, e.g., inevitable intellectual hierarchy (Chubin, et al.), the resolution of conflicts (Bella and Williamson), management options (Bass), integration of project pieces (Rossini, et al.), and the transcendent ordering function of "interfield theories" (Darden and Maull). The sum of these excerpts is a prospectus on fruitful lines of inquiry and outstanding issues of policy significance begging for attention.

For those eager to survey the literature on IDR themselves, we have provided a 147-item bibliography with annotations. These items are, in a sense, the raw data of this book. They are provided so that each reader, in his or her own way, can sample and digest IDR further. The pace and longevity of the "banquet" will depend upon appetite, fortitude, and ultimate purpose (e.g., teaching vs. research). To guide you through the various courses, we have prepared a menu of sorts, a bibliographic essay that presents some qualitative and quantitative patterns in the literature we have retrieved. It derives, or if you prefer, imposes some order on 30 years of titles, sources, and findings. It tries to answer the question of recognition and interpretation: How do we know what is IDR?

A concluding essay by Julie Thompson Klein, a professor of humanities at Wayne State University, is offered as an antidote to our collective myopia. Toward the end of our search, we fortuitously encountered a kindred soul dwelling in another kingdom, that of the Association of Integrative Studies. So we invited her to complete the journey with us by supplying an independent assessment of what she sees when she looks at IDR. She graciously complied and in doing so grants us a fresh perspective on "The Broad Scope of Interdisciplinarity." In cataloging intellectual and organizational "movements" of IDR, Klein steals the last scene, so to speak, in our dream of interdisciplinarity (Book 1). We applaud her effort and await her own sequel which currently is in preparation.

PART II

WHY IS IDR IMPORTANT?

2

INTERDISCIPLINARY RESEARCH MANAGEMENT*

Lowell H. Hattery

Background

Interdisciplinary research has taken on continuously greater significance, as a function of the complexity of societal and scientific problems insoluble by single disciplines and single experts. Policy decisions, whether public or private, almost universally involve matters in the domains of several disciplines. Such decisions need to be buttressed by interdisciplinary studies. Fundamental research also generally intersects theory, methodology and data from more than a single discipline.

The distinctive characteristic of IDR is generally identified as *an integrative research process which takes place among researchers with different disciplinary backgrounds*. In contrast, "multidisciplinary" and "polydisciplinary" do not connote the continuous integrative communication and accommodation processes as subsumed in "interdisciplinary."

Attention to the *management* of interdisciplinary research has tended to diverge into two relatively separate areas of concern - *external management* which includes such matters as selection of personnel, organizational structure, organizational interfaces; and *internal management* which includes such matters as project planning, supervision and coordination, team communication, and evaluation of performance. Most reported research on interdisciplinary research

* Adapted from a paper presented at the First International Conference on Interdisciplinary Research Groups held at Schloss Reisenberg, Federal Republic of Germany (1979) and printed in the proceedings, *International Research Groups: Their Management and Organization* (Richard T. Barth and Rudy Steck, editors). Much of the background work for this article was performed as a part of the RMI Program evaluation project supported by a grant from the National Science Foundation to American University. The author was Principal Investigator for that project.

(IDR) management has been targeted primarily on external management.

Although much general management research has been devoted to internal management (e.g., small group relationships and effectiveness), the findings are seldom differentiated by function. Findings from such generalized research *may* be applicable to IDR, but of this there is no adequate demonstration or proof. Furthermore, the differences between the small group research function and other functions are sufficient as to throw into question all generalized management assumptions.

Classification of IDR Management

The elements of the generic topic of the Management of Interdisciplinary Research (MIDR) can be classified and arrayed according to various schema. The most obvious schema are built under the subtopics of:

—ORGANIZATION (including institutional arrangements);

—MANAGEMENT (including both macro and micro aspects);

—ADMINISTRATION (relating especially to support, e.g., accounting and auditing); and

—RESEARCH PROCESS (from project definition to evaluation, dissemination and utilization of output).

Confusion in approaches to IDR and the management of IDR is frequently the result of failure to differentiate significant differences in the nature of the research, scale, performing institutions, organizational arrangements, sponsorship, time-frame, etc.

Much of IDR is performed in the universities—but even among universities there are essential differences: e.g., state v. private, large v. small, traditional v. non-traditional, theoretical v. applied, graduate emphasis v. undergraduate emphasis, rich v. poor, well-managed v. less-well-managed.

Those who are studying the management of IDR, or undertaking the sponsorship of IDR, or monitoring and evaluating IDR and MIDR should be sensitive to institutional/situational variables such as those cited. It is useful to prepare a checklist of those variables which are relevant to the mission (sponsorship, evaluation, etc.) for comparative analysis or for ad hoc guidance and decision. An approach to such a checklist is presented in Exhibit I.

Checklist of Differentiating Elements for PERFORMERS of IDR

Descriptor	Variables
Type of Institution	Public university
	Private university
	Not-for-profit research
	Consultant
	Industry/Business
	Other
Tradition	Disciplinary
	Interdisciplinary
	Stable, static organization
	Flexible, dynamic organization
	Other
Size	Large, well-staffed
	Medium
	Small, need to recruit for projects
	Other
Leadership	Stable
	High turnover
	Management-oriented
	Research, science-oriented
	Other

Checklist of Differentiating Elements in IDR PROGRAMS AND PROJECTS

Descriptors	Variables
Nature of Research	Basic, fundamental
	Applied
	Developmental
Scale	Large - over $1 million/year
	Medium - $250,000 - $1 million
	Small - under $250,000
Degree of Disciplinarity	One dominant discipline
	Hard and soft sciences
	Hard sciences only
	Soft sciences only
Time Frame	One-year completion
	1- to 3-year program
	Long-term program

EXHIBIT I

This paper is directed to *unfulfilled needs for research on the management of interdisciplinary research*. It rests on a state-of-the-art assessment of what is known about the management of IDR, and is based specifically on: (1) general review of the relevant literature; (2) findings from related projects supported by the National Science Foundation Research Management Improvement Program; (3) participation in conferences concerned with the issue (especially conferences conducted by the American Association for the Advancement of Science and Stanford University); and (4) consultation with many individuals who are thoughtful about the subject.

Research Needs

Research needs in IDR management can be expressed in several ways, e.g.,

Theory to be conceptualized and stated

Hypotheses to be tested

Sectors, topics to be investigated

Data to be collected, arranged, and analyzed

Findings to be evaluated

We have for a number of reasons taken the topical approach, without assuming that this is the most valid. It is the product of a review of the resource material. It is also what would seem to be most immediately useful to sponsors of IDR, and others related to the process.

Some generalizations illustrative of those which should be included in such a theory, and to which research support should be related, are:

1. It is important to foster and nurture interdisciplinary research and interdisciplinary educational programs.

2. Individual faculty members are personally committed to interdisciplinarity in principle.

3. However, power politics in the university environment are hostile to the very existence of interdisciplinary programs. These programs are natural targets for attack or neglect in the university power struggle.

4. This is one of the reasons why research is separated out from the basic university structure into semi-independent research institutes or foundations.

5. This separation arrangement, however, tends to seal off the potential benefit of a research program as enrichment to the educational program.

6. There are many lacunae of knowledge about IDR, and selective support should be targeted to build a better base for understanding, planning, operation, and management of IDR.

Themes and Topics for Research

Derived from the background input as described above from the literature, twenty problems or topics are recommended for research support.

These topics are grouped under seven "themes," and are presented in the following arrangement:

A. Sponsor Role
    1. Sponsor monitorship
    2. Seed money and IDR
    3. Serialization of research
    4. Agendas for IDR
B. University organization
    5. Disciplinary organization of the universities
    6. Research institutes
    7. Effects of tenure and research
C. Other organizations
    8. IDR in the think tanks
D. Education and training
    9. Opportunities for education for ID thinking

      10.   ID education for research
      11.   IDR as educational experience
  E. Operational management
      12.   Characteristics of the IDR team
      13.   IDR leader as facilitator
      14.   Reducing "startup" time for IDR projects
  F. Dissemination and utilization
      15.   Dissemination of results of research on IDR
           management
      16.   Journal outlets for IDR outputs and peer
           recognition
      17.   Utilization of IDR
  G. Evaluation
      18.   Evaluation of IDR
      19.   Resistance to evaluation
      20.   The beatitude and the reality
  H. Historical Studies
      21.   Historical studies of IDR

The set of research topics recommended for priority attention by sponsoring agencies is presented below.

A. SPONSOR ROLE

The role of the sponsor is obviously important in planning and selecting research to be supported. Importance of the roles of monitoring, quality control, leadership, motivation, evaluation and dissemination is not so clear. We believe the latter are significant responsibilities of sponsors, varying in method and emphasis with the circumstances.

We note, however, that little research attention has been given to the role of R&D sponsors with the possible exception of the very special matter of peer review for project selection.

1. *Sponsor Monitorship*

Sponsor monitorship of both grant and contract research has been a highly confused and disputed matter, marked with variation in practice, misunderstandings, and sometimes conflict.

At the root of the problem is the often polar positioning of research performer and sponsor. Differences in point of view occur at every point in the grant process—from proposal to report evaluation.

The traditional and strongly culture-based view of the researcher is maximum freedom to perform. Equally strong is the stewardship culture of the provider of funds—the sponsor's responsibility to assure that funds which he distributes are converted into satisfactory performance.

The case history of monitoring by sponsors is highly mixed - from happy to unhappy. Happiness does not always accompany the rule of "the monitor who monitors least, monitors best."

There are elements of mutual respect, professional understanding, mutual confidence, mutual helpfulness, and many others which seem to affect the nature of the sponsor-performer relationship.

Two conditions exacerbate the sponsor-university relationship. Whereas there is heavy pressure from sponsors to assure quality return for expenditures, universities and research institutes resist sponsor audit and control. The friction is inimical to the interests of both sponsor and performer.

Research sponsors should undertake and support a major investigation of this area with a view toward the eventual development of guidelines and standards applicable to the array of sponsored research situations.

2. Seed Money and IDR

Repeatedly, at an exploratory workshop held at Stanford University (1978), the desirability and need for "seed money" for IDR was emphasized.

In the *disciplinary* environment of the university, the initiation of IDR is, to a degree, unnatural and is certainly beset with barriers to individual initiative to achieve proposals and projects which cross disciplinary boundaries. Seed money, that is, financial support for initiating exploratory work, can provide the breakthrough to achieve interdisciplinary action. It is to be hoped that the initiation of a sound IDR project will provide the base to achieve additional support as necessary for a significant IDR activity.

3. Serialization of Research

The bane of research, generally, is the interruption of investigative processes for non-science reasons: budgetary; administrative policy; loss of leader interest; transfer of leadership; inadequate integrative supervision; weak dedication and insight into potential value of research; and a host of other administrative, personal and fortuitous circumstances. The growth of sponsored research, with annual budgetary review, turnover in sponsor staff, and changes in "institutional policy" are all major contributions to sputtering discontinuities in the process of investigation.

Yet the history of science and technology shows that many investigations lead to useful findings only after years of continued, continuous research. Studies of the reasons why longer-term serial research is not planned and supported (especially in the United States), and conditions necessary to achieve changes in practice are recommended.

4. Agendas for IDR

"More research is needed on *what* is needed," it was concluded at a conference on IDR sponsored by the American Association for the Advancement of Science (1977). Priority-setting is necessary.

We recommend that comprehensive studies leading to IDR research agendas in various fields be commissioned, similar to the studies in the sciences which the National Research Council of the United States has produced from time to time. Such analytical, evaluative and prescriptive statements should be highly useful in leading the attention of researchers, and in guiding support actions by sponsors.

B. UNIVERSITY ORGANIZATION

5. Disciplinary Organization of the Universities

Testimony is overwhelming that the disciplinary structure of university curricula, faculty, research and thought is archaic, irrational and antithetical to research on real-life problems. Yet efforts to change the systems are generally weak and minimally successful.

Major, commissioned projects to review the background, present status, advantages and limitations in the present university disciplinary system and steps to be undertaken for reform are badly needed.

6. *Research Institutes*

Large and important universities have established semi-autonomous institutes for the performance of sponsored research. The reasons for this action are generally related to administrative advantages — accounting, legal, employment, tenure, etc. Underlying some of the administrative considerations are problems related to the disciplinary structure of the university educational mission whereas the research program is, to a considerable degree, interdisciplinary.

More should be known about the comparative relationships and effects of IDR on university disciplinary structure when (a) IDR is carried out within the formal university or (b) in a research institute affiliated with the university.

7. *Effects of Tenure on Research*

"Research can be basic because tenure protects," said one participant at the Stanford University workshop. "Tenure" has become a whipping boy for many problems of universities and of academic research. Charges of deadwood protection and lost motivation are common. On the other hand, the risks of doing research that may not be very productive can be born more readily by tenured professors. So can the risks of losing disciplinary recognition by engaging in IDR.

The implications of tenure, its weakening, and its possible elimination for IDR and R&D in general should be studied, and recommendations to university governance should be developed on the basis of such studies.

C. OTHER ORGANIZATIONS

8. *IDR in the Think Tanks*

Research attention to IDR and MIDR has been directed primarily to the universities. Superficially, at least, it seems that while IDR has been subject to a myriad of financial, administrative, organizational and personal problems in the universities, it has proceeded with harmony and effectiveness in several not-for-profit "think tanks,", e.g., the Rand Corporation and the Mitre Corporation.

To verify this observation, intensive case studies of the experience of think tank organization and management are recommended.

D. EDUCATION AND TRAINING

9. *Opportunities for Education for "ID Thinking"*

Although there is a commonly accepted need for university curricula to develop appreciation for and skill in interdisciplinary thinking and approaches, there is little study and little knowledge about how to accomplish these objectives.

There is an opportunity for research and experimentation in the curriculum structure, instructional syllabi and educational methods for such achievement.

One of the writer's most challenging and exciting educational experiences was a semester course in "Political Science Concepts in Sociological Terms." The course consisted of a series of exercises in rewriting political science literature in the language of sociology. It required rigorous comparative study of conceptual equivalents, and it forced understanding of the theoretical structure and concepts of another discipline. Further, it resulted in a more critical review of the primary discipline.

Similar experimentation should be sponsored, documented and evaluated. The effects of courses in the history of science and technology, and other interdisciplinary courses should likewise be studied and evaluated.

10. *ID Education for Research*

It follows logically that if IDR is needed, qualified researchers are needed. This leads to the idea of systematic curricular graduate education for IDR with, possibly, graduate ID degrees.

Some universities have instituted ID graduate program options. Descriptive and evaluative studies of IDR graduate education programs should be conducted. Both institutional case studies and comparative studies should be supported.

11. *ID as Educational Experience*

One critic of ID curricula has said they are "too broad, too applied and too complex." This observation is interesting and deserves attention. The hypothesis should be challenged and verified or refuted. The results of such investigation should provide important insights not only for IDR but also for university academic structure and educational theory and method more generally.

E. OPERATIONAL MANAGEMENT

Hypotheses to be tested or topics to be explored in the operational management of IDR can extend to a long list. It is suggested that topics which are less readily guided by findings from the general body of management research and literature be selected for special IDR study. Examples are: effect of electronic communication developments in interdisciplinary research, e.g., computer conferencing; incentives-disincentives; more precise studies of related impact of incentives/disincentives in different organizational/management/ project models; detailed case studies of small groups in IDR projects.

12. *Characteristics of IDR Team*

The microstudy of IDR has been most neglected. Only one of the National Science Foundation Research Management Improvement grants supported the study of the IDR team. Professor Bernard Cohen of Stanford University believes this to be a most important entry point for research on IDR management, but one in which only a beginning has been made.

There are many hypotheses which might be tested; e.g., there is an upper limit to the number of researchers who can be integrated effectively into a research team: the optimum system of rewards is different for researchers from various disciplinary origins; planned colloquia and other deliberately contrived arrangements are necessary to achieve effective communication among IDR team members.

13. *IDR Leader as Facilitator*

Much has been said and written about the anomalous position of the research supervisor who is often less expert than members of his research team — at least in their specialties. He may also be less qualified as a researcher, and less prestigious.

At the same time, it is his responsibility to provide a favorable research environment, to facilitate accommodation and creative association in IDR situations, as well as to tend to the institutional/administrative necessities of personnel, finance, reporting, evaluation, etc.

More research is needed to determine objectively the characteristics of the successful IDR project supervisor, how to select leaders with these traits, how to train in the associated skills, and how to evaluate performance.

14. *Reducing "Startup" Time for IDR Projects*

Because of the particular difficulties associated with the interaction of persons from different disciplinary backgrounds, the relatively long startup period identifies a significant problem, especially for the project which is limited to a year or so.

Research is needed to identify ways to facilitate and accelerate the initial, formulative steps in a research project. This is not a simple problem since it entails management policies, planning, supervision, intergroup relations, documentation, definitions, and perhaps other processes and elements.

Findings from the recommended research, though directed especially to R&D projects, should be very useful in application to other processes.

F. DISSEMINATION AND UTILIZATION

15. *Dissemination of Results of Research on IDR Management*

Professional workers in scientific disciplines are generally uninformed and untrained in management. More information is needed about (a) the general problem of the dissemination of results of management research to R&D managers in general; (b) dissemination of results of management research to IDR managers; and (c) dissemination of results of IDR management research to IDR managers.

16. *Journal Outlets for IDR Output and Peer Recognition*

Publication in refereed professional journals has long been a standard for judging scholarly performance.

It is natural that the editorial staffs and peer referees of disciplinary journals, themselves discipline-oriented, should favor publication of discipline-related papers over IDR papers.

Despite some shift in attitude, interdisciplinary journals, growing in number, are judged less favorably by disciplinary scholars. Since academic tenure and promotion, scholarly prizes, and professional society offices tend to be controlled by discipline-oriented persons, the IDR specialist is often underrated and underrecognized. From one interview survey, the consensus was: "Stay out of IDR or pay the price."

The performance of scholarly journals as to acceptance of IDR papers should be studied. The record of professional society officerships held by IDR scholars should be examined. A thorough survey of comparative academic recognition should be undertaken.

17. *Utilization of IDR*

Utilization of the results of IDR is a part of the more general problem of research utilization which John Salasin reported in his study of *The Management of Federal Research and Development*. Fostering utilization of R&D results is an unsolved problem, Salasin says. He suggests that methods for assessing impact on utilization might be developed by:

1. Identifying an array of process and outcome of effects desired from utilization activities.
2. Identifying appropriate measures from these effects, and techniques by which measures might be developed, and,
3. Pilot testing assessment methods on various areas to determine their feasibility and utility for providing information needed to improve the utilization function.

G. EVALUATION

18. *Evaluation of IDR*

Evaluation of research is elusive in definition and method. It is an unsolved problem in R&D management.

Evaluation of IDR poses difficulties for evaluators beyond those of disciplinary R&D. Different standards must be applied to measures of publication and of citation indexing. Peer evaluators may be more difficult to find.

Nevertheless, evaluation of IDR performance is the essence of many policy and management decisions related to IDR programs, projects and personnel.

The need for methodology for evaluating IDR is a prime target for research and experimentation. Pilot tests of various approaches and designs should be supported. Theoretical studies should be encouraged.

19. *Resistance to Evaluation*

Both IDR researchers and administrators resist evaluation. The basis for this resistance should be explored.

By its nature, the outcome of research is uncertain. As one approaches basic research, the precision of cost/benefit ratios declines. An appreciation of this fact and a fear that evaluators will not understand complexities and uncertainties may be at the root of researcher resistance to evaluation. Other factors may also be present. It is not unusual that a scientist believes no one else is qualified to understand and evaluate his work.

There is also the almost omnipresent conflict between researcher and administrator about the time-frame of evaluation. Administrators are pressed to evaluate on a short-term basis for periodic decision-making. Researchers tend to believe that evaluation requires a long-term perspective.

The attitudes of IDR researchers should be studied to provide a better base to develop evaluation methods and approaches which will cope with or remove researchers' resistance.

20. *The Beatitude and the Reality*

Although there are many barriers to effective interdisciplinary research, and there is often internecine opposition to specific interdisciplinary programs and projects, there is nevertheless almost no one who opposes interdisciplinary research in the abstract.

In practice, however, there is considerable reluctance and resistance to participation in IDR. This fact suggests that there are limitations, weaknesses or other unfavorable attributes of IDR. There is a widespread view that IDR is of inferior quality, though this belief seems to be impressionistic.

Evaluative studies of IDR research and research results on a more aggregative scale than those recommended above should be useful to test the hypothesis that IDR is scientifically inferior. This information could be used to improve the design of IDR research and its management.

H. HISTORICAL STUDIES

21. *Historical Case Studies of IDR Management*

The history of science and of technology have shown growth and development as scholarly disciplines. Each has a strong professional society and the scholarly output is substantial both in the United States and internationally. However, attention to the elements of "management" is generally neglected in the historical studies of science and technology. Specific attention to management of *IDR* is neglected almost completely.

Documentation for the study of the management of science and technology is increasingly available—in primary sources especially, but also here and there in secondary sources (case studies, administrative histories of organizations, and more general historical studies of the sciences and technology). Actual work in the historical study of IDR and the management of IDR should be encouraged and supported.

CONCLUDING COMMENT

The 21 targets for research attention cited above are presented in the leanest form—each is susceptible to fuller rationalization and description as a basis for research proposals and sponsorship and performance.

The principal message which seems to be woven throughout the literature, thought and analysis is that the interdisciplinary research mission is significant, troubled, uncertain in academe; much is known about the academic climate—much more needs to be known about a host of relevant factors to achieve productive IDR. Because of the special linking role of IDR between science and application, more research about IDR should be supported, in a systematically developed plan for international exploration.

3

ETHNOCENTRISM OF DISCIPLINES AND THE FISH-SCALE MODEL OF OMNISCIENCE†*

Donald T. Campbell

This paper is a preliminary exercise in the sociology of science—an exploratory application of principles of groups and intergroup organization to group processes in the institutionalization of science. Our goal in this book is a comprehensive, integrated multiscience. The obstacle described in this paper is the "ethnocentrism of disciplines," i.e., the symptoms of tribalism or nationalism or ingroup partisanship in the internal and external relations of university departments, national scientific organizations, and academic disciplines. The "fish-scale model of omniscience" represents the solution advocated, a solution kept from spontaneous emergence by the ethnocentrism of disciplines. The slogan is collective comprehensiveness through overlapping patterns of unique narrownesses. Each narrow specialty is in this analogy a "fish-scale." Figure 1 illustrates the title. Our only hope of a comprehensive social science, or other multiscience, lies in a continuous texture of narrow specialties which overlap with other narrow specialties. Due to the ethnocentrism of disciplines, what we get instead is a redundant piling up of highly similar specialties, leaving interdisciplinary gaps. Rather than trying to fill these gaps by training scholars who have mastered two or more disciplines, we should be making those social-organizational inventions which will encourage narrow specialization in these interdisciplinary areas.

The diagram of Figure 1 is of course an oversimplification, an analogy in two dimensions of what should be n-dimensional.

† The preparation of this paper has been facilitated by the Council for Intersocietal Studies, which operates under a grant from the Ford Foundation to Northwestern University.
* From *Interdisciplinary Relationships in the Social Sciences*, edited by M. Sherif and C. W. Sherif, (Aldine Publishing, Co. 1969), pp. 328-348, reprinted by permission of the author.

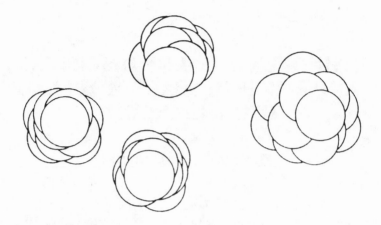

Fig. 1a-Present situation: Disciplines as clusters of specialties,
leaving interdisciplinary gaps.

Fig. 1b-Ideal situation: Fish-scale model of omniscience.

Particularly likely to be dyscommunicative are the exaggerated gaps
between the disciplinary clusters. The real situation is perhaps more
often one of unrecognized overlap. The disciplinary clusters may at
their edges overlap other clusters, but as ships that pass in the night,
they fail to make contact. The clusters, as it were, may overlap but lie
on independent planes. Such an alternate diagramming might be

possible, and the reader is invited to substitute it in his mind's eye in what follows. The issue, too, is not one of total absence but of relative density of interdisciplinary specialties.

COMPREHENSIVE TRAINING AND THE LEONARDESQUE ASPIRATION

Too often in discussions of interdisciplinary training one hears calls for *breadth*, for *comprehensiveness*. Too often we attempt the production of multidisciplinary scholars, professionals who have mastered two or more disciplines, rather than interdisciplinary specialists. This orientation I will parody as the "Leonardesque aspiration": the goal of creating current-day Leonardos who are competent in all of science. As a training program it is bound to fail in one of two directions. At its worst it produces a shallowness, a lowest-common-denominator breadth, an absence of that profound specialization which is essential for scientific productivity. At best it is evaded in the direction of the interdisciplinary narrowness here advocated.

THE BURGEONING LITERATURE AND THE OBLIGATIONS OF INTERDISCIPLINARIANS

One of the several background facts that lies behind my emphasis is the enormous past and burgeoning present literature. Speaking for myself—any volume like this raises guilt feelings in that it acquaints me with the existence of scientific literatures of obvious relevance to my work which I have neglected. William McGuire's paper, for example, lies in an area of high relevance to my work, and yet I have not read or read-at even half of his citations, and was not at all aware of the existence of another sizeable proportion. But it is not only multidisciplinary conferences that have this effect. Unidisciplinary conferences remind me that I am failing to keep up in areas once central—and so does the arrival of one of the few journals I take (and read only 10 per cent of), or chance inspection of one of the many journals equally relevant to which I do not subscribe.

What seems to me essential is that moving into an interdisciplinary problem area not increase this obligation and guilt—that for every new literature we pick up we are excused from or drop some other literature, so that the interdisciplinarian be free to remain as narrow, as specialized, as any other scholar.

THE MYTH OF UNIDISCIPLINARY COMPETENCE

Lying behind many models of interdisciplinary competence is an unrealistic notion of unidisciplinary competence—the image of scholars competent in one discipline. It will clarify the discussion of interdisciplinary competence to recognize at the outset that there are no such persons. What we have instead is a congeries of narrow specialties each one of which covers no more than one-tenth of the discipline with even a shallow competence. Yet individual disciplines do have some integrity, some comprehensiveness—at least in comparison with social science as a whole or with specific interdisciplinary areas. What must be recognized is that this integration and comprehensiveness is a collective product, not embodied within any one scholar. It is achieved through the fact that the multiple narrow specialties overlap, and that through this overlap a collective communication, a collective competence and breadth, is achieved. This approach is our only hope for a unified and complete behavioral science. The present social organization of science impedes it.

THE LOCUS OF SCIENTIFIC KNOWLEDGE IS SOCIAL

Philosophy of science and epistemology have not yet assimilated the fact that the problem of knowledge must, in the end, be stated at the social level—though Charles Sanders Peirce and James Mark Baldwin, for example, were making this point at the turn of the century. Moving the problem of knowledge from a solitary viewer's vision to language is a step, but the implicit model is still usually a single native speaker with perfect knowledge of a stable language. Sufficient attention is not yet given to the social and incomplete conditions of language learning, to the fundamental idiosyncrasy and errorfulness of functional individual lexicons, to the very partial distribution of words that are still somehow "in" the language, to the effective redundancy which makes imperfect language as competent as it is. When these have been assimilated, the locus of "truth" and "knowledge" will have clearly shifted from individual "minds" to a collective social product only imperfectly represented in any one mind. Similarly in the philosophy of science, the competence, the discipline, the verification, the integration are all in the end social products, imperfectly and incompletely represented in the work of any one scientist. Michael Polanyi writes to this point in *The Tacit Dimension* (Doubleday, 1966) identifying the locus of scientific authority as the "Society of Explorers" itself:

> . . . the *principle of mutual control.* It consists, in the present case, of the simple fact that scientists keep watch over each other. Each scientist is both subject to criticism by all others and encouraged by their appreciation of him. This is how *scientific opinion* is formed, which enforces scientific standards and regulates the distribution of professional opportunities. It is clear that only fellow scientists working in closely related fields are competent to exercise direct authority over each other; but their personal fields will form *chains of over-lapping neighborhoods* extending over the entire range of science. It is enough that the standards of plausibility and worthwhileness be equal around every single point to keep them equal over all the sciences. Even those in the most widely separated branches of science will then rely on each other's results and support each other against any laymen seriously challenging their authority. (p. 72).

PRESENT DISCIPLINES AS ARBITRARY COMPOSITES

While it is probably not essential to the perspective, it is certainly relevant that the present organization of content into departments is highly arbitrary, a product in large part of historical accident.

Thus *anthropology* is a hodgepodge of all novelties that struck the scholarly tourist's eye when venturing into exotic lands—a hodgepodge of skin color, physical stature, agricultural practices, weapons, religious beliefs, kinship systems, language, history, archeology, and paleontology.

Thus *sociology* is a study of social man in European industrialized settings, a hodgepodge of studies of institutional data in which persons are anonymous—of individual persons in social settings, of aggregates of person data losing both personal and institutional identity, and of interactions which are neither persons nor groups.

Thus *psychology* is a hodgepodge of sensitive subjective biography, of brain operations, of school achievement testing, of factor analysis, of Markov process mathematics, of schizophrenic families, of laboratory experiments on group structure in which persons are anonymous, etc.

Thus *geography* is a hodgepodge of land-surface geology, of industrial development, of innovation diffusion, of social ecology, of political territoriality, of visual perception of areal photographs, of subjective phenomenology of mental maps.

Thus *political science* is a hodgepodge of political entities as actors and persons as actors, of humanistic description and scientific generalization, of history and of social psychology.

Thus *economics* is a hodgepodge of mathematics without data, of history of economic institutions without mathematics or theory, of an ideal model of psychological man.

There are no doubt many natural divisions within the domain of the social or behavioral sciences—but they are not employed in the allocation of content to disciplines. A hierarchy of levels of analysis exists in which the focus of differential description at one level becomes the assumed undifferentiated atoms of the next: this is the atom-molecule-cell-organ-organism-social group-etc. model. On this hierarchy, sociology, political science, geography, and anthropology are all mixed across the individual and group levels, and so is experimental social psychology. The experimental laboratory work of Sherif, Lewin, Lippitt, and Bavelas in many instances represents psychologists doing experimental sociology, experimenting with social structure, developing laws about social norms in which persons are treated as undifferentiated atoms, and in which the resulting laws relate social, structural and group-product variables.

Another natural division is between the descriptive-humanistic, on the one hand, and the scientistic, on the other. On this dimension, too, our departments and disciplines are mixed, with all save history having both strong scientific and strong descriptive-humanistic factions.

There are ways of describing the internal logic and coherence of disciplines, but this cannot be done with singular principles and still capture both the reason for the content within one discipline and the reason for the same content's appearance or exclusion in others. And certainly the dimensions so used would be only a partial sample of potential classificatory criteria.

The specialties within disciplines are more coherent, and eventually such specialization takes over, each scientist allowing the congeries of irrelevancies within his own disciplinary knowledge to atrophy, journals to go unread, subscriptions to lapse, etc. The temporary disciplinary breadth transiently achieved in graduate school is of course not undesirable—the objection here is rather to the repetitious duplication of the same pattern of breadth to the exclusion of other breadths equally relevant but organizationally unsupported.

ETHNOCENTRISM OF DISCIPLINES

Effects of Organizing Specialties into
Decision-making Units

Consider what would happen if we took a large domain of specialties and aggregated adjacent dozens into "departments," as collective-decision-making units. In this hypothetical example, let us suppose that the aggregation has been arbitrary except for the requirement of adjacency, that all specialties are equally well staffed to begin with, and that any specialty can belong to only one department. We are now interested in the effect of this second-level organizational structure, this superimposition of departmental boundaries upon the specialty boundaries. We are particularly interested in differential effects upon the future growth of the "central" specialties versus the peripheral or marginal specialties, this centrality or marginality being in this hypothetical case a purely arbitrary byproduct of where the administrative boundaries happened to fall. Figure 2a is an effort to portray this starting point. (In Fig. 2, Ap, Bp, Cp, are examples of peripheral specialties, Dc and Ec of central ones.)

Consider first purely internal decision-making. For most issues there are differences in priority and preferences which are associated with specialty points of view, and overlapping specialties are apt to have overlapping preferences. The situation will also be that collective decisions will be achieved only by a consensus of a plurality of specialties within the department. The accidentally central specialties have more natural allies within the department, and find it easier to achieve support for their concerns. The natural allies of the peripheral specialties lie in other of the arbitrary departments, and are organizationally prevented from effectively presenting their consensuses. The incidentally central specialties are also more frequently the compromise candidates, and when an ideology is needed to rationalize the historically arbitrary departmentalization it is the concerns of the central specialties that are chosen as epitomizing the true common denominator, as the essence of the initially arbitrary aggregate. Centrality becomes reinterpreted as common root, trunk, and fountain head when initially it meant only remoteness from the boundaries with other departments.

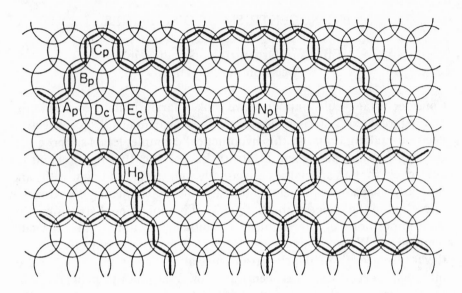

Fig. 2a—Hypothetical pattern of specialty overlap at the time of superimposition of arbitrary "departmental" boundaries (heavier lines).

Here are some considerations which would illustrate these purely
internal dynamics. The selection of a chairman in a peaceful
department will follow these lines—only if a peripheral is a compromise
between two strong factions each with some central specialties will he
be a chairman. Deciding on a core curriculum to be required of all
students, the minimum essential to their being sound, well-grounded
X-ologists, will go in this direction. Pressure there will be to require one
course from each specialty. Demands for time to meet the needs of
specializing will preclude this in any but the smallest departments. The
process of choosing a smaller set will involve the elimination of
peripheral specialties because inherently in the arbitrary organizational
structure there are fewer other specialists in the department who deem
them important. This tautology may of course be expressed
ideologically as "that's not really X-ology—it even comes close to being
Y-ology." The setting of qualifying exams and dissertation committees
will exercise a constant centralizing bias on the training of graduate
students in peripheral specialties. Going across departmental lines in
study programs is wasted effort as far as these important hurdles are
concerned. The peripheral specialist himself will be anxious that his

students show up well on the central core content, and will be willing to see equally or more relevant crossdepartment content be neglected, since no punishment is involved in its neglect, no institutional reward in its achievement. This is a minor problem if these departmental hurdles are low. But there is great pressure on departments to achieve excellence, and there is a perverse tendency to see this as implemented by high standards in the achievement of passive regurgitative mastery of past achievements in the literature. Under the institutional decision-making arrangements here described, the inevitable effect of higher standards in training is greater neglect of peripheral and crossdepartmental content. And this is without the byproduct of increasing the profundity of specialized training for any but the central specialties.

Deciding who in the department merits a raise or is ready for promotion, whose competing offer it is essential to meet and whose the department has not the funds to match, whose specialty needs additional staff and space, all show the effect of the arbitrary location of departmental boundaries on what becomes defined as central or peripheral. In my professional career at four universities I have repeatedly seen men who were of exceptional creativity and competence, and who were absolutely central as far as social science or behavioral science was concerned (occupying positions like those designated as H or N in Fig. 2a), be budgetarily neglected and eventually squeezed out because the departmental organization of specialties made them departmentally peripheral. That in some cases these were arrogant men does not explain the result, because their detractors were also arrogant men, but more centrally located. However, a selective feedback may well be at work, it may be that of all those who are initially attracted to peripheral, boundary-crossing specialties, only the arrogant persist in bucking the institutional pressures which would otherwise move them to more centrally defined specialties.

The dynamics just described are internal to our hypothetical departments. These arbitrary budgetary units compete with each other as budgetary entities, for budget increases, space increases, personnel increases. The specialties within the arbitrary departments thus come to share common fate, and become joint actors in competition with the other arbitrary aggregates of specialties. This common fate, though arbitrary in its initiation, is real enough in practice to provide the basis of an ingroup identification against competitive outgroups. There also develops implicit or explicit competition for the most talented students, and indoctrination procedures designed to maintain the loyalty of those who have tentatively joined. Characteristic of ingroup-outgroup relations in other settings, these indoctrination procedures not only emphasize ingroup virtues and ideology but also contrasting outgroup faults. Philosophy and sociology departments have frequently maintained internal solidarity by teaching about the wrongness of behavioristic psychology. Sidney Aronson in his paper for this volume has documented the manner in which historians build ingroup morale by deprecating sociologists. (It is even symptomatic of ethnocentrism that the first illustrations that come to his and my mind are ones in which our own departments are being wrongly disparaged by outgroups, rather than vice versa.)

If we add to our hypothetical example the feature that on most university campuses the arbitrary aggregations into departments be parallel as to which specialties are combined, further institutional pressures emerge. Departments' students must be prepared to appear adequate to centrally dominated hiring committees at other universities. The new faculty appointments to the department must be ones that inspire admiration on the part of the parallel departments of other universities.

Effect of Departmental Organization on Scientific Communication and Specialist Competence

In this topic we come to the most direct effect of departmental organization on scientific knowledge. Each scientist's competence, his participation in the collective activity of science, is based upon communication. The hypothetical departmental organization under consideration affects communication patterns in many ways. In our hypothetical example, suppose that those specialties aggregated into an arbitrary department be housed adjacently, but that departments be scattered at random. Incidental oral and paper-passing communication links thus become predominantly intradepartmental, and the extradepartmental aspects of peripheral specialties suffer great relative neglect in comparison with their intradepartmental overlaps. Shop talk, reading of dissertations, reading of each other's preprints and reprints, looking at laboratory setups and research instruments, all illustrate primary modes of communication seriously warped. The bias extends also to books and journals read. One is rewarded socially for shared detailed reading of exciting new developments. No such reward occurs for unshared reading, and thus the literature in the crossdepartmental aspects of a specialty loses ground to the reinforced intradepartmental reading.

With a parallel arbitrary organization occurring at other universities and in national and international disciplinary organizations, still other boundary effects occur. Professional organizational membership and their journal discounts to members lead to stereotyped patters of journal subscription with most members limiting themselves to journals within one field—these are invariably so voluminous that one excuses himself for not reading in other fields by noting that this would be foolish when he is not even able to keep up in "his own field." "Own field," needless to say, tends to become defined in terms of these arbitrary departments whenever it goes beyond the narrow specialty. Abstracting sources, annual reviews, handbooks, etc., further the redundant repetition of intradepartmental patterns of breadth at the expense of equally relevant crossdepartmental ones.

(The annual reviews and handbooks do another disservice from the fish-scale model. Even within departments, each scholar's coverage must be partial, collective competence being assured by different partialities for each. Annual reviews and handbooks become crutches leading large numbers of scholars to the *same* partiality, and the inevitable neglect of other partialities. The degree of this partialness is generally underestimated, impressed as we must be at the long bibliographies appended.)

The departmental grouping of communicators allows unstable language to drift into unintelligibility across departments. A basic law is that speakers of the same language, once isolated into separate communities, drift into local idiosyncrasies and eventually unintelligibility, once the discipline of common conversation is removed. This tendency produces departmental linguistic idiosyncrasy even for shared contents and referents. Furthermore, as Edmund Leach and others have noted, such idiosyncrasy may be exaggerated as an ingroup solidarity device. What is despised as jargon by the outgroup may be the shibboleth of adequate professional training by the ingroup.

Resulting Ethnocentrism of Disciplines

Figure 2b shows the results of these dynamics. A few isolated specialties have been lost and the peripheral specialties have allowed their crossdepartmental edges to atrophy, producing departmental discreteness and interdepartmental gaps.

What started out as a hypothetical case has occasionally in the previous paragraphs drifted into the description of current actualities, perhaps blurring the point being made: Even if the true nature and the historical starting point had been one of a homogeneous texture of overlapping specialties, the organizing of specialties into departments and disciplines for decision-making and communication purposes would have produced disciplinary discreteness, cohesiveness, and interdisciplinary gaps such as exist at present. These features therefore should not be judged to justify as natural the existing arrangements of specialties.

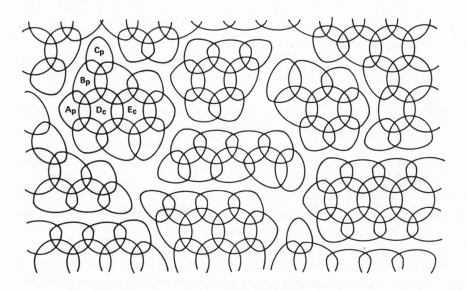

Fig. 2b—Resulting modification of specialty overlap as a result of organizing decision-making and communication along the arbitrary "departmental" lines. ("Departmental" boundaries omitted to facilitate inspection of specialty overlap pattern.)

The historical origins of departments and disciplines are of course quite other than those of our hypothetical example. The actual histories add historical depth to the tribal myths of origin and no doubt provide a greater true commonality to departments than in our hypothetical instance. Yet no matter what the degree of valid core and discreteness, the dynamics described here would inevitably have the effect of artificially enhancing it . . . .

A MISCELLANY OF REFORMS

A New Ego Ideal for the Scholar as Student

At the present time the ego ideal of the scholar calls for competence, for complete knowledge of the field he claims as his. In his everyday interaction with fellow specialists, he tends to feel guilty when he finds that he has not read what they have read. While he inevitably learns to live with such guilt feelings, this ego ideal spells the direction of his guilt. If the scholar takes to heart the notion that scientific competence can never be embodied in single minds—that his guilty neglect is not his unique shame but the inevitable predicament of all, and that science is somehow achieved in spite of this, he may come to substitute a quite different ego-ideal, a quite different focus of guilt. Rather than praying, "May I be a competent and well-read X-ologist, may I keep up with the literature in my field," he will pray. "Make me a novel fish-scale. Let my pattern of inevitably incomplete competence cover areas neglected by others." Each scholar would then try to have a pattern of journal subscriptions unique to his department, university, or profession. Noting that he and a colleague were reading the same set of journals, he would feel guilty and vow to drop one of these in favor of some other. Recognizing that the interdisciplinary links in the collaborative web of knowledge are the weakest, he would give up some ingroup journal in favor of an outgroup one. He would feel guilty if he did not cut attendance at ingroup conventions to attend relevant outgroup ones, etc.

There is a secondary payoff in crossdisciplinary reading and conventioning. Scholarly reading for the true scholar is ideally recreational, something he enjoys doing and would choose to do reactionally even if he had some other profession. The social system of science, particularly in graduate school and in the first stages of a scientific career, associate such activities so strongly to the reward and punishment system of competitive evaluation that they cease to be relaxing or effectively recreational. In the current disciplinary organization, the scholar will often find that the journals and conventions of a neighboring discipline can still serve this recreational function—particularly if he accepts his role as smatterer and does not assume the obligation of "mastering" that literature. If our fish-scale model were to become the norm, such reading would of course tend to become more obligatory and run the risk of ceasing to be recreational.

(While on the themes of recreational reading and the duplication of fish scales, it seems appropriate to deplore the tendency of social scientists to feel that they all should read current newspapers, particularly the *New York Times*. Certainly the collective perspective would be better if most spent the equivalent time with newspapers of other epochs, or with historical, anthropological, archeological, or literary descriptions of quite other samples of social milieus. Rather than the ego-ideal of keeping up with the current worldwide social developments, the young scholar should hold the ideal of foregoing current informedness for some infrequently sampled descriptive recreational literature. Too often our ego-ideals call for uniform omniscience, knowledge of both past and present, of both here and there, and too often we settle for the same pattern of compromise all our colleagues are settling for. Compromise from the Leonardesque aspiration there must be, but even in leisure reading let us hold as ideal the achieving of unique compromises.)

An Ego-Ideal for the Scholar as Teacher

Under the ideology of disciplinary competence, a department feels that its staff should be able to provide competent guidance in the Ph.D. programs it offers, that students should bend their interests to the locally available specialties or go elsewhere, that to train a student properly the faculty should be more competent than the student in the student's area of study. Combining this with the organizational advantages of one-headed decision-making units in dissertation direction, etc., a strong tendency toward duplicating of identical fish scales within departments results.[2]

Under the fish-scale ideology, the professor would feel guilty when he turned out "chips off the old block," Ph.D.s who showed the same pattern of overlap as he. The goal instead would be to encourage each new Ph.D. to select such a novel specialty that he could indeed within his graduate training become one of science's leading experts, a fully contributing specialist. Note the difference between this approach to instant expertness and that of exhaustive mastery of an exceedingly narrow realm within one specialty. The latter asks the graduate student to be narrower than his mentor, to subspecialize within his mentor's range. The former asks him to achieve a novel range, not necessarily broader or narrower than the mentor's. One greatly needed implementation of this goal is to encourage the Ph.D. to give up some traditional intradisciplinary subfield in favor of mastery of a crossdisciplinary one of relevance. A common reason given for rejecting this is that for such a content we X-ologists would have no way of checking his competence—a typically ethnocentric reaction, illustrating again the way in which, given our present organization into departments, concern over evaluation of competence decreases the crossing of departmental bounds in specialization.

Using the Advantages of Smallness and Bigness

Generally speaking, the larger the university, the wider the variety of specialists available and the more likely that the full range of possible specialties be represented by actual persons. This being so, one might expect the interdisciplinary gaps to be less and interdisciplinary collaboration to be more frequent. In actual practice, the contrary is more apt to be the case (though we need studies to verify this), and the laws of group organization and size applied to departmental organization explain this. The larger the department, the more obligatory relationships there are intradepartmentally, and the more the totality of obligatory and informal relationships is predominately intradepartmental. The larger the department, the more required courses there are for graduate students within the department (Aronson in this volume cites a study by Sibley to this effect), and the less opportunity and the greater jeopardy for crossdepartmental study. In the smaller department, the loyalty demands are less, informal communication and friendship links are more frequently crossdepartmental, collaboration across departmental lines is less apt to involve loss of intradepartmental esteem, and graduate students are more apt to feel sufficient mastery in their home departments to have time to explore outside. Northwestern University has had an exceptionally productive period of interdisciplinary collaboration in recent decades, at a time when most universities have been finding such relationships increasingly impracticable. The explanation lies in part in the chance accumulation of a few key leaders with this orientation, such as Richard Snyder in political science, but more significant, I believe, has been the smallness of its departments combined with low teaching loads and a full commitment to research and graduate training. Most places this small are focused on undergraduate training. Most places focused on research and graduate training combine this with largeness. In contrast stands the University of California at Berkeley where interdisciplinary contacts have steadily decreased as departments grew, and where once interdepartmental institutes have become annexes of single departments . . . .

Reprise: bigness increases the isolation of departments, decreases the interdepartmental fish scales, unless organizational reforms are devised to prevent this.

Ad Hoc Interdisciplinary Training Programs

Even at Northwestern, what crossing of disciplines we achieve is mostly at the faculty level. My own graduate students are as unidisciplinary as any and rarely do more than a required course or two outside of psychology. Were I to push them to a real mastery of some relevant-to-them cross-disciplinary specialty—be it time-series analysis in economics, analysis of ideology in sociology, or child rearing customs in anthropology, I would be adding to an already inhibiting burden of requirements. But if I could at the same time relieve them of the need to master some physiological psychology, or the sensory discrimination literature, or the like, such programs would be possible. They are also much needed, not because they would be better than the present mix but because they individually might be as good and because the combination of some of these plus some of the standard would be collectively stronger than the present all-of-one-type.

At a place with relatively good (though minimal) interdepartmental contact like Northwestern, one should be able to train hybrid specialists such as these, with an ad hoc assembly of core courses, fields for prelims, and dissertation committees tailor-made for each student. The adviser and student would assemble an ad hoc training advisory faculty and schedule of courses. Perhaps a divisional review committee would have to check the program, to assure that it was as exacting and as coherently specialized as the standard programs required in the overlapping departments. Such a committee would also conduct written and oral qualifying exams, and guide the dissertation. If the possibility of use to evade difficult requirements emerged, the program might be restricted to only the top half of entrants. If perceived as a vehicle for inadequate professors, the prerogative of advising on such programs could be limited to an elite of proven unidisciplinary capability, etc. To coordinate with the labels of the disciplines nationally, the Ph.D. would be designated according to the department of his senior advisor. If departments objected to thus annointing an inadequately trained X-ologist, a dual labeling could be adopted, Ph.D. in X-ology (Divisional) for the new type, Ph.D. in X-ology (Departmental) for the old. In the present academic market, we should have no difficulty placing such Ph.D.s. Thus with no such drastic reorganizations as creating new rigid interdepartments, with no new budgetary units, no new staffs, a congeries of new specialties each as coherent and narrow as our present Ph.D. programs could be achieved.

Paralleling such ad hoc training programs for graduate students, ad hoc decision groups substituting for departments in deciding on raises, promotions, and tenure might well be established for interdepartmental faculty appointments, with some divisional funds allocated for such purposes separate from departmental budgets.

Organizational Alternatives for Journals and Conventions

Our academic professional organizations publish journals and offer them to their members at reduced rates. There results a repetitious patterning in the several journals each scholar takes. If our associations would make these same rates available to the members of other disciplinary associations (as indeed some do), novel journal sets would become more frequent. In the creation of new journals, broad interdisciplinary scope should be eschewed for novel narrowness. The new *Journal of Verbal Learning and Verbal Behavior* sets an excellent example. It is much narrower than the *Journal of Experimental Psychology*, which it overlaps heavily, but it juxtaposes work by experimental psychologists and by linguists so as to eventually nurture some novel fish scales.

Our professional conventions are too large, have too many simultaneous meetings, cover too wide a range of specialties, and last too long. If our conventions instead were held at different times by each specialty (e.g., by divisions within the American Psychological Association), and if the scholar did his annual conventioning by attending several of these shorter ones, he would be much more likely to cross disciplinary lines.

SUMMARY

Interdisciplinary programs have been misled by goals of breadth and multidisciplinary training. Even within disciplines, disciplinary competence is not achieved in individual minds, but as a collective achievement made possible by the overlap of narrow specialties. This fish-scale model of collective omniscience is impeded in interdisciplinary specialty areas by the ethnocentrism of disciplines, by the organization of specialties into departments for decision-making and communication. For an integrated and competent social science, we need to invent alternative social organizations which will permit the flourishing of narrow interdisciplinary specialties.

FOOTNOTES

: . . .

[2]For total careers, there is, of course, considerable freedom to redefine personal specialties within disciplines. This, combined with the needs for autonomous personal identity within face-to-face departments, reestablishes the needed texture of overlap within disciplines.

4

THE DIFFERENTIATION
OF DISCIPLINES*

W. O. Hagstrom

Segmentation begins with cultural change, the appearance of new goals in the scientific community. Of course, new goals do not spontaneously 'appear': scientists actively seek them. Those who discover important problems upon which few others are engaged are less likely to be anticipated and more likely to be rewarded with recognition. Thus scientists tend to disperse themselves over the range of possible problems.[1] The behavior is analogous to competitive behavior in the animal world:

> But the struggle will almost invariably be most severe between the individuals of the same species, for they frequent the same districts, require the same food, and are exposed to the same dangers. In the case of varieties of the same species, the struggle will generally be almost equally severe, and we sometimes see the contest soon decided. . . . (Darwin, 1958, p. 82.)

In many disciplines, dispersion to avoid competition takes place not only over the range of problems available but over the range of institutions, with the result that few identical specialists will be found in the same organizations. 'Complete competitors cannot co-exist.' (Hardin, 1960.)

Dispersion may lead to isolation, both geographical and social. Scientists working on the most unusual research problems, not being encouraged elsewhere, may be concentrated in a few research establishments. Social isolation results when pursuit of different goals leads to the development of different terminologies, techniques, and modes of organization. Eventually communication between specialties may be difficult and uncommon. Research in one area will have only

* Reprinted by permission of Basic Books, Inc., Publishers from *The Scientific Community* by Warren O. Hagstrom, 1965, pp. 222-226. Copyright 1965 by Warren O. Hagstrom.

remote effects on research in another, and programs of instruction may become differentiated; the social equivalent of crossbreeding will occur less frequently:

Isolation, also, is an important element in the modification of species through natural selection. In a confined or isolated area, if not very large, the organic and inorganic conditions of life will generally be almost uniform; so that natural selection will tend to modify all the varying individuals of the same species in the same manner. Intercrossing with the inhabitants of the surrounding districts will, also, be thus prevented. (Darwin, 1958, p. 106.)

Dispersion and isolation may encourage cultural differentiation, but here the biological metaphor breaks down. Differences between specialties may be viewed as deviance by members of specialties that are traditional or central to the discipline, and attempts may be made to sanction such deviance.

Initially, attempts may be made to establish conformity by the use of formal sanctions - with regard to appointments, instruction of students, and access to communication channels. The exercise of these sanctions tends to be implicit. Unsuccessful candidates for jobs may not be told specifically why they were not appointed, papers may be rejected by journals for vague reasons, and a professor may find his students failing because of their 'incompetence', or their 'attitudes'. Whether or not the recipient of the sanction is informed of the standards used in judging him, the matter does not become public.

Further development of the deviant specialty leads to overt social conflict. Those likely to be sanctioned publicly question the legitimacy of the standards used. Thus goals and standards are made explicit, and scientists and others will be made aware of the conflict. At first, organizations may attempt to reduce the resulting strains by primary adjustments. These usually amount to a limited range of permissiveness for the allegedly deviant group; they will be permitted a maximum number of appointments, limited access to channels of communication, and a higher degree of autonomy in instructing their own advanced students. Primary adjustments may make it possible to cope with conflict, but sometimes specialties will continue to diverge from one another, and the disadvantages of primary adjustments may lead to continued dissatisfaction. Such organizations as university departments and scientific societies will be made more rigid, scientific standards usually expressed by the award of recognition may become relaxed, and programs of instruction may suffer. Dissatisfaction with these failings may stimulate formal differentiation of disciplines.

Such differentiation requires special communication channels, the development of a disciplinary utopia, and successful appeals outside of existing disciplines. Leadership of an unusual sort in science - leadership unwilling to shrink from organizational controversy - will be necessary if these steps are to be successful. The establishment of communication channels and the development of a utopia make it possible for scientists to identify with the emerging discipline and to claim legitimacy for their point of view when appealing to university bodies or groups in the larger society.

At first, organizations may respond to these claims by structural innovations to which they need not be committed, innovations which they may abandon. In the university setting, this means such things as research institutes and interdisciplinary teaching programs, but not departments of instruction. Later on, separate departments for the new discipline may be established. This represents an almost irreversible differentiation, for universities are strongly committed to departments of instruction, and, through their graduates, the departments have reproduced themselves and established ties with groups in the larger society that employs them.

Structural change, especially departmental differentiation, is unlikely to occur unless the emerging discipline is marginal to at least two existing disciplines. When the emerging discipline is confined to a single existing discipline, it is apparently difficult for it to legitimate appeals outside of the disciplinary structure, especially appeals for structural change.

This analysis of social change can be conveniently presented in the schematic form in Figure 1.[2]

Differentiation results in the re-establishment of disciplines and specialties as the basic communities in science. New disciplines have internal structures similar to those from which they have differentiated, and this internal organization is characterized by the relatively great importance of informal relations.

From the point of view of the larger scientific community, however, continuing structural change implies a qualitative change in the organization of science. Modern science is no longer like the science of the seventeenth and eighteenth centuries. There are no universal scholars, and interdependence between disciplines and even among

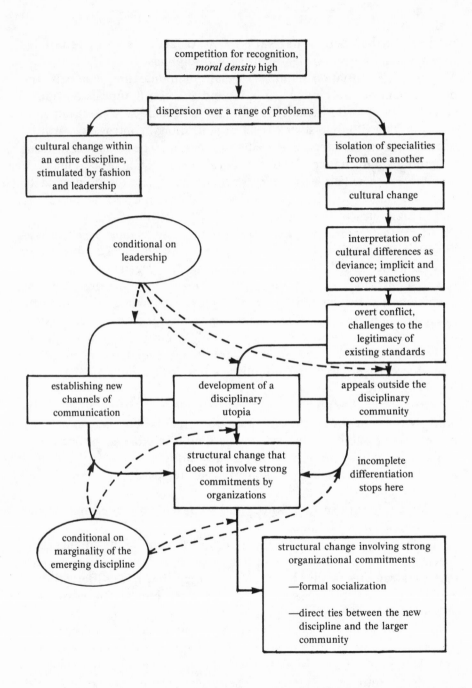

Figure 1 Differentiation in science: segmentation

specialties within disciplines is small. This degree of specialization has implications for the organization of science that are reflected in the current problems of organizing university instruction and in allocating research facilities among disciplines. It also has implications for the place of science in the larger culture. Science no longer presents a unitary picture of the world to the nonspecialist, and the place of the scientist as a cultural leader is thereby dubious. This is expressed in a somewhat disillusioned passage written by Oppenheimer (1958):

Today (as opposed to Plato's Greece), it is not only that our kings do not know mathematics, but our philosophers do not know mathematics and - to go a step further - our mathematicians do not know mathematics. Each of them knows a branch of the subject and they listen to each other with a fraternal and honest respect; and here and there you find a knitting together of the different fields of mathematical specialization. . . . We so refine what we think, we so change the meaning of words, we build up so distinctive a tradition, that scientific knowledge today is not an enrichment of the general culture. It is, on the contrary, the possession of countless highly specialized communities who love it, would like to share it, and who make some efforts to communicate it; but it is not part of the common human understanding. . . . We have in common the simple ways in which we have learned to live and talk and work together. Out of this have grown the specialized disciplines like the fingers of the hand, united in origin but no longer in contact.[3]

References

DARWIN, C. (1958), *The Origin of Species*, Mentor, 6th edn.
DURKHEIM, E. (1947), *The Division of Labour in Society*, trans. G. Simpson, Free Press.
HARDIN, G. (1960), 'The competitive exclusion principle', *Science*, vol. 131, pp. 1292-7.
OPPENHEIMER, R. (1954), *Science and the Common Understanding*, Simon & Schuster.
OPPENHEIMER, R. (1958), 'The tree of knowledge', *Harper's*, vol. 217, pp. 55-57.

FOOTNOTES

[1]Compare Durkheim's concept of moral density (1947, pp. 256-64).

[2]This scheme would seem to be applicable to other types of segmentation in communities, such as the segmentation of religious groups, families, and nations.

[3]See also Oppenheimer (1954).

5

THE ARBITRARY DISCIPLINES*

Norman Birnbaum

For years an official critique of the division of the world of learning into disciplines has accompanied the growth of ever more rigid compartments of the mind. The very men who as scholars, teachers and administrators perpetuate the academic division of labor argue persuasively that it is nonsense. Committees of inquiry, essays, treatises and speeches have abounded, yet the organization of our academic lives is unchanged. Now there is a revolt within the disciplines: younger scholars—and some not so young—have challenged the authenticity and legitimacy of the established routines. In a number of scholarly societies, determined groups of younger academics (acting with varying degrees of coherence and skill) have demanded immediate and profound changes in the scope and direction of scholarship. The critique is neither abstract nor polite: they propose to terminate the governance of the learned societies by oligarchies of department chairmen—even if the younger scholars are often unclear about what to do with the power they intend to take. Their revolt mirrors, in distorted fashion, the crisis of the disciplines, even though it is a revolt *in* the disciplines and is not in the first instance directed *against* them. It is a sectarian phenomenon in the kingdom of learning, and not a new intellectual ecumenism. Nevertheless, it can tell us much, if at times something other than what the revolutionaries want us to hear.

The very notion of a scholarly discipline contains a fundamental ambiguity. Is a discipline a method of approach to part of our experience, or is it a way of apprehending the totality of our experience? The study of literature, for instance, seems confined to one type of human activity. Literary scholars, however, have not hesitated to use that activity as a means of analyzing the roots of human nature, the

---

* From *Change*, July/August 1969, pp. 10-21, a publication of the Helen Dwight Reid Educational Foundation.

human condition and human history itself. History studies the past—but it encompasses areas treated separately by economics, sociology and literature. Philosophy is divided precisely between those who see it as a totalizing discipline and those who insist on its more limited character, who regard it as an activity criticizing and codifying the processes of knowing and evaluation in other disciplines.

To these difficulties must be added those which come from the preconditions of successful work within a single discipline: an economic description of market behavior entails some psychology; a psychology interested in learning must have some systematic relationship to the study of society; philosophical treatments of scientific discourse rest on certain linguistic assumptions. No doubt it can be argued that there is a distinction between a discipline commanding the resources of other disciplines for its own purposes and the simple dissolution of all disciplines into a total process of knowing without boundaries or limits. Yet ambiguity attaches to the term, *for its own purposes*, and nowhere more strikingly than when specialists attempt—as some still do—to communicate with others.

The situation seems less confused in the physical sciences. There, rigorous reasoning and a strict accountability to fact would appear to exclude the ambiguities of the humanities and the social sciences. It does not take more than a reading of *The Double Helix*, however, to discover that disciplinary lines in the sciences are in flux: indeed, Crick and Watson won their Nobel prize precisely by intruding into domains for which they were technically unprepared. Those with more technical capacity, on the other hand, were so blinded by their specialization that they often did not envisage the possibilities and implications of their findings.

At first glance, then, the division of academic work into disciplines entails inconvenience as well as convenience, and complicates our task as much as it simplifies it. How explain its persistence? The origins of the disciplines go back at least to the medieval universities. Theology reigned supreme, but it was understood in a broad way which by no means precluded the allocation of important intellectual tasks to ancillary disciplines like rhetoric, or the development of subdisciplines like logic. Moreover, the medieval universities exhibited a considerable respect for the world of praxis: their faculties of law and medicine were closely tied to the actual exercise of these professions. Common impressions of the abstractness of scholasticism are false: the debates among the philosophers and theologians had direct relevance to the world of praxis, in politics and technology, and the connection between abstract activity and its practical consequences was fairly evident to the learned community (which was of course small). The division of academic labor into disciplines expressed the division of labor in the larger society; a uniform clerisy shared a few important tasks.

The increased division of labor in the larger society that came in the period between the Middle Ages and the emergence of industrial capitalism had important consequences for the division of labor within the university. The processes of production in the economy included a technological component which accelerated and intensified that systematic reflection about nature long present in medieval philosophy. In the early modern period, however, thought about nature tended to move out of the universities; indeed, much significant work in philosophy itself—as it detached itself from theology—also emigrated from the universities. Learned societies, courts and salons became for a period the sites of significant intellectual activity.

The reconstitution of the universities (in Germany in the eighteenth and nineteenth centuries, in France with the Napoleonic reforms, in Britain in the middle of the nineteenth century, in this country at the end of the nineteenth century) had significant consequences. The organization of the new fusion of reflection, humanistic studies, science and technology followed disciplinary models which had developed as older and more unified fields of inquiry decomposed between the Middle Ages and the industrial epoch. At the same time, the necessity of perpetuating tradition in scholarship entailed continuation of the procedures of apprenticeship, journeymanship and mastership.

In the medieval university, however, faculties exercised collective mastership over learning. In the nineteenth century, in a parody of bourgeois individualism, the masters were individual scholarly *virtuosi*. Faculty organization, the corporate organization of the university, the state or public sponsors and treasurers of the universities, legitimated the *virtuosi*. The disciplines became their private arenas. Precisely when the new industrial organization of society seemed to demand a new flexibility in the universities, new combinations of subject matters and new modes of work, a defensive rigidity pervaded the centers of learning. The contradiction was not fortuitous: it reflected the resistance of the cultivated bourgeoisie to the use of knowledge in the newer forms of market organization. Disciplinary organization, in this setting, was a means for the perpetuation of the cultural and academic domination of the *virtuosi.*

It is striking that the role of the *virtuosi* was least conspicuous in those university systems which were founded, or reformed, in direct response to the pressures of the new industrial epoch: the American land-grant universities, the Czarist universities at the turn of the century, even the German technical universities. These had the explicit function of conducting useful research and of preparing students for technical roles in the new productive apparatus. But even in these systems, disciplinary notions and forms were taken over from the past and from the most prestigious of the older universities. The newer systems exhibited that paradoxical combination of intellectual bureaucratization and professorial individualism which in exaggerated form constitutes the pathology of the university today.

We have been confounding the organization of the disciplines with the powers exercised by the professoriate, and this in turn with the question of the universities' relationship to the larger society. The only way to understand what has become of the disciplines is to understand the use made of their intellectual products. As the division of labor multiplied outside the universities, a strange combination of retrograde traditionalism and farcical adaptiveness resulted in the multiplication of the disciplines. The process was continued because society found profit in it.

Obviously, trained and specific capacities are required by a complex society; and the disciplinary organization of knowledge was one way in which to produce them. Trained capacity, however, entailed trained incapacity in another respect. The increasing narrowness of the disciplines meant that persons with generalized knowledge were rare. The ancient British universities, the French faculties of letters, did produce men learned in philosophy and convinced that they could apply it in the governance of society. In each case, however, the philosophy in question was harmoniously adjusted to the requirements of governing elites (the imperial magnates in Britain, the bourgeois rulers of the Third Republic in France). It was not, in other words, a critical philosophy, and it became increasingly sterile as time went on. The other humanistic disciplines evolved in the direction of what has been termed a mandarin culture, educating persons who could speak only to each other in an increasingly circumscribed language or set of languages. Where knowledge was power, it was power in the limited sense that it could be put at the disposition of others. Where it was critical, it seldom had access to the universities. Marx, Darwin and Freud did their work outside the universities, and in our own time men of orginality and distinction have had no easy career in the universities. The case with the physical sciences was different of course—but the scientists had entered into an implicit compact with society not to challenge the technological uses to which scientific discovery was put.

It is certainly true that work in the humanities and in the social sciences did influence an educated public. Through the education of publicists, teachers in the secondary schools, politicians and state bureaucrats—and the intervention of the professoriat in political controversy—ideas developed in the universities entered the public domain. What is striking about all of this is how little the public cared about the methodological controversies and refinements associated with the disciplines. The public attended, as best it could, to the ideas at issue in the universities. The mandarin-like character of many of the controversies within and between the disciplines troubled the public little, and the resultant insulation from public resonance convinced many in the disciplines of the value of the esoteric nature of their concerns. I am not, of course, referring to the distinction between high culture and mass culture, or between high culture and vulgarization: much of the creative force in high culture in this period was provided by nonacademic intellectuals who found in the universities an atmosphere of intolerable constraint.

At the same time, the multiplication of disciplines reflected public processes. For example, the social sciences as such were not taught in the American universities at the middle of the century: there was instruction in history and in moral philosophy. But in mid-century, the American Social Science Association was founded (in Boston) to deal with the new problems of immigration and urbanization, and out of it grew university instruction in economics and sociology. The sociologists split off from the American Economic Association to form their own society because the economists paid insufficient attention to factors other than the market in the organization of society. In each case, disciplinary developments in the universities expressed a change in the social consciousness of the epoch—new views on social problems developed by new elites. In each case, however, the relevance of the connection to political reality was in the long run lost; a controversy with an original political meaning was made academic, emptied of significant moral content and reduced to the status of esoterica.

The emergence of sociology in the German universities had a similar history. The great controversies over the academic status of sociology pitted sociologists (many of whom perforce taught political economy and philosophy) against historians and jurists. The sociologists held that Germany's inner social problems were serious, that the threat of socialism had to be met by structural reforms. The orthodox academics were also orthodox politically; for them, the central institution in society was not the class system but the state, and the strengthening of the state demanded the concurrence of history and political jurisprudence, not potentially subversive discourse on the conflict of the classes. But methodologically the dispute rarely attained this level of consciousness.

The mandarinism of the disciplines, then, developed for two rather different reasons. Within the universities, it was a mode of domination exercised by ruling professorial oligarchies, by elder generations, by established cliques. It provided ostensibly objective criteria for judging younger scholars. The very notion of a discipline, in its modern academic form, convinced those who worked within it that they were indeed partaking of the great and continuing Western tradition—no matter how miniscule or inane their own activities within it might appear to untutored observation. The codification of disciplinary procedures, indeed, relieved scholars of the one burden most of them found anguishing—that of thinking for themselves.

The sponsors of the universities—the elites who paid for the activities of the professors—took a rather different view. For one thing, they hesitated to challenge the professorial claim that the academic estate was the sole legitimate heir of Western culture's high traditions—from which it followed that criticism of the estate was either ignorant or irrelevant. For another, they were aware that in fields like the sciences and their technological applications, disciplinary organization proved useful. (This conviction has been extended, more recently, to the behavioral social sciences—despite the increasingly fraudulent status of some of them.) Finally, the sponsors of the universities were (and are) well served by a state of affairs in which the division of the kingdom of learning into rigidly compartmentalized fiefdoms prevents it from becoming a republic of virtue, a counter-society within the larger society, capable of mobilizing moral and intellectual resources to change it. This is the very point at which recent criticism of the disciplines within the academy has set in. It is, frankly, a political point: it has become so important because the crisis in the disciplines has been linked to a crisis of generations, of academic authority, and in the relationships of the universities to the world.

Not without a certain melancholy, we may recall that serious men have attempted for more than a generation to obtain a hearing for critiques of the current form of disciplinary organization often far more profound than the cliches of many of today's academic radicals. Robert Hutchins for decades has insisted that the disciplines must become relevant to the concerns of educated men in search of wisdom. The celebrated report of the Harvard Committee on General Education in 1945 proposed educational innovations (at least, innovations for Harvard) which were intended to nullify some of the nefarious consequences of excessive concentration on disciplinary distinctions. Columbia College had developed before that a series of introductory courses which did precisely what Harvard expected its new courses to do. The Hutchins reforms at Chicago, although they left a deep impress upon a gifted generation, were gradually undone by a counterrevolution of the specialists. The experiments at Columbia and Harvard, moreover, were confined to their undergraduate colleges, while their graduate schools (of more influence on American education) allowed the disciplines to run amok.

Remember, too, that considerable efforts were made recently to redeem the disciplinary principle by promulgating a sham negation of it. During the past decade or two, "interdisciplinary" programs have become popular: Russian studies, Chinese studies, mental health studies, African studies, Latin American studies, defense studies, peace studies, poverty studies, urban studies, black studies and—no doubt, its counterpart—studies of civil disorder. These programs involve an entertaining sort of academic alchemy: the collaboration of five sorts of specialist was needed to produce a sixth. No sooner risen, the new academic homunculus behaved precisely like his predecessors and alleged the existence of a new specialization with its own language, methods and "discipline."

Most of the interdisciplinary programs were responses—of a very limited sort—to the demands of praxis: immediate service to interested sponsors and clients able to pay for them. They did not arise out of the inner necessity of the evolution of thought. (Thought, of course, has always evolved in response to the demands made upon it by history.) The immediate nature of these interdisciplinary responses, in institutions not otherwise sensitive to the demands of their times, suggests that there has been something superficial, even contrived, about them. In fact, all of these groupings have had little intellectual effect on the universities; they have left the disciplinary structure intact. Moreover, they have produced an administrative sort of expertise in their own fields, rather than original thought or scholarship. They have not, in other words, expanded our view of the world, but rather have constituted routinized responses to changes in that view which were determined elsewhere—in the society's centers of decision and power.

An antithetical approach to the relationships between the disciplines was provided by the experiments at places like Chicago, Columbia and Harvard. There, men genuinely devoted to teaching attempted (with elite students) to convey some of the essential elements of our cultural tradition. They often enough defined tradition in ways which made implausible, irrelevant or simply ludicrous the customary disciplinary distinctions. Yet they themselves, for perfectly comprehensible reasons, could not sever their own ties with their disciplinary colleagues. They were allowed a protected space to experiment, but were not allowed to carry their experimentation into the strongholds of the disciplines. The able undergraduates they taught later accepted disciplinary conventions—or found no place in the universities. If excessive adherence to practice generally marked the interdisciplinary efforts in problem-solving for the larger society, excessive belief in theory marked the anti-disciplinary educators. They supposed that their compelling example of intellectual excellence would in fact overcome the forces of academic inertia and spiritual sloth. In fact, however, circumstance and interests combined to perpetuate through the 1950's and 1960's a rigidly disciplinary framework in most universities.

We have experienced a period of enormous expansion in higher education, and the end is not yet in sight. The graduate schools, in these circumstances, found themselves in a position of great influence. They controlled the rates of production of new university teachers. They agreed to increase the rates, but exacted the price of doing so in their own way. The multiplication of candidates with theses to write hardly produced a reconsideration of the utility of the thesis, or new thoughts about its function and content. Instead, it produced a further fragmentation of knowledge—often in many fields simply spurious or gratuitous. New centers of graduate instruction invariably patterned themselves on the more established ones.

The problems and contradictions of this process are now becoming visible. The graduate schools have been sending to teaching posts in the undergraduate sector large numbers of younger scholars painfully aware of the gap between their preparation and the tasks they are called upon to perform. It is true that part of the problem is one which neither the graduate schools nor, for the moment, anyone else can solve: the irreducible philistinism and anti-intellectualism of the American population, now represented in institutions of higher education by millions of offspring who have had no relationship to high culture. These students are certainly malleable—but they cannot be moved by crude or vulgarized versions of graduate school culture. The disciplinary organization of undergraduate studies, if it does anything, often reinforces their resistance to education.

The sense of futility and impotence experienced by the younger teachers in their new circumstances has been intensified by factors not directly connected to the implicit tyrannies and absurdities of academic intellectual organization. The great movement of protest, criticism and revolt in American society has divided the universities. One of the expressions of that division has been the demand that learning be made relevant to life—life being defined, variously, as the tastes of a new generation, the needs of underprivileged groups for services hitherto supplied by the universities only to the privileged, and the conflicts of a society capable neither of halting change nor of accepting it.

Many of the demands for relevance, many of the criticisms of traditional academic culture, are tributes by the American Left—quite unintended—to the philistine Right. The movement of protest and revolt in America is sufficiently indigenous to engage at times in the systematic denigration of the activities of criticism and reflection, to demand that ideas be simple and immediately comprehensible, to insist that all intellectual activity be connected to an immediate payoff. The word is in itself significant: rarely has a political movement led by intellectuals exhibited such a lack of literary felicity. The revolt against established culture has depressing components; it is in part a revolt against the moral strenuousness and intellectual rigor of high culture itself, a historical fantasy on the part of the children of television whose early conditioning did little to develop their capacities for the authentic

imaginative transcendence of immediacy. Meanwhile, those students
who have come to the university from highly educated families cry
loudly that they have been revulsed by the uses to which their parents
put education . . . .

The central issue in all the revolts within the disciplines is the social
and political relevance of knowledge. Surprisingly little discussion of
the problems of teaching has taken place, apparently for two reasons.
Many of the radical scholars so despair of the university as an
institution that they feel their activity as teachers within it to be
presently meaningless. Others frankly seem to care rather little about
teaching: they are more intent on establishing contact between the
universities and social groups hitherto excluded from its services. Some,
to be sure, express familiar views on student participation in
curriculum decisions and the educational process. But if they were to
apply to this effort half the critical energy they now expend on the
foibles of their elders, they would surely emerge with a radical new
theory (and possibly even a practice) of university education as a whole.

What is disappointing about the entire discussion within the
disciplines is its lack of concern with the problem of the continuity of
cultural tradition, as important a reason for the existence of universities
as any other. Perhaps there is something American about this
deficiency; at any rate, it blunts the cutting edge of the revolt of the
radical younger scholars.

The radical critique of the existing disciplines could constitute the
beginning point of a radical critique of the system of disciplines in
general—but those who utter the critique are often incapable of
proceeding beyond it. Often enough, they propose counter-disciplines
by offering themselves as candidates for posts in revolutionary
governments to replace the conservative ones which now rule the
separate academic nations. Their notion of a new relationship to praxis
is important, but they often ignore the mediating function of culture. A
direct relationship to praxis may not alone replace conservative or
ossified structures of thought with new ones: it may only tend to
relegate thought to an entirely secondary status. Radical ideas, indeed,
frequently are those which by any immediate criterion appear most
impractical; Marx held that philosophy could become actuality, not by
changing the universities, but by changing society.

In any case, the younger radical scholars who demand new criteria
of relevance in their disciplines have aligned themselves with the

student movement in a number of countries. The more articulate American students, as well as those in France, Germany and Italy, have promulgated extremely negative analyses of the curricula now offered to, or imposed upon, them. The idea that scholarship should be vitalized by response to the demands of history itself is in principle easy to accept. In pedagogic practice, however, a number of severe problems arise.

The present intellectual horizons of the students are shaped, after all, by a limited historical moment; what they may need (even if they do not always know it) is a form of liberation from what a colleague, George Kateb, calls the tyranny of the present. Twenty-year-old students will live out another fifty years of history: their education will have to prepare them for fifty years, nor merely the next five. If the students do not know what they need to know, there will obviously be difficulties with arguments for the immediate and total democratization of the processes by which curricula are devised. Can one seriously imagine Herbert Marcuse or Henri Lefebvre sitting down with students to persuade them that they ought to be allowed to teach Hegel and Marx?

One answer to this problem is to pluralize the universities in fact, and not merely in the self-congratulatory ideology of academic liberals who on no account will consent to changing what they have been doing all their lives. This would entail arrangements for a spectrum of teaching systems at any one university: students would have to pass through some student-taught sequences, some in which they work with their teachers to determine the subject matter to be studied, and others in which they would be taught in more traditional ways. No amount of mechanical innovation, however, can replace the development of new conceptions of the content of university education; at best, innovation can only allow the content to emerge from many trials, and many errors.

No doubt this touches upon the terrible problem of the discrepancy between high culture and democratization—much in evidence in all discussions of increasing access to the universities for those whom the class system normally excludes from high culture. It is easy enough to declare that high culture is a class culture and that therefore it ought to be abandoned if not condemned—a position which ignores the fact that in America, at least, a good part of the culture of those in the bottom part of the class structure is manufactured for it according to market criteria. One of the grotesque aspects of the present situation in the universities is that the disciplinary system in the graduate schools rests on a vulgar democratic notion of the facility with which culture can be acquired. The graduate schools assume, in general, that the preparation needed for the doctorate is technical and not general: anyone, with a bit of luck, can acquire the technique. But the kind of general culture which can enable a student to rise above the trivialities and limitations of graduate work cannot be acquired overnight.

The main innovating force with respect to change in our notion of the disciplines is still to be found in the undergraduate programs. An increasing number of independent study plans, schemes for broad rather than narrow types of concentration, and an extension into the upper years of undergraduate work of the assumptions which animated the earlier general education courses constitute in fact (if not in theory) an attack on the sovereignty of the disciplines.

Related developments are evident in other countries. In France, the Faure educational reforms of 1968 provide for the termination of the traditional French faculties, with their rigid disciplinary demarcations, and their replacement by Unités d'Enseignement et Recherche (Units of Teaching and Research). In Germany, two of the new universities, Konstanz (already opened) and Bielefeld (now being planned), have done away with the traditional system of institutes organized exclusively around the particular interests of one professor of one discipline. In Britain, the new universities of Essex and Sussex have had considerable success with new syllabi which cross customary lines. The success of these teaching programs will have to be measured eventually by their impact on the scholarship of those teaching in them or graduating from them.

Perhaps the difficulty resides in this: we no longer have an effective conception of the general core of culture. Knowledge has accumulated so rapidly and so heavily that the demand that anyone acquire the rudiments of knowledge in the several areas of human inquiry appears utopian. The perpetuation of the disciplines may be a desperate expedient in a situation threatened by intellectual vacuum or sheer chaos. In current circumstance, one solution may lie in postulating the acquisition of intellectual discipline and method as the aim of education—even of advanced education of the doctoral type. This would free the student from bondage to a single discipline, but not from the demands of rigor, precision and mastery supposed to accompany disciplinary specialization.

There is an objection; namely, that as between the several fields of human knowledge (historical knowledge, the study of nature, those sorts of social science which bear at once upon the administration of institutions and more ancient canons of wisdom), no unitary conception of discipline or method can apply. Precisely: the student can rise to intellectual maturity by recognizing the discontinuities in the present stage of the organization of culture, by appreciating the limits of his own mastery of a subject matter. This could have the effect of changing the emphasis of work within the several areas of inquiry from the production of technicians able to turn out finished intellectual products to the education of scholars capable of apprehending the structure of a problem. The education in question would be far from empty of content; indeed, it would place more strenuous demands for the mastery of specific subject matters upon students than they now face, since today these demands can often be met by performances increasingly stereotyped and ritualized.

Designs for academic utopias are cheap; concrete programs for academic change are expensive. The heaviest price will have to be paid by the present professorial generation which will have to give up those illusions of omnipotence it cultivates by encapsulating itself in the disciplines as presently defined. Put another way, the professors will have to abandon not only some of their psychological gratifications, but also some of their power. Again, a certain amount of experimentation may make the transitional process feasible. A social scientist studying the social effects of technology need not fear loss of status by assuming the role of student to a colleague in a technological discipline. An historian interested in revolutions might well find a student-directed seminar on modern American society fruitful: revolutionaries are traditionally voluble, but not all of them are so available for questioning. If we can accept challenges of this sort, we may yet convert the university into an institution in which learning is continuous for ourselves as well as for others—an indispensable preliminary to the transformation of society into a university, a utopian goal made possible by the present role of knowledge in the social process.

For the moment, however, the fragmentation of the disciplines renders all of us passive before a world become increasingly obscure and arbitrary. Originally instruments of mastery, the disciplines have become—despite our volition—means of perpetuating the irrationalities inherent in contemporary society's use of knowledge. The solution does not consist of discarding mankind's accumulation of knowledge as so much pernicious ballast, but in creating new systems for codifying it—not as an immediate political act, but as a way of transmitting to the future a heritage of learning which alone can serve as the basis for a rational polity.

6

DISCIPLINED RESEARCH
AND UNDISCIPLINED PROBLEMS†*

Richard Rose

Far better an approximate answer to the right question, which is often vague, than an exact answer to the wrong questions, which can always be made precise.

Professor John W. Tukey

Because social scientists study the conditions of man in society and governments seek to influence these conditions, there is a logical relationship between the interests and activities of social scientists and public officials. There is a cash nexus because the activities of social scientists are to a very large extent dependent upon support from government funds. There are also links in terms of personnel, for many high-ranking public officials are themselves graduates in the social sciences, and many high-ranking academic social scientists at some stage in their career have held official posts in government, concurrently act as official advisers to government ministries, or maintain unofficial contacts with those in government whose concerns are immediately relevant to the problems that they study in universities.

Notwithstanding these many points of contact, there is an uneasy relationship between social scientists and public officials in many countries where major efforts have been made to utilize the social

† This article draws upon discussions at an international round table on the market for policy research, conducted by the Committee on Political Sociology, IPSA/ISA, and the Institut fur Empirische Sozialforschung (IFES, Vienna) in Vienna, 29 September—3 October 1975, with financial support from the Ford Foundation and the Austrian Government. As co-covenor, I am grateful to the participants for their stimulating comments, but none should be considered responsible for the conclusions drawn herein.

* Reprinted by permission of Unesco from the *International Social Science Journal*, Vol. XXVIII, No. 1, 1976, pp. 99-121. Copyright 1976 by Unesco.

sciences in government. Social scientists complain that their work is ignored by public officials, or the opposite—that government departments are trying to exercise too much supervision or control of their work. The growth of non-university research institutes, both profit-making (e.g. the management consultants, McKinsey & Co.) and non-profit-making (e.g. the American Brookings Institution), as 'middlemen' between university-based social scientists and government departments is further evidence that something is missing in the relationship between government and academic social scientists. Government officials complain that social scientists fail to interest themselves in the real problems facing their country; they are said to worry instead about abstractions that interest specialists of a given discipline. When social scientists do come forward with data, ideas and, even more, prescriptions about what government ought to do, this may not be appreciated by those with the formal authority and power to take decisions. Social scientists may be accused of prescribing naive or politically 'impossible' ideas, and told to go back to the universities, where their academic (in the pejorative sense) knowledge belongs.

The object of this article is to examine the organizational causes of the uneasy relationship between social scientists and government officials and the extent to which the intrinsic character of the 'undisciplined' problems of contemporary societies make this relationship both relevant and difficult. The third section considers, in the light of the limitations identified, strategic measures likely to increase benefits or, at least, reduce waste and frustration in relationships between two overlapping but far from integrated spheres.

Different organizations and divergent disciplines

The social scientist thinks of himself as a free professional whereas the official in government thinks of himself as a bureaucrat. Like any ideal-type distinction, these definitions emphasize one point of difference, notwithstanding many similarities among the two groups and many dissimilarities within each category. The distinction remains crucial, however, in understanding how organizational factors influence the different outlooks of the two groups. As the Washington aphorism known as 'Miles's law' puts it, 'where you stand depends upon where you sit'.

To describe a social scientist as a free professional, capable of exploring ideas unconcerned by their implications for organizations is not to claim that social scientists are unconstrained by social influences, but rather, that the constraints are very different from those operating upon politicians and civil servants working in the bureaucratic structures of formally organized government departments. The daily work of a social scientist differs from that of a bureaucrat because the former is unconstrained by laws stipulating his functions, nor would a social scientist consider that elected representatives had the technical knowledge to direct his research. While academics are increasingly burdened with committee work as the price of university expansion and reform and the 'heavier' forms of social research require research grants typically negotiated with government-sponsored funding agencies, the model social scientist none the less remains an individual scholar, seated gazing contemplatively out of the window, or looking down at a musty book or the day's latest computer printout.

The social scientist is responsive to an 'invisible college' of professional peers, a group that rarely if ever meets collectively, for its members are scattered throughout universities in many lands, and dispersed among universities within his country of residence. The normal mode of social scientific communication is scholarly publication, and the language of discussion is analytic. The social constraints and norms that affect a social scientist's work do not come from government but, rather, from within his profession. The skew distribution of social scientists between countries, the growth of international professional associations and journals, and international mobility toward 'international learning centres' for post-graduate study mean that for many parts of the world the setters of professional standards will be resident in another country or continent.

Whereas society is unitary, the social sciences are subdivided into many specialisms, and development has meant the increasing differentiation of specialisms, both as between disciplines, e.g., economics, sociology, and political science, and within disciplines, e.g., macro- and micro-economics, or the eternally expanding categories of 'the sociology of. . . .' A decade or a generation ago, many professors in the social sciences did not have a university degree in the subject that they professed, because such a degree had not been offered when they themselves were undergraduates. The rapid expansion of universities and of post-graduate training in the social sciences has increasingly meant, as part of professionalization, the employment of individuals with disciplinary training in academic posts concerned with that discipline. Greater depth within a specialism usually means less awareness cutting across specialisms. The focus of social scientists conducting research within disciplinary categories tends to be narrower than that of politicians concerned with the undisciplined ramifications of a problem, or with the interconnectedness of many problems.

University departments initially influence the perception of embryonic social scientists through the systematic instruction and training of post-graduate students. The effect of this training is to give a qualified graduate both professional expertise and a particular definition of what his discipline is about. This definition is sustained by employment in a university or discipline-oriented research institution, where both his initial appointment and promotion prospects are evaluated in terms of his competence in the subject-matter of his discipline. While there is no agreement within a discipline about many matters of major concern, professional associations and the 'invisible college' none the less provide reasonably reliable criteria specifying how colleagues and superiors can tell whether a given individual is doing good work at his discipline. A 'good' economist or a 'good' sociologist is a person who is good at doing what groups of his fellow professionals think is worth doing, and worth doing well.

Professional social scientists are products of the enlightenment, and they tend to define their role, not in terms of profit, as might an entrepreneur, or higher wages, as might a manual worker, but rather in terms of knowledge in the abstract. The enlightenment of society leads to a more knowledgeable society; this is assumed to be *ipso facto* a better society.[1] The utilization of such knowledge is not a principal concern of a social scientist, as it is for someone trained in the law and practising as a lawyer, or trained in medicine and practising as a physician.

Public officials, whether career civil servants or elected or appointed partisans, are important by virtue of their position in the organization of government. Almost invariably the office that a man holds antedates his own appointment, and the bureau and ministry of which it is a part is also well established. The first thing that a public official must do is to become effectively socialized into the norms and values of his office, learning what the organization of which he is a part expects of him.

Whereas the social scientist's work is primarily concerned with ideas, the work of a public official is much more concerned with the allocation and management of tangible resources; the money, personnel, laws and administrative decisions that collectively make up the outputs of his organization . . . .

Public officials tend to define their work in terms of the problem immediately confronting them. In this, they are like engineers, rather than the philosophers and speculative scientists of the enlightenment. They wish to apply knowledge within the policy process, rather than achieve an understanding which, however elegant theoretically, is not relevant to the task before them. A public official does not define problems in terms of a body of abstract theories and concepts, but rather by looking at the pile of papers placed on his desk each morning, or by answering the telephone and learning of another crisis that must be coped with. Policy makers in Washington want to know 'who has the action' in terms of a current issue and public officials wish to 'get a piece of the action'. While no one official expects to control all of the action, he will, like an engineer, want to know whether what he does can produce the effect intended within his relatively narrow, specific and identifiable range of concerns.

As long as public officials and social scientists stay within the boundaries of their own discipline, whether academic or bureaucratic, there is little or no communication or communication problem. Problems of communication arise only when social scientists try to participate in the governmental policy process while remaining academic social scientists, or public officials become involved with social scientists in the hope that this will help government, as well as social science disciplines. Common interests do not make for common appreciations of what is important about a given problem area. The divergences between the disciplines of bureaucrats and social scientists creates confusion and misunderstanding. An Austrian survey of attitudes towards social science research found that public officials did not criticize it on academic grounds, but rather in terms of the inappropriateness of research for their organization; 63 per cent said that the results involved political difficulties and 51 per cent that the results were not concrete enough (i.e., they did not refer to means for managing the problems before them). Criticisms sometimes involved contradictions, e.g., some respondents complained that the results of social science research told them nothing new, and yet concurrently asserted that they disliked novel results that did not fit with the opinions of those inside government.[2]

The enlightenment model of social science gives little attention to the problem of utilizing the findings of research in specific organizational contexts. Social scientists tend to assume that their knowledge can transfer freely, simply because it is difficult to inhibit the movement of anything so intangible as an idea. Good ideas (that is, the learning that constitutes the conventional social science wisdom) are expected to drive out bad ideas, even after allowing for cyclical setbacks arising from the repudiation of conventional wisdom by new intellectual discoveries. The transference of knowledge into government is not a responsibility of social scientists. The appropriate image for transferring ideas comes from meteorology: social scientists are concerned with the climate of opinion. The most highpowered do so by 'cloud seeding' devices making rain. Even when they succeed, there are still many uncertainties about who the rain falls upon, and what effect it has upon those who indirectly feel its impact. The average social scientist adapts to the climate of opinion—within his discipline if not within his society as a whole . . . .

The problem of social problems

To speak of relating social science to social problems inevitably invokes a model of the application of physical sciences to problems of the physical universe. In the latter instance, theoretical understanding of the physical universe and a technology stipulating techniques for applying theoretical propositions lead to changes in real world phenomena. In this paradigm, science and technology are combined leading to results that lead one often to say in the mid-twentieth century, 'science can work wonders'.

Universities train professional scientists and technologists by giving them instruction in theories, techniques and applications to a given standard in a professional qualifying examination. A chemical engineer or a surgeon is a man who has a certificate attesting to his possession of knowledge, and this qualifies him to solve a set of problems defined within the field of that competence. Within academic quarters, highest prestige is usually given to those professionals who are most proficient at theory, rather than applications. The same is true internationally; for example, Nobel prizes are awarded for work in pure science, and not for work in the various subdivisions of engineering technology. In the world of public affairs, highest prestige is usually given to those professionals who are most proficient in applying their skills to specific problems affecting their clients. A man with a legal problem does not want the wisdom of a professor of jurisprudence, but the shrewdness of a lawyer who can find a loophole in an embarrassing document. Similarly, a head of State does not want to employ military theorists whose books are read around the world, but rather, generals who will win battles and wars. The 'quick technological fix' may well date from the time, millenniums ago, when lawyers were first employed to find loopholes in municipal or divine laws so that a monarch could do what had hitherto been thought impossible.[4] The traditionally most honoured professions—the law, the army and the church—were and remain those where the theoretical bases for action are least clear. This is irrelevant among clients who judge professionals in terms of their results, rather than their assumptions.

The paradigm of science and technology depends for its success upon many assumptions. Specially relevant here is the assumption that the scientific theory in question provides understanding of relationships amenable to manipulation by scientists. This is not, however, always the case. For example, for many centuries astronomers have studied the solar system, without being able to alter it. Moreover, the knowledge of astrophysicists runs well ahead of the capability of technologists to build devices sufficiently powerful to test at first hand what they study at a distance. Meteorologists have also been incapable of developing a technology to control the weather which they seek to understand. Moreover, the phenomena that it deals with (e.g., will it rain tomorrow?) are less amenable to accurate forecasting than are phenomena of interest to astrophysicists. The distinction between the virtually certain application of mechanical technology and the probabilistic application of other technologies presents problems for both professionals and their clients. Ironically, where success is most important to individuals, namely the practice of medical science, clients appear ready to accept the fact that a doctor's knowledge offers, at best, only a probability of successful treatment.

A second assumption in the paradigm is that there is a consensus about the subject-matter of the science and the object of its applied technology. Biologists and computer scientists each can specify what they are studying, and that their subject-matter differs from each other.

Biologists agree professionally that it is desirable to understand vital processes of the human body, and computer scientists agree professionally that it is desirable to invent ways in which computers can do their existing work more efficiently, and to develop techniques so that computers can be applied to problems currently outside their scope. Each of these scientific disciplines is clear about what is considered a good thing to do within its field of professional competence.

Logically, assumptions about consensual objectives and an applicable technology imply four possibilities, for a scientific discipline can have consensus or lack consensus about its objectives, and it may provide a good technology for the application of its understanding or lack this. Four possibilities of variable properties of scientific disciplines are given below:

	Consensual examples	Non-consensual examples
Applicable understanding	1. Mechanical engineering	2. Nuclear physics
Lacks applicable understanding	3. Medical research	4. Psychoanalysis

1. The normal model of a scientific discipline presupposes a clear consensus about what professionally qualified practitioners should do, and an understanding applicable to real world phenomena. Most of the engineering sciences fit into this category.
2. The 'politicizing' of a discipline occurs when a dispute arises within it (or is imported from outside) concerning the objectives to which its undoubted understanding should be applied. In the years following 1945, there were disputes among nuclear physicists about whether and in what circumstances their skills should be applied to the development of military weapons. Today, in nations where industrial development has been accompanied by pollution, there are disputes about the application of well-understood chemical techniques polluting the environment.
3. Professionals applying themselves to clearly agreed goals, but without the ability to achieve ends, often enjoy ready support for their efforts. For example, medical researchers concerned with cancer are agreed upon preventing the occurrence of the disease and its fatal consequences. The fact that no advance has been made comparable with immunization for smallpox or poliomyelitis has not deprived cancer researchers of their scientific status, or of funds to continue their work.

4. Professional scientists who disagree about the objectives of their work and about the technology appropriate for undertaking it may have their status as scientists challenged. Psychoanalysts often are so challenged, even when there is evidence that their work may sometimes produce cures (that is, satisfied clients). There is no agreement among psychoanalysts about the objectives of their discipline nor is their technology so well defined or applicable as to produce probablistic-type statements about the consequences of their activities.

In a governmental context, the important point that follows from the foregoing distinctions can be expressed in terms of the following hypothesis: government will make use of professionals in so far as they demonstrate consensus about their objectives, and have a technology to apply their theories to real world phenomena. The hypothesis is important because it explains two types of phenomena, both of which can be readily observed in societies with a large number and variety of scientists. The first is that governments are very large employers of many types of professionally qualified men, ranging from lawyers through engineers to physical scientists and life scientists. Equally, it explains why governments are unlikely to give employment to many professionals whose objectives are in dispute among themselves, and whose understanding is suspect, e.g., psychoanalysts or sociologists . . . .

The subject-matter of social science is 'undisciplined' for many reasons often mentioned in the literature of the philosophy of social science. Social scientists who claim to belong to the same discipline disagree about many fundamental questions concerning theories and objectives of research. These disagreements are most obvious in international gatherings, given the enormous variation in social environments among nations, and in political ideologies shaping perceptions of social phenomena. In recent years, especially in the United States, the international centre of many social science disciplines, domestic disagreements have become prominent, and 'political' caucuses have formed within professional associations. Even when social scientists seek to apply their theories, they usually concern probabilistic relationships. Any prescription given for action must contain a *ceteris paribus* clause; but in complex contemporary societies 'all other conditions' rarely remain equal.

The problems and theories of interest to social scientists are heterogeneous. Within this agglomeration it is important to note the extent to which disciplines vary in terms of consensus about objectives and in the development of an applicable technology. Some variable properties of social science disciplines are given below:

	Consensual examples	Non-consensual examples
Applicable understanding	1. Operations research	2. Economics
Lacks applicable understanding	3. Classic public administration	4. Sociology

1. Consensual fields with a high understanding of what to do to achieve results are peripheral subjects in the social sciences, and may not even be regarded as such. For example, traffic engineering may be considered a branch of operations research, a 'hard' science rather than a social science. Alternatively, consensual topics may be considered not to belong to government public policy since politics is about conflicts between differently valued choices. For example, a prime minister is unlikely to feel that his job is made easier if a specialist in linear programming can determine the optimum allocation of typists in government offices operations research and, in its politically most peripheral aspects, management consultancy, typically apply understanding to consensual objectives.

2. Even though economists are notorious for disagreeing about many matters, public officials are none the less ready to consult with them. The route that leads public officials, especially elected officials, to high office often does not give them training in the technicalities of economic policy. Yet high office gives public officials responsibility for major decisions about the economy, decisions that can have a pervasive impact upon public policy. The fact that economists lack a consensus about what government should do is less significant than the fact that, within such branches of economics as public finance, public expenditure, investment appraisal, money supply, etc., economists do have an understanding that is applicable to the otherwise 'undisciplined' problems confronting politicians.

3. Classic public administration involved consensual goals of 'good' government. Good administration, like good health, was taken for granted as a consensual objective, and academies and schools of public administration promoted the subject. The proponents of classic public administration doctrines also claimed that they had discovered principles of administration which, if properly understood, could be applied in practice. It was assumed that a sharp distinction could be drawn between politics and

administration. Events since the Second World War, both in government and in universities, have disproven these assumptions. Empirical studies of government have emphasized the impossibility of distinguishing clearly between politics and administration, and comparative studies have emphasized how culture-bound and narrow were classical definitions of good government. The attempt to apply principles as prescriptions made it evident that the absence of theoretical justification was not a token of practical efficacy, but rather, often accompanied practical inadequacy. As public administration has become more self-conscious about these shortcomings, its new leaders have tended to 'go political', that is, emphasize non-consensual elements of their work.

4. Any reader of national sociology journals will be well aware that the discipline is non-consensual. Sociologists may challenge the claim that they lack understanding of society. It could even be argued that the very variety of theories and explanations abounding in the discipline is probabilistically an indication that some of them are likely to be right. What is important here is that the theories of sociologists are rarely capable of development into a technology which a government can apply to reduce the social problems that public officials face. In so far as sociologists state that their purpose is not to change the world, but rather to understand it, then the lack of a social engineering capability is no fault in their claim to academic status—but it is a fatal weakness to utilization within government.

The work of social scientists is potentially relevant to the work of public officials, especially high-ranking politicians, in so far as it deals with issues about which there is dissensus. The reason is simple: politics is about the management of conflicting opinions. Activities of government about which there is no dispute are non-political, and therefore, not relevant to the directors of government.[5] The consensual activities of natural scientists and life scientists may be financed by government grants, but they are of little or no concern to high-ranking government officials, until such time as their social implications become evident, and controversial. Government officials are concerned with the social, economic and political elements of scientific activities and not with laboratory work *per se*. For example, medical research is non-political, as long as life scientists are seeking to understand biological processes. It becomes political when efforts are made to apply this understanding through decisions of government, for example, through fluoridation of drinking water or government-sponsored birth control programmes. The political importance of dissensus is illustrated by the fact that economists who work on such controversial questions as unemployment and inflation are more likely to have the ear of public officials than do economists whose recommendations concern such agreed goals as the optimum allocation of floor space in a government building. The fact that the economists have (or claim to have) an understanding applicable to controversial issues gives them effectively more relevance than sociologists, who often address controversial issues and reflect dissensus, but conclude their critiques without making any recommendations that government can act upon. For example, generalizations about the inexorable consequences of industrialization or the importance of changes in cultural values do not interest public officials, because they are not immediately applicable through their existing resources and institutions . . . .

In search of improvements

Any proposals likely to improve the utilization of social science research by government must accept limitations imposed by the institution of government and of social science, if suggestions are to be immediately practicable. Social scientists must accept that public officials are not going to reorganize their institutions, their jobs or their work habits to make possible the application of social science techniques. For example, the economist's model of rational allocation of resources through a central decision-maker implies a government with a single centralized decision-making official or agency. In governments where power is not so centralized, public officials want social scientists to redefine their models to fit existing institutions, rather than change institutions to suit models whose assumptions in the abstract do not fit their own circumstances. Equally, in countries where social science disciplines have become institutionalized, within departments of universities, academies and institutes, and through professional associations with internationally recognized and defined roles, social scientists have a strong interest in maintaining institutions as important to them as established bureaux are to bureaucrats. In countries without a well developed and established range of social science disciplines, a government would find it difficult to create professional cadres of personnel outside the framework of internationally recognized disciplines, for imported staff or students sent abroad for training are likely to acquire conventional social science outlooks.

A second inhibition to the utilization of any type of policy-oriented research arises from properties intrinsic to politics. Social scientists may seek to improve their understanding of the causes of poverty, ill health, unemployment and other major social concerns of the contemporary world. They may even arrive at theories, apply these theories to real-world phenomena, and deduce prescriptions for action that appear more coherent or more efficacious than the theories and applications of government. But this is as far as social scientists can go on their own, and it is not far enough to make their work effective within government. Any conclusions arising from research must be tested by political standards, as well as by the criteria of social (or natural) science disciplines. Political standards imply conflicts about ends as well as questions of means. Social scientists cannot, qua social scientists, remove conflict and create consensus in the political process. In the absence of consensus, they cannot hope for unanimity about the specification of desirable goals. To resolve conflict or to determine specific programme objectives is a political not a social scientific act.

The importance of the political content of social science subject-matter is made evident if one considers the likely demand for policy research in three different types of political systems.[8] In a system characterized by a very high level of consensus and clarity about political goals, there would probably be little or no political demand for new government policies and programmes. Policy-relevant research would then be concentrated upon classical concerns of efficiency experts: time and motion studies of routine clerical tasks of low echelon bureaucrats, the forecasting of future manpower needs to assist civil service recruitment, etc. Management scientists would claim that they have the technology appropriate to improve, if not resolve, many of the problems that arise in routine operations of government directed at clear, consensual objectives. Such disciplines can be found within universities, but usually they are classified as part of business studies, rather than as central disciplines of the social sciences. In a political system with a high degree of conflict about fundamental values the primary need is for political philosophies or ideologies justifying competing and very different approaches to the activities of government. The fact that scholars, after centuries of meditating upon how the State ought to be governed, have reached no agreed conclusions, does not detract from the political relevance of their activities in societies where political philosophies are competitive and very much in conflict. In a third, intermediate type of State, with some disagreement and uncertainty about goals, the demand for new policies will be greater than in a completely consensual system, and the demand for workable policies greater than in a high conflict system where arguments may concentrate upon ends for their own sake. In such a system, one would expect to find social scientists divided about whether their chief role was that of philosophers or ideologists, expounding and defending the choice of specifically valued objectives, or, alternatively, experts with technical skills, seeking to explore the implications of a variety of programme alternatives, leading to conclusions about consequences which may be evaluated differently by different groups in society. The comments that follow are chiefly directed to situations of this third type.[9]

The most straightforward strategy for social scientists to adopt, confronted by demands and problems outside their discipline, is to withdraw from involvement in the problems of government. Withdrawal can take many forms, from concentration upon philosophical and speculative questions well beyond the immediate capability of government to effect, through empirical work with little or no policy relevance to theories offering explanations of long past historical circumstances, without regard to the possible application of these findings to specific problems confronting contemporary governments. The larger and more secure the social science discipline is, within a country or internationally, the greater the likely priority of 'reflexive research', that is, work that feeds back into the discipline, rather than being intended primarily to affect those outside the discipline in society at large . . . .

Effectively, social scientists seeking greater relevance for their work in government must choose between giving priority to a role within an academic discipline, where the demands of the policy process are secondary, or else, a role in the public bureaucracy, where organizational demands come before the demands of academic professions. The simplest improvement that one can suggest is for individuals who are adept at both roles to move freely back and forth between these two worlds. As long as they are good bureaucrats when in government and good social scientists when in a university post, their colleagues are happy. As long as one role is taken at a time, those in question need suffer little tension and gain in breadth and depth of understanding.

For a government to use social scientists *qua* social scientists is difficult, because it requires both an environment congenial to social scientific work, and the identification of issues or elements of problems amenable to social scientific analysis. The logic of the preceding analysis implies the creation of organizations independent of government, insulating social scientists from immediate political pressures and independent of universities, insulating them from the pressures of university departments and professional associations. The staff of such an organization would not be free from constraints in approaching problems; instead, the organization would be structured to create constraints conducive to the desired output—policy relevant research.

Such organizations are typically called research institutes, albeit labels differ greatly both between language areas and within single nations. The crucial conceptual attributes are twofold: (a) a 'public problem' orientation, e.g., concern with health, housing, traffic, education, transportation, etc.; (b) a multidisciplinary and interdisciplinary approach to research. The problem focus differentiates a research institute from university departments oriented toward single elements of a problem whether economic, sociological, administrative, political or psychological. Specialists in such disciplines are found within research institutes, but they are not expected to pursue problems as defined by professional associations, but rather, as defined by public policy concerns. Academic problems tend to be esoteric, relating to the world of an academic discipline; policy problems tend to be exoteric, relating to the larger world of political discourse. An institute will draw together specialists in several disciplines to study several social science elements not only in isolation, but in specific contextual relationships. The structuring of activities in such institutes may seem unconventional to an academic, but that is only because the structure of government departments rather than universities are followed. In the United States, the distinction between academic research and institute research is made very evident by the fact that the nation's capital city, Washington, D.C., is the location of dozens of research institutes, but not of one front-rank university[11]. . . . The catalogue of potential uses for social science does not promise to relieve all the problems of any government or society. Social scientists should ask themselves: Why should it? Even when they have good grounds to believe that their understanding is superior to government policy of the day, they cannot expect, as social scientists, to mandate these views upon society through government action. This can happen only in a technocracy, that is, a political system dominated by experts whose standing is defined by technical skills related to specific bodies of subject-matter. A technocracy is inconsistent with the politician's view of government as the prerogative of political leaders, men whose expertise is very differently derived than that of social scientists, and validated by different means, e.g., popular election or seniority within the civil service rather than by formal social scientific research procedures. If a social scientist wishes to apply his knowledge within the structure of government, he can do so—but he must first change roles, from that of social scientist to that of politician, and demonstrate capability in that sphere . . . .

If public officials think social scientists, in their political naiveté, expect more influence than their expertise and status warrants, social scientists may retort that public officials often assume that their power and status gives them greater knowledge than the consequences of their actions imply. In a world in which governments are very much on the defensive, because of the multiplicity of problems that have to date proven unamenable to discipline by either governmental action or social scientific analysis, neither group is in a strong position to criticize the other. The argument for social scientists to undertake research of policy relevance is not that such work can resolve essentially political conflicts, but rather a more modest, but for the same reason, stronger argument. Reviewing the difficulties arising from established policies determined within government, social scientists can invoke the law of comparative advantage: 'there must be a better way'.

FOOTNOTES

[1]cf. Daniel Bell, *The Coming of Post-Industrial Society*, New York, N.Y., Basic Books, 1973; and Samuel P. Huntington, 'Post-Industrial Politics: How Benign Will it Be?', *Comparative Politics*, Vol. VI, No. 2, 1974.

[2]See Karin Knorr, 'The Policy Instrumentation of Non-Profit Research, or Policy Science and the Non-Profit Research Institute', a paper presented to the Committee on Political Sociology, IPSA/ISA International Roundtable on the Market for Policy Research, Europa Haus, Vienna, 1975, henceforth cited as Vienna Roundtable. For the United States, see Nathan Caplan, 'Social Research and National Policy', below.

. . . .

[4]Sometimes, the fix failed to take. See, for example, Sophocles' *Oedipus Tyrannus*.

[5]Since dissensus requires that political figures be aligned on both sides of an issue, social scientists will have their statements ignored if there is a negative consensus among public officials that their views are impractical, nonsensical or incomprehensible.

. . . .

[8]This paragraph reflects ideas set out in Arnold J. Meltsner, 'Policy Research, Analysts and the Bureaucracy', Vienna Roundtable, 27. For Meltsner's detailed discussion of the influence of organization upon policy analysts in the American context, see his forthcoming book *Policy Analysts in the Bureaucracy*, Berkeley, Calif., University of California Press, 1976.

[9]The Vienna Roundtable, which provided the stimulus for this paper, tended to register agreement among American, Austrian, British and German participants on one point: unique national character or cultural differences are of little or no significance in accounting for differences in the relationship of social scientists and government. Moreover, what are sometimes labelled national differences, as if intrinsic to a culture, in fact are often institutional differences (e.g., the contrast between federal and unitary states) that create variation cross-nationally—but by the same token argue against theories of national uniqueness.

. . . .

[11]Participants in the Vienna Roundtable, after reviewing papers on profit-making and non-profit-making research institutes, tended to conclude that the distinction was not central for relationships between government and social scientists. In so far as government influences such research by acting as the funding contractor, its influence will be greatest *vis-a-vis* institutions requiring contracts to meet fixed overhead costs. It should be noted that some non-profit institutions, including university-based research institutes in the United States, may rely upon government contracts to meet non-profit overheads. Some commercial organizations may have a surplus of potential clients as against staff numbers so that they can select among potential clients those whose problems most interest the firm, and avoid pressures to take on tasks solely for pecuniary reasons.

7

THE DIALECTIC AND RHETORIC OF DISCIPLINARITY AND INTERDISCIPLINARITY*

Julie Thompson Klein

The Disciplinary Paradox

... The first part of the paradox—the essential use of disciplinarity—leads to the second—the essential role of disciplinary behavior and structure in interdisciplinary inquiry. Kenneth Boulding addressed the problem for general systems, oft touted as one of the most promising of interdisciplinary approaches. One might expect philosophers would have had a place for general systems. Yet they were "hostile," viewing it as "an amateur threat to professional interest." Necessarily then, to gain respect and a place, general systems faced an inevitable dilemma, which Boulding not surprisingly conceives in organic, systemic terms:[8]

> Unless, therefore, general systems itself becomes a discipline, and an intellectual species, the other species in the intellectual ecosystem are likely to regard it more as a virus that threatens them than as a food to sustain them.

What, however, is the price? Boulding already recognized a certain loss of generality:[9]

> The identification of general systems with systems science and especially with large-scale computer modeling may threaten its philosophical growing edges, even though systems science itself has a great deal of validity as a discipline.

The only choice, Boulding suspected, may well be to practice both disciplinarity and interdisciplinarity. There might be "a niche," he

---

* From *Issues in Integrative Studies*, Vol. 2, 1983, pp. 35-47. Copyright 1983 by Association for Integrative Studies.

thought, for general systems as a "kind of quasi-masonic order, a quasi-secret society, among those who have to be good little disciplinary boys and girls outside the lodge in order to survive, but who have a hankering for a larger view, a broader perspective than can be found in single departments or disciplines."[10] That would recognize the importance of discipline itself as a process of detecting error and distinguishing good from bad work. Yet it would also show that discipline is inadequate if it is "too self-contained and too much closed to information from the outside."

Becoming disciplinary in this sense is justified for several reasons. It means moving from the catalyst stage so popularly associated with interdisciplinary exploration to the substantive stage of interdisciplinary inquiry. When tied to the detection of error and the value of an epistemic community for testing new work, "discipline" has an undeniably positive value. When tied to the danger of prematurely settling upon one working paradigm to demonstrate solidarity or dealing with the problems attendant to maintaining departmental status, it has negative connotations. In those cases "discipline" signals the threat to invention and exploration which gave rise to the interdisciplinary alternative in the first place. What is most important is the problem of self-containment and it is here that the paradox is firmly seated. Containment is necessary for consolidation and development. Yet it sets in motion the definition of parameters.

A few examples are in order.

The first is that of immunopharmacology. It emerged as a specialty out of recognized needs and interrelationships. The overlap between pharmacology and immunology was acknowledged some time ago. Research of "an immunopharmacological nature" was conducted early in the century by Paul Erhlich, who was working with antitoxins in search of specificity of treatment. The resulting specific receptor concept established links between immunology and pharmacology in the early 1900's. Later, some of Erhlich's contemporaries applied the receptor theory more widely and then, in the 1940's, structural chemical approaches to immunological specificity were founded. Other early and later investigations further forged these links but the emergence of a subspecialty depended, as it so often does, on the fuller development of both parent fields.[11] Immunopharmacology advanced from its early role as an appendage to bacteriology to a much wider view in teaching, research and administration. It was able to grow from simply practical applications (vaccines, skin tests, diagnostic antisera, blood groups and allergic reaction) to exploration of its theoretical structures when chemists, zoologists and geneticists started building a new conceptual structure for the field. Several publications and a new journal now support the concentrated study of immunopharmacology. There were two books bearing the title published in the mid 70's, one in 1975 and the other in 1977. Then in 1979 the *International Journal of Immunopharmacology* was created to provide a forum for disseminating and testing new work in the field.

The success of future work in immunopharmacology will depend on immunologists and pharmacologists becoming more sophisticated in knowing each other's work. They must also become more knowledgeable about the principles and new techniques of chemistry and physics, so they may better understand chemical manipulation of the immune system.[12] That progress, however, will raise new problems in training in immunopharmacology.

Janice Lauer considered these problems when she thought about how graduate students could be trained in the study of written discourse. The majority of theorists in this new field are members of English departments who have been investigating, as Lauer defines it, "the causes of increasing illiteracy and developing 'new rhetorics' to account for the processes of pedagogy of written discourse, especially those kinds of discourse ignored by literary studies."[13] From the start, their study has had a "multidisciplinary cast." They saw the field not as a *tabula rasa* but as a place for building on relevant work in other fields and for using investigative methods refined elsewhere.[14] Their questions about the nature of the writing process, the interaction among writer, reader, subject matter and text as well as their speculations about "the epistemic potential of writing and its implications for improving powers of inquiry" led them into foreign domains. They moved into classical rhetoric, transformational and tagmemic linguistics, semiotics and speech-act theory. They made psychological studies of creativity, problem-solving and cognitive development. They also ventured into philosophical studies like those of Gadamer, Johnstone, Perelman, Toulmin, Polanyi and Kuhn. There they found theories which helped them deal with the problem domain defined by the dissonance they had experienced "between their responsibility for composition and the inadequacy of their understanding and training for it."[15] They also used several modes of inquiry: historical studies, theoretical research, linguistic analysis, hermeneutic studies and empirical work.

Their "multimodality" has its risks and advantages. The vastness and density of their problem domain has a certain "subtle seduction," Lauer explains. Multimodality helps to avoid near-sightedness and cultivates a "fruitful reciprocity among modes":[16]

> Historical studies have kept the field from reinventing the wheel; theoretical work provides guidance and hypotheses for empirical research, which, in turn, offers one kind of test or validation of theory. Hermeneutical and linguistic studies buttress and act as heuristics for theory development.

In addition, connected as they are to praxis in the classroom, composition studies enjoy a constructive interplay between empirical and theoretical modes. Yet, there are problems. The "burden of comprehension" demands knowledge of not just what is borrowed from another field but its context, history and status in that field. Then, training must be defined and negotiated with English departments.[17]

Multimodality can create further problems in that camps may develop around certain modes and certain disciplinary dominances. That happened in both social psychology and in American studies. Social psychology is probably the most frequently cited example of an interdiscipline. Characterized in its early days by the work of Allport, Sherif, Champman, Volkmann and others, it deals with problems lying between sociology and psychology.[18] Yet there is a controversy about the two social psychologies, one psychological and the other sociological. They have different methods, theories and foci. Sociological social psychology has tended to use survey research, with an anti-experimental, anti-laboratory bias. Psychological social psychology tends to center in laboratories and favor experimentation, with more interest in intra-personal, cognitive concerns than extra-personal, social-structure concerns. What has resulted in most discussions is what Thomas Blank calls "a dichotomy on the basis of disciplinary identification."[19] David Wilson and Robert Shafer even concluded after a survey to determine differences between the two social psychologies, that they weren't very interdisciplinary after all.[20] Still, social psychology has moved in directions which separate it from its parent disciplines. Moreover, concepts such as symbolic interaction have been borrowed back in the parent disciplines, demonstrating the kind of influences that can develop between original disciplines and new interdisciplinary inquiries.

Both the problems of disciplinary dominance and premature settling upon one holism plagued American studies. It was accused of becoming "disciplinary" because it took on departmental trappings, and it concentrated at an early point on a search for *the* American mind as well as the critical method of myth and symbol analysis. Since American studies grew out of interactions between English and History departments, it also retained those disciplinary dominances, with the relegation of social-science methods to a periphery. Those biases have come under vigorous attack from several quarters, including the attack on the consensus search for *the* American mind in history, the analysis of limitations to myth/symbol criticism in literature departments and American-studies forums, as well as the complaints from ethnic and minority groups that their voices were excluded not only by traditional disciplines but by American studies as well.

Although the debates have been rather tense at times, they have taken place before multiple audiences, a phenomenon characteristic of interdisciplinary inquiry and ultimately productive of wider dialogue. There is debate directed at external critics of American studies, generally in the form of demonstrations of current working premises, new research and information-rich retorts to outside attacks. There is debate between American studies and the minority forum which split off to develop their own deeper and wider forums for developing and testing new perspectives against the current American studies philosophy, not altogether different from the kind of debate that often develops between subspecialties and mainstream disciplinary views. The debate has been genuinely productive in several ways. Women's studies has published some of its analyses of the American studies/women's studies relationship in important American studies journals and is usually regarded as the most developed of the ethnic/minority studies. Ideas and concepts about American culture which were developed in American studies teaching and research are finding their way back into History, Literature and even Anthropology departments. Unfortunately, now that a lot of the studies programs are being dismantled in budget cutbacks, their efforts are undermined and the debate severely limited. Yet, discussion continues not only in what interdisciplinary journals and associations do survive, but in the new perspectives which have penetrated traditional disciplinary research programs.

What comes through these examples most clearly is the power of community in defining, conducting and evaluating interdisciplinary work. Ronald Grele defined a "community of interest" in oral testimony, a field among those whose work and practice "is dependent upon knowledge of the contextual analysis of the spoken word."[21] Like immunopharmacology, oral testimony emerged because of particular developments in its two core disciplines, in this case linguistics and anthropology. Moreover, the possibilities for intellectual integration were recognized among the subdisciplines of psycholinguistics, sociolinguistics, ethnohistory and ethnomethodology studies. In older, more traditional disciplines, such new methodologies and practices as oral history, English as a second language and the linguistic study of poetics fostered new awareness of the voice as "a medium through which information is conveyed." Finally, there were other forces encouraging the study of people face to face in the field: the academic revolution of the 60's, the declining job market and a concern for broad cultural analysis.[22] Oral testimony had, Grele explained, "its own impetus toward interdisciplinarity" because the material could not be exploited within the narrow conventions and methods of specialties. While the disciplines and subdisciplines of oral testimony have not emerged as an integrated field of study, their interpenetration is becoming more obvious and Grele himself has outlined a framework for incorporating the interpenetrating disciplines. Two points about his proposal are noteworthy. First of all, his critical review of the field appeared in *American Quarterly*, a major journal for American studies which regularly features bibliographical essays on important subspecialties as well as an annual bibliography which alerts scholars to work in various fields. Second, Grele stipulates that field workers in each discipline concerned with oral testimony must learn what kinds of information other investigators need and familiarize themselves with the technical needs of those in other fields. Finally, they must collectively produce materials usable by the widest range of investigators. They must assume Lauer's "burden of comprehension." They must also recognize their liability for other disciplinary and subspecialist interests in the material under interdisciplinary investigation. They must work through forums which not only serve the needs of their "community of interest" but also continually reappraise those needs in light of the multiple audiences which comprise the interdisciplinary dialogue.

They must, in short, practice discipline with regard for the breadth of their community and the complexity of their domain . . . .

... Interdisciplinarity is metaphorically structured by more than one concept; but the most obvious, the surface structure, is that of geopolitics. Geopolitical language is not uncommon in discussions of knowledge. We have been mapping knowledge into spheres, world, fields, provinces and kingdoms for some time. In fact, when they studied the relationship between the curriculum and the disciplines, Arthur King and John Brownell found a world of "methodological imperialism" between fields.[46] In that world the chief activity is dispute over territory, not just in education and research but even in medical-care teams, where a patient becomes the "turf" of specialists. In the logic of the geopolitical metaphor as it appears across interdisciplinary discourse, a discipline is "private property" with "no trespassing notices,"[47] a "domain" with its own "turf." A field is an "empire," and a graduate division a "territory."[48] Each separate scientific domain is a "balkanized region of research principalities,"[49] "feudalized" like other scientific disciplines into separate "fiefdoms."[50] Locked in their "autonomous fiefs,"[51] their "bastions of medieval autonomy," the disciplines nurture their "academic nationalism," keeping departmental turf "jealously protected"[52] and "domain assumptions" firm.[53]

However, "floundering expeditions into territories already explored by other disciplines" disturb the status quo. So do ventures to the "borderlands" and the "frontiers" of knowledge, advanced as they are by "cutting-edge questions."[54] Where once "no interdisciplinary interlopers invaded,"[55] there is "alien intrusion."[56] The map now shows "enclaves" of interdisciplinarity, "little islands"[57] occupied by interdisciplinarians who argue for "transdisciplinary cosmopolitanism,"[58] for new structures and "global strategy."[59] Yet, with the "annexing" of "satellite disciplines,"[60] there is resistance, for no disciplines willingly abdicate their "mandated sovereignty."[61] Interdisciplinarity faces a full-scale problem of "foreign policy,"[62] and "bi-lateral treaties"[63] may be in order ....

Given those circumstances, it is not surprising to find the rhetoric of belief affixed to the rhetoric of suzerainty and war. To experiment with disciplinary knowledge is to tamper, to "meddle with" the "preordained,"[67] to disturb the "intellectual idols," to suggest tearing off the "labels which still decorate the pediments of the university temples,"[68] even to challenge the "awe-inspiring pontiffs."[69] The "sheer force of orthodoxy" drives disciplinarity into a fixed hole, like an ostrich with its head in the ground.[70] Disciplinarians who "sing out of the same prayerbook"[71] find "right doctrine" in their journals.[72] Yet, the interdisciplinary impulse is to "convert" the specialists into generalists, just as they were once "baptise[d]" into specialists. The specialists may have "worked their alchemy,"[73] but the generalists too enjoy certain powers and even had a "Bible" in the Harvard redbook on general education.[74] Interdisciplinarians have staged "revivals" and dispatched their own share of "missionaries." They even have their own "frequent strain" of "millenial interdisciplinarity," advanced by a "scornful prophetic minority" with its corner on "some special Truth."[75]

The belief turns ideological for those who see interdisciplinarity as the "implement for a blithe liberation"[76] and for those who use it as a "vehement protest" against fragmentation.[77] Universities are described as "prisons with hermetically sealed cells for inmates with the same record,"[78] disciplinary jargon as "suitable discourse" for translating new "arsenal concepts,"[79] and laboratory research in psychology not just as a paradigm of practice but "the most efficient and powerful weapon" in the "social psychological research armamentarium."[80] Little wonder, once the dust has settled, that some will have "moved their careers to safety within traditional departmental boundaries."[81]

The arguments for change are both provocative and productive because the imperialism cuts both ways. While resisting attempts to usurp their data and theory in the name of interdisciplinarity, disciplines may well be asserting their own imperialistic claims. Rhetorician Wayne C. Booth sees such imperialistic claims forcing matters into "the courts of communal discourse,"[82] where separate rationalizations are "transmuted." Just as cross-pressures in voting can free individuals from traditional positions, the "intellectual cross-pressures" of interdisciplinarity may yield new outlooks.[83] Disciplinary imperialism is not altogether unhealthy, Andre' Lichnerowicz advises, for it obliges other disciplines to "receive, accept and modify points of view and to use concepts, methods and techniques that have come from elsewhere." The "master words" and "master concepts" of one discipline are less likely to turn into "intellectual idols."[84]

Beneath the combative surface picture, there is another conceptual structure which goes beyond the geopolitical circumstances to describe the epistemology of interdisciplinarity. At first glance, we find just what we might expect. The physicist looks at interdisciplinarity in terms of elements and particles of knowledge, the mathematician in terms of subsets, the biologist of symbiotic ideals and fecundity, the economist of market strategies, the anthropologist of disciplinary ethnocentrism and tribal rivalries, the systems theorist of feedback and cybernetic relation, the sociologist of sibling rivalries . . . and predictably so on. Still, there is a distinct pattern of language and argument. The languages of mathematics, physics, biology and general systems have been particularly prominent in the discourse. Knowledge is mapped as clusters of lines and coefficients, sets and subsets, and as "powerful vectors" present along a continuum "from subatomic particle to gallaxy[sic].[85] There is an easy union of mathematical, formal logical and physics languages, talk of the "locus," "vectors" and "clusters" of knowledge not just among disciplinary users of such language but increasingly among others who have found them appealing, if not downright fashionable. "Sets," "subsets" and "material fields" are described at their "overlapping patterns," their "nexus" points and even at a "center of gravity." Most of all, they are not static sets. Knowledge is usually pictured in interdisciplinary discourse as a dynamic system moving vigorously at the "frontiers of convexity" and advanced by "fission" and "fusion," the two most popular scientific terms for describing change.

In the second half of this century, particularly, there has been an oscillation between the metaphors of the machine and the organism. There is a lot of talk about "interfacing," the most popular term borrowed from the language of computer systems.[86] When questions and problems arise, it takes an "interfacing" of knowledge and practical approaches to solve them. Stored programs must be adapted to new information,[87] the "through flow" of people used productively, the "operator" and the "entrepreneurs" marshalled. But to do that, Nevitt Sanford argues, generalists must synthesize and address the "dynamics of specialized knowledge, whose sudden thrusts within a limited sector of a social system create imbalances in the whole."[88] Leo Apostel, one of the early theorists who uses cybernetic language, has in fact developed an elaborate market productivity metaphor to illustrate the best possible "operations" for interdisciplinarity in society as a whole.

Still, the dominant metaphor of a system is an organism. The organic metaphor has enjoyed favor in interdisciplinary discourse because it establishes interdisciplinarity as a natural, ingenerative process. That metaphor stresses evolution and fluctuation of knowledge rather than structural foundations or states of equilibrium. The image of an organism puts knowledge in "live relationships," a combination of macroscopic relationships in which the mental complexity of the human mind finds for several writers a ready analogue in the workings of the ecosystem. The "hybrid vigor" of interdisciplines, the "symbiotic ideal" of the Meikeljohn curriculum, the "symbiosis" of an interdisciplinary curricular model: all demonstrate the synergistic value of interdisciplinarity. In a recent book entitled *Interdisciplinary Teaching*, general education is described as "in the wind," a "growing swell."[89] It becomes easy, in fact organically proper, for biologist Lewis Thomas to see a poem as a healthy organism.[90] The natural model of the bodily paradigm regains its appeal in Carl Hertel's article, "Toward an Energic Architecture," while language in poetry is likened to the molecule with its functional information.[91]

The organic metaphor further invites the metaphor of pathology in writing upon education. The wrong kind of knowledge is *dead* knowledge. The "dreaded poison" of specialization requires the "antidote" of interdisciplinarity. The university is beset by "hardening of the arteries" and the patient needs "surgery."[92] However, there is a risk. As Michaud and Briggs put it, "how can new organs capable of changing the whole organism be transplanted without killing him?"[93] If specialization is a disease, interdisciplinarity is not progress but "a symptom of the pathological situation in which man's theoretical knowledge finds itself today."[94] In the most extreme version of the metaphor, professors are "authoritatively performing their appropriate mortuary rites," cast as undertakers in charge of corpses of dead knowledge and threatened by changes which ought to be seen as natural, "benign developments," not "destructive disasters to be resisted."[95]

Growing use of the organic metaphor seems almost a fulfillment of the forecast C.C. Abt made in his working papers prior to the 1970 Centre for Educational Research and Innovation seminar:[96]

It seems that consideration of the dynamic life cycle of a discipline has more insights to offer than the static, taxonomic view of the division of scholarly labor. Viewing disciplines as organic entities may prove to be a more productive analogy than architectural ones offer. We can at least look for what feeds the growth or poisons the survival of a discipline, and what groups of disciplines coexist in harmonious fecundity spawning new disciplines through interdisciplinary intercourse, using the organic analogy.

Contiguous disciplinary relations are described in language accentuating natural relations: their "links," "symmetry," "convergence," "conjuncture," "interactions," "integration" and "interface." Interdisciplinary work is perceived as a process of natural mediation along "intercultural," "interdependent," "interstitial," "intersectional," and "interdepartmental" lines. Problems anthropomorphically elude the "grasp" of a single discipline and "refuse" to stay within boundaries. Ultimately the organic metaphor corresponds to the geopolitical metaphor in that it is a definition of the "natural" place and the "inherent" need for interdisciplinarity in that geopolitically conceived environment. It is the identification of natural place against historically-determined divisions . . . .

. . . Two final metaphors deserve summary comment because both speak to the tension between analysis and synthesis which is such a prominent theme in the discourse. Julian Huxley used a popular image when he advocated reforming science on a "centripetal, convergent pattern," to alleviate the damage of its present "non-pattern" of centrifugal and often divergent trends. Les Humphreys and many others have likewise argued that interdisciplinary thought has "centripetal power." [105] Huxley himself was uncomfortable with interdisciplinary terminology. He felt changing to a centripetal pattern required a problem focus, "a concentrated attack on specified problems." To avoid using the "fashionable" term of "multidisciplinary," he would prefer to call it just "plain cooperative." Terminological quibbles aside, Huxley arrived at the centripetal position for the same reasons many interdisciplinarians do. Intercommunication, cross-contact and cross-fertilization constituted "a kind of reproductive union, producing new generations of scientific offspring, like biophysics or cytogenetics." The separate sciences, on the other hand, were behaving like galaxies in an expanding universe: "diverging at increasing rates from some central position towards some limiting frontier." [106]

Both Huxley and B.M. Kedrov spoke at the same international colloquium on the theme of science and synthesis, organized by UNESCO to mark the tenth anniversary of the deaths of Albert Einstein and Teilhard de Chardin as well as the fiftieth anniversary of the theory of general relativity. Kedrov posited a metaphorical model for the advancement of science, a symmetrically truncated cylinder: [107]

According to the angle it makes with the plane, its projection on the plane may be a circle, a triangle, a square, or all three at once—like shadows projected upon the ceiling and two different walls.

Thus,

From the point of view of simple analysis, the aspect of the object-model changes according to the standpoint from which it is viewed. But from the synthetic point of view, the different aspects of the model can be seen to belong to the same object by relationships which can be determined.

Integration depends upon synthesis and synthesis takes account of analytic data. By first studying the projections individually, by breaking down the geometrical image of the body into its "constituent elements," then reconstructing on a theoretical level, science can move, Kedrov concludes, "from the one to the many, and from the simple to the compound."

Huxley's view is more organic in that he sees interdependencies and intercommunication as centripetal *forces*, as established processes of reproduction. Kedrov's view is more mechanical in that he achieves integration by manipulating the cylinder and by moving from the part to the whole. That manipulation corresponds to the image of loosening horizontal lines and choosing to work in the zones between the established vertical pillars of knowledge. The difference is important. The organic image assumes there are linkages which have been obscured or even damaged by divisions which developed out of historical contingencies. The view that those natural connecting forces will reestablish connecting links is the dominant ideal of interdisciplinary discourse. Yet, it is for the most part just that, an ideal against which efforts towards integration and the mediation of potential solutions to problems are measured. The day-to-day reality of interdisciplinary work is that centripetal power does not function of its own accord. The interdisciplinarian therefore manipulates projections of synthesis and resolution. In that final sense, the root organic metaphor is a description of philosophical premises, while the geopolitical metaphor is a definition of the circumstances which make interdisciplinarity an architectonic, constructive art of resolving the tension between analysis and synthesis.

The interdisciplinary idea appears in a considerable variety of circumstances, from high-level presumptions of unity across the sciences and powerful holistic paradigms to more modest searches for relationships among disciplinary clusters and instrumental resolution of conflicting approaches to a single problem. However, despite that variety, there are common claims and goals which the metaphoric conceptual structures expose in their own rich and various textures. The most central claim is that of place and the dominant method is that of discerning the means to achieve integrative and synthetic thought amidst disciplinary structures and strategies which are seen as both complement and contradiction in the eyes of different theorists. Regardless of the theorists' ultimate philosophies, however, it is very clear that the dominant conception of interdisciplinarity is that of a productive art of restoring and discovering the grounds for interdependence and relationship.

FOOTNOTES

. . . .

[8]Kenneth Boulding, "The Future of General Systems," *Interdisciplinary Teaching*, ed. Alvin M. White (San Francisco: Jossey-Bass, 1981), p. 109. Number 8 of the *New Directions for Teaching and Learning Series*.

[9]Boulding, p. 109.

[10]Boulding, p. 109.

[11]Peter W. Mullen, "Editorial, An Immunopharmacology Journal: Reflections on Its Interdisciplinary and Historical Context," *International Journal of Immunopharmacology, 1:1* (1979), p. 2-3.

[12]Mullen, p. 3.

[13]Janice N. Lauer, "Studies of Written Discourse: Dappled Discipline," a manuscript copy of the introductory essay for a forthcoming collection of essays on studies of written discourse. This essay is a printed version of an address Professor Lauer made before The Rhetoric Society of America at the 34th Annual Meeting of the Conference on College Composition and Communication in Detroit, Michigan on Thursday, March 17, 1983. I thank Professor Lauer for making a copy of the manuscript available to me.

[14]Lauer, p. 8.

[15]Lauer, p. 2-4.

[16]Lauer, p. 8.

[17]Lauer, p. 9.

[18]Wolfram Swoboda, "Disciplines and Interdisciplinarity, A Historical Perspective," *Interdisciplinarity and High Education*, ed. Joseph J. Kockelmans (University Park: The Pennsylvania State University Press, 1979), p. 65.

[19]Thomas O. Blank, "Two Social Psychologies: Is Segregation Inevitable or Acceptable," *Personality and Social Psychology Bulletin, 4:4* (1978), p. 553.

[20]David W. Wilson and Robert B. Schafer, "Is Social Psychology Interdisciplinary," *Personality and Social Psychology Bulletin, 4:4* (1978), p. 548.

[21]Ronald J. Grele, "A Surmisable Variety: Interdisciplinarity and Oral Testimony," *American Quarterly 27* (August 1975), pp. 276-277.

[22]Grele, pp. 276-277.

. . . .

[46]Arthur R. King, Jr. and John A. Brownell, *The Curriculum and the Disciplines of Knowledge, A Theory of Curriculum Practice* (Huntington, New York: Robert E. Kriefer, 1976), pp. 74-75.

[47]Stanley Milgram, "Interdisciplinary Thinking and the Small World Problem," *Interdisciplinary Relationships in the Social Sciences*, ed. Muzafer and Carolyn W. Sherif (Chicago: Aldine, 1969), p. 119. In the narrative amalgram of metaphorical expressions, I am citing for the most part works which summarize dominant attitudes.

[48]William Mayville, *Interdisciplinarity: The Mutable Paradigm* (Washington, D.C.: American Association for Higher Education, 1978), p. 1. *AAHE-ERIC Higher Educational Research Report #9.*

[49]Robert Dubin, "Contiguous Problem Analysis: An Approach to Systematic Theories about Social Organization," in *Interdisciplinary Relationships in the Social Sciences*, p. 68.

[50]Rustum Roy, "Interdisciplinary Science on Campus, The Elusive Dream," *Interdisciplinarity and Higher Education*, ed. Joseph J. Kockelmans (University Park: The Pennsylvania State University Press, 1979), p. 162.

[51]J. R. Gass, "Preface," *Interdisciplinarity, Problems of Teaching and Research in Universities* (Paris: Organisation for Economic Cooperation and Development, 1972), p. 9.

[52]Marvin W. Mikesell, "The Borderlands of Geography as a Social Science," in *Interdisciplinary Relationships in the Social Sciences*, p. 237; Ernest L. Boyer, "The Quest for Common Learning," in *Common Learning, A Carnegie Colloquium on General Education* (Washington, D.C.: The Carnegie Foundation for the Advancement of Teaching, 1981), p. 18.

[53]Used by Alvin W. Gouldner in *The Coming Crisis of Western Sociology* (New York: Basic Books, 1970) and by Rustum Roy, p. 168.

[54]Used by Arnold A. Rogow, "Some Relations between Psychiatry and Political Science" and Kenneth D. Roose, "Observations of Interdisciplinary Work in the Social Sciences," in *Interdisciplinary Relationships in the Social Sciences*, p. 278 and 324 respectively.

[55]Rustum Roy, p. 168.

[56]Martin Landau, Harold Proshansky and William H. Ittelson, "The Interdisciplinary Approach and the Concept of Behavioral Science," *Decisions, Values and Groups*, ed. Norman Washburne (New York: Pergamon Press, 1960), p. 11.

[57]Pierre Duget, "Approach to the problems," in *Interdisciplinarity: Problems of Teaching and Research in Universities*, p. 13.

[58]William J. McGuire, "Theory-Oriented Research in Natural Settings: The Best of Both Worlds in Social Psychology," in *Interdisciplinary Relationships in the Social Sciences*, p. 28.

[59]Leo Apostel, "Conceptual Tools for Interdisciplinarity: An Operational Approach," in *Interdisciplinarity: Problems of Teaching and Research in Universities*, p. 164.

[60]Heinz Heckhausen, "Discipline and Interdisciplinarity," in *Interdisciplinarity: Problems of Teaching and Research in Universities*, p. 87.

[61]Joseph J. Kockelmans, "Why Interdisciplinarity?" *Interdisciplinarity and Higher Education*, p. 135.

[62]John Higham, *Writing American History, Essays on Modern Scholarship* (Bloomington: Indiana University Press, 1970), p. 28.

63Geoffrey Squires, "Discussion" in response to Guy Berger's "Introduction," *Interdisciplinarity Papers Presented at the Society for Research into Higher Education Symposium on Interdisciplinary Courses in European Education, 13 September 1975 (At City University, London)*. (London: Society for Research into Higher Education, Ltd., August 1977), p. 9.

. . . .

67Gass, p. 9.

68Andre Lichnerowicz, "Mathematics and Transdisciplinarity," *Interdisciplinarity: Problems of Teaching and Research in Universities*, p. 121.

69Muzafer Sherif, "Crossdisciplinary Coordination in the Social Sciences," *Interdisciplinarity in Higher Education*, p. 214.

70Muzafer and Carolyn Sherif, "Interdisciplinary Coordination as a Validity Check: Retrospect and Prospects," *Interdisciplinary Relationships in the Social Sciences*, p. 8.

71Dubin, p. 67.

72Murray Wax, "Myth and Interrelationship in Social Sciences: Illustrated Through Anthropology and Sociology," *Interdisciplinary Relationships in the Social Sciences*, pp. 86-87.

73Edward Joseph Shoben, Jr., "General and Liberal Education: Problems of Person and Purpose," *Interdisciplinary Perspectives, 4:1* (Spring 1972), p. 8.

74Ernest L. Boyer, "The Quest for Common Learning," *Common Learning, A Carnegie Colloquium on General Education* (Washington, D.C.: The Carnegie Foundation for Advancement of Teaching, 1981), p. 6.

75Scott, p. 319

76Guy Berger as quoted by Guy Michaud in "General Conclusions," *Interdisciplinarity: Problems of Teaching and Research in Universities*, p. 287.

77Kockelmans, Why Interdisciplinarity?," p. 149.

78Kockelmans, "Why Interdisciplinarity?," p. 149.

79Lichnerowicz, p. 122.

80McGuire, p. 22.

81Donald T. Campbell, Ethnocentrism of Disciplines and the Fish-Scale Model of Omniscience," *Interdisciplinary Relationships in the Social Sciences*, p. 339.

82Wayne C. Booth, "Mere Rhetoric, Rhetoric, and the Search for Common Learning," *Common Learning*, p. 37.

83Milgram, p. 103.

84Lichnerowicz, p. 122.

85Jack Lee Mahan, Jr., "Toward Transdisciplinary Inquiry in the Humane Sciences," An Unpublished Dissertation. United States International University, San Diego, 1970, p. 136.

86See especially the work of Rustum Roy and Kenneth Roose as well as Nancy Anne Cluck, "Reflections on the Interdisciplinary Approaches to the Humanities," *Liberal Education* (Spring 1980).

87Silvan S. Tomkins, "Personality Theory and Social Science," *Interdisciplinary Relationships in the Social Sciences*, p. 201.

88Nevitt Sanford, "The Human Problems Institute and General Education," *Daedalus* (Summer 1965), pp. 646-647.

89See *Interdisciplinary Teaching*, ed. Alvin M. White (San Francisco: Jossey-Bass, 1981), p. 7. #8 (December 1981) of the New Directions in Teaching and Learning Series.

90Lewis Thomas, "The Natural World," *Common Learning*, p. 112.

91Carl H. Hertel, "Toward an Energic Architecture," *Interdisciplinary Teaching*, p. 86.

92Asa Briggs and Guy Michaud, "Perspectives: Context and Challenge," *Interdisciplinarity: Problems of Teaching and Research in Universities*, p. 191.

93Briggs and Michaud, p. 191.

94Kockelmans, "Why Interdisciplinarity?," p. 146.

95Vincent Kavaloski, "Interdisciplinary Education and Humanistic Aspiration," *Interdisciplinarity and Higher Education*, p. 229; and Clark C. Abt, a restricted document of the Centre for Educational Research and Innovation, "One Description and One Ideal Model and Implications for University Organisation for General, Professional and Lifelong Education and Research (Note by the Secretariat)," p. 6. Abt presented these papers at the 1970 Centre for Educational Research and Innovation seminar on interdisciplinarity but they do not appear in the 1972 published book from the seminar. For providing me with this and other documents and granting me permission to quote from them, I thank Helen M. Benyahia of the Paris office for the Organisation for Economic Co-Operation and Development.

96Abt, working paper, pp. 5-6.

. . . .

105Les Humphreys, *Interdisciplinarity: A Selected Bibliography for Users*, p. 3. Available as *ERIC* document ED 115 536.

106Sir Julian Huxley, "Science and Synthesis," *Science and Synthesis*, (New York: Springer-Verlag, 1967), p. 32.

107B. M. Kedrov, "Integration and Differentiation in the Modern Sciences, General Evolution of Scientific Knowledge," *Science and Synthesis*, p. 72.

BIBLIOGRAPHY

Abt, Clark C. "One Description and One Ideal Model and Implications for University Organisation for General, Professional and Lifelong Education and Research (Note by the Secretariat)," (A restricted document of the Centre for Educational Research and Innovation, presented at the 1970 Centre for Educational Research and Innovation Seminar on Interdisciplinarity).

Briggs, Asa, and Michaud, Guy. "Perspectives: Context and Challenge," *Interdisciplinarity: Problems of Teaching and Research in Universities*. Paris: Organisation for Economic Co-Operation and Development, 1972.

Cluck, Nancy Anne. "Reflections on the Interdisciplinary Approaches to the Humanities," *Liberal Education* (Spring 1980).

Humphreys, Les. *Interdisciplinarity: A Selected Bibliography for Users*. Available as *ERIC* document ED 115 536. Mimeo. Boston State College, 1975.

Kavaloski, Vincent. "Interdisciplinary Education and Humanistic Aspiration," *Interdisciplinarity and Higher Education*, ed. Joseph J. Kockelmans. University Park: The Pennsylvania State University Press, 1979.

Kedrov, B. M. "Integration and Differentiation in the Modern Sciences, General Evolution of Scientific Knowledge," *Science and Synthesis*. New York: Springer-Verlag, 1967.

Sanford, Nevitt. "The Human Problems Institute and General Education," *Daedalus* (Summer 1965): 646-647.

Sherif, Muzafer and Carolyn W. "Preface," *Interdisciplinary Relationships in the Social Sciences*, ed. Muzafer and Carolyn W. Sherif. Chicago: Aldine, 1969.

Sklar, Robert. "American Studies and the Realities of America," *American Quarterly, 22* (Summer 1970 Supplement): 597.

PART III

WHO ARE THE PARTICIPANTS?

8

MULTIDISCIPLINARY TEAM RESEARCH †*

Gordon W. Blackwell

What are the features which distinguish multidisciplinary team research from other kinds of research undertakings? What problems may be anticipated in multidisciplinary team research and how may they be met? Exploration of these questions is the purpose of this paper. Largely omitted from consideration are such matters as organizational setting of the research, source and extent of financial support, and contrasting values of applied investigations and basic research.[1] Illustrations will be drawn largely from recent research in the Institute for Research in Social Science at the University of North Carolina.

Three dimensions of a research undertaking are relevant to multidisciplinary team research: (1) the number of people doing the research (exclusive of assistants, computers, clerks, secretaries, and similar ancillary personnel); (2) the kind of action involved in the research process; (3) the number of disciplines involved in the research.

Let X represent the number of researchers (X_1 = one person; X_n = more than one person). Let Y represent the kind of action in the research process (Y_1 = separate action; Y_n = varying degrees of collective action). And let Z represent the number of disciplines (Z_1 = one discipline; Z_n = more than one discipline). It is obvious that these dimensions may be arranged in eight possible combinations. Two of these combinations would require *one* person in *collective* action which is impossible. The remaining six combinations of these dimensions may be placed on a descriptive continuum of research as illustrated in the accompanying chart.

† Read before the 17th annual meeting of the Southern Sociological Society, Atlanta, Georgia, March 26, 1954.
* From *Social Forces*, Vol. 33, May 1955, pp. 367-374. Copyright 1955 by University of North Carolina Press.

CONTINUUM OF TYPES OF RESEARCH UNDERTAKINGS

$X_1Y_1Z_1$	$X_1Y_1Z_n$	$X_nY_1Z_1$	$X_nY_nZ_1$	$X_nY_1Z_n$	$X_nY_nZ_n$
Lone researcher working in one discipline	Lone researcher using more than one discipline	Two or more researchers working separately in same discipline	Two or more researchers working as a team in same discipline	Two or more researchers working separately in different disciplines	Multidisciplinary team research

1. *Research by the lone scholar working in one discipline* has included most work in the social sciences. Through this type of research have come most of the major contributions in the development of each discipline. One thinks of Durkheim studying the nature of suicide, Cooley observing his own children, or Odum developing a theory of the folk out of his empirical regional studies. The occasional great flashes of insight usually have occurred in the mind of one individual with maximum opportunity for reflection and solitary study. Probably no other kind of research has been more important in the development of each of the social sciences.[2] Donald Young has expressed this point of view as follows:

> It is assumed with good historical reason that basic innovations in social science may rarely be expected from large-scale projects; initiation of such projects has usually been stimulated by the findings of some previous innovator working on a modest scale. There seems to be no alternative to continued dependence on the individual worker for new ideas and pioneering studies.[3]

To quote Alfred McClung Lee:

> In order that he may have maximal flexibility and minimal embedment in institutional obligations, tensions, and other influences during his hours of research, the individual researcher needs to feel above all and as much as possible that his only criteria of achievement in research are those he associates with (1) his own drive to satisfy his own curiosity, (2) his own desire to extend or broaden human knowledge of society, and (3) his own conception of a scientist's personal integrity.[4]

2. Occasionally one finds *an individual capable of using two or more disciplines* in an attack upon a research problem. Not many social scientists have been able or have had opportunity to master more than one discipline. There have been exceptions, however, such as MacIver has evidenced in *The Web of Government*[5] which contains so much that is sound in both political science and sociology; or Vance in his *Human Geography of the South*[6] combining concepts from geography,

ecology, economics, and sociology. The use of an interdisciplinary advisory committee has sometimes aided a researcher in using more than one discipline in a study. Recent attention to the fruitfulness of combining anthropology, psychology, and sociology should increase the quality and quantity of personnel with multidisciplinary understanding and skills in these fields. [7]

3. It has not been uncommon for *two or more researchers in the same discipline* to combine forces in a research project, though *working separately*. Unless there is considerable joint endeavor in developing the research design, this type of decentralized collaboration may be largely a matter of division of labor often based upon the specialisms of the participants. There is also the danger of fractionation of the object of inquiry as contrasted with study of a dynamic functioning entity. An example of this kind of research is *Church and Community in the South*[8] by Blackwell, Brooks and Hobbs in which each of the researchers independently undertook designated segments of the study: rural communities, urban communities, and field studies of church-community relationships.

4. A step further along the continuum away from the lone scholar type of research is the situation in which *two or more persons in the same discipline* tackle a research problem *as a team*. In this case collective action involving cooperation, coordination, and communication characterizes the research process from initial planning through data collection and into much of the analysis and writing, though in the latter stages some division of labor is usually desirable. Here one has the features of team research without the added complications of multidisciplinary effort.[9] The study of rural public housing in the South by Vance and Blackwell is an example of this type.[10] Lee[11] has pointed out that there are some who "see group research as a profitable but bungling and overrated bureaucratic device which comes to end-products of greater political than scientific significance." However, to balance this we have the view of Robin Williams writing about his World War II experiences in a research branch of the War Department.

Considered organizationally, one of the most striking features of this war-time governmental research is that it was *group research*, rather than *individual research*. From our experience on this point at least two main conclusions seem justified: (1) team research is feasible and productive to a degree which would not have been generally acknowledged as possible in many academic circles a few years ago; (2) collaborative group research introduces important *new* problems of organization, motivation, and of research standards and ultimate purposes.[12]

We shall return later to problems of team research.

5. Moving another step along the continuum, *two or more researchers in different disciplines* may attack a research problem, though *working separately*. Here one may face problems of multidisciplinary research if the effort is to involve real interdisciplinary collaboration, yet the features of team research are lacking. The use which is made of the respective disciplines is often determined by the director of the project. There is variation as to how much the concepts from different disciplines are merged and how much such concepts are merely used individually in the effort to achieve understanding. Indeed, one discipline is usually dominant in the formulation of the problem. Interaction between the researchers is kept to a minimum after a plan of study is agreed upon. Here is the point on the continuum for the interdisciplinary symposium of which *Recent Social Trends*[13] was a classic example. Another illustration is the volume edited by Vance and Demerath on *The Urban South*.[14] This project has drawn upon contributions from twelve sociologists, one demographer, one city planner, one social worker, and three political scientists. Still another example is the recent volume, *For a Science of Social Man*,[15] edited by Gillin, which has as its contributors three anthropologists, two psychologists, and two sociologists. This is, of course, not a presentation of empirical research. Rather, the objective has been to "bring to light certain agreements and convergence, especially in theory, among these sister disciplines and to point to promising possibilities that will . . . contribute to the further development of a science of social man." (pp. 4, 5) This project involved two conferences in which the contributors first developed a plan for the book and later went over together the manuscripts which had been prepared separately.

6. Finally, at the last point on the continuum there is *multidisciplinary team research* in which two or more researchers in more than one discipline work collectively on a problem. Here the features, difficulties, and advantages of the two previous types of research undertakings are combined.[16] Perhaps the difficulties increase geometrically rather than arithmetically as a result of combining the multidisciplinary feature with the team feature. Sometimes it seems so. Bronfenbrenner and Devereux have given this testimony relative to a Cornell project: "The welding together of an interdisciplinary team has been for us a slow process by no means free from anxieties and conflict."[17] Collective attack on a research problem

by persons from two or more disciplines may be justified by the need to use either the methods or theory, or both, from more than a single science. Examples of this kind of research are becoming more numerous, perhaps in part because of increased availability of funds for large social science research projects.

The three-year study of Human Factors in Air Force Base Efficiency undertaken by a group at the University of North Carolina under the direction of Demerath, Blackwell and Noland (for one year) for Human Resources Research Institute of the U.S. Air Force affords an example. The senior staff was comprised of an anthropologist (one year), a specialist in public administration (two years), a social psychologist (one year), a statistician (one year), and three sociologists (one for one year, two for three years). Consultation was sought from students of complex organization and business management. Team operation characterized the project throughout. A theoretical model applicable to analysis of the functioning of a complex instrumental organization was hammered out as a group product, drawing upon functionalism in sociology, the concept of informal structure as developed in public administration and business management, motivation, morale, and leadership theory in social psychology, interaction theory in sociometry, and the concept of cultural pattern in anthropology. Toward the close of the project the group worked on theories in small group organization and in clinical psychology in an effort to strengthen the theoretical model for complex organization analysis. Also particular attention was devoted to development of experimental designs for both laboratory and field research with psychologists proving to be particularly helpful.

It is clear that our experience in this project has been more rewarding than that of Dorothy S. Thomas who has written: "I have not found it profitable to approach interdisciplinary research by trying to merge disciplines at the 'conceptual' level."[18] Furthermore, Howard W. Odum in his *American Sociology* has given a balanced discussion of the hazards and limitations inherent in efforts to integrate the social sciences in research undertakings.[19]

We would tend to agree, however, with Harry M. Weaver writing about progress on research on poliomyelitis:

Reliance on group thinking to guide research can be, from an administrative point of view, a disappointing experience. However, if those concerned are principally motivated to achieve success in the total program; if the individual contributors are allowed the right to range without penalty along lines that may be ahead or even contrary to the thinking of the group; and if the conferences can be conducted in a spirit totally divorced from any employer-employee relationship—under these conditions, the effectiveness of group thinking is a stimulating experience to behold..[20]

One finds also so sceptical a social scientist as J.J. Spengler taking this position:

> The specialization [of the separate social sciences] consequent upon the analytical decomposition of man as a social totality has borne fruit. It has also exacted a price. (1) Important modes of collective behavior have escaped significant analysis because no unseen hand has been present to coordinate the activities of diverse specialists and insure analysis of *all* significant forms of interpersonal behavior. (2) Developments within fields of specialization frequently have weakened and sometimes have nearly destroyed interfield communication. . . .How many social sciences may contribute is governed both by their comparative state of advancement and by the narrowness with which the situation under analysis is defined.[21]

But, merely because of what we believe to be success in our multidisciplinary team research on Air Force organization (and others could be cited from our program), we do not want to overstate the case for this kind of research nor minimize the significance of contributions of the lone scholar working in a single discipline. To repeat, the lone scholar may continue to make most of the major contributions in the development of each of the social sciences.

Based on experience in this project and several other multidisciplinary team research undertakings of the Institute for Research in Social Science, as well as preliminary reports by Margaret B. Luszki on the study of interdisciplinary team research in mental health being conducted by the National Training Laboratory in Group Development,[22] the following outline of potential problems and possible adjustive mechanisms in research of this kind has been drawn up. Some of these problems grow out of the effort to bring together two or more disciplines in a joint enterprise; others are derived from difficulties inherent in the functioning of a group in the research process.

In conclusion, we have presented a discussion of the features of multidisciplinary team research which distinguish it from other kinds of research undertakings; we have pointed out some of the more important problems which may be encoutered in this complicated way of doing research; and we have suggested some ways of minimizing these difficulties. A more definitive statement must await further experience and scientific study of the multidisciplinary team research process.

ASPECTS OF MULTIDISCIPLINARY TEAM RESEARCH

Potential Problems	*Adjustive Mechanisms*

A. Selection of a research problem suitable for multidisciplinary team research.

Criteria for selection of problems for multidisciplinary team research:

(1) Any single discipline appears to be inadequate to handle the problem.

(2) The problem falls theoretically in a fringe area between disciplines.

(3) Previous research by more than one discipline suggests leads on the problem.

(4) Conceptual integration of previously distinct conceptual frameworks is needed.

(5) The problem is of such magnitude that team research is needed.

(6) Relevant disciplines appear to be ready to collaborate.

(7) Staff from relevant disciplines who meet criteria for multidisciplinary team research are available.

B. Multidisciplinary research may be undertaken merely for sake of multidisciplinary research; faddism; assumption that multidisciplinary research has greater power than does individual research; group activity as an end in itself.

Focus upon a specific research problem, perhaps in a pilot study; make the research multidisciplinary only if it will help; careful attention to criteria for selection of problems for multidisciplinary team research; avoid shotgun wedding of disciplines.

C. Semantic difficulties; "jargon."

Conscious attention to group process in staff seminars and planning; provision of adequate time for reading; preparation of glossary of selected terms with carefully developed definitions.

D. Problems in theory and methodology; danger of lowest common denominator in theory and method; assumption that consensus is good in and of itself; failure to use the most sophisticated and most powerful tools and concepts of each discipline when attempt is made to merge the

Development of procedure within the staff for directing attention to theoretical integration and methodological matters:

(1) By seeking out the potential contributions of each discipline.

ASPECTS OF MULTIDISCIPLINARY RESEARCH (*cont.*)

Potential Problems   *Adjustive Mechanisms*

disciplines or equate them as to their value in a specific research undertaking.

(2) By determining whether a merger of concepts is needed in accomplishing the research or merely separate use of concepts from several disciplines.

(3) By development of supra-concepts or broad integrative theories.

(4) By exploring empirical situations early in the project rather than prolonging the usually sterile discussions at the theoretical level.

(5) By seeking agreement on specific criteria of evidence.

(6) By trying out various methods, perhaps in pilot studies, using spontaneously developed subgroups in the team.

(7) By using outside consultants.

Staff consideration and choice between such alternatives as these, suggested by Luszki, may be helpful.

(1) Prior conceptualization *vs.* emergence of theory from the data.

(2) Reliance upon several sources *vs.* reliance upon a single source for theory.

(3) Emphasis upon development of new concepts *vs.* use of concepts accepted in the literature.

(4) One principal investigator with staff of researchers *vs.* senior staff with equal responsibility in research planning.

E. Curtailment of really significant research contributions; originality of researcher may be limited; too little opportunity for reflection; infertile situation for "flashes of insight."

Selection of research staff with theoretical interest in fringe areas between disciplines; staff seminars; budgeting of time so individual reading and reflection are encouraged; recognition of legitimacy of the *Verstehen*

ASPECTS OF MULTIDISCIPLINARY RESEARCH (*cont.*)

Potential Problems	*Adjustive Mechanisms*
	method; avoidance of insistence on consensus, at least early in the project.
F. Feeling of limitation on scholarly productivity of staff; anxiety that researcher may produce less in his own field, perhaps less *in toto*; differential professional rewards.	Keep administrative red tape at a minimum; hold down size of project so as to minimize time devoted to administration; encourage staff individually and in subgroups to follow leads in their own disciplines and to publish articles in their own fields.
G. Competing interests between basic research, applied investigation, therapy, and training due to (1) differences between disciplines and (2) nature of sponsorship of project.	Careful staff selection in view of nature of project; careful definition of project objectives through detailed, thorough staff planning; constant attention to needs and interests of each staff member consonant with team goals.
H. Problems relating to organization of research team:	Criteria for selection of staff for multidisciplinary team research:
(1) Staff selection.	Intellectual attributes:
	(1) Recognized competence in at least one discipline.
	(2) Broad training in the social sciences; respect for the contributions of each of the disciplines.
	(3) Versatility and flexibility in semantics.
	(4) Flexibility in theoretical orientation; not doctrinaire.
	Personal attributes:
	(1) Emotional maturity.
	(2) Demonstrated ability to function effectively in group activity.
(2) Administration.	Clear definition of leadership responsibilities in project; both sound administration and democratic participation required; neither dictatorship nor anarchy; creation of social situation in which group processes can function effectively.

ASPECTS OF MULTIDISCIPLINARY RESEARCH (cont.)

Potential Problems	*Adjustive Mechanisms*
(3) Internal communication.	Staff meetings and conferences; staff memoranda; working papers; occasional progress reports; free informal communication between all staff members, yet with as little administration and red tape as possible.
(4) Status differences between staff members (seniority, rank, salary, etc.).	Status structure of research group must be appropriate to situation and to demands of the research process; careful staff selection *re* emotional maturity; attempt to foster group integration through focus on common goals.
(5) Status differences between disciplines.	Careful staff selection *re* personality and perception of other disciplines; staff seminars with aim of increasing understanding of what each discipline can contribute; attempt to foster group integration.
(6) Differential motivation among staff members varying in age, personality, intellectual maturity, discipline, and so on; problems of morale.	Recognition of differential motivation through staff assignments of roles; provision of opportunities for individual achievement; attempt to foster group integration; development of loyalties of individuals to creating and using a common, shared body of theory and data.
(7) Credit for authorship.	Specific agreement in advance relative to authorship credit, giving due recognition to junior as well as senior staff.
(8) Problems derived from external conditions.	Carefull attention to communications and public relations; use of advisory committee device; cultivation of personal relationships with those having authority or influence over the project; avoidance of over-dependence upon outside sources of support; maintenance of freedom of inquiry and publication.

FOOTNOTES

[1]These matters have been discussed recently in the literature. For contrasting points of view see Charles Y. Glock, "Some Implications of Organization for Social Research," *Social Forces*, XXX (December 1951), 129-34; Alfred McClung Lee, "Individual and Organizational Research in Sociology," *American Sociological Review*, XVI (October 1951), 701-707; N.J. Demerath, "Initiating and Maintaining Research Relations in a Military Organization," *Journal of Social Issues*, VIII, No. 3, pp. 11-23.

[2]For a deprecating view of the "lone wolf researcher," see Philip M. Hauser, "Are the Social Sciences Ready?" *American Sociological Review*, XI (August 1946), 382.

[3]*UNESCO International Social Science Bulletin*, Paris, I (1949), 100.

[4]*Op. cit.*, p. 702.

[5]R.M. MacIver, *The Web of Government* (New York: The Macmillan Company, 1947).

[6]Rupert B. Vance, *Human Geography of the South* (Chapel Hill: University of North Carolina Press, 1932).

[7]The establishment of the Department of Social Relations at Harvard, combining cultural anthropology, clinical and social psychology, and sociology, is a case in point; also the large number of interdisciplinary social science research institutes and centers established in universities in recent years. See also John Gillin (ed.), *For a Science of Social Man* (New York: Macmillan, 1954).

[8]Gordon W. Blackwell, Lee M. Brooks, and S.H. Hobbs, Jr., *Church and Community in the South* (Richmond: John Knox Press, 1949).

[9]William Kolb, in his oral discussion of this paper, pointed out with keen insight that the significant breaking point between individual and team research probably is not at one person as contrasted with more than one person, but rather at the point when the research team comprises perhaps four or five persons rather than fewer researchers.

[10]Rupert B. Vance and Gordon W. Blackwell, *New Farm Homes for Old* (University, Alabama: University of Alabama Press, 1946).

[11]Alfred McClung Lee, *op. cit.*, p. 703.

[12]Robin M. Williams, Jr., "Some Observations on Sociological Research in Government During World War II," *American Sociological Review*, XI (October 1946), 574.

[13]*Recent Social Trends in the United States*, 2 vols. Findings of the President's Committee on Social Trends (New York: McGraw-Hill Book Company, 1933).

[14]Rupert B. Vance and Nicholas J. Demerath (eds.), *The Urban South* (Chapel Hill: University of North Carolina Press, 1954).

[15]Gillin, *op. cit.*

[16]Margaret B. Luszki is project coordinator of a study of multidisciplinary team research in mental health, conducted by the National Training Laboratory in Group Development under the sponsorship of the National Institute of Mental Health. The project has issued several preliminary reports and gives promise of being the most exhaustive investigation of the subject yet undertaken. A final publication entitled, Methods and Problems in Interdisciplinary Team Research, is nearing completion and will be published in 1955.

[17]Urie Bronfenbrenner and Edward C. Devereux "Interdisciplinary Planning in Team Research on Constructive Community Behavior," *Human Relations*, V, No. 2 (1952), p. 188. See also William Caudill and Bertram H. Roberts, "Pitfalls in the Organization of Interdisciplinary Research," *Human Organization*, X (Winter 1951), 12-15.

[18]Dorothy S. Thomas, "Experiences in Interdisciplinary Research," *American Sociological Review*, XVII (December 1952), 669.

[19]Howard W. Odum, *American Sociology* (New York: Longmans, Green, 1951), pp. 455-459.

[20]Harry M. Weaver, "Progress on Research on Poliomyelitis," *Public Health Reports*, LXVIII (July 1953), 673.

[21]J.J. Spengler, "Generalists Versus Specialists in Social Science: An Economist's View," *American Political Science Review*, XLIV (June 1950), 360.

[22]"Work Conferences in Mental Health Research," Progress Report, April 21, 1952, 38 pp., mimeographed; Second Report, February 9, 1953, 23 pp., mimeographed.

9

DO YOU SEE WHAT I SEE?
THE EPISTEMOLOGY OF
INTERDISCIPLINARY INQUIRY[1] *

Hugh G. Petrie

Since the answer to the question in the title is, for members of
interdisciplinary groups, not always and obviously "yes", an
examination of why this is so and how it might be overcome appears in
order. The impetus for this investigation and, indeed, part of the
content arose out of my participation in the Sloan Program of the
College of Engineering at the University of Illinois over the past years.
That program was in large part designed as an interdisciplinary effort
to examine the role of the social sciences and humanities in an
engineering curriculum. The method was interdisciplinary faculty
seminars, and my particular interest was in the processes of those
seminars. I was a general participant in the meetings which brought in
a series of speaker-discussants on the topics, "How does X view the
world." X was each week replaced by the name of the speaker's
discipline. In addition, I chaired an interdisciplinary subgroup whose
topic was the interdisciplinary research and teaching process. Much of
what I will say in the following is a result of these experiences, and
although a philosopher, I will be making some nonphilosophical claims
in what follows. That I dare to do this is part of what must result, I
think, if interdisciplinary work is to succeed.

Harry Broudy has surely been one of the most persistent advocates,
at least of late, for the importance, not to say the necessity, of
interdisciplinary work.[2]   Basically the argument is that a complex
technological society requires interdisciplinary solutions to its
problems, and I don't think it requires much restating. One needs only
consider the problems of pollution, world-wide inflation, energy

* From *Educational Researcher*, Vol. 5, No. 2, February 1976, pp. 9-15. Copyright 1976 by
American Educational Research Association.

production and conservation, and so on to get the flavor. In addition, if one adds the increased sensitivity of professional schools to their broader social roles as evidenced by other papers, the importance of interdisciplinary work becomes apparent.

Unfortunately, the importance of interdisciplinary work has seldom been matched by its fruitfulness. All too often grandly conceived interdisciplinary projects never get off the ground, and the level of scholarship seldom exceeds that of a glorified bull-session. Frequently, and with some justification, people look upon interdisciplinary projects as a dumping ground for the less than disciplinarily competent. I shall argue, however, that the most competent disciplinarians are required for an interdisciplinary group to be successful. It is in hopes of contributing to a higher rate of success for interdisciplinary projects that I offer the following "profile" of interdisciplinary inquiry— research or teaching.

First, however, a few preliminary distinctions need to be noted. I distinguish between interdisciplinary and multidisciplinary efforts. The line is not hard and fast, but roughly it is that multidisciplinary projects simply require everyone to do his or her own thing with little or no necessity for any one participant to be aware of any other participant's work. Perhaps a project director or manager is needed to glue the final product together, but the pieces are fairly clearly of disciplinary size and shape. Interdisciplinary efforts, on the other hand, require more or less integration and even modification of the disciplinary subcontributions while the inquiry is proceeding. Different participants need to take into account the contributions of their colleagues to make their own contribution.

Take the energy crisis, for example. If the heating engineer as a member of a group looking at energy consumption in housing is simply asked to design houses that are more thermally efficient, it can be done in an almost wholly disciplinary way. One needn't worry about the energy cost structures or legal restrictions, etc. On the other hand, if the group is considering significant changes in social organization and life-style to meet the energy crisis, the same engineer will have to take projected altered living styles and arrangements, different patterns of energy consumption, and so on, into account in order even to do his disciplinary work. And, of course, conversely with respect to the nonengineering participants. It is the interdisciplinary, as opposed to the multidisciplinary, process with which I shall be concerned in this paper.

The other distinction I want to make here is that I shall not be concerned with the individual who acquires more than one disciplinary competence. In the first place, such a person's problems will be mirrored, I think, in what I shall say about the workings of interdisciplinary groups. But second, such a solution is simply out of the question for most people, given the demands of time and energy placed on attaining even one disciplinary competence. If we cannot stop short of making Renaissance persons out of a good deal of our population, then the interdisciplinary mode will *not* be able to contribute to the solutions of our pressing societal problems. Thus, I shall talk about groups instead of individuals.

With these preliminaries out of the way, let me sketch the course of the paper. First I shall note several very important nonepistemological factors that seem to be particularly relevant to the success or failure of interdisciplinary inquiry. These include the notion of idea dominance, psychological considerations, and the institutional settings in which interdisciplinary work is carried on. Next, I shall turn to the epistemological and methodological constraints on interdisciplinary work. Here I shall concentrate on the problems raised by the apparent fact that different disciplines use different observational categories and occasionally mean quite different things by the same linguistic terms. I shall suggest that the kind of knowledge exhibited by knowing the observational categories and meanings of the key terms of any discipline is fairly close to what Broudy calls the interpretive use of knowledge. I shall then expand on this notion of interpretive knowledge as a universally necessary condition for successful interdisciplinary inquiry. I shall indicate how one can, in principle, tell when it has been obtained, and I shall conclude by noting the key pedagogical concept necessary for coming to understand the language of a wholly different discipline, viz., metaphor.

Nonepistemological Considerations

Idea Dominance

One of the central considerations necessary for interdisciplinary success seems to be what I will call the dominance of an idea. That is, there must be a clear and recognizable idea which can serve as a central focus for the work. It can be embodied in a single individual who leads the project through force of personality or importance of a perceived mission. The dominant idea may be imposed by some external necessity clearly perceived by all participants. Certain kinds of mission-oriented projects fit here. Finally, it may be an idea embodied in a new and powerful theoretical concept or model—a concept that does not find a natural home in an established discipline.

Closely associated with the idea dominance is the necessity for some kind of achievement. The need for achievement also appears under the heading of psychological characteristics, but here it is primarily directed toward the logical requirement of some kind of feedback to confirm the clarity and force of the idea originally conceived. Thus a dominant personality begins to lose dominance if he or she cannot lead the group to some sort of achievement. A mission unachieved raises doubts as to whether it was properly defined. And, a powerful new theoretical idea will ultimately be shelved if it fails to achieve results.

The notion of idea dominance seems to admit of degrees—there can be more or less of it. To this extent, I would predict that, other things being equal, the stronger the idea, the more chance of success. A caveat must be entered here. In some cases it may be extremely difficult, if not impossible, to judge the strength and dominance of an idea independently of whether it turns out to be successful. However, at least a gross empirical handle does seem possible here in that this criterion would seem to rule out interdisciplinary projects undertaken simply for the sake of being interdisciplinary.

Psychological Characteristics of Participants

The second major category of nonepistemological factors is the psychological characteristics of the participants in a successful interdisciplinary effort. Of course, successful people here are very much like successful people in any endeavor, but several characteristics, attitudes, and motivations stand out. The persons must, first of all, be secure in their original endeavors. Interdisciplinary efforts seldom work if the participants are not fully competent in their own fields. Second, the participants must have a taste for adventure into the unknown and unfamiliar, i.e., they must not be tied too closely to their secure home base. Of course, there is a sense in which a really good disciplinarian is, *ipso facto*, adventurous. It is a taste for *new* adventure that I am talking about here. Third, their interests must be fairly broad, if not in terms of their spheres of competence, at least in terms of what they feel is of importance.

It should be noted that disciplinary competence and security are sometimes at odds with broad interests and imaginative speculation. Given the current pattern of graduate education, the kind of people attracted to any discipline will tend to be those who are good at a fairly narrow thing. Furthermore, the rewards to a successful academic tend to reinforce the narrow, albeit incisive, disciplinary focus. Thus, on the whole one tends to see good disciplinarians uninterested in interdisciplinary efforts and many who are interested seem to have marginal disciplinary competence. A useful blend of competence and broad interest is rare.

The need for achievement enters into the psychological realm as well. Not only must there be achievement in the sense of the development and confirmation of the dominant idea as already mentioned, the participants must also feel that they are achieving something. This need magnifies the difficulties of combining in one person security of disciplinary competence and broad interest, for the external signs of achievement upon which people depend generally do not go to the person interested in interdisciplinary work. Thus the ability to get internal satisfaction and a sense of achievement are crucial in the early stages of interdisciplinary work. Providing signs of achievement might also be a very effective way for administrators and those concerned with the social setting of the effort to protect the very fragile nature of interdisciplinary projects in their early stages. (See the discussion of the institutional setting below.)

The precise mix of disciplinary competence, adventurous spirit, and broad interests may be very difficult to determine. What does seem clear is that no one of these can be allowed to predominate. By this I do not mean that the extremely competent disciplinarian would not make a good participant in an interdisciplinary effort, but rather that if one is not also extremely adventurous and extremely interested in the project, the rewards which accrue simply due to disciplinary competence are likely to pull an individual away from the interdisciplinary effort. Likewise, the person of extremely broad interests, but lesser disciplinary talent may feel the project is going well, when in fact it never gets beyond the superficial. And the adventurous spirit is needed for learning, where necessary, parts of new disciplines.

Another set of psychological issues involves the simple dynamics of working in a group. Members of Sloan subgroups have remarked over and over that they seem to spend almost all semester simply learning what each other is like and getting their biases and interests on the table, before they feel they can really get to work. Whether or not they really could get to work is not at issue here. What is important is that such a "shakedown" of attitudes and modes of behavior is almost always necessary with new groups before they can get to a more substantive level of functioning.

The Institutional Setting

This third category involves the institutional setting for the interdisciplinary work. Under this head is included first of all administrative support for the project. This involves seed money, released time, encouragement, and so on. Closely related to administrative support is the necessity for peer recognition somewhere. This can come from the original parent guild of the participant, from a larger community that deems the interdisciplinary work important, or from the interdisciplinary group itself. These features are connected with the achievement need mentioned under idea dominance and psychological characteristics.

Thus I would predict generally that the more administrative and social support that can be given to interdisciplinary groups, the more successful they are likely to be. Complicating the situation, however, is the need to recognize the operation of the dynamics of the group. With very strong idea dominance, some of the early settling in may be avoided; but in the main, one will simply have to be realistic about how much can be accomplished in a given time under conditions in which the members of the group are, almost be definition, strange to each other.

Epistemological Considerations

I turn now to the category of epistemological considerations. This general area is involved with the modes of inquiry appropriate both to the parent disciplines of participants and to the interdisciplinary effort. In the first place the participants need to recognize that different disciplines do have different cognitive maps and that these maps may well get in the way of successful interdisciplinary inquiry.[3] By cognitive map here, I mean the whole paradigmatic and perceptual apparatus used by any given discipline. This includes, but is not limited to, basic concepts, modes of inquiry, problem definition, observational categories, representation techniques, standards of proof, types of explanation, and general ideals of what constitutes a discipline. Perhaps the most striking of these, and also often the least-noted, is the extent to which disciplinary categories of observation are theory and discipline relative. Quite literally, two opposing disciplinarians can look at the same thing and not see the same thing.[4] I hope to illustrate this thesis in a few moments.

The present point, however, is that if disciplines do differ in their cognitive maps, then quite plainly until these maps are shared by the interdisciplinary participants, they will be unable to see the relevance of their colleagues' points of view to the problem at hand. If they do not learn the other disciplinary maps, at least some of the discussion will be necessarily misunderstood for it will be processed in terms of the participant's *own* map which may not be the same as that of the person who offered the comment in the first place. Thus learning at least a part of other disciplinary maps is a necessary condition for turning multidisciplinary work into interdisciplinary work.

It might be objected here that learning another discipline's cognitive map cannot possibly be a logically necessary condition for successful interdisciplinary work, since we can point to numerous cases in which the nature of the problem itself clearly called for the insights afforded by another discipline.[5] Thus at a certain stage in the development of biology, the problems clearly called for the insights of physics. The examples could be multiplied. Of course, I do not deny the existence of such historical examples. What I do wish to dispute, however, is that there really was no learning of the cognitive maps of the other relevant discipline. After all, not all biologists saw the need for physics. Could it be that those who did had already learned the necessary minimum about physics?

Alternatively, I would imagine there are cases where it appeared to people that the insights of another discipline were relevant to their current problems, and yet found upon investigation and more familiarity with the other discipline that their early faith was misplaced. History seldom records such failures, but they would seem to indicate that problems "call" for other disciplines only when enough of the other disciplines is known to make the call *appropriate*. In short my claim that learning (or having learned) at least a part of other disciplinary maps is a necessary condition for interdisciplinary work is a conceptual rather than an historical claim.

I would also hypothesize that a failure to undertake such learning helps explain the relatively naive level of so much interdisciplinary work. Failing to realize the significant differences in cognitive maps and yet faced with the necessity for communicating with each other on *some* level or other, the participants retreat to the level of common sense which *is* shared by all. But *ipso facto*, such a level cannot make use of the more powerful insights of the disciplines. On the other hand some very successful interdisciplinary work has occurred because the overlap of cognitive maps was large to begin with as, for example, in nuclear engineering or biophysics. The problem is paramount when the maps are far apart as, for example, when the team involves humanists and scientists.

Given this difference of cognitive maps, the question arises of what kind of learning of another's disciplinary map is required for the interdisciplinary team member. Broudy gives us a clue here in distinguishing four uses of learning—the associative, the replicative, the applicative, and the interpretive.[6] Roughly these uses of learning are as follows. One uses learning associatively when, on the occasion of use, the learning provides a context of associations. Aesthetic learning in the appreciation of art often functions associatively. One uses learning replicatively when one replicates the learning on the occasion of use in just the form in which it was learned. Spelling is a prime example of replication. One uses learning applicatively when one *does* something in light of the learning. A great deal of expertise is required here both to know the theory, how to apply it, and when to apply it. Persons exercising their full disciplinary competence probably are using their learning applicatively. Finally, one uses learning interpretively when the situation of use is interpreted with the aid of the learning. It is *seen* in light of the learning.

Broudy also suggests that the interpretive uses of learning or knowedge should be understood primarily in terms of Polanyi's concept of tacit knowing.[7] I cannot even begin to do justice here to Polanyi's rich and fertile discussions of tacit knowing. It will be sufficient for my purposes to note two points. First, I take my development in the remainder of this paper to be in the spirit of Broudy's interpretive use of learning and Polanyi's notion of tacit knowing.

Second, I shall make direct use of one central feature of tacit knowing. This feature is the contrast between tacit and focal knowing as that is exemplified by the Gestaltist's figure-ground relationship. Polanyi's claim is roughly that the figure in perception is known focally while the ground is known tacitly. Furthermore, as one shifts to perceiving the ground focally, the former figure recedes into the ground and becomes tacit. It is clear that tacit knowing would prove to be a valuable addition to Broudy's theory of interpretive uses of knowledge. For if the interpretation is tacit it would explain both the importance of the interpretive use as well as the difficulty of justifying that use in an age in which everything seems to have to be made focal in behaviorist terms in order to be recognized as important.

Tacit knowledge used interpretively can also be seen as extremely suggestive for my problem of how much and what kind of the others' disciplines must be learned for successful interdisciplinary work. One needs to learn enough so that this knowledge can be used to interpret the problem in the other disciplinary categories. Interpretive knowledge is almost surely used tacitly by the disciplinarian, and this explains why it is so easy to overlook its importance in interdisciplinary work. Further, one often retreats to a common sense that is tacitly used by all when the going gets rough. My claim is that one *can* and probably must make this interpretive knowledge focal so that all can learn it well enough to permit tacit functioning from then on in the operation of the group.

The minimal constituents of the amount of learning needed of the others' disciplines seem to be the following: First one must learn the observational categories of the other discipline and, second, one must learn the meanings of the key terms in the other discipline. Note that this would seem to allow one to interpret the problem in the others' terms, but stops short of the full-fledged knowledge of theory, modes of inquiry, and ideals of the discipline, which the disciplinarian himself would possess. It would allow one, however, to understand the import of certain claims or recommendations made from the disciplinary point of view. Such knowledge by the participants in an interdisciplinary group is certainly not sufficient for success, but as I have argued, it is necessary, and, clearly, has been largely overlooked in the past.

Let me try now to illustrate what I mean by observational categories and meanings of key concepts. Consider the following so-called "ambiguous figures."[8]

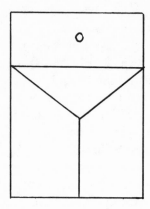

Figure 1

Do you see the martini-bikini in the first figure? Do you see the duck-rabbit in the second figure? Now consider the third figure of the young-old woman. This one is hard for many. The old woman is looking down and to the left. The young woman is looking away from the viewer and to the left. The old woman's mouth is the choker around the young woman's neck. Notice how, as Polanyi claims, what is focal for one interpretation becomes tacit for another. Note too, how the cognitive orientation seems to give meaning to the lines or parts of the drawing rather than the other way around. Imagine what it would be like to be a member of an interdisciplinary group discussing a problem in which the young-old woman, or something analogous, played a part. What would happen if your discipline allowed you to see the young woman, while another's discipline interpreted it as an old woman and you didn't realize the difference? Would you be tempted to retreat to your own narrow discipline and categorize those other folks as just silly? My suggestion here is quite simple. It often happens that when different disciplines look at the same thing (the same lines on the paper) they *observe* different things. Thus, it is necessary for people engaged in interdisciplinary work to understand each others' observational categories.

Figure 2

The second example concerns different meanings of key concepts and was derived from a discussion section of a course I teach. I was sitting in on the section as an observer and the teaching assistant was trying to explain the difference between facts and values. He gave as an example, "Blacks score 10-15 points below whites on standard I.Q. tests," and asked whether this was a statement of fact or a statement of value. A class-member responded that it was a statement of value. This was *not* the correct answer. As discussion proceeded, it became clear that a very understandable difference of meaning was being attached to the concepts, "fact," and "value" by the student and by the T.A.

Figure 3

By "fact," the T.A. meant any statement which *purported* to describe what is the case, whether we know if it is true or not. Thus controversial claims and even false claims were all "facts" to him at least as opposed to values which purport to say what *ought* to be the case. For the student, "fact," was limited to true, noncontroversial facts and all else was vague. Again if different disciplines have different meanings for the same terms and this is not taken into account, one can predict almost certain failure for interdisciplinary projects.

But now if the interpretive use of tacit knowledge is what is required in the interdisciplinary situation, almost by definition it will be a difficult task to determine when the appropriate knowledge of observational categories and theoretical meaning will have been attained—at least short of full disciplinary training. This problem is particularly vexing when one considers just how systematically ambiguous varying interpretations of the world might be among several disciplines. Think of the young-old woman again. Two different disciplinarians might talk about "the woman" for a long time without realizing they were talking about different things.

The route to identifying a person's set of observational categories and theoretical meanings is in principle deceptively simple: Introduce what would be a disturbance into the situation being observed and see if the person counteracts the disturbance.[9] If the disturbance *is* counteracted, the appropriate categories and meanings probably have been learned. What does this mean? Consider again the young-old woman. If one is attempting to determine if someone has learned to see the old woman, one might suggest that despite her age, she certainly has a lovely nose. If one can actually see the "old" woman, that should, for most, constitute a disturbance which would be resisted by some such disclaimer as, "You call *that* nose lovely? You're out of your mind." In the case of the teaching assistant and the student who disagree on the meaning of "fact," the assistant can introduce examples of true facts, false facts, and controversial facts to see what sort of resistance the student puts forth. If all of these count as facts while a paradigmatic value statement is not, and vice versa, then the student probably understands the fact-value distinction.

A real-life example occurred once in one of our general sessions during the Sloan project. Professor Nicholas Britsky was speaking to us on how the artist views the world and was showing us a series of slides of his own and others' work. Recall that we were a thoroughly interdisciplinary group with scientists, engineers, social scientists, and humanists. Professor Britsky came to a slide of one of his own abstract works. He was asked whether a certain predominant color area on the canvas could have been anywhere else, and his response was negative. Some in the audience agreed. To move that area would have constituted a disturbance from the perspective of the observational categories of those who understood and appreciated the art. Others could not see the difference that would have been made. They had not yet assimilated the appropriate observational categories. The principle of introducing a disturbance to test for the presence of categorial and meaning knowledge is thus clear even if the application is often extremely difficult.

I have now identified the minimal cognitive level necessary for successful interdisciplinary work—namely, come to use the observational categories and meanings of the other disciplines interpretively. I have also indicated, in principle, a test for when this use of knowledge has been attained. In conclusion, I want to sketch briefly the key pedagogical tool I think needs to be employed to bring people to this minimal level of understanding of another's discipline. The tool I have in mind is metaphor, where "metaphor" is conceived of broadly as encompassing visual metaphors and even theories—models as they are often called in the sciences.[10]

Notice that the interdisciplinary situation is, by hypothesis, one which seems peculiarly apt for the kind of language that has surrounded metaphor.[11] The participants are familiar with one set of observational categories and meanings, their own, and they want to gain an insight into another system of observational categories and meanings. Metaphors traditionally have enabled us to gain an insight into a new area by juxtaposing language and concepts familiar in one area with a new area. One begins to see the similarities and differences between the literal uses of the metaphor and the new area to which we have been invited to apply the "lens" or "cognitive maps" supplied by the metaphor.

The notion of correcting disturbances enters again into the actual pedagogical use of metaphor. The students in the group begin by utilizing the inferences, concepts, and observational categories surrounding the literal use of the metaphorical term in the new to-be-learned area. Of course, certain adjustments are made due to the dissimilarities already perceived by the student between old and new areas of discourse. However, since the learning is being conducted in the presence of an already competent disciplinarian, if the student makes a wrong move with the metaphor, this creates a disturbance for the disciplinarian-teacher. The disciplinarian's reaction shows the student that the move under discussion is part of the difference between the literal use of the metaphor and the new use. Gradually both come to react to disturbances in the same way as already described.

I cannot begin to give many varied illustrations of pedagogically useful metaphors, primarily because it follows from my discussion that only competent disciplinarians can locate their own best metaphors. However, I shall suggest two. My own presentation here has used the ambiguous figures as visual metaphors for the important notion of theory-dependent observational categories. I have found by experience that this metaphor is effective pedagogically.

A second example I still remember from high school geometry. A very dear, old-fashioned teacher used it to explain the concepts of point as location, line as distance, and rectangle as plane surface. She held up a pencil and said, "Imagine this pencil sharpened as sharp as possible—and then sharpened much sharper than that. That's a point." Then she took this "point" in her fingers and drew it apart, saying, "Now, if I take the point and draw it apart like this, that's a line." Then she pulled the line down in front of her saying, "And if I pull this line down like so, that's a plane." For me that metaphor worked beautifully, and I think most disciplinarians would be able to come up with appropriate pedagogical metaphors for their own fields.

An important pedagogical point here is that through use and assimilation, metaphors die and take on simply an alternative technical meaning. When disciplinarians fail to realize that terms they use in a technical sense—as dead metaphors—may be taken as quite live metaphors by their students, communication problems are almost certain to result. Thus the conscious and imaginative use of appropriate metaphorical devices seems to be required to bring the members of an interdisciplinary group to the requisite minimal level of understanding of each other's disciplines. Once more we return to one of Broudy's long-standing interests—the importance of humanistic education in general and, to the extent that metaphor is central to aesthetic education, to aesthetic education in particular. (Although I'm not quite sure that Broudy will approve of *that* much stretching of aesthetic education.)

Summarizing, I have argued that for interdisciplinary as opposed to multidisciplinary efforts, the factors of idea dominance, psychological characteristics of the participants, and the institutional setting are all extremely important. With respect to epistemological considerations, I have urged that some mixes of disciplines require as a necessary condition for success that the participants learn the observational categories and meanings of key terms of each others' disciplines. This knowledge is then tacitly used in an interpretive way on the problems facing the group. One can tell when this minimal learning has been achieved by noting when disturbances are corrected. Finally, I have suggested that a conscious attention to a very broad notion of metaphor is the key to bridging the gap between the differing categories and concepts of the different disciplines. Only when you see what I see does interdisciplinary work have a chance.

FOOTNOTES

[1]This paper was originally delivered at a colloquium entitled "Uses of Knowledge," September 1974 at the University of Illinois, Urbana, honoring Harry Broudy.

[2]See, for example, Harry S. Broudy, *The Real World of the Public Schools*, New York: Harcourt Brace Jovanovich, 1972, Ch. 7, and Harry S. Broudy, "On Knowing With," *Proceedings of the Philosophy of Education Society*, Studies in Philosophy and Education, Southern Illinois University, Edwardsville, Il., 1970, 89-103.

[3]Thomas Kuhn's work is probably the best-known current position on the differences in cognition among different disciplines. See Thomas Kuhn, *The Structure of Scientific Revolutions* (2nd ed.) University of Chicago Press, 1970.

[4]There is a large literature on the theory-dependence of observation. A classical source is N.R. Hanson, *Patterns of Discovery*, Cambridge University Press, 1958. A view that accepts much of the theory-dependency thesis yet objects to some of the more radical interpretations of it can be found in Israel Scheffler, *Science and Subjectivity*, New York: Bobbs-Merrill, 1967. For some of the pedagogical implications of this view, one might consult Hugh G. Petrie, "The Believing in Seeing," in Lindley J. Stiles (ed.) *Theories for Teaching*, New York: Dodd-Mead, 1974.

[5]This problem was suggested to me by Dudley Shapere.

[6]See Harry S. Broudy, B.O. Smith, and J.R. Burnett, *Democracy and Excellence in American Secondary Education*, Chicago: Rand McNally, 1964.

[7]See Broudy, "On Knowing With," cited in Note 2, Michael Polanyi, *Personal Knowledge*, University of Chicago Press, 1958, and "The Logic of Inference," *Philosophy*, 1966, 40, 369-386, will get one started on Polanyi's views of tacit knowledge.

[8]The martini-bikini was drawn for this paper. The duck-rabbit and the young-old woman were taken from N.R. Hanson in Willard E. Humphreys (ed.) *Perception and Discovery*, San Francisco: Freeman, Cooper and Co. 1969, p. 90.

[9]This notion of a disturbance and counteracting a disturbance which I am here using in a hopefully nontechnical way received a most illuminating and far-reaching technical treatment in William T. Powers, *Behavior: The Control of Perception*, Chicago: Aldine, 1973. In ten years this book will have generated a revolution in philosophy and psychology.

[10]See my paper, "Metaphorical Models of Mastery: Or How to Learn to do the Problems at the End of the Chapter in the Physics Text," presented to the Philosophy of Science Association meeting, Notre Dame, Nov. 1-3, 1974, for a detailed analysis of the role of metaphor in pedagogical situations logically equivalent to the one obtaining for the interdisciplinary work. This paper is scheduled for publication in *PSA 74: Boston Studies in the Philosophy of Science*, Vol. 32, 1975. Two other recent papers on metaphor illustrate the renewed interest in this subject, Andrew Ortony, "Why Metaphors are Necessary and Not Just Nice," *Educational Theory*, Vol. 25, 1, Winter, 1975, pp. 45-53, and Felicity Haynes, "Metaphor as Interactive," *Educational Theory*, Vol. 25, 3, Summer, 1975, pp. 272-277, are especially noteworthy.

[11]The account of Metaphor upon which I am relying is a fairly standard one as found, for example, in Max Black, *Models and Metaphors*, Cornell University Press, 1962.

10

COMMUNICATIONS BETWEEN HARD & SOFT SCIENCES*

Tom Wilbanks

Let me tell you why I am interested in communications between hard and soft sciences. Basically, it's because I have always thought that academic disciplines are less than adequate to deal with interesting intellectual and social issues. Essentially, disciplines are administrative conveniences—suiting the needs of academic institutions and perpetuating themselves as social organizations. But when it comes to such basic questions as how to assure that people get enough food to eat, or how to assure a stable and secure society, or how to understand the meaning of the universe, these subdivisions get in the way more often than they help out.

It was this kind of point of view that resulted in my choosing to specialize in geography, a field that seemed to close fewer doors than most. Geography has direct links with the social sciences and the earth sciences. Its intellectual sibling is probably physics when it comes to theory building, and its analytical tools are shared with such fields as communication theory, plant ecology, and crystallography.

At the University of Oklahoma, I spent four years as part of the Science and Public Policy Program (S&PP), an interdisciplinary technology-assessment program. At S&PP, I worked every day with nuclear engineers, ecologists, civil engineers, political scientists, philosophers, law school faculty, and many others.

Now, at Oak Ridge National Laboratory, my job mainly involves two goals: (1) to help build a first-rate social-science-research capability in a research institution that has always emphasized the physical sciences, life sciences, and engineering specialties; (2) to help integrate this social science work with the rest of the expertise there.

* Reprinted by permission of Oak Ridge National Laboratory from *Oak Ridge National Laboratory Review*, Spring 1979, pp. 24-29.

I have had a real professional stake in communications between the hard and soft sciences—both in trying to talk to them and in trying to understand what they say. And I think the challenges in this kind of communication include overcoming

- Disinterest
- Niche-Seeking
- Acculturation
- Stereotypes

These challenges are substantial ones.

Disinterest

First of all, most people are busy with their own affairs. Their hands are full trying to be good in their specialties, and it's hard to find the time to engage their minds in someone else's field—except as a sort of recreation, if it interests them. In other words, I might be interested enough in "black holes" to read a lot about them, regardless of whether an astronomer wants to communicate with me. But digging into the chemistry of coal conversion, which sounds like work (not fun), might be a different thing altogether.

It's my impression that substantive communication between fields of science is more work than is staying within a familiar community. For one thing, it can involve some costs. For example, the time you spend learning a little sociology to talk to the other person could be spent keeping up with the proliferating professional journals in your own field. Time is one of our most precious personal resources, and allocating it to one kind of communication means that it's not available for another.

So I think the first challenge is that we can't assume that hard and soft scientists consider it a high priority to communicate with each other. They don't object to it, as long as it doesn't interfere with more important things. But they don't get around to it very often, and that doesn't worry them much.

Niche-Seeking

Next, although I wouldn't want to carry this too far, I think that there may be a little bit of self-selection that operates as people choose one field of science over another for themselves. The college student gravitates toward fields in which he or she finds other students who seem to be kindred spirits.

To the extent that this is true, trying to communicate across boundaries between professional groups is like talking to people from a different country or a different culture—people who picked a life that is hard for the communicator to imagine choosing. The campus politicians are all of a sudden trying to talk to those strange people who actually *liked* spending hours in those laboratories, and vice versa. It's not easy, after you get finished covering the weather and the fortunes of the local football team.

Acculturation

The third challenge is professional acculturation. I am convinced that one of the main objectives of graduate school is to train people how to play a particular professional role—how to react to situations. Many times, it's almost a classic example of behavior modification: reinforcement here, penalties there. Unless a person is pretty tough, he or she comes out of all that a *different* person—one who is comfortable playing the role, and uncomfortable operating outside it.

One of the most important parts of the acculturation is learning the jargon of one's own discipline. In a way, jargon is a kind of professional shorthand that speeds up and clarifies communication within the community. But as you know, and as I have found out myself, it's pretty unsettling to try to work professionally in a situation where others not only don't understand your jargon but aren't even willing to grant that it's useful! Communicating from one field of science to another usually requires people to rediscover the regular English language. Yet, we have been trained to think that the regular language isn't adequate for professional work. Although it's our *lingua franca* as citizens, it's not the way we communicate as scientists. So this sort of deeply ingrained attitude makes it harder to communicate with other types of scientists as fellow professionals.

Stereotypes

Finally, there is the problem of stereotypes: the nuts-and-bolts engineer, the narrow-minded physical scientist, or the wholly minded social scientist. We tend to approach people who chose another kind of specialty as representatives of a narrow disciplinary image instead of as the complex individuals that they usually are. We tend to try to communicate in terms of what we think that other person can do, rather than to try to learn more about his or her real interests and skills. But, stereotypes are always too narrow, and they are usually off-target.

These are some of the challenges: People aren't often very interested in communicating; they find it easier and more comfortable talking their own language with people like them; and they often fail to connect with the other person because they are trying to communicate with a stereotype rather than a person.

Such problems are obviously multiplied when a third party wants to communicate with both hard scientists and soft scientists at the same time. Here, the challenges are also complex:

- Getting Their Attention
- The Perils of Simplifying
- Toe-Stepping
- "You Can't Please Everybody"

Getting Their Attention

Disinterest is compounded when a third party tries to reach two or more disinterested people, and it's even worse when the medium of communication is written rather than face to face. We are all immersed in things to read, when, in fact, very little reading gets done. So coming up with a theme, a gimmick, or something else that will attract the attention of a bunch of dissimilar people is the first challenge.

The Perils of Simplifying

Second, talking to a lot of specialists at the same time means that all jargon has to be avoided. But this means using simple language to communicate things that some of the people will think really require complicated language. And, in fact, some of the technical meaning will probably get lost—or distorted a little.

Toe-Stepping

Third, when a third party tries to talk about a cross-cutting subject to a wide range of people, he or she is probably going to step on some toes. Often it's because some of the audience have a vested interest in decisions that the communication might influence. For example, try presenting a balanced summary of the issues surrounding the use of nuclear power in the United States in such a way that nuclear engineers, ecologists, and sociologists will understand one another's bases of information and points of view. Almost surely, somebody is going to say that his or her interests have not been represented as strongly or effectively as somebody else's—which brings up the last point . . .

"You Can't Please Everybody . . ."

I think it takes more than a little bravery to communicate to a diverse scientific audience. A person has to be prepared to look a little foolish, to be considered a little naive, to be judged as being a little superficial, to take a little criticism.

Well, where do we stand at this point? We have concluded that it is just about impossible to get hard and soft scientists to communicate with each other as professionals, and we have concluded that it is even harder for a third party to communicate with both. Is there any hope?

I not only believe such communication can take place but I have seen it happen, being lucky enough to have participated in it firsthand. Feature this: a group of five people—a nuclear engineer, a systems ecologist, an operations-research specialist, a political scientist, and a geographer—charged with writing a book together about science and technology policy. Nearly two years later, when the time comes to decide what the conclusions are, they find that they not only have arrived at the same conclusions but that they also are speaking the same language, that their thoughts are just about interchangeable, that they no longer can remember which of the ideas in the book started with which person. *That's* communication between hard and soft scientists.

Before I try to draw some lessons from that experience and other evidence, let me quickly indicate some popular approaches that I think *don't* work very well. One is suggesting that one group attend courses to learn about the other. Disinterest and niche-seeking and acculturation are just too much to overcome. What's the incentive, anyway? Another approach is putting together multidisciplinary programs, courses, or research efforts, where each specialist does his or her thing as part of an overall scheme of things. In spite of noble intentions, I think it is very rare for much cross-disciplinary communication to take place—except perhaps inside the heads of students or coordinators. People get busy, do what is required to meet their own specific commitments, and that's all. I have directed a program like that, and I could make it sound truly integrated when I wrote an annual report or a new proposal for funding. But it was really a bunch of independent activities under a fragile umbrella which was largely cosmetic and which existed mainly because of a combination of opportunism and utopianism.

Another approach that doesn't work very well is the introduction of fancy methodologies, including formal group-interaction procedures. People—especially well-educated people—are so aware of being "processed" that they seldom let their guards down to communicate freely under these circumstances.

What does work is some combination of these things:

- Mutual Focus on a Technology or Policy Issue
- Reviews of Draft Materials
- Joint Responsibility for Written Reports
- "Living Together"
  Physical Proximity
  Group Review Processes
  Field Trips
- Exceptional Gatekeepers

This is drawn from the Science and Public Policy Program experience at Oklahoma—truly an epistemological experiment, and a successful one. It reflects a range of other things: the experience of advisory panels for government agencies; a number of successful interdisciplinary policy studies (such as the very innovative National Coal Policy Project, jointly arranged by a senior official of the Dow Chemical Company and a former president of the Sierra Club); the work of the American Association for the Advancement of Science

(AAAS) and its remarkable journal, *Science*; and others. There is nothing really amazing about any of these approaches; but they work, and the successes can be documented.

Mutual Focus

First of all, it's necessary to cut across niches and break through disinterest by focusing the attention of both hard and soft scientists on a technology or policy issue to which they all agree is worth paying attention. The issue needs to be complex enough in its ramifications so that everybody can see a way to contribute, and it needs to be important enough so that people are willing to work in some unconventional ways in order to be involved. There are lots of such issues in science policy: energy conservation, recombinant DNA, communication and privacy, quality of urban life, resource scarcity, solar energy—and many more. Basically, you ask everybody to think of himself or herself as, perhaps, an *energy* specialist rather than as a mechanical engineer or as a political scientist. Once everyone redefines his or her niche, even just for awhile, communication is not only possible but also necessary. This, I think, is the secret behind the effectiveness of *Science* and the AAAS.

Draft Reports

A second avenue is to use written materials to communicate—by asking for *responses* to them. I have found that even when somebody in a well-defined niche is busy, he or she will usually read and comment on something you write—*if* you ask *and* as long as there is some kind of overlap of substantive interests—especially if the paper is eventually going to be read by policymakers (such as a biologist when the paper deals in some way with environmental impacts). But there are some secrets to this. You get more feedback if the written materials really *look* like drafts, if they aren't too polished or finished-looking. People want to think they can have some effect on the document, that they can get gaps filled or can remove inaccuracies or mistaken emphases. A polished paper looks as if it's too late for any of this. At Oklahoma, we developed a national reputation for our coffee-stained, dittoed drafts with hand-written inserts, typos, and gaps. It was deliberate, and we got terrific response. Furthermore, once this opened up a communication channel, a lot of the time we could *keep* it open, especially if the next draft showed we had listened to the comments on the first one.

Joint Responsibility

A third avenue is to get hard and soft scientists to *write* something together—not separate contributions to an edited volume, but something that will be jointly authored so that each person is responsible for all that is said. This works especially well if a management process is used that assures a lot of interaction. The way we worked it at Oklahoma was to integrate this joint responsibility with the review procedure. Essentially, a four- to six-person diverse core team is formed to write something about a technology or policy issue. The territory is split up and farmed out for each member to write a rough first draft of some part of it, preferably one that is *not* in his or her area of specialization. Then, each of the drafts is reviewed in detail by the groups—general concept and coverage, writing style, word usage—eventually almost sentence by sentence. It helps if the deadlines for doing the first drafts are so tight that nobody feels that he or she has done anything that approaches perfection. If it's clearly thrown together, nobody's ego gets too tied up with specific wording. Then, you juggle the assignments and have revised drafts written by people other than the ones who wrote them the first time. All along, the group meets to talk about whether the whole thing is moving in the right direction and whether it is subdivided in the right way. These early stages are what we called "the wallowing around period," and it helps if there is time to let it proceed without rushing. As you can see, it is a matter of using the first two avenues, structured just a little and oriented toward a joint publication, to get people with very different professional backgrounds to spend a *great deal* of time together as fellow professionals. I am using a similar approach at the Laboratory now, in order to provide DOE with assessments of the environmental and social impacts of some ideas that are being considered for the second National Energy Plan. The core team includes an engineer, a physicist, an ecologist, a social scientist, and me. Again, it's working very well. We are communicating daily; a lot of the time the communication is intensive, and it's highly professional. I think it is a much more interesting way to work than with one's own discipline alone.

Living Together

I think what I have described is, in many ways, just a structured way to assure this next point: In order to communicate well, hard and soft scientists have to spend a lot of time together—to break down stereotypes, to learn to converse without relying on their own individual jargons, to reorient their definition of niches. An especially effective way to move this along is "field trips"—several people with different backgrounds traveling together, going to see things or to talk to people. The National Coal Policy Project found that it was on long weekends in Montana or in West Virginia, over dinner or in airport lounges, or in the bar in the evening, that the industrialists and environmentalists really started to talk to each other and to identify things they could agree upon.

Exceptional Gatekeepers

Finally, I think we need to recognize that communication between the hard and soft sciences depends a great deal on what sociology calls gatekeepers—exceptional individuals who play a special role in connecting a community with the outside world. There are nuclear engineers, such as David Rose, who talk with theologians. Or economists, such as Lester Lave, who talk with engineers and physical scientists. Or political scientists, such as Don Kash, who talk with earth scientists—people with a special gift for communication and a desire to communicate. I am not talking about the John Kenneth Galbraiths or the Isaac Asimovs or the Carl Sagans, although they help, too. I am talking about scientists who spend a great deal of their time building and maintaining bridges to groups of professionals outside their own fields. You can't program this, and I am not sure that people can be trained to do it. But it is surely possible to encourage and reward it.

We live in a society that isn't working as well as it ought to, and I think the main reason is that we have gotten so compartmentalized. We need to learn to build bridges between all sorts of compartments. The private sector and the public sector need to be able to work together without suspicion and rhetoric. Management and labor should be able to work as partners rather than as adversaries. Ethnic groups and neighborhoods and regions need to understand each others' concerns. All of mankind would benefit by hearing what is being said by all of womankind. Hard sciences and soft sciences as compartments are only one example of a much larger problem, and it behooves all of us to help solve the larger problem as well as the smaller one.

11

BUILDING AN INTERDISCIPLINARY TEAM*

James B. Taylor

Complex societal problems have emerged with special urgency in the last 50 years. It is apparent now, with the advantage of hindsight, that modern technologies have led to vast but unanticipated effects in all areas of modern society. By their very complexity and interdependence, such effects are hard to analyze. Concepts relevant to a particular problem are generally fragmented among a variety of separate disciplines, each having its own perspectives, language, and methods. Any cohesive, rational attack on the current problems of society is frustrated by such fragmentation.

One obvious answer is to bring together different disciplines to work on such complex societal problems. The notion is not new: major efforts were made in the 1930's and 1940's to develop interdisciplinary groups of social and behavioral scientists. Much exciting work resulted, but the attempts generally proved to be short-lived. Most interdisciplinary institutes either disappeared, or evolved away from interdisciplinary effort into more traditional forms of scholarship. The past history of interdisciplinary work in the behavioral sciences thus seems first promising and ultimately disappointing . . . .

And what might be done to overcome the difficulties? To examine these questions, it is necessary first to draw on the essential distinction between well-defined and ill-defined problems.

"Well-Defined" vs "Ill-Defined" Problems

Interdisciplinary teams are set up to solve problems. We may distinguish between two classes of problem: the "well-defined" problem

---

* From *Perspectives on Technology Assessment*, edited by S. Arnstein and A. Christakis, (Jerusalem: Science and Technology Publishers, 1975), pp. 45-60. Copyright 1975 by Academy for Contemporary Problems (now the Academy for State and Local Government).

and the "ill-defined" problem. Well-defined problems are those in which one can be truly specific about what is to be accomplished and the steps necessary to get there.

A well-defined problem may fall within the province of a single discipline when the lore of a single discipline encompasses the component tasks. A well-defined problem may also be multidisciplinary when the component tasks require lore from different disciplines. For example:

> If an energy plant, utilizing water cooling, is set up by a river, the cooling process is likely to influence the river ecology. What ecological changes in the river are likely to emerge, given a defined set of design options? Assuming that one wishes to minimize ecological disruption, what is the preferred design for the plant?

This is a complex problem requiring cooperation between biologists and engineers. Admittedly, the problem is not completely defined—what, for instance, is an unacceptable degree of ecological disruption? And what kinds of trade-offs are possible between engineering cost-effectiveness and ecological disruption? But it does fit our definition of a relatively well defined problem.

In passing, it should be noted that most normal R & D effort is concerned with relatively well-defined problems, as in most of what Kuhn calls "normal science" [2] With well-defined problems, some degree of cooperation is common across disciplines. The major problem with cross-disciplinary effort in such cases is largely technical: the different specialists seldom use the same language, methods, and concepts. As we shall see, additional and more vexing problems arise when different disciplines cooperate in solving ill-defined problems.

In the ill-defined problem it is hard to be very specific about the optimal outcome, or the steps necessary to its achievement. An ill-defined problem is, of necessity, ambiguous, and may or may not be perceived as multidisciplinary. Three examples of relatively ill-defined problems follow:

> — Society at present is malfunctioning. Human wants are unmet, injustice is common, and remediable misery is uncared for. How can one achieve a utopian social order, free of want, injustice, and remediable misery?

— Since wars begin in the minds of men, how can we improve human morality so as to make war unacceptable?

— How does one win a chess game?

As the three examples show, ill-defined questions may arise from practical problems of polity, from basic theoretical problems in a scholarly discipline, and from moral or value positions. And, as the last example suggests, certain kinds of games may provide a convenient model whereby we can examine the ways in which ill-defined problems are solved.

A systematic examination of the relatively ill-defined problem is provided by the work of H. A. Simon and his colleagues on computer modeling of chess-playing ability.[3] A chess game involves one specified undesirable outcome—to checkmate. A vast number of other desirable or undesirable events are possible during the course of the game, but are not specifically predefined. The moves necessary to achieve the optimal outcomes also cannot be predefined, and for all practical purposes the choice of moves may be seen as infinite. In spite of these ambiguities, a grand master will always defeat a novice. In attempting to model the chess playing process, Simon has specified a number of information-processing strategies. These strategies also seem applicable to other kinds of relatively ill-defined problems. We shall draw generally upon his work in the following discussion.

To say that a problem is relatively ill-defined does not imply that it is trivial. It does not imply that it is useless as the starting point for scientific work. But it does imply that it will not be approached by the same processes which serve for well defined problems. The current push for "interdisciplinary synthesis" seems motivated primarily by the need to solve relatively ill-defined problems . . . .

Arbitrary Choice

Ill-defined problems necessarily require arbitrary choice. Even the most expert chess players will differ in the moves they choose: no two grand masters will ever play identical games. This means that certain of their decisions will be more-or-less arbitrary.

Similarly, a team concerned with urban issues may need to be somewhat arbitrary in deciding on the initial problems to be included in their first stage scan. In the second stage, when they look at specific cases, they will again need to be arbitrary. They may, for example, decide to restrict their attention on the problems of a west coast port with much automated industry. They may do so because they believe that the future lies with automation and west coast migration. Or they may hope to improve their understanding by considering the kind of international trade issues that affect a seaport. Or they may have had relevant experience that bears on this kind of a city. These decisions are arbitrary, yet they too are reasoned and reasonable. No two individuals will apply selection criteria in exactly the same way; nor will they scan in the same way, nor will they conceptualize patterns among variables in the same way. Therefore, solutions to the ill-defined problem are necessarily indeterminate. No agreed-on criteria will define the "right" answer. Ordinary language reflects this fact: in such problems we seldom speak of "true solutions," but only of "the best solution currently available." The major theories of science have this same quality of indeterminacy, and in such theory the judgmental criteria of "elegance" and "surprise" play a recognized role.

Individual Competencies

In spite of indeterminacy, different people exhibit different degrees of competence in solving ill-defined problems. In pure science, some researchers have a "talent" for hitting on the crucial questions among an infinite variety of possible questions. Similarly, any chess master can generally trounce any novice. We are therefore led to look at the nature of competence in solving ill-defined questions.

From examination of chess, we know that the competence of the chess master depends upon his ability to perceive patterned relations among pieces. Usually these patterns are coded by a label: "three pawns in second rank," for example, or "a finchettoed bishop." Once identified, the pattern may be matched against coded and stored patterns from prior games. The grand-master may have a repertoire of 50,000 stored chess patterns to call upon: the novice is likely to have only 3 or 4. The highly competent player thus brings a background of appropriate patterns to apply to his chess task. These will have been derived from past experience and from recorded chess lore.

Associated with the patterns are certain heuristic rules for optimal play: "In an open file, place a rook" for example. The grand-master has developed these heuristic rules from thousands of games; the novice has few. When the able player analyzes the specific chess problem before him, he draws upon these stored patterns and heuristics. His analysis shows whether or not the heuristic rules are applicable to the particular case confronting him.

The competent chess player scans, perceives patterns, considers heuristics, and analyzes specifics in a reiterative fashion. He does not focus on a single piece at random and explore all its possibilities before going on to the next piece. Rather, he quickly brings all he knows to bear on the most central issues, analyzing first one possibility, then another.

Chess vis-a-vis Ill-Defined Problems

In the general case, the problem-field first needs to be scanned in order to identify the issues and to specify them in a highly differentiated way. Patterned relationships among issues should be sought. High competence comes from a high awareness of possible patterns. This awareness may come from preexisting knowledge based on direct experience, or from professional lore. It may also come from the application of heuristic theory. Competence in this process thus depends upon the solver's preexisting awareness of relevant paradigms, and the ability to apply them to the problem at hand.

The chess analogy implies that the scanning, chunking, and analyzing process should involve broad gauge but short-term reiterations and approximations. Ackoff has similarly suggested that interdisciplinary systems research similarly requires broad gauge, short-term reiterations:

> "Systems are not fundamentally mechanical, chemical, biological . . . or ethical. These are merely different ways of looking at such systems. Complete understanding of such systems requires an integration of these perspectives. By integration I do not mean a synthesis of results obtained by independently conducted uni-disciplinary studies, but rather results from studies in the process of which disciplinary perspectives have been synthesized. The integration must come during, not after, the performance of the research".[4]

Guidelines for a Concrete Example

So far, our analysis has been abstract. We shall now consider a concrete example. In what follows, we suppose that a single person sets himself the task of planning an ideal city, an urban place which minimizes the problems endemic now in Los Angeles, New York, and other cities in the U.S. We suppose that this single person adapts a frankly Utopian approach. We further suppose that our planner is a polymath, having encyclopedic familiarity with a variety of relevant disciplines.

The Ideal Polymath

These suppositions are admittedly unrealistic. No such ideal polymath will ever exist. Later on we shall consider the special issues confronting a team-in-an-organization which sets itself a similar task. But for now it is useful to examine the simplified case. We shall follow our polymath as he applies the problem-solving strategies sketched out above.

1. Our polymath begins by scanning the problem field to identify the general kinds of issues relevant to his proposed utopia. Since his goal is defined by exclusion—to build a city free of current problems—he first needs to specify what he means by "current problems." He makes a preliminary list:

   traffic congestion
   polluted air
   polluted water
   high crime rates and lack of safety on the streets
   deterioration and abandonment of whole areas fringing on
      the business district
   city deficits exceeding the tax base
   mounting welfare rolls
   racial injustice
   unwieldy, bureaucratic governance
   poor medical care for low and middle-income families

insufficient reservoirs of available power to handle peak
electrical demands

high rates of unemployment among youth and minority
groups

lack of regionalized government

inefficient compulsory schooling which may leave up to
40 percent of the grade school graduates functionally
illiterate, etc.,

etc.

This process of scanning-and-listing is analogous to the initial
scanning of the chess board to see what squares are filled.

Having arrived at the most exhaustive listing possible, our
ideal polymath then moves towards greater specificity. What, for
instance, defines the first item, "traffic congestion"? Is it simply
a vast quantity of cars in limited space? No, for every parking lot
has this. Is it the slowness of vehicular traffic? No, for
horse-drawn carriages move as slowly, yet in 18th century
London no one complained of the slow speed. What then are the
key elements which make up the traffic congestion problem?

This move to specify and to identify the salient features is
analogous to the specific identification of specific pieces on the
chess board. It is a process which our polymath applies to all of
the issues listed.

When any problem is specified with some clarity our
polymath may find that certain solutions suggest themselves.
These heuristic solutions may be fairly general, or quite specific.
As he proceeds he would record such possible solutions for later
analysis.

As the problems are made more specific larger patterns may
become apparent. It may be that the same solutions emerge in
different problems. Or it may be that some specific solutions
suggest further, patterned consequences. Our ideal polymath
would be sensitive to interdisciplinary links in such patterns,
since his perception is informed by a vast lore of relevant
knowledge and theory from all disciplines.

Once these steps are accomplished, he would be in a position
analogous to the chess master who has scanned the board,

recognized the pieces, and chunked his information into patterned form.

2. But this is only the first step. The ideal polymath cannot possibly explore all ramifications of all possible patterns under all conditions. Instead, he is advised to focus on those issues with the "highest priority" under more limited and specified conditions. He needs something analogous to the specific chess game.

   To meet this need he has two options. First, he may focus upon planning a certain kind of city at a certain specified location, taking into account the realistic options and contingencies as they exist at that site. Alternatively, he may decide to plan a hypothetical city and pre-impose whatever contingencies and options seem useful. Either way, the concrete case provides a necessary arena for further exploration and learning.

3. Finally, in the concrete case, the ideal polymath weighs alternatives, probabilities, and consequences. He makes a concrete decision. As this decision is implemented the nature of the problem will change, and the entire process will be repeated again.

When ill-defined problems are attacked by an interdisciplinary team, additional complexities arise. In order to clarify the tasks of our special case, we have postulated an ideal polymath with all necessary knowledge and skills. No ideal polymath exists. In the imperfect world of reality we may approximate the ideal polymath only by bringing together different people with different skills. We shall now consider the case of the group which attempts to do the same job as the ideal polymath, and with the same competence.

It must be recognized that the ideal polymath has several advantages over any group. He knows how he relates to himself, how he thinks about things, and what his competencies are. Members of a newly-formed group are not integrated or acquainted in the same way. The ideal polymath knows how much he can trust himself; the beginning group has no such trust. The ideal polymath can coordinate his efforts in accord with his own plans; the new group lacks such coordination. The ideal polymath is free to make whatever arbitrary decisions are necessary to the task; the beginning group may find itself in conflict when confronted with arbitrary choice.

Moreover, the ideal polymath is forever a single person communing full-time with himself; the incipient group is faced with decisions about how many people should be involved, to what extent and for how long. The ideal polymath has all the knowledge he needs; the incipient group must decide on the knowledge it needs and recruit accordingly. The ideal polymath stays in one body during his lifetime; a group loses some members and gains new ones, causing problems of disruption, socialization, and continuity. Finally, the ideal polymath is untroubled by external pressures and pulls, while the beginning group is very much subject to pressures and pulls from the surrounding organization.

All of this creates a high degree of complexity. We shall here examine some of the particular complexities, and some ways of resolving them, in the early stages of team formation.

Building an Interdisciplinary Team

In what follows, we assume that a small planning group has been formed, attempting to build a team to do the job previously assigned to the ideal polymath.

The problem here is to bring together members to form the optimum team. The optimum team contains individuals who (1) have the major skills necessary for the task, (2) are motivated to engage in the task, (3) have adequate time to devote to the task, (4) have reasonable aptitude for the task, (5) will be engaged long enough to provide continuity to the task, and (6) include the most important skills within a group small enough to allow intensive, task-focused interaction to take place.

The first thing the planning group must do is to identify the relevant skills. This means that the planning group itself must go through an initial scanning exercise, the kind of exercise proposed for the ideal polymath. Initial scanning led the polymath to a listing of major city problems; the planning group too would emerge with such a list, from which it may become apparent that rather specific areas of knowledge would be useful. Some problems will require the skills of the environmental or civil engineer, some will require an urban or labor economist, some will require a person knowledgeable about the sociology of organizations. By making the skill requirements as explicit as possible, the criteria for recruitment are clarified.

The next step will be to scan the available talent, within and (perhaps) outside the organizational context. Those who seem to meet the criteria are potential recruits.

At this point, the size of the group should be decided. In general, any intensive, interactive, task-focused groups should not contain fewer than five or more than twelve people; the range of 7-9 is optimal. With larger numbers the information processing necessary exceeds the channel capacity of individuals, discussion becomes amorphous, and the group tends to segment.[5]

Recruitment then proceeds, with a (usually informal) attempt to maximize motivation, aptitude, time availability, and continuity in choosing the members.

In discussing recruitment, we noted "motivation" and "aptitude" as criteria for group membership. The nature of motivation and aptitude in this context is by no means obvious; we know relatively little about the aptitudes and motivations conducive to solving ill-defined problems. However, what is known suggests certain interesting speculations.

Most normal science is concerned with "well-defined" problems. Such problems seem to require a good share of what some psychologists have called *convergent thinking*:

> The individual is set a problem in which he is required to find the right answer; and he is frequently invited to choose this right answer from a list of alternatives . . . His reasoning is said to *converge* on the right answer. A typical intelligence test question might run:
> *Brick is to house as plank is to . . . orange, grass, egg, boat, ostrich.*
> Only one of the five alternatives satisfactorily completes the analogy: boat.[6]

In contrast, certain of the steps necessary to solve "ill-defined" problems seem to require a good share of *divergent* thinking ability.

Consider now a typical question from a 'creativity' test: *How many uses can you think of for a brick?* Here the individual is invited to *diverge,* to think fluidly and tangentially, without examining any one line of reasoning in detail. [7]

The scanning and patterning processes called for in solving ill-defined problems would especially seem to require this form of reasoning. However, the later steps, requiring disciplined rigor, would also seem to call for convergent thought.

These two kinds of thinking are not randomly distributed across disciplines. Early evidence suggests that scientific and technological pursuits appeal mainly to convergent thinkers, while divergent thinkers are drawn more towards humanistic pursuits and the social sciences. [8]

The two types of thinking seem to be associated with different personality traits. Early evidence suggests that convergent thinkers are much more likely to have views which are conservative and respectful of authority: they tend to have strongly focused but narrow intersts; they are apt to be more interested in the impersonal aspects of life and less interested in human relations; they are relatively cautious in the expression of feeling; they tend to avoid interpersonal stress and controversy; and they are concerned with practical matters. A number of investigators have pointed out that such personality characteristics are typical of engineers and technicians.

The personality traits of the pure divergent thinkers are in many ways opposite. They prefer the unconventional and the ambiguous, are more liberal or anti-authoritarian in their views, focus upon personal relationships, dislike precision, enjoy emotional display, and may value a certain unbuttoned messiness. The strongly divergent thinker is made uncomfortable by highly specific problems which call for highly disciplined solutions. [9]

This evidence suggests several problems which are likely to arise in recruitment and in team process.

— It may be that ill-defined team efforts are especially attractive to predominantly divergent thinkers. In ill-defined problems the issues are ambiguous and "messy," the topics are often related to liberal concerns, and team efforts are often highly personal. It is likely however that divergent thinkers will be limited in their efforts by their difficulty in accepting arbitrary decisions, and by their dislike of disciplined problem-solving approaches.

— It may be that ill-defined team efforts will prove especially *un*attractive to predominantly convergent thinkers. For such people, the ambiguity of the work is likely to prove uncongenial and threatening. They may tend to cut short the scanning and patterning stages by striving too early for clarity, concreteness, and discipline.

— Since the two types, in the extreme, hold antithetical views and values, their incorporation into a single team is likely to produce continuing conflict. Since the two types tend to be drawn to different disciplines, it is likely that this conflict will be seen as a conflict between disciplines. This militates against interdisciplinary cooperation.

In building an interdisciplinary team, the ideal solution would be to recruit when possible, from the "all-rounders": those equally competent and comfortable with both approaches. Such a solution is not always possible. When it is not, some attention may need to be given to specialized assignment of task, with the divergent and the convergent thinkers working on those stages of problem solution most congenial to their underlying styles.

Time and effort needs to be given to the stages of group formation. Let us assume that nine people have been recruited to the interdisciplinary team. Nine people do not constitute a working group. A working group will exist when these nine people have developed a solid base of reciprocal understanding—both among themselves, and with the surrounding organization. A competent group will exist if these reciprocal understandings promote, rather than hinder, the task at hand. The period which produces the reciprocal understandings we may call the "stage of group formation."

Much can go awry during this stage. Two related problems typically emerge. The first problem arises from the management of conflict and lack of trust among members; the second, from issues of leadership and authority. Both types of problems are especially apt to emerge when the group is faced with ambiguous and unclear tasks. The first task of the new group then is to develop reciprocal and realistic understandings about each other, and about the leadership-authority function.

Some Prescriptive Guidelines:

— Trust is developed in two kinds of group settings: work settings which allow a joint exploration of task-related ideas, concepts, and interests; and informal social settings which allow a wider acquaintanceship to develop.

— In work settings, trust will develop most quickly when the group starts with well-defined and reasonable modes of leadership and authority. Not all leadership modes are "reasonable" in this context. "Imposed-authoritarian" leadership based upon pre-existing status in the organization is clearly not reasonable. Leadership based on expertise, or upon socio-personal attraction, is not reasonable initially because it has not had time to emerge. The sole reasonable kind of leadership at this stage may be called "coordinative leadership": the mode of leadership which sets agendas, defines tasks for further discussion, focuses group thinking, makes final assignments of work and responsibility, forces decision and mediates conflicts. Leadership in this mode may be highly participatory, but nevertheless very real and very unambiguous.

— Acquaintanceship and trust is more likely to develop when the group meets frequently in an informal way, free of objective task demands or office constraints. Such meetings provide an arena for the working out of personal feelings and group process issues. Specific trust-building exercises as developed in encounter groups, may have a place in such meetings. Often this sort of thing occurs spontaneously in project parties; it may also be planned as a specific part of the subject.

— The more ambiguous the group task, the more the group is likely to exhibit conflict between members and dissatisfaction with leadership. Ill-defined problems necessarily are reflected in ambiguous group tasks. Therefore, groups working on ill-defined problems are likely to exhibit a relatively high degree of membership conflict and leadership dissatisfaction during the initial stage. The tactics listed above can reduce these conflicts and dissatisfactions, but will not eliminate them. On the other hand, the successful weathering of such storms is likely to lead to high group morale and commitment.

In short, ill-defined problems are apt to produce special strains during the period of group formation. These special strains may be partly ameliorated, but cannot be bypassed. However, once the group has worked through such issues, it may function effectively as a unit. *The true interdisciplinary team needs to be able to perform—as a group—the scanning, identifying and patterning functions of the ideal polymath; it must be capable of making and accepting arbitrary decisions, and it must be capable of working intensively together on problems which it identifies as interdependent.*

FOOTNOTES

. . . .

[2]Thomas Kuhn, *The Structure of Scientific Revolutions* (2nd Ed.) Chicago: University of Chicago Press, 1970. Kuhn suggests that most normal science is guided by accepted disciplinary paradigms, which define the important problems and the criteria for their solution. "Scientific revolutions" arise when these normal paradigms prove insufficient - a state of paradigm crises. We suggest that ill-defined problems are characteristic of sciences undergoing a paradigm crisis.

[3]Herbert Simon, W. Chase, *Amer. Scientist*, 61, 394, 1973; H. Newman, H. Simon, *Human Problem Solving* (Prentice Hall, Englewood Cliffs, N.J., 1972).

[4]Russell Ackoff, General Systems Yearbook, 5, 1 (1960), p. 6.

[5]Complexity of interaction in an undifferentiated group is multiplicative, according to the formula $\frac{1}{2}N$ (N-1). Interactions in a 10 person group thus are approximately four times as complex as in a 5 person group (J. Klein, *The Study of Groups*, Routledge & Kegan Paul, London, 1956, p. 42).

[6]Liam Hudson, *Contrary Imaginations: A Psychological Study of English Schoolboys.* (Methuen, London, 1966.)

[7]*op. cit.*

[8]*op. cit.*

[9]These characterizations are overdrawn in the interest of brevity, and based primarily on extreme samples of individuals with pronounced divergent or convergent modes of thought. In fact, the bulk of individuals come close to balancing the two modes, and the correlations between thought process and personality are at best moderate. Still, with all the qualifications stated, the research findings are supported by common observation as exemplified for instance by Snow's notion of "Two Cultures."

12

THE 'BRIDGE SCIENTIST' AND HIS ROLE*

Michael Anbar

The history of science and technology teaches us that a majority of significant developments were the result of a polydisciplinary approach. Adaption of technical information or concepts from one discipline to another invariably resulted in a "jump" or step function in the development of the adapting discipline. Breakthroughs in science and technology require, by definition, diversion from conventional thought and methodology, and the best innovators are people from other fields. As modern science utilizes computers for storage and retrieval of information, and as many experimental techniques become automated and less dependent on the individual skills of the experimenter, the classical specialists give way to "polydisciplinary" scientists who may help to diversify knowledge by transfer of concepts from one discipline to another.

But bringing together professionals with different disciplinary affiliations generates profound problems of interpersonal communication. These problems arise not only from the different languages of the participating disciplines, but also from the differential evaluations (that is, differential status) of the disciplines and of the individual professionals. The successful performance of a "bridge role" in the management of such teams may mitigate these problems of communication. In other words, the successful operation of a polydisciplinary research team requires building a special role into that team and recruiting a scientist or engineer competent to perform that role.

Although agreement generally exists about the importance of polydisciplinary research, little effort has been applied to analyze its constituents and the conditions of its success. This article describes our

* From *Research/Development*, July 1973, pp. 33-37, reprinted by permission of the author.

effort to define the "bridge role" and presents guidelines to aid in selecting a scientist to fill it.

Multidisciplinary or Interdisciplinary?

In the operation of polydisciplinary research teams, composed of scientists from different disciplines, we distinguish between the *multidisciplinary mode*, where a monodisciplinary team leadership formulates the plan of the project and specifies the contribution of each of the participants, and the *interdisciplinary mode*, where each of the disciplines represented on the team interacts on an equal footing to formulate the plan of action and to specify the contributions of each of the participants. . . .

The interaction among scientists of different disciplines will result in new combinations of ideas that will not occur in the absence of intense team interaction. This interaction will lead to the asking of questions that would never be asked from a monodisciplinary perspective. And, finally, these new combinations of ideas and the asking of new questions will generate a greater range of proposed solutions to the team problems. . . .

Ideas are not enough

While novelty of questions asked and of solutions proposed are gains to be desired, they are not the sole criterion for the successful solution of a research problem. It's quite conceivable that a team can produce many ideas, and yet fail to make any contribution to solving a problem. The ideas generated can drive the team simultaneously in several directions, making it impossible to pursue research or even to formulate a preliminary research plan. To function as a team, some consensus on evaluation of ideas and on criteria for selecting avenues to be pursued are necessary. To achieve this consensus and a sense of direction for the team imposes special demands on the team leadership. Insofar as these problems occur in multidisciplinary teams, the centralization of authority and responsibility provides a mechanism for resolution. Where the team structure is participatory, mechanisms for resolving these issues must be generated from within the team itself. Quite obviously, different demands are made both on the team leadership and on the participating scientists in each mode of operation.

Both the multidisciplinary and interdisciplinary modes of operation of research teams are confronted with a special set of management problems. The greater the conflicts over language, prestige, ability and the value of the individual scientist's contribution, the poorer the quality of the team product. The more successful the management of these conflicts, the higher the quality of the team product. The more intense the interaction among team members from various disciplines, the more salient are issues of differential prestige of the disciplines. Because participation is greater in the interdisciplinary mode, the range and magnitude of problems arising in interaction—particularly the problems of differential prestige—are likely to be greater and more pressing for solution than in the multidisciplinary mode. It is in connection with management of intra-team interaction that we regard the "bridging role" as crucial.

Interdisciplinary bridging crucial

The demands of interdisciplinary team leaderships are considerably greater than the demands of multidisciplinary team leadership. For the interaction *among* specialists from different disciplines to be fruitful, the leadership must be sensitive to a number of potential barriers and innovative in dealing with obstacles. On the one hand, the leadership must guard against imposing so rigid a structure as to prevent synergistic activity. On the other hand, the leadership must guard against creating so loose a structure that the only result is the proverbial camel—the horse designed by a committee.

Language barriers, disciplinary prestige, and the individual prestige impose severe restrictions on interdisciplinary teamwork unless one finds a way to match the team member with the problem and the team members with each other. This function of matching, which becomes more important as the team becomes larger and more diversified, calls for a scientist with the technical knowledge and personal persuasion needed to bridge the gaps between disciplines.

The role of the "bridge scientist" is often to initiate the project, to translate the need of the project into terms of the different disciplines *without* assigning any specific task to any discipline, to enhance the interdisciplinary interaction between the team members *without* imposing any authoritative view, and ultimately to be in charge of or at least be strongly involved in the integration phase of the project. . . .

Constraints on performance

The performance of interdisciplinary teams is subject to a number of important constraints, which have to be tackled by the bridge scientist.

1. Multiple sets of criteria and values in teams functioning in an interdisciplinary mode, which make it difficult for team members to evaluate each other's stature and performance. This leads to a situation where the appreciation by one member is not always received as a reward by his colleague, who may not consider him to be competent to pass judgment, negative or positive. In many cases, the team members attach more importance to the opinion of their peers in their respective fields than to that of their collaborators inside the team.

2. A hierarchy of disciplines superimposed on the hierarchy of individual stature, which determines the inter-relations among the team members.

3. Interdisciplinary communication between team members. Problems have to be presented to all team members in most general terms with a minimum of preconceived bias.

4. Conceptualizing a problem and choosing among different solutions. These functions are limited not only by language barriers but also by the different types of reasoning that are typical for people of different training and background.

5. Nonhomogeneous attitudes toward the problems and objectives of the team. What may look to one team member like a fundamental contribution to basic knowledge in a given field, may look to another team member from another discipline like a second-rate, trivial contribution.

6. Uneven distribution of resources, which is a major factor in the motivation of team members. Facilities and equipment may serve one group of team members, but may be of no use to others. In many cases, allocation of resources is not merely a utility function, which facilitates the accomplishment of specific assignments, but also an important reward. A nonhomogeneous distribution of this type of reward may insert a strong bias in the conceptualization and initial planning phases.

This list of problems, which is not comprehensive, illustrates the need for special management criteria and management tools in the operation of interdisciplinary teams.

On the basis of an analysis of the special problems of the interdisciplinary mode, we concluded that the more intense the interaction among team members from various disciplines, (a) the greater is the likelihood of conflicting evaluations of products of individual team members, (b) the more salient are issues of differential prestige of the disciplines represented and (c) the more salient are issues of differential prestige of individual scientists. The bridge scientist, however, by his sensitivity to paradigm conflicts, can contribute to the solution of these interactional impediments, which are much harder to overcome than language barriers.

The formulation of the bridging role emphasizes the "translator" aspects of the bridge scientist. Indeed, when a bridge role is present in a multidisciplinary team, it will deal almost exclusively with problems of language, serving to translate the formulation of the needs of the research problem from one monodisciplinary perspective into another. However, in the interdisciplinary mode, the bridging role extends far beyond resolving terminological conflicts. The bridge scientist in the interdisciplinary mode must be sensitive to paradigm conflicts among disciplines and to the varying evaluational standards contained in these conflicts. This sensitivity enables him to cope with the special problems that arise from the intense interaction of the interdisciplinary team. Thus the personality of the bridge scientist rather than his professional training plays a crucial role in his performance.

Find four types of bridge scientist

A number of "bridge scientists" have been identified in a study at Stanford Research Institute (SRI) through a critical analysis of a large number of polydisciplinary projects. From these findings we gained substantial understanding of the characteristics of bridge scientists.

Bridge scientists can be classified according to their backgrounds or according to their mode of operation. According to background, we find four characteristic types:

a. Professionals who are strongly grounded in a particular discipline and, having obtained satisfaction in terms of scientific curiosity and recognition by their peers, have become adventurers. They now receive satisfaction by stimuli from others who have different backgrounds and attitudes. These people look at the world from an even wider viewpoint, and, as time goes on, they become ideal generalists who are still deeply rooted in one or two fields of specialization. These people generally will be the most active and creative bridge scientists.

b. Professionals who are strongly grounded in a particular discipline and might like to stay in it, but who feel *forced* to get involved in other disciplines because their own discipline is becoming obsolete and nonmarketable. Being less enthusiastic, these professionals are less likely to act as bridge scientists in spite of their readiness to get involved in interdisciplinary research.

c. People who had some rather superficial training in one or more disciplines, who now find that they can get work and consequent recognition as generalists. They are best utilized in organization and marketing rather than in project generation and management.

d. People who have moved into managerial, sales or other essentially bridge positions, who have not been prepared to fulfill a bridge role. Yet their present job requires them to become involved in interdisciplinary research activities. In the absence of other bridge scientists, they take this role. People of this type, whose attitudes are far from those required by bridge scientists, may become the most serious obstacles to interdisciplinary research.

Characteristics to look for

Certain characteristic features of type a became evident in the course of our study. These include the following:

a. Many have depth in at least one discipline; some have made substantial contributions to two, or even three disciplines.

b. Many have taken an unconventional set of courses in college.

c. They have realized early in their professional career that a range of disciplines is required to solve any important problem in science or technology.

d. They go out and seek involvement in diverse kinds of problem solving and enjoy it beyond the call of duty.

e. They have a wide range of interests, and are regular readers of generalist journals.

f. They have multiple connections to various societies—scientific, social and cultural.

g. They have aspirations different from those of the majority of professionals. They try to understand *nature*, not physics or chemistry.

They hope to become directors of research institutions rather than chairmen of university departments. They wish to achieve a Nobel prize for an unforeseen innovation rather than become world experts in a certain field.

h. They are oriented toward problem solving, and are quick to abandon an old specialty if a new one seems more promising.

i. They show intense interest in whatever area they are investigating at the moment and "forget" it when they attack a new area.

j. They are able in an interpersonal sense—good listeners, emphatic and accepting, able to generate enthusiasm. Being optimistic and persistent, they tend to encourage their peers. They are ready to accept inputs from others, are critical but trustful.

k. They are generally good salesmen of ideas and projects with an easy perception of the needs of others, and they excel in demonstrating the value of their ideas in meeting these needs.

These characteristics could provide the basis for selecting bridge scientists. However, we do not anticipate complete success in fitting individuals to this role. Some scientists who possess many of these characteristics will nevertheless not be effective in the bridging role. The quality that seems most critical for an effective bridge function is quality j, the personal interaction quality. Scientists who have this type of personality trait are almost guaranteed to success as bridge scientists if they are interested in this function and especially if they also have traits a, e or h. This strengthens our conclusion that the role of the bridge scientist is primarily that of *a people mediator* rather than *a concept translator*.

This brings us to three major questions from the standpoint of a top management that is interested in the success of interdisciplinary projects:

1. Is it possible to identify potential effective bridge scientists according to a personality profile?

2. Is it possible to train existing senior personnel to become effective bridge scientists?

3. Is it possible to generate bridge scientists at the university level by a special set of courses?

Our findings at SRI, though rudimentary, strongly suggest that a potential bridge scientist could be rather easily identified. It should be mentioned at this point, however, that such individuals are rather uncommon. SRI is one of the outstanding interdisciplinary institutes in the world. Yet only one of every fifty professionals at SRI could qualify as a bridge scientist, and only about one-third of these could reach excellence in this function.

Is training feasible?

This scarcity of good bridge scientists brings us to the second question—is it possible to train staff scientists to fulfill this function? Our opinion is that scientists who fulfill quality j—interpersonal ability (which ought to be characteristic of all good project leaders)—could be motivated and trained to become good bridge scientists. The major problem here is motivation, because most good project leaders hold positions of excellence in their own discipline. It is hard to persuade them to give it up in favor of an interdisciplinary activity to which they were less inclined in the first place. Here, management has to undertake a campaign of persuasion to recruit qualified candidates for bridge positions.

The last question of specialized university training is not as easy to answer. Good bridge scientists are mature persons who have demonstrated expertise in at least one discipline and in many cases in more than one. A set of generalistic courses in science and technology plus appropriate courses in sociology, psychology and management could generate "professional" bridge scientists. However, it is hard to estimate their success in this complex and difficult role. For one thing, these "synthetic" bridge scientists will lack quality a—the depth of experience in research. But in spite of this uncertainty, it would be worthwhile for at least one or two universities to offer curricula aimed at producing this unique type of research manager.

An even better approach would be to offer at universities courses that emphasize the advantages of interdisciplinary research efforts and include anecdotal information about personality and team management problems. Such courses, given by lecturers with first-hand experience, would draw the attention of the best students during their formative stages of higher education and would prompt those students interested in technical management to take up appropriate additional courses in management and in other social sciences. The result would be professionals who would then pursue their monodisciplinary careers, but who could, when they mature and the opportunity appears, take up a bridge scientist position.

If we could just double the fraction of effective bridge scientists in our research laboratories, it is quite likely that we would more than quadruple the output of innovations.

PART IV

WHERE IS THE INSTITUTIONAL SETTING?

13

MESHING INTERDISCIPLINARITY WITH INTERNATIONALITY*

Bernhard Wilpert

Introduction

From an a priori point of view it can be argued that outputs of research groups are as much an outcome of social processes as of intellectual activity; they are similarly influenced and determined by power relations, affective relationships, interpersonal perceptions and attitudes, situational constraints and opportunities as the output of factory workers in a production line. The plausibility of such an argumentation derives from the fact that teams are micro-organisations with common purposes and objectives that are implemented through decisions. And decision making and decision implementation are social processes. The sociologists of knowledge in Karl Mannheim's tradition have long since recognized the impact of social fabric and societal dynamics on the generation of knowledge. But their insights are restricted to a macro-sociological level.

It is almost platitudinous to say that research results depend on the methods employed. This is why scientists bend over backwards to account for the possible methodological and measurement errors in their findings. Ethics of science and our socialization in the paradigms of our disciplinary research demand it thus. But why, if research results are affected as well by the social dynamics through which they are produced, why do we rarely ever account for them? I would surmise that two factors contribute to that blind spot[1]:

* From *Interdisciplinary Research Groups: Their Management and Organization*, edited by R.T. Barth and R. Steck, 1979, pp. 168-179. Proceedings of the First International Conference on Interdisciplinary Research Groups, Schloss Reisensburg, Federal Republic of Germany, April 22-28, 1979.

(1) We have been reared as researchers in an environment of aseptic objectivity where we assume or even claim that the human factor is cancelled out by methodological rigour.
(2) Probably in consequence of that upbringing we lack a microanalytic framework to take note and to account for the group-dynamical and situational parameters of research production.

While I know from experience and logical deduction that the assumption in (1) is largely unwarranted, I feel that such a micro-analytical framework (2) is urgently needed for the sake of development of science in general and of social sciences in particular.

We presently observe an outstanding mushrooming of multi-national comparative and collaborative research in the social sciences (Roberts, 1970; Petralla, 1974; Almasy, Balandier and Delatte, 1976). Similarly, a growing concern with the needs and modalities of interdisciplinary research can be noted (CERI, 1972). One reason for both developments may be that social problems nowadays pose themselves in an order of magnitude which transcends both national and disciplinary boundaries. But international collaborative and interdisciplinary research pose interpersonal problems of a very special kind or at least pose them also in different order of magnitude than encountered in any kind of collaborative research. So it is not surprising to observe that it is particularly from international or interdisciplinary collaborative experience where a new impetus started to reflect those internal and external factors that influence the functioning and end results of the research process itself (Mabry et al., 1966; Szalai and Scheuch, 1972; Castri, 1974; Blaschke, 1976; Jennings and Farah, 1977; Szalai and Petralla, 1977; Glaser, 1977). These appear to be healthy signs of renewed self reflection in the social sciences. I hope the following contributes to this process.

Models of International Collaborative Research

Organizational structures of research teams have enjoyed little attention from organization sciences. And yet, as a longstanding body of literature shows, structures impact outputs (Bavelas, 1955). Among the few references may be mentioned Claessens' (1962) discussion of the desirable personality mix in teams and, taking off from his study, Muller-Fohrbrodt's information flow and structuring needs in research teams (1973). Fisch (1977), in his review article, also reports mainly studies on personal characteristics of team members and their effects on research outcomes. Joerges (1977), in his very perceptive review of conditions for scientific creativity, reports little to no research on the micro-structural aspects of research groups. An organization psychological framework by Bilitza (1978) comes closer to that by analyzing the structure of research institutes, their leadership and group dynamical properties and the impact of the environmental scientific community.

Rokkan (1969) addresses himself explicitly to a comprehensive typology of approaches to "gathering of information and the analysis of data across a number of distinct cultures, societies or political entities". He distinguishes four major categories (Figure 1):

sites/units of study

		within one nation	within several nations
Research Organization	In one nation only	I The typical single nation study	II Typically secondary analysis of data already available for several nations
	In several nations	III Cooperative international national research in one nation	IV The typical co-operative cross-national study

Figure 1: Models of cross-national research (Rokkan 1969)

He further differentiates project organizations according to the main functions (design development, data collection, data analysis, data interpretation) which can be carried out by individual national teams or jointly by international teams. Thus, it might be (Fourcade and Wilpert, 1975) that projects are either *centralized-hierarchical* (with central funding, leadership, and responsibility for all project functions), *semi-decentralized* (with part of the functions centralized, others in the responsibility of cooperating national teams) or *decentralized-collective* (all functions collectively agreed upon but decentrally carried out). It is the decentralized-collective type of research that steers clear from any safari-type of research where jet-set data collectors sweep in and out of a country in the pursuit of multi-national research.

Thus we can order various organizational models of multi-national research along a continuum from no or little international diffusion of leadership and responsibility to maximum diffusion and collective accountability. It is quite clear that such differences in formal structures of project organizations will imply noticeable differences in motives of collaborating researchers, their commitment to and identification with the research, the risks they take vis-a-vis their home country institutions, comprehensiveness of design and in the depth and validity of data interpretation.

Models of Interdisciplinary Collaborative Research

Integrating Jantsch's ideas (1970, 1972) about inter- and trans-disciplinary cooperation and coordination, di Castri (1978) arrives at a set of different organizational models ordered along a continuum of increasing interaction and cooperation between disciplines and policy making (Figure 2).

While his models of multi- and pluridisciplinarity impose no major demands on the various members of a scientific discipline, this changes with the emergence of the latter models of cross-, inter- and transdisciplinarity. Here members are required to subordinate themselves to constraints that are traditionally external to an idealized notion of scientific activity. Individual disciplinary inputs become functionally integrated into some purposive planning or action orientation. Again it must be assumed from a priori positions that these model differences with their respective behavioral requirements will put social and psychological forces into motion that are likely to impact on the final research outcomes.

What then happens if one brings both together—the intrinsic complexities of international and interdisciplinary research models?

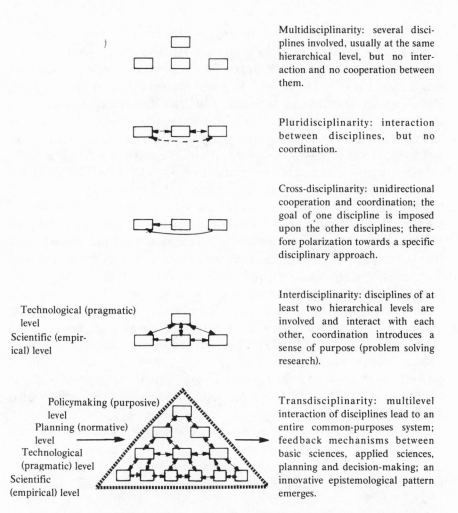

Multidisciplinarity: several disciplines involved, usually at the same hierarchical level, but no interaction and no cooperation between them.

Pluridisciplinarity: interaction between disciplines, but no coordination.

Cross-disciplinarity: unidirectional cooperation and coordination; the goal of one discipline is imposed upon the other disciplines; therefore polarization towards a specific disciplinary approach.

Technological (pragmatic) level
Scientific (empirical) level

Interdisciplinarity: disciplines of at least two hierarchical levels are involved and interact with each other, coordination introduces a sense of purpose (problem solving research).

Policymaking (purposive) level
Planning (normative) level
Technological (pragmatic) level
Scientific (empirical) level

Transdisciplinarity: multilevel interaction of disciplines lead to an entire common-purposes system; feedback mechanisms between basic sciences, applied sciences, planning and decision-making; an innovative epistemological pattern emerges.

Figure 2: Steps in the increasing cooperation and coordination of research and management (based on Jantsch, 1970)

Towards a Micro-Analysis of International, Interdisciplinary Research Teams

(1) Data Base

What follows is a composite account of the "natural history" (Mabry et al., 1966)—if there is such a thing—of two international social scientific research projects. One is a comparative study of managerial leadership and decision making in eight countries (Heller, 1971; Fourcade and Wilpert, 1975; Heller and Wilpert, 1977) in which some ten scholars collaborated over a period of five years (Project A). The other (IDE, 1976) is a study of twelve national industrial democracy schemes and their impact on organizational behavior in which some 25 scientists from 13 countries cooperated over a period of six years (Project B). According to the models described above Project A would have to be called a cooperative cross-national study of the semi-decentralized variety, Project B (still ongoing) is a cooperative cross-national study of the decentralized-collective type. In terms of disciplinary background, team members came from a considerable variety of fields (general and organizational sociology, industrial relations, organizational and industrial psychology, business administration, engineering, political science). Since the focus of both projects was on organizations, their model in terms of disciplinary cooperation would probably fall somewhere between cross- and interdisciplinarity.

The members of both teams differed considerably in terms of age (early twenties to late fifties), professional experience and status (young assistant researchers to internationally reputed scholars), scientific interest and methodological orientation. Their interpersonal and language skills (lingua franca of both projects was English) varied similarly in both teams.

All meetings of both international teams were monitored by tape recordings and extensive minutes.

(2) Structural Parameters

In the two projects eight (A) or twenty (B) national research centers cooperated actively in the research, financially supported by some 10 or 30 national funding organizations. Thus the research implied the buildup and maintenance of considerable personal and institutional networks. Given that funding agencies vary in their evaluation standards and procedures for project proposals, the decentralized funding of both ventures inevitably led to discrepancies in takeoff time giving those country teams that were earlier in the field an edge over latecomers. Differences in access to national resources (institutional backing, funds, and access to companies) similarly set boundary constraints to overall balanced equalities. Net result of such factors is an intrinsic ambiguity in the time horizons of such multisited projects which at times causes considerable friction with national funding bodies.

International collaboration over extended time and space dimensions quickly surpasses the 'normal' magnitude of technical problems found in smaller ventures. Letters delayed in postal strikes and slowdowns, wrongly marked "surface" rather than "air", coding instructions misunderstood by junior assistants who had not been present at plenary meetings, data tapes incorrectly specified—all are deleterious characteristics of boundary transcending projects. A case in point were "fool proof" coding instructions. In one project, data were to be read directly from coding sheets by an optical scanner in the central data processing center. Hence, instructions read that coding was to be done "as you write" (i.e. for most Europeans from left to right), since all necessary recoding would automatically be carried out by the scanner. No wonder we could make no sense out of the data received from our Israeli colleagues!

In view of all these structurally determined uncertainties, both projects would have been doomed from their very inception without at least some central funding of international overheads which facilitated regular plenary meetings, a modest coordination budget to guarantee standardized procedures, controls, and data analysis.

(3) Process Dynamics

The choice of a particular organizational model, characteristics of team composition, and infrastructural parameters set the frame for the evolving research processes in international, interdisciplinary teams. A socio-biographic approach of the projects concerned may help to highlight the factors which at various project stages appear to have influenced the final outcome of the research.

Presumably any biography, and certainly the biography of a research project, may be described in terms of a cumulative process of reducing options. In the phase of problem definition the range of options seems to be widest. But here the projects already differed in the sense that Project A was centralized in the sense that it was based on a national study which was to be carried out as an extended and somewhat modified replication in other countries. Project B was genuinely developed "from scratch" by the collective of the international team. This difference in the project organization almost inevitably led to differences in the motivational states. While in one case the project idea had to be "sold" by the initiators and "bought" by prospective collaborators, in the other case the idea was owned by all from the beginning. Crucial at this stage proved to be that each participant was fascinated by the issues posed, that the intellectual styles of participants stimulated rather than blocked each other, and that personalities involved seemed to fit. It appears that little can be done about planning such a coincidence. In both projects we could observe the development of a distinct project-"lingo" which facilitated easy communication among team members, increased group coherence but made it difficult for late-comers to the team to be fully integrated.

In the design stage significant strides are made to limit options. And these decisions determine largely the ultimate nature of the research. Should one focus on macro-level factors such as societal and historical contexts or national policies? What is more appropriate, an inter-organizational or intra-organizational research perspective? Case studies or cross-sectional methodologies? Consensus, at this stage, is crucial. But it so happened that commitment to disciplinary paradigms posed the first barriers to easy agreements. It is here where we experienced interdisciplinary friction most. Given that consensus on design decisions is absolutely mandatory, every team member virtually holds a veto position which is likely to result in extended, sometimes seemingly endless discussions. Usually compromise solutions are inevitable. They require an often taxing readiness to compromise. Hence, apart from the time requirements to these decision processes through frequent meetings, compromises may result in diluting theoretical stringency. These may be high costs. But on the benefit side is the high level of commitment to the decisions taken and—hopefully—a more meaningful ultimate design in terms of its real life relevance. The reason for this expectation can be seen in the fact that differences in paradigmatic focus of disciplines usually reflect different analysis levels and, if they are brought together in an integrative research design, they might thus comprise a more meaningful chunk of reality to be investigated.

The stage of operationalization imposes decisions on choice of methods, procedures and instrumentation which all limit increasingly the freedom of action. Once more the battle is resumed to recapture ground lost in the design phase. We noticed the rush of national teams and members of different disciplines to save 'pet ideas' at least through the back door of operationalizations. At least in Project B, due to its greater openness in organizational premises, many a hotly debated decision on instruments and procedures could only be solved through feasibility tests in a pilot study. An excellent conflict resolving device proved to be the possibility to declare a particular methodological extension to be "optional" rather than "obligatory".

Field work phases, according to our experience, tend to be relatively straightforward with hardly any international or interdisciplinary conflict. "Handbooks for field researchers" helped considerably to bridge distances in times, space and common understanding.

However, planning of strategies and procedures for the final data analysis is once more likely to raise the level of internal conflict and bargaining. Constraints on time, funds and required expertise usually prevent analysis planning in plenary. Choosing members to an analysis planning committee implies choosing among theoretical biases (for instance regarding preferred levels of aggregation!) and the formation of such a committee implies the acceptance of different power positions in the team. It helped to alleviate internal tensions by a brief of the plenary meeting to the analysis committee that all recommendations by nonmembers had to be seriously considered and if possible to be incorporated. Furthermore, both project teams developed a "social contract" which, among others, implied collective data ownership and the opportunity to later alternative data analyses.

The writeup phase once more introduces influence and power differentials by virtue of differing resources in time and expertise that various team members are able to offer for the drafting of reports. Even if one chooses a strategy whereby this task is widely spread and whereby the whole team has the ultimate right of approval, the likelihood that parts of the resulting drafts are radically rewritten is rather unlikely. Lack of time of individual members, deadlines of reports to funding agencies and the professional status of the drafters within the team make such drastic revisions difficult to implement. It may be symptomatic for the consequences of organizational model and motivational states in both projects to see that all team members in Project B waived their individual authorship rights in favor of a collective authorship while this was not the case for Project A.

Any group with common purposes requires some kind of leadership. The leadership function in the two projects was strongly affected by the respective group culture which was preconditioned by the organisational form chosen. While it was more centralized in Project A, it was rather diffused in Project B where leadership was variable in the sense that different persons or teams took on a leading role in shifting and moving decisions into certain directions very much as a consequence of the nature of the problem, strength of interest and expertise. The virtual veto position of individual members in team B was so real that no one could claim that a single locus of leadership existed. The necessary central administrative function (central administration of international funds, record keeping, etc.) can, of course, also imply a certain kind of leadership through the preparation of meetings and minutes. Central data processing with the ensuing need frequently to make crisis decisions (which are unavoidable as anyone knows with some experience with data crunching) also creates some leadership position which is only legitimated by full accountability to the team as a whole.

Finally, the more informal dynamics that are evident in any research team as in any social system. It would have been challenging and revealing to record and analyze, as it was amusing to note when stereotypes surfaced such as "the Scandinavians think . . .", "the French want . . .", "how British can you get . . .?", "what's the use of such global culturological explanations . . .?", "Can't you stop psychologizing . . .?" Also nicknames readily and fittingly available for individual team members undoubtedly influence, like national or disciplinary sterotypes, the interactions, relationships and outcomes of team work. Satiric after-dinner speeches and hilarious travesties of events in the team, as were characteristic for both research groups, can certainly be understood as devices for tension reduction and inoffensive feedback. It is worth noting that everyone involved will agree to the claim that comprehensive attention to the likely group dynamic effects of any proposed idea and plan are essential group maintenance requirements for international, interdisciplinary teams.

Conclusions

The total configuration of infra-structural, organizational, personal and group process elements are decisive in shaping the course and final results of a research venture that opts for involvement of participants from different countries and disciplines. From experience in two large projects I have tried to delineate some factors that provide constraints and opportunities for the successful pursuit of such research. A micro-analytic awareness of these processes requires attitudinal changes among scientists and a shift of focus in our training institutions. Ultimately it calls for a systematic framework which would enable us to pinpoint how structural and processual elements have co-determined results in research reports similar to the precautions we take to protect us and our readers from errors due to specification and methods. The development of such a systematic analytical framework is far from being complete. But if it is correct, as limited and casual experience suggests, that a full understanding of given research results requires an understanding of the social fabric and dynamics under which they were generated, then I see no reason why we should not request that our ethical code to conduct research be rewritten to include norms for their public account.

FOOTNOTE

[1]As a beginning to overcome that blind spot, see Bell and Newby (1978).

REFERENCES

Almasy, E., Balandier, A., Delatte, J. (1976). *Comparative Study Analysis: An Annotated Bibliography* 1967-1973. Sage, Beverly Hills, London.

Bavelas, Alex (1955). "Communication Patterns in Task-oriented Groups", in: Lazarsfeld, P. and Rosenberg, M. *Language of Social Research*. Glencoe, Ill.

Bell, Colin; Newby, Howard (eds.) (1978). *Doing Sociological Research*. London: Allen and Unwin.

Bilitza, Klaus (1978). "Organisationspsychologische Aspekte der Forschung", *Gruppendynamik*, 9 Jg. (1), 11-22.

Blaschke, Dieter (1976). *Problems interdisziplinarer Forschung*, Wiesbaden: Franz Steiner.

Castri, Francesco di (1978). "Planning international interdisciplinary research", *Science and Public Policy*, Vol. 5 (4), 254-266.

CERI - Centre for Educational Research and Innovation (1972). Interdisciplinarity Problems of Teaching and Research in Universities. Paris: OECD.

Claessens, Dietrich (1962). "Forschungsteam und Personlichkeits-struktur", *Kolner Zeitschrift fur Soziologie und Sozialpsychologie*, Vol. 14, 487-503.

Fisch, Rudolf (1977). "Psychology of Science", in: I. Spiegel-Rosing and D. de Solla Price (eds.), *Science, Technology and Society - A Cross-Disciplinary perspective*. London: Sage, pp. 277-318.

Fourcade, Jean-Michel, Wilpert, Bernhard (1976). Group Dynamics and Management Problems of an International Interdisciplinary Research Team. Report IV/76-1, International Institute of Management, Berlin.

Glaser, William A. (1977). "The Process of Cross-National Survey Research", in: Alexander Szalai, Riccardo Petrella in collaboration with Stein Rokkan, Erwin Scheuch: *Cross-National Comparative Survey Research*. Oxford: Pergamon Press.

Heller, Frank A. (1971). *Managerial Decision Making*. Assen: Van Gorcum and London: Tavistock.

Heller, Frank A., Wilpert, Bernhard. (1977). "Limits to Participative Leadership: Task, Structure and Skill as Contingencies - a German - British Comparison", *European Journal of Social Psychology*, Vol. 7 (1), 61-84.

IDE - International Research Group (1976). "Industrial Democracy in Europe - An international comparative study", *Social Science Information*, Vol. 15 (1), 177-203.

Jantsch, Erich (1970). "Inter- and Transdisciplinary University: A Systems Approach to Education and Innovation", *Policy Sciences*, Vol. 1 (4).

Jantsch, Erich (1972). *Technological Planning and Social Futures*. London: Cassell Business Programs.

Jennings, M.K., Farah, B.G. (1977). "Continuities in Comparative Research Strategies: The Mannheim Data Confrontation Seminar", *Social Science Information*, Vol. 16 (2), 231-249.

Joerges, Bernward (1977). "Wissenschaftliche Kreativitat - empirische und wissenschaftsprak-tische Hinweise", *Zeitschrift fur Allgemeine Wissenschaftstheorie*, Vol. 8 (2), 381-404.

Mabry, John H., Cartwright, Ann, Pearson, Joyce, Silver, George, Vukmanovic, Cedomir. (1966). "The Natural History of an International Collaborative Study of Medical Care Utilization", *Social Science Information*, Vol. 5 (1), 37-55.

Muller-Fohrbrodt, Gisela (1973). "Darum ist es so schwer, ein Team zusammenzuhalten", *Analysen*, Vol. 10, 30-33.

Petrella, Riccardo (1974). La Recherche Comparative Transnationale de Type Cooperatif. Contribution VIIIe Congres Mondial de Sociologie, Toronto, 19-25 Aout, 21 p.

Roberts, Karlene H. (1970). "On Looking at an Elephant: An Evaluation of Cross-Cultureal Research Related to Organizations", *Psychological Bulletin*, Vo. 74, 327-350.

Rokkan, Stein (1969). Cross-cultural, cross-societal and cross-national research, in: Rokkan, S. (ed.) *Main trends of research in the social and human sciences*. Part one: Social Sciences. New York: Uni. Pub. Inc., pp. 645-689.

Szalai, Alexander, Petralla, Riccardo (eds.) (1977). *Cross-national Comparative Survey Research. Theory and Practice*. Oxford, New York: Pergamon.

Szalai, Alexander, Scheuch, Erwin (1972). "The Organizational History of the Multinational Comparative Time-Budget Research Project", in Szalai *et al.*: *The Use of Time*, The Hague, Paris: Mouton, 15-29.

14

IMPACTS OF LARGE RECREATIONAL DEVELOPMENTS UPON SEMI-PRIMITIVE ENVIRONMENT*

Anne S. Williams
G. A. Nielsen
H. F. Shovic
D. G. Stuart
J. W. Reuss

INTRODUCTION

In February 1970, public announcement was made of a proposed year-round resort development, Big Sky of Montana, Inc., to be located in a semi-primitive environment in southwestern Montana. Recognizing a unique research opportunity to assess the significant impacts of such a commercial recreation development upon a sparsely populated and fragile ecosystem, a group of researchers at Montana State University began preparing a large-scale, interdisciplinary research project to examine the environmental and social consequences of the proposed resort development. In March 1970, a group of 32 research scientists joined together for the purpose of gathering baseline data on the biological, physical, social, and economic conditions existing in the study area prior to development of the resort. Funding was received from the National Science Foundation in July 1970, with present work on the project expected to terminate September 1976.[1]

* From *Guidelines for Conducting Interdisciplinary Applied Research in a University Setting*, MSJ-NSF Gallatin Canyon Study, Montana State University, Bozeman. Prepared for the National Science Foundation, April 1976. NTIS PB-260 503. Any opinions, findings conclusions or recommendations expressed in this publication are those of the author(s) and do not necessarily reflect the views of the National Science Foundation.

Throughout this time period, considerable effort has been directed toward examination and analysis of the interdisciplinary research processes employed by the study team members. The results of this continuing analysis are presented here in the hope that this experience will be instructive to future researchers engaged in similar interdisciplinary efforts.

EVALUATION

Two internal studies were conducted to evaluate the effectiveness of the interdisciplinary framework employed by this research project. In late 1972, a pre-structured, attitudinal questionnaire (including both open- and closed-ended questions) was administered to all project members to determine their opinions concerning the management of the project and the research framework and to assess participants' knowledge and understanding of the interdisciplinary research objectives.[2]

A second, more intensive evaluation was completed in late 1973. Using a pre-structured questionnaire, interviews were conducted with University administrators, principal project members, and key support personnel associated with the project. The objectives of this second evaluation were to measure the extent to which problems of communication, management, budgeting, reward, "boundary maintenance,"[3] and so on, were perceived as obstacles to successful project functioning.[4] Results from both studies have been used in developing the following recommendations concerning the initiation, management, and integration of large-scale, interdisciplinary, applied research projects.

INITIATION

There are a number of ways in which large-scale, interdisciplinary research efforts can be launched. The most usual method is sometimes called the "shopping list" approach in which a number of researchers independently develop disciplinary sub-proposals which are then collected, stapled together, and submitted as an interdisciplinary proposal. This method, which is essentially inductive, never seems to result in a viable interdisciplinary effort and there are obvious conceptual reasons why such an approach generally fails. The foremost disadvantages of the "shopping list" or "inductive" approach are that:

(1) it provides no clear framework concerning which sub-projects are of lower or higher priority; (2) it does not provide a guideline for determining the sequence (time phasing) in which sub-project results need to become available for input into related sub-projects; and most importantly (3) it offers no conceptual framework for interrelating total project activities with the result that interdisciplinary research never happens. Instead, to the extent that the project succeeds, it will have been a multi-disciplinary effort in which the participating scientists have all focused on a common problem but clearly have not achieved a highly integrated cross-disciplinary research effort.

The Gallatin Canyon Study Experience

A variety of institutional arrangements had previously been established within the University for the conduct and administration of limited, small-scale interdisciplinary research efforts. Among these were the Center for Environmental Studies and the Center for Planning and Development. The former was directed by biological and physical scientists while the latter was directed by social scientists. With the decision to undertake an impact study of the Big Sky of Montana resort, these two Centers became the logical coordinating arms for this interdisciplinary effort. One individual (a physical scientist) was named director of the project and a team of four additional faculty members was asked to consult with the director concerning administrative and management matters. This team consisted of two social scientists from the Center for Planning and Development, one biological scientist from the Center for Environmental Studies, and an industrial engineer.

A series of meetings were held at which time interested scientists were invited to prepare disciplinary project proposals, in the format specified by the NSF-IRRPOS program (Interdisciplinary Research Related to Problems of Our Society). The five-member management team agreed to review the disciplinary proposals and to develop a research strategy and proposal for the IRRPOS program. This approach to initiating an interdisciplinary project could be labeled "inductive," since a systematic, conceptual framework had not at this time been developed and decisions concerning the appropriateness of the various disciplinary proposals were made primarily on an intuitive basis. The project directors believed that decisions could be made without first developing a sophisticated conceptual framework, since the objective of the research project was simply to establish baseline measures of the pre-development situation, with the conviction that in later years (perhaps ten years hence) post-development measures on the same variables could be obtained and the "impact" of the resort development would then become clear.

In June, 1970, the University was advised that the National Science Foundation would support the project but at approximately one-half the funding level requested. The "inductive" approach to project initiation now posed serious problems for the project manager—it provided no clear framework for making decisions concerning which projects were of lower priority and which projects were essential to the conduct of the research effort; none of the five project managers agreed completely with one another on research priorities. After a series of meetings in which the five project managers individually ranked the priorities of the various disciplinary research efforts, and strenuously argued their individual points of view, decisions were made to eliminate five of the proposed research efforts and to reduce substantially the amount of funding requested by the remaining 27 scientists.

The project (locally known as the Gallatin Canyon Study) was funded as a one-year pilot study, beginning July 1, 1970.[5] Each of the 27 individual researchers received an individual budget and control over the expenditure of his sub-project funds with the charge that his disciplinary research effort must be completed within one year's time.

During the first year of research activity, a number of problems were evident. Coordination of the various disciplinary sub-projects was exceedingly difficult since responsibility for the biological and physical studies rested with the Center for Environmental Studies, while coordinative responsibility for the social science research rested with the Center for Planning and Development. As a result, cross-disciplinary communication among researchers in the biological and physical sciences on the one hand, and the social sciences on the other, was not enhanced. Finally, a decision was made to combine the two Centers into one unit which was named the Center for Interdisciplinary Studies.

The principal investigator of the research project had very little free time to conduct and manage the affairs of the project. His teaching, student advising, and other academic responsibilities had not been reduced when he became the project director, nor had project funds been budgeted to support a full-time project manager. As a result, the burden of project management was assumed on an ad hoc basis by two of the other five members of the management team. However, because of the informal nature of this leadership, the project members did not look to these individuals for direction. As a result, for approximately the first ten months of the research effort, no concerted effort was made to pull the participating researchers together into an interdisciplinary team. This problem was observed and noted by the principal investigator, by the other four members of the management team, and by the upper administrators at the University. As a result, a decision was made to officially recognize the leadership structure of the project. This reorganization resulted in the appointment of a new principal investigator with two-thirds time available for managing and directing the project activities, and the formation of an Executive Committee composed of twelve individuals representative of the various disciplinary activities in which the project was engaged. The function of the Executive Committee was to give guidance and advice to the principal investigator as he began to consider the problems of integration of the disciplinary projects and also the important task of developing an integrated, problem focused renewal proposal for the National Science Foundation program.

During this first year, a decision was made at the National Science Foundation to abandon the IRRPOS program and to replace it with the RANN program (Research Applied to National Needs). This decision had a major impact on the research team since it implied a substantial redirection of project objectives. The RANN program placed considerably more emphasis on problem-solving research and requested that the project team address impact problems, generalizable to the region, and communicate policy relevant research results to natural resource managers in the Rocky Mountain Region. This new focus was a dramatic change in the initial project objective which, as stated above, was merely to establish baseline measures of the pre-development situation; and progress on this objective had been proceeding as originally planned.

With the concurrence of the principal investigator and the Executive Committee to the project, two members of the original management team developed a renewal proposal to the NSF-RANN program with major emphasis on problem-solving research activities and strategies for communicating research findings to identified, critical resource managers in the region. This second proposal was funded for a two-year period with work beginning July 1, 1971.[6]

The project managers now recognized the failure of the "inductive approach" as a framework for applied interdisciplinary research. Somehow, the project managers had to develop a conceptual framework for the conduct of the research activity, requiring that the research follow from identified problems associated with development of the resort complex. Accordingly, a seven-member Steering Committee was selected from among the members of the Executive Committee, and charged with developing such a conceptual framework. It had become clear that a small staff was needed to develop the conceptual framework for the project; trying to develop conceptual themes within a group of 27 individuals was simply impossible due to problems of communication, differences in motivations of the individual researchers, and levels of understanding concerning the applied nature of the research activity. It was also noted that the individual personalities of some researchers were simply not amenable to interdisciplinary research. A few of the project participants were clearly "loners" and, although competent in their own disciplinary fields, were not able to understand or appreciate the linkages among and between the various disciplines.

The seven-member Steering Committee worked diligently for approximately five months and developed a "problems area framework" to be used in identifying critical research gaps and linkages among the disciplinary research sub-projects. This conceptual framework identified in detail the prominent *actors* (political decision-makers, significant landowners, external impinging forces, relevant natural resource managers, etc.), the critical environmental and social variables (*baselines*) which were likely to change given the *activity* of recreationists, agriculturalists, and commercial operators in the area. Seven major interdisciplinary problem areas were identified as well as five secondary problem areas. Conferences were held with project participants (individually and in groups) in an effort to identify the particular disciplinary input they might have in addressing the most critical impact problems. Finally, teams of researchers were organized as task forces for the purposes of communicating and interrelating their disciplinary expertise.[7]

The Steering Committee then used this problems area framework to develop an interdisciplinary, applied research proposal to NSF-RANN, in which funding was requested for a final two-year period, beginning July 1, 1973. It was interesting, but disappointing to the project directors, to learn that the disciplinary scientists reviewing the project could not clearly identify the disciplinary inputs into the problems area framework. Criticisms were received suggesting that the traditional, disciplinary project proposal was reviewed more favorably than the interdisciplinary, problems area proposal. Even so, the most recent proposal was funded for an eighteen-month period beginning July 1, 1973.[8]

Based on the above experience, it is recommended that a small group of disciplinary scientists (three to seven members seem to work best) should be convened and charged with: (1) defining the problem(s) to be examined; and (2) identifying the level and type of disciplinary research necessary to address the policy-relevant problem(s). Decisions concerning disciplinary input should follow from the nature of the problems being addressed. Accordingly, a conceptual framework (which integrates the various disciplinary inputs to the proposed project) should follow from, and be defined by, these policy-relevant problem(s).

A careful search should be made for those disciplinary scientists who can function most effectively using a task force approach. Interdisciplinary research projects seem to be most successful when they are limited to a relatively small number of well-funded sub-projects which can be organized effectively around the identified research problems.

MANAGEMENT

. . . In interdisciplinary research projects, there is a tendency to simply ignore the management role because the participants in such projects are primarily specialists focusing upon a particular disciplinary problem. Disciplinarians often fail to appreciate the need for, and requirements of, centralized project management, nor are many interested in assuming this role. The management role is clearly a full-time responsibility and should be budgeted as such. Further, this role should be performed by a skilled management expert whose time is not diverted by involvement in disciplinary, sub-project activity.

In such projects, the individual disciplinary scientist must be prepared to enter into a "contract" with the project manager in which the scientist agrees to research identified policy-relevant questions and to deliver an agreed upon product in accordance with an established time sequence. University researchers seem to work most comfortably when they have personal control over their individual sub-project budgets; this suggests that research funds should be "contracted out" to disciplinary scientists charged with sub-project responsibility. Care must be taken, however, in making decisions concerning the allocation of money to specific sub-projects. One authority notes that: "Depending upon the institutional environment, the flexibility of the individual, and the nature of the original (financial) commitment, attempting to alter the nature of a commitment may present various kinds and degrees of problems.[9] The experience on the Gallatin Canyon Study indicates that, once funding commitments have been made, discontinuance of a disciplinary sub-project is difficult and sometimes almost impossible to obtain. Interpersonal commitments, friendships, and disciplinary allegiances tend to nullify objective decisions to withdraw funding from disciplinary scientists and particularly so if they are one's own colleagues.

In order to maintain project activities on a schedule which will ultimately result in timely delivery of policy-relevant research products, the project managers should develop a scheme for time-phasing the various disciplinary inputs. Such scheduling might take the form of detailed flow charts which define the sequence in which tasks need to be completed and which identify those tasks which seem most critical to the successful completion of other project tasks and to the overall project effort. However, one authority argues that: ". . . .in my view, the advantages of university-level involvement in research, i.e., its potential for innovation and inquiry with high risk and potentially high pay-offs, may be nullified by controls of this kind."[10] Since exact estimates of required effort for various segments of the project cannot be made, and since estimates must be continually revised as the project evolves, scheduling should not become so definitive that the project becomes inflexible to future demands. Nevertheless, without some scheduling of research activities, projects such as this tend to "drift" and ultimately fail to accomplish their stated goals.

It seems clear that complete flexibility or, on the other hand, rigid scheduling are not desirable in the management of large-scale, interdisciplinary research projects. In many respects these two elements are compatible, however. Sub-project activities must be organized and managed on a time-scheduled basis which defines the sequence in which tasks need to be completed and which identifies those tasks which are most critical to the overall project effort. However, care must be taken to reserve some project funds for unexpected contingencies as the project evolves; clearly, a reserve fund should be maintained to insure financial flexibility to accept new and more pressing future research assignments.

INTEGRATION

. . . Terms used by one scientific discipline often have different meanings in other disciplines. Accordingly, key participants in interdisciplinary research efforts must learn the languages of the various disciplines with which they must work. Evaluation results of the Gallatin Canyon research experience indicate that after working together in small groups over a period of four to five months, the "jargon" problem was no longer perceived as a significant obstacle to project success. However, communication among the team members was a persistent problem because the project managers failed to budget time and money for what turned out to be a crucial component of the total effort. The experience on the Gallatin Canyon Study indicated that for most members of the research team, communication, coordination, and integration required substantially more time than was budgeted and, in some cases, more time than was required for disciplinary sub-project research. Also, funds must be budgeted so that key project members have time to integrate the disciplinary sub-project findings into comprehensive problem analyses comprehensible to identified "user groups."

Physical facilities are critical in this regard. Unless team members have working space in close proximity to one another, the opportunities for communication are severely limited. In the Gallatin Canyon Study experience, project participants were housed throughout the campus in their various disciplinary departments. However, as the research effort evolved, smaller groups of key project participants were allocated joint office space so that the fertilization of cross-disciplinary ideas proceeded more rapidly and the conceptualization and integration of the various disciplinary project activities were facilitated.

By the third year of activity on the Gallatin Canyon Study, four interdisciplinary computer simulation models were in the developmental or operational stages. Modeling activity offers the notable advantage of making explicit to all research team members how the various disciplinary sub-tasks interrelate with the overall research program. In addition, modeling efforts have the added strength of clarifying research gaps which must be filled in order to satisfy project goals. However, computer simulation models are not suitable to all types of policy research; therefore, decisions concerning the utility of modeling efforts should be made on a project-by-project basis, after considering the nature and requirements of the research problem being addressed.

REWARDS

Many of those individuals who initially became most deeply involved in the Gallatin Canyon Study were senior faculty members who had established reputations within their respective disciplines. Interviews with project members in late 1972 indicated that roughly one-half of the participants foresaw little significant professional advancement as a result of involvement in the Gallatin Canyon Study. Eight members of the research team were substantially disturbed by the potential lack of reward and indicated they were considering withdrawing from the project for this reason. The 1973 evaluation results were essentially the same. The majority of the project members felt that no significant professional rewards had accrued to them after three years of project involvement. The only personal benefits derived from their involvement were summarized as "furthered interdisciplinary communication" or "enhanced interdisciplinary knowledge and experience." Neither of these was considered a valuable contribution to their future professional advancement.

It is our contention that constraints within the traditional university structure account for this situation. . . .

There is strong motivation for faculty involved in interdisciplinary, applied research projects to attempt to develop their disciplinary sub-projects in accordance with established disciplinary norms so that the results will be acceptable for publication in their respective academic journals. Theoretical or basic research questions are often examined in considerably more detail than is required to fulfill the objectives of the interdisciplinary research project. In this respect, a strong disciplinary orientation is often counter-productive to achieving the interdisciplinary research goals. Therefore, in traditional university settings, the reward system is, in this respect, inappropriately developed to encourage participation of the brightest and most enthusiastic disciplinarians in interdisciplinary projects.

. . . the professional disciplinarian is not likely to maintain credibility with his disciplinary peers if he engages solely in interdisciplinary activities due to the non-traditional nature of interdisciplinary research. Interdisciplinarians contemplating future changes in professional employment are likely to encounter such traditional attitudes and be hampered by this loss of disciplinary credibility. On the other hand, it is our belief that interdisciplinary scientists and especially skilled managers of interdisciplinary research projects will be in increasing demand in future years. However, the professional researcher must recognize that by becoming fully involved in interdisciplinary research activities, he is essentially making a career decision, i.e., to abandon his traditional disciplinary research focus and to assume an interdisciplinary approach to research activities, requiring skills in team-building and in the management of such projects. . . .

SUMMARY OF GUIDELINES

Initiation

1. A small group of disciplinary scientists (three to seven members) should be convened and charged with (a) defining the problem(s) to be examined; and (b) identifying the level and type of disciplinary research necessary to address the identified problem(s).

2. The conceptual framework (which integrates the various disciplinary inputs to the proposed project) should follow from, and be defined by, the identified policy-relevant problem(s) being addressed.

3. The disciplinary inputs required to solve the identified policy-relevant problem(s) should be clearly specified.

4. The "inductive approach" to the initiation of large-scale, interdisciplinary research projects is inefficient and often interferes with the attainment of policy-relevant research goals.

Management

1. Large-scale, interdisciplinary research projects require "strong" management direction; decisions concerning sub-project goals,

selection of participating scientists, funding levels for sub-project activity, time-phasing and so on, must be the final responsibility of a chief investigator or small groups of investigators.

2. The management role is a full-time responsibility and should be performed by a skilled management expert whose time is not diverted by involvement in disciplinary, sub-project activity.

3. In developing the budget for large-scale, interdisciplinary research activities, care must be taken to insure that ample funds are allocated for performance of the management role.

4. Large-scale, interdisciplinary research projects appear to be most successful when a relatively small number of well-funded sub-projects are incorporated into the research activity and the number of participating disciplinary scientists is limited. However, decisions concerning disciplinary input should follow from the nature of the problems being addressed.

5. University researchers seem to work most comfortably when they have personal control over their individual sub-project budgets; this suggests that research funds should be "contracted out" to disciplinary scientists charged with sub-project responsibility.

6. Care must be taken to reserve some project funds for unexpected contingencies as the project evolves; a reserve fund should be maintained to insure financial flexibility to accept new and more pressing future research assignments.

7. Sub-project activities must be organized and managed on a time-scheduled basis which defines the sequence in which tasks need to be completed and which identifies those tasks which are judged to be most critical to the overall project effort.

Integration

1. Since the ethnocentric attitudes of many disciplinarians are major obstacles to successful interdisciplinary research, care should be taken to select disciplinary research personnel who are sympathetic to, or knowledgeable of, the potential contributions of the diverse and specialized fields of study.

2. Communication problems among the disciplinary scientists can be reduced by budgeting ample time for this activity and by co-locating key project members' office and working space.

3. Funds must be budgeted so that key project members have time to integrate the disciplinary sub-projects into a comprehensive problem analyses, comprehensible to identified "user groups."

Rewards

1. University administrators must be prepared to modify the traditional university structure so that disciplinary scientists can be recognized and rewarded for their interdisciplinary research activities; otherwise, successful integrated problem-solving research will not be feasible within the university setting.

Application

1. Definitive "user groups" must be identified and input received from them as the research proposal is conceptualized and written.

2. At project inception, a clear strategy must be developed for communicating project results in a timely fashion to identified user groups.

3. The project managers must develop an unequivocal position concerning the extent to which project participants are expected to become involved in "advocacy" roles to affect policy decisions; this position must be clearly communicated to potential team members and their concurrence obtained as a condition of involvement in the proposed project.

FOOTNOTES

[1]Initial funding was received from the National Science Foundation IRRPOS Program (Interdisciplinary Research Related to Problems of Our Society); this program was discontinued after approximately one year, and succeeding grants were funded by the NSF-RANN Program (Research Applied to National Needs). Further information concerning the scope and prominent findings of the project research is available in "Impacts of Large Recreational Developments Upon Semi-Primitive Environments: The Gallatin Canyon Case Study," Research Report No. 66, Institute of Applied Research, Montana State University, Bozeman, June, 1974.

[2]C. Robert Emerson, William R. Lassey, and Theodore Weaver, "Investigator Attitudes Toward Involvement in the Gallatin Canyon Study," Discussion Paper (mimeograph), Center for Interdisciplinary Studies, Montana State University, Bozeman, 1972.

[3]"Boundary maintenance" is here defined as the tendency of specialists to protect their particular areas of disciplinary expertise from intrusion by scientists of another discipline. Boundary maintenance takes many forms, including the use of jargon to confuse and exclude the intruder, ridicule, and outright hostility toward invaders.

[4]Henry F. Shovic, "Management Characteristics of Interdisciplinary Research: A Case Study of the Gallatin Canyon Study," unpublished Master's Thesis, Department of Industrial and Management Engineering, Montana State University, Bozeman, December, 1973.

[5]For additional information concerning the project objectives, see "The Impact of a Large Recreational Development Upon a Semi-Primitive Environment: A Case Study," Research proposal submitted to the National Science Foundation, Montana State University, Bozeman, May, 1970.

[6]See "The Impact of a Large Recreational Development Upon a Semi-Primitive Environment: A Case Study," Research Proposal submitted to the National Science Foundation, Montana State University, Bozeman, December, 1970.

[7]For additional information concerning the integrative framework, see "The Impact of a Large Recreational Development Upon a Semi-Primitive Environment: Gallatin Canyon Study," Integrated Progress Report on National Science Foundation Grant GI-29908X1, Montana State University. Bozeman, February, 1973.

[8]For an overview of project goals and summary of preliminary research results, see "An Overview of the MSU-NSF Gallatin Canyon Study," Research Monograph No. 1, Montana State University, Bozeman, June, 1973.

[9]Hamilton, H.R., S.E. Goldstone, J.W. Milliman, A.L. Paugh III, E.B. Roberts, and Z. Zellner, *Systems Simulation for Regional Analysis: An Application to River-Basin Planning*, The M.I.T. Press: Cambridge, 1969, p. 283.

[10]McEvoy, James, III, "Multi- and Inter-disciplinary Research: Problems in Initiation, Control, Integration and Reward," *Policy Sciences* 3 (1972), p. 204.

BIBLIOGRAPHY

Campbell, Donald T., "Ethnocentrism of Disciplines and the Fish-Scale Model of Omniscience," in *Interdisciplinary Relationships in the Social Sciences*, edited by Muzafar Sherif and Carolyn W. Sherif, Alden Publishing Company, Chicago, 1969.

"Impacts of Large Recreational Developments Upon Semi-Primitive Environments: The Gallatin Canyon Case Study," Research Report No. 66, Institute of Applied Research, Montana State University, Bozeman, June 1974.

15

INTERDISCIPLINARY RESEARCH— A DILEMMA FOR UNIVERSITY CENTRAL ADMINISTRATION*

Borje O. Saxberg
William T. Newell
Brian W. Mar

... Research Design

In the work reported here, we designed a research project specifically aimed at exploring and examining management of large scale interdisciplinary research in the university setting. Under Phase I of this project we conducted field research at judgmentally selected sites involving university central research administrators, directors of research centers and institutes, and principal investigators and project team members. We wanted to know how universities interpreted their involvement in interdisciplinary research to solve societal problems. Specifically we were interested in the degree of support central university research administrators were giving to such research. We were also interested in their judgment regarding the nature and quality of interdisciplinary research and the specific difficulties that such research faced. Finally, we wanted to establish what are perceived as criteria of success in interdisciplinary research management given that the management and organization dimensions are at the core of our research. Our findings are from interviews conducted with university central administration officials at the University of California, Berkeley and Los Angeles (UCLA); University of Southern California (USC); Stanford University (Stanford); University of Illinois (Illinois); University of Wisconsin (Wisconsin); State University of New York at

* Reprinted by permission of the Society of Research Administrators from *SRA Journal*, Vol. 13, Fall 1981, pp. 25-43.

Albany (SUNY); Massachusetts Institute of Technology (MIT); and the University of Washington (Washington).

Interviews were conducted with Vice-Presidents of Research or Deans of Graduate Schools, depending on the administrative focus for interdisciplinary research. In addition, Directors of Grants and Contracts were interviewed for clarification about the processing of research proposals. In some cases appropriate officials of accounting and finance functions were also included in the interviews. The interviews were open-ended though an effort was made to cover similar areas of interest at each institution. . . .

Universities' Emerging Role in Interdisciplinary Research on Societal Problems

It is clear from our research interviews that it is not something new for universities to become involved in research on societal problems. They contain the academic and research talents that are needed. The agricultural college and its extension service are prime examples of a long history of contributions that institutions of higher learning have been making to life around them. In 1962, the land-grant colleges and universities celebrated the centennial of the Morrill Act. Faculty members of these as well as of other public and private universities have played an important role in meeting the demand for their services in research laboratories, on national and governmental commissions, and in governmental offices. On the other hand, the heavy dependence of all universities on legislative budgets and other public resources at the local, state, and national levels, suggests that the university is also expected to make a contribution to the solutions of society's problems in order to enjoy continued support. [1]

Thus far research grants of federal funding agencies have been mainly limited to non-profit organizations including universities, but this convention is currently being challenged. These agencies encourage for-profit organizations to compete with universities for research contracts, placing additional pressure on universities competing for scarce research funds.

There are many outside pressures on the university and the academic community to move into applied research. Such a move becomes inevitable once a university receives funds from governmental agencies for applied research as the trend has been toward an emphasis on funding for research with concrete results or demonstration projects at the end. . . .

University Central Research Administration—
Views on Interdisciplinary Research Issues

We found that university administrators are in agreement that the academic community is made up of faculty members who are independent scholars who rarely, if ever, join in group efforts involving research. Collaborative or cooperative efforts are at most with colleagues within the department. In the status system prevailing in the university community, single authorship of articles, monographs, books, and others, carries greater weight than multiple authorship.

There is an implicit conflict recognized between faculty and university administration related to the outward look and professional identification of the former, compared to the inward look and institutional identification of the latter. Consequently, faculty members emphasize personal and local autonomy, colleague authority, and a cosmopolitan professional orientation. University administrators are more concerned with bureaucratic authority and a local institutional orientation.

Discipline Orientation of University Organization

The traditional departmental structure reflects existing academic disciplines as the basis for university operations currently. Faculty members leave their discipline-oriented research focus at their own peril. A policy statement on interdisciplinary research centers contains the following statement:

> The challenge facing those who would stimulate and perform interdisciplinary research is to do this in a way that is compatible and actually adds strength of the main line function of the University.

The main line function refers to the strength of the departments where teaching and research are viewed as optimized.

The whole university reward system—merit, advancement, and tenure—rests within the departmental structure. The weight of senior departmental faculty and the chairman of the department is critical in determining who will be recommended for merit, promotion, as well as for tenure. These decisions affect particularly junior faculty members who are working to achieve the security that goes with a tenured appointment.

Quality of Interdisciplinary Research

In a number of instances university officials pointed to the danger that a faculty member incurs in interdisciplinary research as his time may be gobbled up by a supportive role on the research team. In basic research involving a team of investigators, each discovery of new knowledge is adequate in and for itself. But a supportive role—instrumentation, measurement, methodology, and others—may cause a researcher over an extended period of time to be left behind the frontier of his own profession, and his professional growth and development as a consequence jeopardized.

Young faculty members embarking on interdisciplinary research thereby remove themselves from their departmental home base which governs their future within the university. We heard statements by university officials to the effect that "there is no substitute for quality, in particular discipline quality." Or, "it appears absolutely irrefutable that in the new generation to be trained there still must remain a competence based on a rock-bed in one discipline." In addition, they found that interdisciplinary research involving national needs and societal problems runs the risk of potential involvement in outside partisan interest groups and their views which may cast doubt on the university's role and jeopardize faculty members' career aspirations within the university structure.

Doubts existed in officials' minds with reference to the review of the quality of interdisciplinary research. This difficulty jeopardizes the preparation of graduate students for significant future contributions requiring special expertise. It is uncertain that the academic market place is ready to employ a graduate of an interdisciplinary program. Rather, the preference might well exist for a discipline specialist who has an appreciation for interdisciplinary work. Several university officials indicated that interdisciplinary research and affiliation may make the students subject to the suspicion of shallowness of research and less than solid competence in the fields involved.

The concern with the nature and quality of the interdisciplinary research effort was reflected in the following statement: "It is important that the interdisciplinary, problem-oriented research done at . . . be of top quality—to match the standards of the University as a whole." This was in fact cited as the main reason for the establishment of one Center for Interdisciplinary Research—to avoid *ad hoc* interdisciplinary projects and programs.

Interdisciplinary Research Centers on Trial

University central administration is frequently in the hands of individuals who have careers and appointments within university departments. University governance is heavily dependent on faculty involvement at departmental, school, and college levels as well as in the Faculty Senate and its various committees. It is slow to change, slow to innovate, and slow to accommodate new organizational structures.

In particular, the position and role of interdisciplinary centers and institutes or Organizational Research Units (ORUs) are still in the process of emerging. University officials emphasized that interdisciplinary research centers had to be seen as contributing to the educational purpose of the university. Research formed the prime target in the establishment of a center and was closely tied to giving the opportunity for graduate students and faculty to do research. "If there are no students served there is no reason to maintain a program even if funding might be available." A number of university administrators suggested it was preferable that a center or institute relate to an appropriate department or school or college. Only in exceptional cases should the organizational reporting relationship bypass a chairman or dean. The review of the center's activities should take note if its character had changed so that it might report to a departmental chairman or dean.

The prevailing opinion was that interdisciplinary research centers should be reviewed periodically for their contribution to the university and its academic and educational purposes.

University officials suggested strongly that they viewed these centers as temporary and likely to disappear when the interest or need was no longer there. Generally the review was to be conducted at three to five year intervals. At some institutions the review included a decision on reappointment or rotation of the director. Except for one university, the review process had not led to the discontinuation of interdisciplinary research centers. . . .

There is great reluctance to allow for the independent existence of interdisciplinary research centers with the right to design their own teaching curriculum, offer their own degree programs, and recruit their own faculty with the possibility of gaining tenure. Officials at some universities emphasized that the granting of degrees, building of curricula, and course offerings are restricted to existing departmental units. In contrast, at Washington, Wisconsin, and Illinois, an emphasis on development of degree programs and offering courses reflected a vital interest in gaining a university budget contribution. This was governed through systems of payment for student credits.

A similar distinction was evident in faculty appointments—some universities preferred that all tenured faculty appointments remain within established departments, but a few have provided interdisciplinary research centers in some cases with a budget for core staff and tenured faculty appointments. However, even the latter have shown great reluctance in making appointments outside the departmental organizational system due to faculty preference for positions within departments, or access to the professional group in a department.

There were doubts expressed by university administration officials about the present degree of integration of interdisciplinary research centers with the university as a whole. The centers were seen to confront a serious problem as they were prone to increase their professional research staff which was not classified as university faculty. As one administrator reflected: "Reading the future, it appears that on one hand the need for interdisciplinary studies and the attack on problems through interdisciplinary studies is on the rise, while on the campus of . . . the research support and services are likely to decline for the interdisciplinary research centers unless they are successful in raising their own outside funds." Many directors of interdisciplinary centers and institutes see their difficulties insurmountable as they are dependent on the goodwill of departmental faculty, chairmen, and deans of schools and colleges to conduct their research and teaching functions. The solution they offer may be in stark contrast to the departmental hegemony now prevailing on university campuses.

In relation to the authority structure of the university, university officials interviewed generally agreed that initiation of research is in the hands of faculty as is the initiation of most other activities of an educational, academic, or research nature. Only veto power is delegated to university administration in the conduct of the day to day affairs of the university.

Interdisciplinary research and teaching relate to the establishment of new disciplines. These must meet the requirements of logical coherence—for learning, for basic research—and faculty interest. This may not necessarily follow in view of the political, technical, and economic factors which are unrelated to the university organization but govern the nature of applied research to solve societal problems. However, business and engineering are examples of schools which have emerged out of a problem orientation.

As a result of these views, we are led to believe that university central administration officials harbored considerable doubt in their minds whether a university is suited to have an action-orientation to solve immediate societal problems. Such an orientation may not be natural to the university organization as traditionally established where basic research and advancement of an academic discipline are in the forefront. . . .

Generally, central research administration officials did not seem to believe in active encouragement of interdisciplinary research. They chose not to actively design, shape, guide, and direct university research activities because they saw the role of faculty as supreme in the research function. Entrepreneurial, creative, and good faculty researchers were seen as automatically defining their academic life around research and therefore successful in obtaining funding for their research. Those who are already thus involved do not need further support beyond that of grant and contract administration to assure that the use of funds is within the legal constraints within which the principal investigator and the university have to operate.

Doubts were expressed that active provision of seed money and other tangible research support to faculty not presently engaged in funded research would be likely to generate successful researchers on funded research any way—disciplinary or interdisciplinary. . . .

A minority of the interviewed representatives of university central research administration held a view opposite to those cited previously. They believed in providing strong direction to research activities including deliberate encouragement of interdisciplinary research by making available seed money and other funding in support of preproposal and proposal activities. They exemplified university administration's active support to generate interest among faculty members to become involved in this research. . . .

The interviews with university officials suggested that few administrators saw management and organization of research as an opportunity to make a contribution to the university's research community. University administration was integrated for compliance with administrative rules and its preparedness was governed by needs of accountability. Little attention was paid to the function of management in planning for the university's role or in formulating its objectives and goals.

Part of the problem may be connected with a confused concept of management. This was evident in a series of discussions held by the Advisory Panel to the NSF convened under the sponsorship of the American Council on Education to advise on research on improvement of university research management. As reflected in the words of the rapporteur:

> Because it conjures up images of industrial models and threats to academic freedom, the RMIP's emphasis on "management" is anathema to many faculty members and academic administrators. Management is perceived as external manipulation and hence is viewed as a potential threat to academic freedom.[8]

The management activity that the Advisory Panel accorded as legitimate to university research administration was "screening of proposals to delete those which do not adhere to university policies and mission." Beyond that limited definition of management, there was included the possibility of identification of research areas which were new and obtaining of information on funding sources, and providing such information to faculty and others.[9] . . .

Lack of University Research Policy

Our findings indicate that the university environment was generally characterized by a lack of university policies to guide or direct interdisciplinary research. Universities operated on an intuitive bureaucratically oriented foundation in dealing with the university's role in research and, in particular, in interdisciplinary research.

The following areas showed relative lack of defined policies:

1. With few exceptions, there is no recognized university position with regard to its particular major and significant role as a research institution.
2. There is no preparedness indicated in relation to involvement in basic vs. applied research or problem oriented research dealing with societal issues and concerns.
3. There are no established standards to be applied in judging research as good or bad.
4. Little work has been done on the creation of an integrated systematic information flow on research and research activities either for the internal university community or for interested parties outside the university.
5. Management and organization of interdisciplinary research have been neglected at all levels—university central administration level, center or institute level, and principal investigator or project team level.
6. There is a lack of coordination between grants and contracts office or administration, including the finance and accounting functions, with needs of principal investigators and other researchers, needs of funding agencies, and needs of others to whom accountability exists.

Universities appeared to "roll with the punches" reacting to faculty research interests and faculty funding agency relationships.

As a result, new faculty members had very little available to them of an informational or educational nature introducing them to research opportunities and research processes. This introduction became a hit-and-miss affair with reliance on guidance by an established faculty member or recourse to individual ingenuity.

The University's Role in Interdisciplinary Research - A Controversy

Interdisciplinary Research - Temporary or Permanent

We found two conflicting views among university administrators concerned with interdisciplinary research, particularly when this involved problem-oriented research responsive to national needs and societal problems. On one hand, they recognized that U.S. Government funding agencies increasingly emphasized applied research. They recognized that faculty interests are likely to move toward available funds. On the other hand, this type of research did not conform to the customary patterns of relationships on a university campus. There was a danger that the university in supporting interdisciplinary research would jeopardize the departmental discipline structure that so far had served the educational aims well. The dangers included in addition considerable doubt about the nature of interdisciplinary research, its quality, and the effect of involvement on young faculty members and graduate students insofar as their careers were concerned. One administrator pointed to the need for a professor to make sure that he worked closely with his department head to keep this individual informed about his work. This was necessary to assure that the department and its chairman recognized that a professor might make available his tools, his specialized knowledge, for use in another field, but that it could still be completely justifiable and defended in relation to the discipline orientation of the department.

On the other hand, viewing the origin of any number of established departments in the university organization would reveal that the field had its origin with a few faculty members striking out on their own against the prevailing conventional organizational structure.

The university may need to review its organizational structure for the purpose of determining whether the interdisciplinary center can be regarded as a vehicle for change. The review process should determine the level of contribution to the university's educational functions. The interdisciplinary center must be considered a temporary organizational unit which ultimately may be either discontinued or else progresses along the path of gaining rights to operate increasingly in a similar mode as a department or school. Eventually, such a center would take its rightfully earned place among the university's departments or schools with a new field of knowledge having been defined.

Departmental Discipline Orientation Versus Interdisciplinary Emphasis in University Organization

Throughout the university, organizational relations cross paths. University discipline-oriented departments, as currently established, represent a functional authority structure for the university in charge of teaching, faculty recruitment, advancement, promotion, and tenure, as well as degree programs and courses. Interdisciplinary research centers represent horizontal program and project relationships across the departmental functional authority lines as the centers draw on faculty and students as well as permission for degrees, courses, and curricula. Authority at the nodes remains undefined and undefinable as it represents negotiations and trade-offs creating a mutually advantageous outcome for the university organization as a whole. At this level, there are particular requirements of managerial and organizational knowledge and skills on the part of the administrative staff and faculty personnel involved.

It is in the hand of central university administration to influence the rate of change and the amount of resources available at any one time to individual faculty members as potential or seasoned researchers, to interdisciplinary research centers, and to departments, and schools or colleges. It can influence and even determine the future course and direction of the university and its research efforts in the life of society surrounding the educational processes.

References

[1]*Science at the Bicentennial,* Report of National Science Board, 1976, Washington, D.C., National Science Foundation, 1976

. . . .

[8]Stauffer, Thomas M. (rapporteur and convener) "Recommendations of Ways The National Science Foundation Can Assist Major Universities Improve Their Research Administration," Advisory Panel, Office of Leadership Development in Higher Education, American Council on Education, Washington, D.C., Sept. 1974, p. 13.

[9]Ibid, p. 11

Acknowledgement

This research was supported by a grant (NM 44380) from the National Science Foundation's Research Management Improvement Program.

16

CROSSDISCIPLINARITY IN THE BIOMEDICAL SCIENCES: A PRELIMINARY ANALYSIS OF ANATOMY†*

Frederick A. Rossini
Alan L. Porter
Daryl E. Chubin
Terry Connolly

I. Introduction and Major Issues

Research which cuts across academic and professional disciplines has often been considered to be predominantly applied, rather than basic (see, for example, Kelly et al., 1978; Rossini et al., 1978, 1981). This study deals with crossdisciplinary work in a basic science—the biomedical science of anatomy. . . .

Peterson's Guide to Graduate Study succinctly describes anatomy as follows:

Anatomy today is a discipline concerned not only with structure, but also with the function and the development of the cells, tissues and organs constituting the animal body. Because the anatomy department is usually at the medical school, it also has an important role to play in bridging the gap between the basic and clinical sciences. Gross anatomy consists of that body of information about structures that can be observed at the gross level, that is, with the naked eye and by dissection. Research at

† An earlier version of this paper was presented at the American Association for the Advancement of Science 147th National Meeting, Toronto, January 1981.

* Reprinted by permission of John Wiley & Sons, Ltd. from *Managing Interdisciplinary Research*, edited by S.R. Epton, R. Payne, and A. Pearson, (London: John Wiley & Sons, Ltd., 1984). Copyright 1984 John Wiley & Sons, Ltd.

this level today is mainly carried out by biological anthropologists, some of whom are located in anatomy departments. Microscopic anatomy consists of studies on the structure of cells and tissues using the light and electron microscopes. Research advances in this area have been dramatic in the past two decades. Because the practical resolution of the ordinary transmission electron microscope is better than 1 nm, molecules can be visualized and the gap between chemistry and morphology bridged (Hay, 1980).

As this description notes, anatomy is moving from a macro orientation to structure visible microscopically. It has reached down from cadavers to large molecules. The transition from gross morphology in anatomy is illustrated in the autobiographical essay of the anatomist G.W. Corner (1958).

... But in biological work especially, the paradoxical situation often occurs that the successful investigator finally cuts off his own ability to advance the subject by carrying his work to the point where further information can only be acquired by new technical methods or new ways of thinking for which he is not equipped. The morphologist, for example, comes to the point at which only biochemistry can help. I have myself more than once wistfully seen my juniors successfully take over problems which I had been keen enough to develop, but was not qualified to solve ...

This shift in the field of anatomy is illustrated by the occasional change in the name of medical school units from "Department of Anatomy" to a label such as "Department of Anatomy and Neuroscience." Such a change and its rationale were described by one Anatomy Department chairman whom we interviewed.

Anatomy is one of the specializations in the developing crossdisciplinary field referred to as neuroscience.

The simplest and most acceptable definition to its practitioners is that neuroscience is the correlated study of brain and behavior. That definition emphasizes the interrelatedness, the interdependence of cause and effect in the organism's life. (Marshall, 1979:3).

The neuroscience literature roughly quadrupled from 1967 to 1977, a period during which the scientific literature as a whole doubled. During the same period, membership in the Society for Neuroscience increased 500% (Marshall, 1979).

Some questions at this point in the research are:

1. What is the current status of crossdisciplinarity in anatomy?
2. What is the general trajectory of crossdisciplinary development in anatomy? What role does the development of neuroscience play in this development?
3. What are the important intellectual and institutional factors which have caused this situation?

To begin to answer these questions, we will first consider some preliminary data.

II. Preliminary Data

We collected data from two sources—advertisements for faculty positions in *Science* magazine, the primary journal in which heads of Anatomy Departments advertise for faculty and also a multidisciplinary journal, and interviews with a number of Anatomy Department heads.

We analyzed position available advertisements in *Science*, both for anatomists and from anatomy related units. The first issue of every other month for a 24 month period back from August 1, 1980 was studied. The search uncovered 46 relevant positions. These were analyzed by field of employing unit, field of person sought, institutional location of the unit advertising the position (medical school or arts and sciences college), and type of position (faculty or postdoctoral).

Tables 1 and 2 indicate the result of these analyses. The usual expectation if disciplinary boundaries were to be strictly maintained is that anatomists would be sought almost exclusively by anatomy units. What appears is that only about 1/4 of the cases fit this pattern. The crossdisciplinary pattern is more pronounced for medical schools than for arts and sciences colleges, perhaps illustrating greater receptivity in professional schools. It is sharper for postdoctoral positions than regular faculty positions, possibly indicating greater impetus for crossdisciplinary activities in temporary and research positions than for permanent and instructional positions. Indeed, conversations with chairpersons indicate a general focus on postdoctoral appointments as

ALL ADVERTISEMENTS
EMPLOYEE'S FIELD

		Other	Anatomy	A+O	
	Other	0	9	11	
EMPLOYER'S	Anatomy	8	11	2	
FIELD	A+O	1	3	1	(N = 46)

(Other is non-anatomy; A+O is anatomy and other)

ARTS & SCIENCES COLLEGES
EMPLOYEE'S FIELD

		Other	Anatomy	A+O	
	Other	0	3	7	
EMPLOYER'S	Anatomy	1	5	0	
FIELD	A+O	0	0	0	(N = 16)

MEDICAL SCHOOLS
EMPLOYEE'S FIELD

		Other	Anatomy	A+O	
	Other	0	6	4	
EMPLOYER'S	Anatomy	7	6	2	
FIELD	A+O	1	3	1	(N = 30)

Table 1   Advertisements by Field of Employer and Employee.
Top table considers all ads. Bottom two tables reflect a
breakdown of ads from arts and sciences colleges and
medical schools.

a means to learn research skills distinct from the area of primary
training.

The crossdisciplinary developments in evidence in the
advertisements were reinforced and expanded by interviews with the
heads of eight Anatomy Departments in medical schools. An initial
instrument was pretested on one department head and was modified as

REGULAR FACULTY POSITIONS
EMPLOYEE'S FIELD

		Other	Anatomy	A+O	
	Other	0	7	10	
EMPLOYER'S	Anatomy	5	11	2	
FIELD	A+O	1	2	1	(N = 39)

POST DOCTORAL POSITIONS
EMPLOYEE' FIELD

		Other	Anatomy	A+O	
	Other	0	2	1	
EMPLOYER'S	Anatomy	3	0	0	
FIELD	A+O	0	1	0	(N = 7)

Table 2   Breakdown of Advertisements by Level
of Position (Faculty or Postdoc)

a result for use with the other units. Table 3 lists the units whose heads
were surveyed and some of their demographic characteristics.

Most critically, the composition of the faculties is already 45%
nonanatomists, while the postdoctoral positions are held by 75%
nonanatomists. In addition to this information, Tables 4 and 5 also list
some of the fields outside anatomy represented. While most of these
fields outside anatomy represented are in the biomedical area, a few,
such as physics and engineering, traditionally stand outside it.

The instructional audience of the Anatomy Departments includes,
in every case, many medical students and relatively few anatomy
graduate students. (A 10-1 ratio is typical.) Half of the departments had
other student audiences—including dental students, osteopathic
students, veterinary medicine students, students of allied health
professions (e.g., nurses and medical technicians), and undergraduates.

Research support came to every one of the departments from
various Institutes of the National Institutes of Health. All had
additional suuport from such organizations as the National Science
Foundation, Muscular Dystrophy Foundation, March of Dimes, various
heart associations, the U.S. Air Force, and private firms.

ANATOMY DEPARTMENTS SURVEYED

Emory University
George Washington University
Medical College of Georgia
Michigan State University
University of Arkansas
University of Maryland
University of Texas
University of Vermont

Faculty
Range   :9-22
Mean±S.D.:16±5

Post Docs
Range   :0-6
Mean±S.D.:3±2

Graduate Students
Range   :5-15
Mean±S.D.:9±3

Table 3 List of Anatomy Departments Surveyed and
Their Characteristics

Crossdisciplinary collaboration was present in all units with other medical school units. Three-fourths mentioned crossdisciplinary collaboration within the unit, while one-fourth indicated such collaboration with other institutions. Crossdisciplinary instruction resided mainly in the neuroscience course, required of all medical students. In most instances this course was staffed by faculty from a variety of departments.

III. Analysis

The data clearly indicate that crossdisciplinary activities (a very wide range was cited by our respondents) are taking place in anatomy departments. At this point in our research there are some things we do and do not know about this situation. We will begin with what we know and develop the rest in the form of a research agenda.

Disciplines of Faculty Anatomy Departments
Anatomy: 70/127 = .55
Non-Anatomy: 57/127 = .45
Non-Anatomy Disciplines Represented on Anatomy Faculties
Biology
Zoology
Pathology
Pharmacology
Medicine
Physiology
Genetics
Cell Biology
Neurosciences
Biophysics
Physics
Psychology
Biochemistry
Chemistry

Table 4 Faculty Disciplines in Surveyed Anatomy Departments
(In a few cases some determinations of the anatomy/
non-anatomy distinction were made in accordance
with the character of the remainder of the unit)

The departments we surveyed varied widely in character. Half were composed predominantly of anatomists while nonanatomists were a majority in others (ranging up to 89% in one department). Yet in both types of units the heads emphasized the importance of a problem focus in which the researcher follows the problem across disciplinary boundaries using whatever techniques are appropriate. The researcher could either master the appropriate techniques or collaborate with those who knew them already. Thus research on important problems was limited neither by knowledge boundaries nor to specific techniques—in contrast to the historical situation reported by Dr. Corner. Research is emphasized and, in the words of one respondent, *all* (anatomy department) research is interdisciplinary today. Or, as another respondent put it: "We teach anatomy; we do biomedical research". This general emphasis leads to interesting practices that differ from much of academia, such as one head's lack of concern with

Disciplines of Post-Docs, in Anatomy Departments
Anatomy: $5/20 = .25$
Non-Anatomy: $15/20 = .75$
Non-Anatomy Disciplines of Post-Docs in Anatomy Departments
Pathology
Biology
Engineering
Physiology
Medicine
Cell Biology
Pharmacology
Chemistry

Table 5 Disciplines of Post-Docs in Surveyed Anatomy Departments
(in a few cases some determinations of the anatomy/non-anatomy
distinction were made in accordance with the character
of the remainder of the unit.)

the anatomy background of his faculty. With high level biomedical research capabilities and outgoing personalities he has found that biomedical researchers can be brought to teach anatomy without any formal background. This also leads to sharp distinctions in research and teaching foci in many cases—as where one does research on neurotransmitters but teaches gross anatomy.

Based on the interviews and the neuroscience inventory analyzed by Marshall (1979) we might speculate that the field is in a state of transformation from anatomy to crossdisciplinary neuroscience. The departments we surveyed were distributed along such a continuum. The prospect of studying a field in transition is interesting from a number of perspectives. However, it leaves many unanswered questions.

One major question which requires treatment is to what extent these crossdisciplinary activities are multidisciplinary and to what extent they are interdisciplinary. This will require analysis on a project by project and course by course level.

Several observations can be made in closing. First, it is important to consider what factors are inducing the apparent transformation of anatomy departments. Speculating, there seems to be an interplay (not accidental) between federal research support opportunities, the organization of medical schools, and intellectual challenge driving research toward neuroscience. One side effect of this movement is the possibility of leaving the function of teaching in the lurch. For instance, two of our departments' titles show a possible evolutionary direction (e.g., Department of Anatomy and Neuroscience). Will this continue to the stage of Department of Neuroscience? If so, what will happen to the teaching of anatomy, already largely a service to the medical school? This question also bears on the individual faculty members. There were indications that those who taught gross anatomy, in particular, tended to be older and less research-oriented. Promotion and tenure criteria emphasize research. In the future who will teach the basics needed for clinical practice? One interesting twist was to request clinicians to teach these for the Anatomy Department (e.g., pathologists to teach histology).

If we are correct in perceiving a transition in progress, how widespread is it? Our pilot survey suggests that it is the dominant, though not exclusive, pattern in anatomy in the United States. We hypothesize that this finding might generalize across the biomedical sciences. We don't know to what extent it crosses the institutional boundaries of the medical school to affect Arts and Sciences units, nor the importance of research institutes and their roles (e.g., Brain Research Institute at UCLA). (We have no data from outside the United States on which to base generalizations in that direction, but we suspect this "interdisciplinarization" to neuroscience to be international in scope.) Were one to feel extremely bold, the speculation might extend into the future to project a spreading wave of redirections into the other sciences. In particular, the social sciences, stressed by declining student bodies of their own, could mold into a service teaching role for the basics and an applied policy research direction encouraged by federal research support opportunities.

The potential impacts of the transformation of institutional arrangements on the face of science are enormous. Our signals are too preliminary to draw any firm conclusions. Instead, they suggest a research agenda first to define more precisely the past trends of change in the biomedical sciences, then to adduce the critical causal forces, and, next, to project the future directions and impacts of any transformations in progress. Finally, such a study should raise critical issues at stake for the intellectual frontiers in science moving through crossdisciplinary bounds vis-a-vis the teaching function, and suggest policy actions to direct the evolution in a desirable way.

References

Corner, G.W. (1958) *Anatomist at Large: An Autobiography and Selected Essays*, Freeport, NY, Books for Libraries Press.

Hay, E. (1980) "Anatomy," in *Peterson's Annual Guides to Graduate Study, 1980 Edition, Book 3, Biological, Agricultural, and Health Sciences*, Edited by K.C. Hegener and S.V. Weaver, Princeton, NJ, Peterson's Guides.

Kelly, P., Kranzberg, M., Rossini, F.A., Baker, N.R., Tarpley, F.A., Mitzner, M. (1978) *Technological Innovation: A Critical Review of Current Knowledge*, San Francisco, The San Francisco Press.

Marshall, L. (1979) "Maturation and Current Status of Neuroscience: Data from the 1976 Inventory of U.S. Neurosciences," *Experimental Neurology, 64*, 1-32.

Rossini, F.A., Porter, A.L., Kelly, P., and Chubin, D.E. (1978) *Frameworks and Factors Affecting Integration Within Technology Assessments*, Dept. Soc. Sci. Final Tech. Rep. NSF Grant ERS76-04474. Georgia Institute of Technology.

Rossini, F.A., Porter, A.L., Kelly, P., and Chubin, D.E. (1981) "Interdisciplinary Integration in Technology Assessments," *Knowledge, 2*, 503-528.

17

RESEARCH CENTERS
AND NON-FACULTY RESEARCHERS:
IMPLICATIONS OF A GROWING ROLE
IN AMERICAN UNIVERSITIES†*

Albert H. Teich

INTRODUCTION

American universities have entered what is likely to be a prolonged period of financial austerity and steady or declining student enrollments. Since there will be fewer openings for new faculty in coming years, many observers have become concerned about the continued vitality of academic science. It has been suggested that as faculties become "tenured in" and begin to age, even the nation's most famous and productive departments will start to feel the effects of intellectual stagnation due to the absence of younger researchers.

How can universities maintain their vitality as research institutions under such conditions? One possible means might be for them to gradually shift their research activities away from regular academic departments to institutes, centers, laboratories, and other "organized research units", and at the same time to develop attractive long-term career patterns for professional researchers outside of the conventional tenure-track faculty. In this manner, universities could hire young scientists and expand or redeploy their research functions in a manner not limited by constraints on the size of their teaching functions.

† Based on research sponsored under grant number PRM 76-82713 from the U.S. National Science Foundation, Office of Planning and Resources Management, to George Washington University. The support of the Foundation is gratefully acknowledged.

* From *Interdisciplinary Research Groups: Their Management and Organization*, edited by R.T. Barth and R. Steck, 1979, pp. 244-259. Proceedings of the First International Conference on Interdisciplinary Research Groups, Schloss Reisensburg, Federal Republic of Germany, April 22-28, 1979.

Certain European concepts—for example, the institutes of Germany's Max Planck Society have been proposed as models which might be adapted to the American situation. A number of initiatives have been proposed to assist or encourage universities to move in this direction (Press, 1975; Atkinson, 1975, 1977; Brooks, 1977), and at least one major institution—the Massachusetts Institute of Technology (MIT)—has begun implementing some of these notions on its own initiative.

Organized research units (ORU's) and non-faculty research professionals are not new to the academic scene in the United States. The proliferation of ORU's during the 1950's and 1960's, in fact, has been a phenomenon widely observed and commented upon (Dressel, Johnson, and Marcus, 1969; Ikenberry, 1970). Yet academic departments and their regular faculties remain the key organizational elements of American universities, and ORU's and their staffs have been treated by most universities in a rather ad hoc manner. Little systematic thought seems to have been given to what might be the consequence for universities and for the scientific community if ORU's and non-faculty researchers—whether by natural processes or by conscious policy choice—were to assume substantially larger research roles relative to academic departments and their faculties. This paper is a preliminary attempt to explore some of the questions involved.

NATURE AND ORIGINS OF ORU'S

The term "organized research unit" encompasses a wide variety of organizational entities in American universities today. ORU's range from tiny, "one-person" or "paper" organizations which consist essentially of a letterhead, a sign on an office door, and an address on a proposal cover sheet, to substantial, multidisciplinary or interdisciplinary laboratories on large sites remote from campus, employing hundreds or even thousands of scientists and engineers and operating with virtually complete autonomy from their parent universities. One recent paper (Friedman, 1977), estimates the total number of ORU's at over 5,000 nationwide, including more than 800 in physical science and engineering. A count of ORU's listed in the *Research Centers Directory* for 52 major research universities reveals a total of 2,096 at just these institutions. In view of the range in size and nature among ORU's, and the definitional questions involved, these figures are neither terribly reliable nor very helpful in developing a real sense of scale. What is clear, however, is that few if any major universities are without a considerable number of such entities.

What forces have led to this proliferation of ORU's? Ikenberry and Friedman, whose survey of some 125 centers and institutes at various universities is the major published work on ORU's, suggest three categories: (1) external, societal pressures; (2) career needs of faculty; and (3) administrators' concerns for institutional development (1972, pp. 11-28). The three are obviously interrelated and often all three are involved in specific instances. . . .

ORU'S AND UNIVERSITY GOVERNANCE

By allowing the university to respond to societal needs, by providing career advancement opportunities for faculty, and by assisting universities in their own development goals, ORU's can play important roles in academic life. Recent experience, however, has raised a variety of questions about the manner in which ORU's function, and about their impacts on the rest of the university.

Departmental and Multidisciplinary ORU's

Many changes have occurred in university structure in recent years, but departments remain the major power centers on nearly all campuses. As Ikenberry and Friedman, among others, note:

Departments continue to exert the principal force in the operational definition of goals and purposes of the university; they largely control faculty reward mechanisms; and they are, through both formal and informal mechanisms, the primary focus of institutional progress and academic achievement (1972, p. 83).

In administrative terms, major differences exist between those ORU's which are closely affiliated with particular academic departments and those which are independent of departments (Day, 1977, p. 1). Departmental ORU's are generally disciplinary in nature and are created to serve departmental objectives, such as providing a convenient organizational framework for faculty members' research, satisfying the needs of an external sponsor, or attracting or retaining a particular individual. An "Economic Studies Institute" affiliated with an economics department and staffed mainly by economics faculty or an "Earth Sciences Laboratory" similarly related to a geology department are examples of such departmental ORU's.

The relationship between this type of ORU and its parent department is not always smooth or trouble free. Tensions may arise over such issues as allocation of faculty time, control of office or laboratory space, and financial support. But on the whole, the departmental ORU is regarded as an extension of the department, subordinate to its interests, and this tends to limit the scope and severity of conflict.

Multidisciplinary ORU's present different problems. They generally exist to serve purposes for which individual departments are not suitable and they are not necessarily subordinate to departments. These ORU's—like the Institute for Social Research at Michigan or the Program of Policy Studies in Science and Technology at George Washington—report administratively to university officials such as vice presidents for research or graduate deans without going through departmental channels. By their nature they create certain tensions in structure and mode of operation. At the root, these tensions derive from the tendencies of the ORU's to seek organizational autonomy in pursuing their activities, and the counter-tendencies of departments to seek to retain some measure of control over them. Departments tend to assume that the ORU's exist to serve the university's (i.e., the departments') purposes. ORU administrators and staff may feel that they do indeed serve university purposes—but these are not necessarily congruent with departmental purposes or preferences. The tensions are manifested primarily in regard to personnel matters, ORU program direction, and quality control. The balance of this discussion applies primarily to such multidisciplinary ORU's.

Staffing and Reward Structures

Most ORU's are free to make professional appointments and promotions on their staff as long as the resources are available and the appointments do not involve faculty status. Only a minority of universities allow ORU's to offer faculty appointments without departmental affiliation (Ikenberry and Friedman, 1972, pp. 85-86). Lacking the power to offer faculty appointments without departmental concurrence, an ORU is limited in its ability to control its own destiny. Departmental power also prevails in relation to control of the reward structure for faculty who divide their efforts between departments and ORU's. Although many universities permit ORU's to initiate recommendations for promotion, virtually all require departmental concurrence in the recommendations (Ikenberry and Friedman, 1972, p. 87).

At the informal level, departmental control over the reward structure for faculty has long been regarded as a barrier to a faculty participation in interdisciplinary research, and hence as a problem from the point of view of ORU management (Alpert, 1969; Stockton, 1972; Roy, 1977). Faculty members who devote too large a share of their efforts to interdisciplinary studies in ORU's sometimes find that the departments with which they are affiliated regard them as less than full members and are less willing to promote them and grant them tenure. While this may not be reflected in formal policy, it seems to be a widely shared impression among faculty and it no doubt inhibits long-term interdisciplinary collaboration and reduces the loyalty and commitment of faculty members to ORU's (Day, 1977; Stockton, 1972).

Programmatic Control and Evaluation

Most multidisciplinary ORU's seem to be relatively free from the direct influence of other elements of the university on the direction of their programs. Ikenberry and Friedman's study found little evidence that administrative superiors or other potentially influential figures in the university shaped ORU activities or program objectives in an immediate sense. Even the advisory committees which most ORU's maintained were not credited with any programmatic role—although some did serve other useful purposes (1972, pp. 90-93).

Freedom from direct programmatic control by other elements of the university does not necessarily equate with a high degree of autonomy for ORU's, however. Departmental control over faculty appointments, university policies which limit the range of functions ORU's can perform (excluding, in most instances, teaching and awarding degrees), and the influence of deans, department heads, and other administrators on resource allocation and other critical matters substantially restrict the ability of most ORU's to "chart their own courses."

Some observers feel these restrictions on ORU autonomy limit their effectiveness. On the other hand, ORU's are regarded by many as opportunistic organizations, and there may be justification to universities' concerns about the need to prevent ORU's from assuming new goals and functions simply in order to perpetuate themselves (Dressel, Johnson and Marcus, 1969; Churchman, 1976). As the Committee on MIT Research Structure noted, ORU's may "take on a life of their own", in which "preservation of the laboratory becomes a goal in itself" (1976, p. 52). This is a well-known trait of bureaucratic organizations, including those engaged in R&D (Teich and Lambright, 1976-77). Churchman (1976) asserts that ORU's ought to be able to "commit suicide" at an appropriate time, rather than continuing to exist without a valid purpose. Few, if any, seem willing to do so, however.

While ORU's at most universities are subject to some form of periodic review and evaluation, not many major universities have made serious systematic attempts to assess their overall ORU structure and its relation to university goals. A recent study of the research climate at the University of North Carolina at Chapel Hill, took note of the variety of expectations that has been vested in ORU's, but then observed that

> There is little evidence that the evaluative function of research administration has been exercised in relation to these expectations or on other issues associated with research institutes. . . .

The MIT study remarked on the ad hoc manner in which ORU's are related to institutional governance structures. Aside from those few ORU's which are integrated into particular departments, it noted that each of the centers and laboratories is a separate "fiefdom", subject to only minimal outside supervision and control (Committee on MIT Research Structure, 1976, pp. 50-52). Even at Berkeley, which has probably paid more attention to the issue of ORU's than any other university in recent years, and where there is a formally articulated policy requiring periodic reviews of ORU's, not a single ORU has gone out of existence or been discontinued by the campus administration (Bolce, 1975, p. 3).

To some extent the tension between ORU autonomy and subordination to university purposes as defined by departments is intrinsic to the nature of the ORU. Compared to an academic department, the existence of which is grounded in a definable body of knowledge, and which is assumed to serve dual function of expansion and transmission of this knowledge, an ORU is an opportunistic entity. There is no denying this. It may be possible for universities to do a better job in assuring that particular ORU's do not develop in a manner inconsistent with larger university goals. But to expect ORU's to behave like academic departments is to deny their nature and unique characteristics. The other side of "opportunism" is "responsiveness". When universities set up ORU's, they are choosing to pursue activities for which departments, for one reason or another, are deemed to be inappropriate. In this sense, ORU's represent a primary means by which universities can adapt to changes in their environments. Attempts at adaptation recognize the potential for failure as well as success. Careful review processes may help make the best use of success while protecting other elements of the university from the consequences of ORU failure. But to allow departments totally to dominate ORU's is likely to prove as dysfunctional for the university as allowing ORU's complete autonomy.

THE "UNFACULTY"

Perhaps the thorniest problems relating to the place of ORU's in the university concern those members of their professional research staffs who do not hold faculty appointments—a class of people that has been termed "the unfaculty" (Kerr, 1963). These individuals, many of whom possess Ph.D.'s, and qualifications comparable to regular faculty members, exist in something of an anomalous state in most universities. Some consider themselves long-term post-doctorals; others are appointed to work on specific projects and remain for follow-on efforts. Some consciously choose the research staff route because they like the freedom and other amenities offered by the university environment, but do not like to teach. Still others are spouses of individuals appointed to the teaching faculty, for whom the university is unwilling or unable to provide faculty positions. In general, these non-faculty researchers are not eligible for tenure; they seldom participate in the decision-making bodies of the universities; and they frequently are denied other perquisites of academic life (Kruytbosch and Messinger, 1968). They are, as many observers have noted, "in the university, but not of the university."

Until recently, non-faculty researchers have received remarkably little attention among educators and science policymakers. Increasing interest, however, is reflected in the publication last year by the National Research Council (NRC) of the results of a survey it conducted of "doctoral research staff" in universities (National Research Council, 1978). The survey revealed that some 4,000 persons—about 3 percent of all Ph.D. scientists and engineers employed in academia were included in this group, and that the group had grown by 20 percent between 1975 and 1977. The report, which termed its investigation preliminary, concluded that "the changing role of doctoral research staff is an important issue that requires continuing attention by federal and university policy-makers" (p. 61). . . .

More needs to be learned about the overall situation of non-faculty researchers in the university before any real conclusions can be reached about their long-term role and its implications for academic life. Nonetheless, some preliminary statements can be made. The status differentials that exist between non-faculty doctoral researchers and teaching faculty are real, and can often be measured in terms of money, privileges, and, especially, job security. Except at the very top levels (e.g., Caltech's senior research associates), they tend to give the non-faculty research track the image—and in some senses the reality—of a second-rate career. This does not mean that individuals on the research track are necessarily any less capable or accomplished than those on the teaching faculty, nor does it mean that the research track itself is inherently inferior to the teaching track. It does mean, however, that there is a definite bias against the research track, one that appears to be prevalent throughout the academic community.

In a perfect marketplace, the best people would get the best jobs, and those who settled for second-best would by definition be second-best. The academic marketplace is hardly perfect, however. It is true that the selection process for tenure track faculty positions is more rigorous and requires a greater degree of peer evaluation than is generally the case for non-faculty research positions. But one cannot automatically conclude from this that differences in selection procedure are inevitably associated with quality differences in personnel.

Yet, the system seems to generate self-fulfilling prophecies. Many non-faculty researchers see their positions as temporary and express an understandable desire eventually to obtain regular faculty appointments (Kruytbosch and Messinger, 1968; Oksala, 1977). It does not appear that many succeed in making the transition. When, occasionally, one does, it may not be on particularly favorable terms. In one (presumably unexceptional) case at Cornell, where a senior research associate did obtain a faculty appointment, it was at the level of assistant professor, despite the individual's experience and the supposed rank equivalent of associate professor.

In many respects, full-time research positions in many universities appear to offer attractions comparable to research positions in in-house or contractor-operated government laboratories, non-profit research institutes, or industrial firms. As their best, they can offer intellectual freedom, good salaries, access to unique facilities, and a stimulating environment for research. On the other hand, the university setting offers the non-faculty researcher few real paths for the kind of career advancement that industrial or government laboratories offer (i.e., into management or policy-making). It also confronts the researcher with the proximity of a more privileged class, the faculty, into which he or she has highly restricted access. If the number of non-faculty university researchers grows, as new faculty positions become even more scarce, this status differential could be the source of serious tensions.

CONCLUSIONS AND IMPLICATIONS

Will the role of ORU's expand as universities enter the steady-state era? Can this trend help universities maintain their vitality in research? The answers are not at all clear. MIT, which in many ways has been a pace-setter among institutions oriented to science and engineering, seems to be embarking on such a path. The Committee on MIT Research Structure, chaired by Frank Press, then head of the Department of Earth and Planetary Sciences, recommended it do so, pointing out that:

In the next decade, expansion of the center and laboratory research modes, closely coupled to departmental and cross departmental groups, may be the principal mechanism by which MIT can enter new fields and bring young researchers into the community (1976, p. 6).

So far, however, MIT seems to be alone in viewing its ORU's in this light. It does not appear that other research universities are following MIT's lead—at least as a matter of stated policy. On the other hand, the results of the National Research Council survey suggest that the non-faculty research staffs of many universities are growing rapidly. Many of these researchers are employed in ORU's, though others are appointed through departments. It may well be that the policy the MIT study advocates is being implemented in many universities as the result of external forces, without any conscious decision. If so, this is a matter that merits serious attention on the part of academic research administrators and policy-makers.

Smith and Karlesky note that ORU's have generally engaged in large-scale team research efforts, rather than traditional "little science" projects. They warn that too strong an emphasis on such projects might adversely affect the educational experience of graduate students— limiting their development as independent investigators—and might also be detrimental to the interests of young faculty. They point out that large-scale ORU efforts might be subject to strong pressure from sponsors to deliver short-term results in high priority social problem areas, thus weakening their links to the university's teaching function (1977, p. 238). Earlier critics of ORU's have charged them with undermining teaching, weakening departments and the authority structure in the university, fragmenting university organization, and more generally epitomizing all that they see wrong with the contemporary university (cited in Ikenberry and Friedman, 1972, pp. 110-112).

To some extent, the importance one attaches to such concerns depends on how one sees the evolving role of the university in society. Weakening the power of academic departments is to some observers a step on the road to the destruction of the university; to others it is the only way to achieve necessary academic reforms (Birnbaum, 1969; Roy, 1977). In any case, such discussions may become increasingly irrelevant as the problems of the university become more severe. The power of academic departments vis-a-vis other elements of the university will not be of great import if the university as a whole declines as a research institution. If ORU's are indeed a means of preserving the university's intellectual vitality, their impact on departmental power is a secondary concern.

The issues raised by Smith and Karlesky (1977) are nevertheless somewhat disturbing. One of the reasons for which many ORU's developed was to provide a framework for coordinated team efforts, somewhat more hierarchical (organized) in structure than those generally found in academic departments (see Steck, 1976). That a shift towards ORU's performing large-scale research might limit the independence of graduate students and young faculty who choose to work there seems partially true. This may not be inevitable, however, and anyway the costs of diminished independence have to be offset against the benefits of participation in such research. Furthermore, it is not necessary that ORU's conduct solely large-scale efforts. An expanded role for ORU's would allow for more "little science" as well as team efforts. A block funding mechanism, judiciously employed by sponsoring agencies, could permit ORU's to develop the kind of flexibility needed for this.

Would ORU's be drawn away from the mainstream of academic life by pressures to serve agency missions and produce short-term results as Smith and Karlesky suggest? The pressure on researchers to serve short-term needs at the expense of long-term work is not just a problem for ORU's, but for the scientific community as a whole (National Science Board, 1976). The nature of ORU's and their dependence on external funds makes them more vulnerable to such pressures than are academic departments, but the extent to which this might become a serious concern probably depends more on the national climate for research than on factors internal to the university. In any case, several approaches might alleviate this problem. These include diversifying sponsorship of ORU's to reduce their dependence on particular agencies, using block grants for ORU research where possible, and integrating funding of ORU's with funding of other units of the university to give them greater stability and resistance to external pressure.

Still remaining is the problem of non-faculty research positions in the university. MIT, following the recommendations of its Committee on Research Structure that it seek to make such positions "attractive to talented researchers so that they would consider intermediate and long-term university careers as professionally advantageous" (1976, p. 93), has recently reformed its non-faculty appointments structure. The reforms are intended to replace the previous haphazard system with a unified hierarchy of positions, to raise the status of these positions, to provide for more careful review of appointees, and to establish a limited number of senior levels appointments which will carry "rolling tenure" (i.e., extended notice of termination). Other universities, including

Cornell, Michigan, Caltech, and Princeton already have or are considering implementing such systems.

These reforms may serve the universities' aims of making research careers more attractive and partially redressing the imbalance between faculty and non-faculty researchers. Nevertheless, unless this hierarchy of positions becomes the true equivalent of the teaching faculty leader, with comparable privileges, selection and review procedures, and job security potential (which seems rather unlikely), the trend seems bound to create a formally two-tiered academic world. If, as the NRC suggests, the number of non-faculty researchers is growing rapidly, the tensions between two classes of researchers might cause serious problems for universities. One cannot but agree with the NRC conclusion that the situation of non-faculty researchers should be watched carefully by academic policy-makers.

Rather than employing too many non-faculty researchers in academic departments or in ORU's closely integrated with campus life, universities might do well to direct the growth of their research efforts into what Harvey Brooks has called "buffer institutions". Some examples of these institutions include the Joint Institute for Laboratory Astrophysics operated by the National Bureau of Standards and the University of Colorado, and the Center for Astrophysics at Harvard, an amalgamation of the Smithsonian Astrophysical Observatory and the Harvard College Observatory. These institutions are sufficiently distinct from their university bases so that their staffs do not see themselves as second class citizens in comparison to regular faculty members, yet they are close enough to contribute to the vitality of the university's research environment. Since parts of the institutions may be considered government laboratories, their senior staffs may even have the job security of civil servants. The "buffer institution" idea clearly merits more careful examination.

REFERENCES

Alpert, Daniel (1969) "The Role and Structure of Interdisciplinary and Multidisciplinary Research Centers", address to the Council of Graduate Schools in the U.S., Washington, D.C., December 5, 1969.

Atkinson, Richard C. (1975) "Remarks to the National Council of University Research Administrators", Washington, D.C., November 7, 1975.

Atkinson, Richard C. (1977) "The Threat to Scientific Research", *The Chronicle of Higher Education*, March 28, 1977, p. 40.

Birnbaum, Norman (1969) "The Arbitrary Disciplines", *Change*, July-August, pp. 10-21.

Bolce, Jane (1975) *The Review Process for Berkeley Campus Organized Research Units*, working paper CP-394, Center for Research in Management Science, University of California, Berkeley.

Brooks, Harvey (1977) "Office of Technology Assessment Invites Comments on Health of Science", *F.A.S. Public Interest Report*, Vol. 30, No. 1, p. 6.

Churchman, C. West (1976) *ORU's and Politics: Or When is Organizational Murder Justified?* working paper CP-398, Center for Research in Management Science, University of California, Berkeley.

Committee on MIT Research Structure (1976) *Report of the Committee*, Cambridge, Mass.: MIT.

Coutu, A.J., and Jones, E. Walton (1975) *Review and Analysis of Sponsored Research at the University of North Carolina*, University of North Carolina, Chapel Hill, N.C.

Day, Douglas, N., Jr. (1977) *The Management of Organized Research Units at the University of California, Berkeley: Size, Politics and Interdisciplinarity*, working paper CP-399, Center for Research in Management Science, University of California, Berkeley, Revised March 1977.

Dressel, Paul L., Johnson, F. Craig, and Marcus, Phillip M. (1969) "The Proliferating Institutes", *Change*, July-August 1969, pp. 21-24.

Friedman, R.C. (1977) *The Continuing Saga of Institutes and Centers*, University Park, Pa.: The Pennsylvania State University, Center for the Study of Higher Education.

Ikenberry, Stanley O. (1970) *A Profile of Proliferating Institutes: A Study of Selected Characteristics of Institutes and Centers in 51 Land Grant Universities*, Center for the Study of Higher Education.

Ikenberry, Stanley O., and Friedman, Renee C. (1972) *Beyond Academic Departments: The Story of Institutes and Centers*, San Francisco: Jossey-Bass.

Kerr, Clark (1963) *The Uses of the University*, New York: Harper & Row.

Kruytbosch, Carlos E., and Messinger, Sheldon L. (1968) "Unequal Peers: The Situation of Researchers at Berkeley", *American Behavioral Scientist*, Vol. 11, May-June, 1968, pp. 33-43.

McMullen, J. Howard (1958) "Our Universities' Research-Associate Positions in Physics", *Physics Today*, Vol. II, No. 8, pp. 14-15.

National Research Council (1978) "Nonfaculty Doctoral Research Staff in Science and Engineering in United States Universities", Washington, D.C.: National Academy of Sciences.

National Science Board (1976) *Science at the Bicentennial: A Report from the Research Community*, Washington, D.C., U.S. Government Printing Office.

Oksala, Lawrence P. (1977) *Professional Researchers at Cornell: An Introductory Study*, internal working document, George Washington University, Graduate Program in Science, Technology and Public Policy.

Press, Frank (1975) "New Arrangements for Science in the Universities", *Science*, Vol. 189, No. 4198, p. 177.

Roy, Rustum (1977) "Interdisciplinary Science on Campus—The Elusive Dream", *C&E News*, August 29, 1977, pp. 28-40.

Smith, Bruce L.R., and Karlesky, Joseph (1977) *The State of Academic Science*, New York: Change Magazine Press.

Steck, R. (1976) "How Can Research-on-Research Contribute to a Better Management of University Research?" *R&D Management*, Vol. 6, No. 2, pp. 81-86.

Stockton, Rex (1972) "University-Based Research Units: A Perspective", *Journal of Research and Development in Education*, Vol. 5, No. 4, pp. 3-13.

Teich, Albert H., and Lambright, W. Henry (1976-77) "The Redirection of a Large National Laboratory", *Minerva*, Vol. 14, No. 4, pp. 447-474.

18

THE INTERACTION OF COGNITIVE AND SOCIAL FACTORS IN STEERING A LARGE SCALE INTERDISCIPLINARY PROJECT*

Jan Bärmark
Göran Wallén

Introduction

The growth of knowledge in science has become a common focus of interest for metascientists and sociologists of science. Their common problem is to map and analyse the steering factors in the development of hypotheses, problems and methods in research programmes. The territory for investigations of the growth of knowledge in science encompasses both cognitive and social factors. From Thomas Kuhn's *The Structure of Scientific Revolutions* we have learned that the growth of knowledge must be seen in its social, psychological, organisational and metascientific contexts.

Paradigms belong to the more important steering factors in the growth of a discipline. Usually, paradigms are not articulated. They function as a "tacit dimension". Our hypothesis is that by studying the growth of knowledge in interdisciplinary projects where disciplines with different paradigms have to confront each other, the importance of paradigms and the interaction of cognitive and social factors will be recognised.

Our task, then, is to investigate the interaction of paradigmatic factors with sociopsychological, sociological and organisational factors. Here we will use the paradigm concept in Håkan Törnebohm's (1977) elaboration where a paradigm consists of world picture assumptions,

* From *Interdisciplinary Research Groups: Their Management and Organization*, edited by R.T. Barth and R. Steck, 1979, pp. 180-190. Proceedings of the First International Conference on Interdisciplinary Research Groups, Schloss Reisenburg, Federal Republic of Germany, April 22-28, 1979.

ideals of science (view on scientific methods, criteria of knowledge, epistemology) and research roles and the required competence to fulfill these roles.

We have found that metascientific problems and psychological factors are strongly interrelated. To do research within a paradigm has psychological consequences. In the same way, paradigmatic factors and organisational problems are strongly interrelated. To study these interrelations we chose to study three interdisciplinary projects: a large ecological project; a project dealing with domestic waste; and a project concerning resource-saving construction of housing.

Our method

The method chosen for these investigations is the case study approach. We interviewed the project leaders and the participants in the projects. We also used participant observations and read the research reports. A paragon for our case study method was Ian Mitroff's *The Subjective Side of Science* and his attempt to integrate psychology of science with philosophy of science. From our investigations on interdisciplinary research we found that in order to get an encompassing picture of the steering factors, it was necessary to study interdisciplinary research from an interdisciplinary point of view, i.e., from theory of science, psychology of science, sociology of science and organisational theory. As we are not competent in all these areas, we consulted people from those areas.

The forest project

Of special importance in our case studies was a large forest ecology project. Our description follows the main scheme of phases in a paper by the project leader, Folke Andersson. We also obtained information from working reports written within the project. As mentioned above, we had in this case study the opportunity to study the project from two points of view, that of the project leaders and that of the participating scientists.

The forest project is the oldest and largest of our projects. It is about seven years old and has occupied about 100 researchers and technical assistants. The basic assumptions of the Eco-system-ecology research programme is that ecological knowledge must be formulated in a mathematical language and that the project must adopt a system-theoretical approach to the "territory".

The project has developed in several phases, with somewhat different views on models, goals, organisation and division of labour. It is also possible to characterize the development in terms of crises. In "Popperian" terms the project developed in phases of "conjectures", rational criticism, revisions of the programme, new conjectures, etc.

Phase 1: **The Initiation Phase** (Aug. 1970-June 1972)

The planning of the forest project began in 1970 and took two years to launch. A great part of this time was spent solving conflicting interests between different research bodies. The project received, in the beginning, special economic support from the Swedish parliament. The total budget suggested was about 27 million Swedish crowns (about 5 million dollars) for seven years.

The forest project was based on a new perspective on ecology and aimed at the development of encompassing models of the coniferous forest by help of system theory. (Eco-system-ecology, where the main interest is in flows of energy, matter, etc., compared to plant communities, populations and organisms.) An important paragon is the "International Biological Programme" in which some of the researchers had been working before.

The main goals of the project were (some subgoals and more "technical" and methodological restrictions are omitted):

1. To provide a scientific basis for the understanding of structure and function of the most important coniferous forest ecosystem of our country . . .
2. To provide such basic knowledge of coniferous forest ecosystems which allows an analysis of the effects of forestry management and of environmental changes . . .
3. To train scientists in multidisciplinary work . . .

Specific aims:

1. To carry out ecosystem studies with regard to energy exchange and turnover of water, organic matter, and nutrients for two types of coniferous forest . . .

Mathematical models and simulation models of ecosystem processes will be elaborated.

Paradigmatic problems in the steering of the project

At the beginning there were some terminological problems. However, these were soon overcome as the scientists discovered that they, to a great extent, shared the same world picture assumptions concerning the territory. There were no conflicts between the world picture assumptions. The ideals of science, on the other hand, were not the same. The empirical scientists here are a heterogenous group in which some are used to thinking in mathematical terms and focussing on processes and flows in their territories. Other scientists came from disciplines where one looked upon mathematics and statistics with suspicion. (One of our informants told us that the courses in statistics were reduced from five to two points in the doctoral studies.)

Phase 2: **Establishing the Project** (July 1972-Dec. 1973)

The project was, in this phase, mainly a cooperative project among researchers from different biology departments, some meteorologists and data-specialists. There were subgroups, for instance, zoologists and microbiologists. The main problem was to formulate operative goals and problems.

The problems of goals

Preconceptions about the character of the project play an important role in the formulation of goals in a project and comprise a very important steering factor. In the forest project one presupposed the project to be analogous to the Apollo Project where it was possible to formulate the goals in operational terms. But this project turned out to be more like the Cancer Research Programme in which the goal is to discover new knowledge in processes. The project has the character of a research programme in pure science where it is not possible to formulate the results beforehand. The goals were formulated like "solutions to the problem . . ." and in terms of an approach: systems thinking and modelling. The project management had intended that the planning of the project should be a systems-technical network model following the scientific ecosystem model. This was, however, never possible. The management ideal of steering a project by objectives implies that the objectives are formulated in terms of output and results and that they are measurable. This is, of course, impossible in a project with so much pure research in which the links between problems and goals are not known. How is it possible to describe discoveries in advance? (You plan for India and find America.)

The following is from a 1976 report from the working committee: "We can now report progress toward the understanding of the concept of operational objectives and their formulation. It seems necessary to try to analyze why the project still after four years activity has not fully succeeded in formulating operational goals." In this report two sources are analysed: the size of the project (it is very large) and a conflict between the demand for scientific explanations and predictions. (In some cases the explanations are not needed for predictions in applications). However, this last reason is a problem of multi-objectives and we think that the main reason the objectives could not be made operative was lack of theoretical knowledge in biology. It is then, of course, much easier to formulate operative goals when you have that knowledge four years later! We think that the effort should have emphasised the precise formulations of problems and methods, and not operational goals which are difficult to formulate in advance. The ambition to formulate operative goals was mainly intended to impress the research councils, and the project was also under pressure from an Advisory Council.

System theory as a steering factor

The methodological side of the goals of the project were systems theory and modelling. All scientists were supposed to learn system theory from engineers skilled in mathematical modelling. But these attempts were not successful since the disciplines concerned were not mature enough for mathematical work. The scientists were neither motivated nor competent to use system models. From their point of view the system models were too complicated, too difficult to learn and of no heuristic use in the research process. The models could not do justice to the data they had collected. The project leaders and the scientists had two perspectives on the system paradigm. The result was a division of work where special scientists were delegated to do the modelling work while others had to do the empirical investigations. There was a division between theoreticians and empiricists.

The research leaders had not taken into account that learning system theory is more complicated than just learning a new method or technique. The adaptation of system theory implies the adoption of new kind of paradigm with new world picture assumptions, ideals or science (criteria of knowledge, epistemology, etc.) and new research roles. Many of the scientists were not used to abstract reasoning in mathematical models. Their interest in attending seminars in order to learn a new paradigm soon faded. They were interested in doing empirical investigations, in measurements, and the process of handling a lot of empirical data. So, instead of adopting new perspectives, they continued their research in the same manner as before.

A note from the psychology of science

The reactions from the empirically-minded biologists towards systems theory is a reminder of the strong interrelations between paradigmatic factors and psychological ones. As in Mitroff's case we found that the two groups of scientists not only had different kinds of paradigms, but also that there are psychological differences between theoreticians and empiricists. The process of changing paradigms comprises the whole personality and that process takes time. It cannot be expected to take place within one research programme. The process of adopting a new paradigm takes at least two research programmes. Some of the scientists had earlier experiences from interdisciplinary science and were not quite unfamiliar with system theory. They could see the idea behind system thinking but preferred to work without the models. The only heuristic value in the models, according to them, was that the models helped in structuring one's own thoughts.

Phase 3: Empirical Dominance (Jan. 1974-Dec. 1975)

The problems of cooperation, together with the difficulties mentioned above, led to a reorganization of the project in 1973 into different problem areas (such as gas exchanges, litter fall, consumption). Although the preliminary models of the ecosystem could not be used to steer empirical work, it was the basis of division into groups according to a preconception of scientific problems. This change from cooperation between disciplines to "problem groups" was successful for planning purposes and for empirical work. At the beginning of this phase, the empirical researchers thought that this reorganization would give them the necessary working conditions, that they would have more opportunity to plan their own work. In other projects we have studied, this change to problem-oriented groups never occurred, and the output of knowledge tends to be coordinated but not integrated across disciplines in these projects.

The change to a problem-oriented structure initiated the third phase of the project, with empirical dominance. The size of the project was so large that it was impossible to steer the subgroups, and the actual field work was not very interdisciplinary at all. The integration was at the planning level: on the theoretical side for the whole project, and for the empirical work on an intermediate level in the problem-oriented groups. The goals and the system theory gradually became steering factors only for the project management and the theoretical biologists. The modelling work was more difficult than expected, largely due to lack of theoretical biological knowledge. The global models of the ecosystem could not be used to direct empirical work and the empirically inclined researchers carried on as usual. Later on they had difficulties in delivering data adapted to modelling and, as we will see, they were not inclined to do so either. There were, of course, also advantages to the relative freedom of the empirical researchers. For instance, important unexpected discoveries of root-production were made. The main steering in this phase was, thus, a reorganization into research-problem-oriented groups. A secondary effect of this was an emerging cleft between empirical and theoretical work.

Some consequences of the division of work

As the scientists were not interested in adopting the system model, a division of work between modellers and empirical scientists occurred. For some scientists this implied that their research roles were diminished (from their point of view) to merely delivering data for the project: their task was to deliver data which then were used in such a manner that their producer could not recognise them when they appeared in the greater context of the model. The process of delivering data was looked upon in different ways by modellers and empirical scientists. The modellers needed data quickly for their work. The empirical scientists, on the other hand, were eager to get longer series of measurements in order to get data which could fulfill *their* criteria of knowledge. The criteria of the empirical scientists were not taken from the modellers' paradigms, but came from their own disciplines with their data-criteria. For some scientists, the task of being a data deliverer was problematic. Time and again they had to choose between the demands for fast results for the project vs. their own disposition, which was to continue a productive line of research by continuing to make experiments and take measurements. For other scientists, the research role as data deliverers was not experienced as unfavourable. These scientists, on the other hand, had very vague ideas of the general goals of the project.

These kinds of problems exemplify a more general problem in steering a large scale project. While it is necessary to steer and coordinate the different investigations, the more the project leaders steer, the less the opportunity for innovation by the participants.

Interdisciplinary cooperation outside the project leaders' planning

Although the attempt to steer the project by means of system theory and global models could not be applied effectively on the field level, other kinds of interdisciplinary cooperation grew spontaneously among the empirical scientists. Some of the participants in the project had earlier experiences with interdisciplinary work and went into the project with the intention of working in teams. Their cooperation consisted of the mutual exchange of methods and results, and help in conducting experiments. The experiment station at Jadraas offered a creative atmosphere for informal discussions and planning of further research projects. In these discussions scientists were motivated to adopt new kinds of competence and to widen their perspectives. Nets of communication were established for future interdisciplinary work. The opportunity to come into contact with colleagues seems to be very important for interdisciplinary work. The informal cooperation between scientists seldom led to integration of knowledge in group work. In most cases, it led to a widening of the individual researcher's competence (which was one of the secondary aims of the project).

Relatively few researchers from different disciplines cooperated in actual research work. It occurred in cases of earlier experiences with interdisciplinary work and due to personal initiative. At the later phases of the project some exchange of information, mostly data, was needed before reporting.

Phase 4: **Modelling** (1976-1978)

In this phase, most of the empirical work continued as before, but the modelling work had been more successful than before and the modellers began to demand empirical data. The first modelling attempts were aimed at providing a global model of the pine-ecosystem. The above description of goals was a compromise and the important aim of building *one* global model of the ecosystem was not specified. As of the beginning of 1976 the idea of a global model was abandoned and a family of partial and more detailed models was produced. These models were closer to field work and the more traditional knowledge of growth in plants. They were at first based on empirical data from the literature due to the fact that the data from the project did not have the same resolution in time or did not fit in other ways, and because of delays in delivery, as already discussed.

A plant stand model for 150 years can function as the desired global model. New kinds of models were built to answer specific questions and some applications were investigated. One, for instance, concerned the effects of acid-rain from burning oil on forest ecosystems. (From this we might learn that in some cases successful solutions to practical problems could be found by problem-oriented models without a complete pure-science background). The term "applications" would thus be misleading. (Compare this point with the discussion on photosynthesis in Phase 5.)

Phase 5: **Synthesis, generalizations and applications** (1979-1980)

In this last phase, the knowledge is to be integrated on the intermediate level in producing synthesising reports and in the model-group. We think that there are certain dangers in synthesising models afterwards (but of course this part of the project is not finished yet). In adding together pieces of knowledge there is a risk of missing system effects. In the modelling work the partial models could be connected together with output from one model used as input in the next one. But some factors are treated as constant and the models are not connected back to the first. The modellers admit that some system effects could occur, but they think that if these were to be anticipated, the models would be too complex. One important system effect has occurred and caused a lot of trouble and discussion: that is the problem mentioned in the discussion of goals. It was found that knowledge about the "mechanisms of photosynthesis" was not necessary on the system level of growth of a whole tree. Of course, it is necessary that photosynthesis occurs, but the trees are "good at photosynthesising", so this is not a limiting factor for the growth. On the contrary, external factors are most important. For the goals of this project, the research on photosynthesis is overly ambitious.

We think that this phase, the end of the project, is the beginning of a new discipline, "Theoretical ecosystem-ecology." (There is no formal name for it yet.) The main theme, ecosystem, could, of course, be traced back to the International Biological Programme, but it is now beginning to institutionalize: the project-leader, a theoretically inclined biologist, and probably some of the researchers on simulation models, will have permanent appointments. The main parts of the equipment will also be preserved.

CONCLUSIONS

(1) This project was too ambitious on the part of research management from the beginning, and the difficulties encountered in fulfilling the goals, and their interpretation, are mainly due to this. In general, we find it necessary to have *realistic preconceptions of the level of knowledge*, both in the research "territory" and in the disciplines, for determining proper ambitions and the way to steer a project. This forest project was initiated by researchers as mainly a pure-science project. The steering problem was internal and close to problems of scientific development in the field, but there are many parallels to the limitations in external steering as found in the literature of "Finalisierung". A traditional management kind of steering is impossible if the relationships between results and problems are now known beforehand. In this, as in other cases of new kinds of research efforts, we think that the research programme must consist of a detailed analysis of the research *problems* and possible *methods*.

(2) The steering factors in interdisciplinary research consist of an interaction of cognitive, paradigmatic factors, socio-psychological, and organizational factors. The paradigms of researchers are not easily changed, and it will often take several projects to establish a paradigm. We think that "soft" ways of steering, like forming *a creative research community* where there are many opportunities for informal communication and cooperation, are important.

(3) It is quite normal to have difficulties in research work, and such difficulties are normally hidden in rationalized research reports. The researchers in the executive committee and the project leader in the forest project have been well aware of the difficulties of steering research. Many of the management problems in this project emerged from the internal development of knowledge. The pressure from the research councils in shortening the initial phase, and pressure from the international Advisory Group on global models and operational goals have, in fact, hindered rapid reorganizations of the project. A limitation to external steering of a project of this kind is expressed by the project leader: *"The organization of the project must be adjusted to the scientific development of the project. In this way, administrative problems cannot be separated from scientific ones."*

REFERENCES

Andersson, F. (1977) "Development, coordination and administration of an integrated ecosystem project" (Paper prepared for the workshop "Initiation of and training for integrated projects", Wenner-Gren Center, Stockholm. 770509-10, organized by the Collaboration Committee of Northwest European Research Councils (NOS) (mimeo)).

Bergman, P.A. (1975) "Development of a large-scale Research project", FEK-report 5, Stockholm 1975.

Bärmark, J., Wallén, G. (1978) "Knowledge production in interdisciplinary groups" (Report no. 37 in series 2, 1978, Department for Theory of Science, University of Gothenburg).

Daele, vd, W., Krohn, W., Weingart, P. (1977) "The political direction of scientific problems", in *The Social Production of Scientific Knowledge, Sociology of the sciences: A Year Book* (vol. 1), 1977, Reidel, Dordrecht, ed. Mendelsohn, E., Weingart, P., Whitley, R.

Johnston, R., Jagtenberg, T. (1978) "Goal direction of Scientific research", in *The dynamics of science and technology, Sociology of the sciences: A Year Book* (vol. 2), 1978, Reidel, Dordrecht, ed. Krohn, W., Layton, E.T., Weingart, P.

Mitroff, I. (1974) *The subjective side of science*, Elsevier, Amsterdam, N.Y.

Steck, R., (1977) "Organisationsformen und Kooperationsverhalten Interdisziplinarer Forschergruppen im Internationaln Vergleich", Referat zur Tagung der Sektion Wissenschaftsforsschung in der deutschen Gesellschaft fur Soziologie, Heidelberg, 2-3 Dezember 1977.

Törnebohm, H., (1977) "Paradigms in fields of research" (Report no. 93, from Theory of Science, University of Gothenburg).

Note: We also used information from interviews and internal reports of the Swedish coniferous ecology project.

19

WORKING WITH OTHER DISCIPLINES†*

Earl R. Swanson

In this paper the term "discipline" refers to a specialized field of knowledge. Each discipline thus defined usually has a professional association and at least one journal. Equating a discipline to a profession is not completely satisfactory for all purposes, but it is consistent with common usage and convenient for the task at hand. Within a university context, a discipline corresponds approximately to an academic department, and disciplines develop when both faculty and administration come to recognize reasonably distinct areas of inquiry.

It is important to recognize that each discipline is usually composed of a set of narrower specializations and that the comprehensiveness of the discipline has at least three properties. First, there is a conceptual model, shared to some extent by individual members of the discipline. Second, there is also a set of phenomena common to the various specializations; and thirdly, the breadth of the discipline is rarely embodied within any one scholar (Campbell, 1969). Cohesiveness of the discipline is achieved through the overlapping of the multiple narrow specialties. This overlap facilitates a greater degree of communication than is possible between disciplines.

Agricultural economists have a long tradition of relationships with other disciplines. These relationships have taken a variety of forms. For many of us, our undergraduate education included a substantial component of the natural sciences, together with an occasional sampling of the social sciences. In graduate study the contact with other disciplines frequently focuses on the so-called tools that can be used by the agricultural economist. These skills and concepts are

† Adapted from the American Agricultural Economics Association's Fellow's Address: "Working with Other Disciplines," published in the *American Journal of Agricultural Economics.* December, 1979, 849-859.

* Reprinted by permission of the Agricultural Experiment Station, University of Minnesota from *Enabling Interdisciplinary Research: Perspectives From Agriculture, Forestry, and Home Economics*, edited by M.G. Russell, R.J. Sauer, and J.M. Barnes, 1982, pp. 19-27.

absorbed into our cluster of specialties and become a part of our collective professional competence.

Our record of joint research with the natural sciences and with engineering is well documented in Association surveys of agricultural economics literature. For at least two decades, a recurring theme of presidential addresses, invited papers, and Fellow's lectures at our annual meetings has been the admonition to borrow from our work with other disciplines, usually other social sciences, in a problem-solving mode.

NEED FOR INTERDISCIPLINARY APPROACH

A fundamental question has been raised in these admonitions: Who should integrate the results of research in the separate disciplines? Should it be the specialists working together in the research process, should it be the decision maker, or someone in between? Clearly, this question cannot be answered in the abstract, but the weight of professional advice has been to shift the emphasis to additional integration in the research process itself. Frequently the biggest contribution of our profession has been to help synthesize results from other disciplines (Nielson, 1974).

Although difficult to document, there has been some response to the call for interdisciplinary research articulated by Association speakers. The fact that reports from cooperative studies with other disciplines do not often appear in the *American Journal of Agricultural Economics* indicates in part that the research output from such projects does not lend itself easily to journal reporting, but also that such studies are not perceived to be in the mainstream of our profession. An informal survey of the *Journal* over the last twenty years indicates that virtually the only kind of joint research reported is that with natural scientists within colleges of agriculture.

This paper focuses on the process of research with other disciplines. An improved understanding of the process should assist us in allocating our research resources and, for that fraction devoted to working with other disciplines, to improve our effectiveness.

THE NATURE OF CROSS-DISCIPLINARY RESEARCH

In analyzing the nature of cross-disciplinary research, the classes of research activity can be distinguished along a continuum. These classes range from unidisciplinary to multidisciplinary to interdisciplinary to transdisciplinary, depending on the degree of integration, a concept introduced by Rossini et al. (1978). Note that this classification refers to a particular research activity or project and not to other relationships among the disciplines.

Castle has provided a more comprehensive analysis of cross-disciplinary relationships dealing with implications for university organization (Castle, 1970). Implicit in the concept of integration is an anticipated trade-off between comprehensiveness and depth of analysis. A narrow disciplinary mix may lead to analytical depth at the expense of comprehensiveness. This balance can only be judged with respect to the objective of the particular research effort. Research output in the form of a published report is the most easily available evidence for evaluating the degree of integration.

Editorial integration in research output is the most elementary level of integration. At minimum, it involves a report or a set of disciplinary reports on the same topic, edited without accounting for differences in terminology and concepts among the disciplines. While the report or reports may share an introduction and a conclusion, these sections may simply describe the history of the research project. A more integrated editorial treatment may involve consistent use of terminology throughout the study and the avoidance of isolated vocabularies. The reports that result from editorial integration may be multidisciplinary, in the sense of a patchwork quilt. On the other hand, interdisciplinary research ideally yields a seamless garment.

Interdisciplinary research is characterized by systemic integration. This implies a common view or representation which permeates and dominates the entire research effort. Evidence of strong integrative links among the various parts of the report is characteristic. Such integration may or may not be achieved by the use of a formal model.

Finally, at the upper limit of our continuum, transdisciplinary integration is theoretically a complete integration (Rossini et al., 1978). This classification implies that individual skills and disciplines are transcended and that scientists from several disciplines work together to create a new common cognitive map of the problem. This classification remains a theoretical ideal for any study of more than a very limited scope.

OBSTACLES TO CROSS-DISCIPLINARY RESEARCH

... Admonitions to work with other disciplines emphasize problem solving, implying that the research output should be useful to public

and/or private decision makers. Given problem-solving as the
rationale for working with other disciplines, a systems perspective
facilitates the following analysis of the knowledge bases in collaborative
research (Figure 1). This version, described by Mitroff, et al. (1979) and
by Mitroff and Pondy (1974), is sometimes referred to as
Singerian-Churchmanian model. Systems analysis in relation to

Figure 1. A Systems View of Problem Solving.

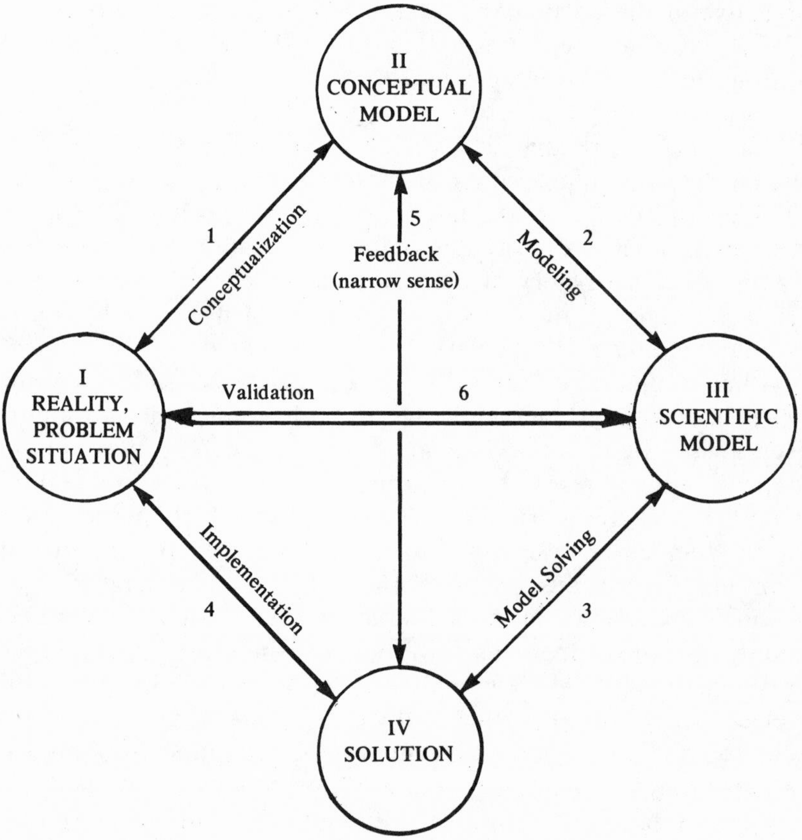

Source: Mitroff et al., p. 48
Note: Figure 1 is reproduced with the kind permission of
INTERFACES, published by the Institute of Management Sciences
and the Operations Research Society of America.

agricultural and natural resource economics has been discussed in volume 2 of the Association of Agricultural Economics' literature survey (Johnson and Rausser, 1977).

A particular research activity may begin with any of the four elements and may end at any of the four elements: problem, conceptual model, scientific model, or solution. Each path between these four elements is bi-directional, implying a wide diversity in the sequence of problem solving processes. In fact, the simple system of Figure 1 has 3,555 total sub-systems that can be formed by considering all possible ways of combining two, three, and four elements.

If, for example, a cross-disciplinary inquiry starts with element I, Reality or the Problem Situation, the transition to element II requires formulation of the conceptual model. In some cases the conceptual model may be formal, a more likely occurrence in economics and the natural sciences than in the other social sciences. The conceptualization process (II) defines and bounds the problem in broad terms, the variables that are to be considered, and the level of aggregation.

Development of the scientific or formal model (III) is the next step. This modeling process includes the translation of the conceptual model into relationships which are then given greater empirical identity. This is followed by the solution (IV) and, finally, implementation brings us back to an impact on the initial problem situation (I). For completeness, note that paths also exist for model validation, between I and III, and for feedback interactions between II and IV. Certainly, the ideal problem-solving loop I-II-III-IV-I is not often found in individual projects. More often, the research process includes a subset of these elements. . . .

Another loop used in agricultural economics is I-II-IV-I. This loop omits element III (Scientific Model). In research which follows this process, there is frequently confusion between conceptualization and modeling and an attempt to substitute a conceptual model for a scientific model. No matter how rich in detail the conceptual model might be, it can seldom substitute for a validated scientific model. Omission of the scientific model implies the loss of the opportunity to develop the logical structure of the conceptual model in a systematic way and to perform the important validation process. Thus the approach implied by the I-II-IV-I loop weakens the potential contribution to scientific knowledge.

To integrate approaches in the system (Figure 1), it is necessary for participants to communicate with others, ideally, in each of the four elements—problem, conceptual model, scientific model, and solution.

Perhaps the most important communication takes place with respect to the conceptual model. Each specialist can be expected to bring a specific paradigm (Kuhn, 1970; Maruyama, 1974; and Johnson and Rausser, 1977) into play as the problem is conceptualized. The degree to which core members of the research team share these paradigms is crucial in determining the level of integration in the final report.

As an example, consider collaboration between scientists using different conceptual models. Suppose that an agricultural economist is using a conceptual approach which combines the unidirectional-causal paradigm and the random-process paradigm, and that he or she is working with a biological scientist who subscribes to a mutual-causal paradigm.

The biological research worker looks for feedback loops in the system and for self-cancellation or self-reinforcement based on concepts of homeostasis. Although the economist may be familiar with related concepts from general equilibrium theory, the concept of the production function from the static theory of the firm does not extend very far toward achieving a common view with the biologist. Until they have at least moderate agreement on the paradigm, their prospects for successful interdisciplinary research are limited.

In this collaboration, the concepts and terms from statistics (Scientific Model, III) may form a useful communication device. Discussing the design of the experiment or the survey may lead back to an improved understanding of the differences and similarities in paradigms originating in the participants' disciplines. This awareness, communicated by both parties, may assist in achieving agreement on a conceptual model. . . .

Without at least a minimum of paradigm agreement among the specialists involved in joint research efforts, the frustrations from communication are likely to be high. In particular, if the communicating parties are unaware that they are using different paradigms and are aware only of differences in vocabulary or language, each party may view the communication difficulty as a result of the other specialist's deceptiveness, insincerity or lack of intelligence. This leads to the second aspect of research with other disciplines, the social process, which has two components—organizational alternatives and approaches to interdisciplinary research.

ORGANIZATIONAL ALTERNATIVES

The institutional setting (Petrie, 1976) is an important organizational consideration for the research team. Research which is to be both problem-solving and interdisciplinary presents great challenges in an academic environment.

In order to encourage cooperative research among disciplines, a number of academic institutions have formed units outside the usual departmental pattern (Ellis, 1974; Capener and Young, 1975). For example, special institutes have been established to study the energy problem, and so forth. Less formal structures such as committees have also been employed, especially within agricultural experiment stations. The problems of a reward and incentive system that follows disciplinary lines and of the attendant risks for younger staff members who participate in such interdisciplinary undertakings have been spelled out (Johnson, 1971; and in Koopmans, 1979).

The most successful interdisciplinary research projects at academic institutions appear to be those that have been externally funded and that have a rather limited group, with no more than four or five disciplines represented. The most desirable institutional environment for such a research team must be one that permits a substantial amount of start-up time and that has flexible hiring arrangements. It is important that institutions contemplating the support of interdisciplinary work understand such special considerations.

In the early 1970's, the College of Agriculture at the University of Illinois received a grant of approximately $600,000 from the Rockefeller Foundation for the project, "Nitrogen as an Environmental Quality Factor". The funds were allocated largely on a departmental or disciplinary basis, with five major groups participating: rural sociologists, agricultural economists, agricultural engineers, agronomists, and veterinary scientists. The common theme of nitrogen and the environment was the connecting link in the five separate efforts (Deeb and Sloan, 1975; Dickey and Lembke, 1978; Swanson, Taylor, and van Blokland, 1978; van Es and Sofranko, 1977; and Welch, 1979). A book on the project is being written by a single author.

This study corresponds to our multidisciplinary category because the separate disciplines approached a common problem, and the integration was at the editorial level, not at the conceptual level. Thus, the grant provided additional funds for departments to do research on the topic but did not necessarily provide the ingredients to integrate the results. The members of the team met to discuss one another's progress only occasionally.

A second project also had an environmental orientation. The project, "Soil Loss from Illinois Farms: Economic Analysis of Productivity Loss and Sediment Damage", was funded at a level of $122,000 by the Illinois Institute of Environmental Quality, a state organization. Six watersheds were studied (Guntermann, 1974). The organizational mode featured economics as the integrating discipline, and a formal model provided the scheme for integration.

This project's organization illustrates the modeling approach discussed above. Contributing specialists included an agronomist, an hydrologist, an agricultural economist, and a finance analyst. All persons were hired to work in the department of agricultural economics, an arrangement that clarified administrative allegiance. Early establishment of a satisfactory economic model permitted the contributors to identify their own objectives and contribution to the project.

The impact of the results on public policy can only be identified indirectly. A member of the Illinois Pollution Control Board mentioned that it would have been helpful if every important policy decision made by the Board could have had a comparable base of information. The usefulness of the report was, in part, a result of the interdisciplinary character of the project.

A third project, sponsored by National Science Foundation-Research Applied to National Needs, was an assessment of hail suppression technology (Changnon et al., 1977; Farhar et al., 1977). The eighteen-month project, carried out under a grant of $260,000, involved agricultural economists and other social scientists including sociologists, a political scientist, and a lawyer. Natural scientists included those from atmospheric science, one of whom served as a team leader, and an environmental scientist.

The organizational approach was a combination of negotiation among experts and scientific modeling. Although the central economic analysis used the usual economic concepts implicit in a national spatial-equilibrium model and the theory of the firm at the individual farm level, these concepts were modified in the course of the project. The modifications represented important inputs from sociologists and the lawyer, as well as others.

It is unlikely that a research team deliberately identifies the intellectual and social components of the projects' organizational patterns in advance. It is more likely that the project's organization evolves into a stable pattern by trial and error. Nevertheless, it is useful to identify four types of approaches to interdisciplinary research and briefly to discuss their strengths and weaknesses (Rossini et al., 1978). These refer principally to teams containing from three to five disciplines. . . . [See Selection 29, Figure 4.]

FOUR EXAMPLES

The type of research team organization that has been used for a given project can seldom be determined by reading the report of the results. Participants in the research process are the only source of information. Consequently, in order to illustrate the use of the classifications and concepts presented, I now draw on some research efforts in which I have recently participated.

In the preparation of the conclusions and policy recommendations, the political scientist and the lawyer had important contributions to make. Among other things, the study recommended that funds for research and development of hail suppression either be substantially increased or eliminated. As a result of the study, National Science Foundation has now discontinued the $5 million line in their budget for hail suppression research. In addition, many of the recommendations have found their way into statements of national policy (report to U.S. Secretary of Commerce from the Weather Modification Advisory Board, 1978). In terms of policy impact the success was due, in a large measure, to the interdisciplinary nature of the study.

A final example is the National Defense University Long-Range Climate Project. This project proceeded in three phases. First, climatologists assessed global temperature and precipitation changes to the year 2000 for different major crop-producing areas of the world. Then, five climate scenarios were constructed. The second phase produced estimates of yield responses to weather variables made by agronomists. This permitted an assessment of the yield consequences of each climate scenario. The final phase was the input of this information into the U.S. Department of Agriculture's grain-oilseed-livestock (GOL) model to determine the impact of the five climate scenarios on location of crop production, international trade, and crop prices. Although the GOL model provided the integrating framework, the climatologists were unaware, or had only very hazy conceptions of how the GOL model operated when they made their assessments. Similarly, the agronomists were not aware of the various aspects of the GOL model when they made their crop response predictions. Nevertheless, this model served as an integrating device for the total project. Organizationally, this project represented a mix of scientific modeling and integration by leader.

CONCLUSION

To sum up, it is my judgment that the modeling approach or integration by leader approach is more likely to provide a satisfactory environment in which agricultural economists may contribute, especially when agricultural economists work with the social sciences, natural sciences and engineering. However, one should not presume that what seems to be a natural integrative role for agricultural economists will automatically be perceived as such by scientists from other fields. These disciplines also have macro models (ecosystems, energy accounting systems, etc.) with integrative potential, and some melding of conceptual models may be required. In many contexts there is an integrating task that is beyond economics. However, if the research has an implementation objective such as the drafting of legislation, it is important to select a conceptual framework which includes modeling and implementation.

On the other hand, an alternative approach which appeals to some agricultural economists involved in joint research involving social scientists is negotiation among experts. Given the diversity in preferences and skills of the participating experts and a limited time frame, this approach may provide a better organizational structure for interdisciplinary research than one such as modeling which requires more complete synthesis.

This paper has attempted to describe the social processes of research which involves more than one discipline. Substantial effort, together with some compromise, is required to prevent research projects with interdisciplinary objectives from becoming multidisciplinary. Although the potential contribution from agricultural economists working with other disciplines remains high, allocation of large segments of our professional resources to such activity should be done with caution. The gains from specialization are too high to be sacrificed casually, and the opportunity costs of doing interdisciplinary research may easily be underestimated. It should be emphasized that the objective of the Association is to further the development of systematic knowledge in agricultural economics. A part of the development of that systematic knowledge requires working with other disciplines, and it is important that we do that part well.

References

. . . .

Campbell, Donald T. (1969) "Ethnocentrism of Disciplines and the Fish-Scale Model of Omniscience." *Interdisciplinary Relationships in the Social Sciences*, ed. M. Sherif and C.W. Sherif. Chicago: Aldine Publishing Co.

Capener, Harold R., and Robert J. Young. (1975) "Interdisciplinary Research in the University." *Nitrogen and Phosphorous: Food Production, Waste and the Environment*, ed. Keith S. Porter. Ann Arbor, Mich.: Ann Arbor Science Publishers.

. . . .

Castle, Emery N. (1970) "Priorities in Agricultural Economics for the 1970's." *Amer. J. Agr. Econ.* 52:831-40.

Changnon, Stanley A., Jr., Ray Jay Davis, Barbara C. Farhar, J. Eugene Haas, J. Loreena Ivens, Martin V. Jones, Donald A. Klein, Dean Mann, Griffith M. Mortan, Jr., Steven T. Sonka, Earl R. Swanson, C. Robert Taylor, Jon van Blokland. (1977) *Hail Supression, Impacts and Issues. Final Report*, NSF Grant ERP75-09980. Urbana: Illinois State Water Survey.

. . . .

Deeb, Barbara S., and Kenneth W. Sloan. (1975) *Nitrates, Nitrites, and Health*. University of Illinois Agr. Exp. Sta. Bull. 750, May.

Dickey, E.C., and W.D. Lembke. (1978) *Wells and Ponds: Water Quality and Supply*. University of Illinois Agr. Exp. Sta. Bull. 758, July.

Ellis, Robert H. (1974) *The Planning and Management of Problem-Oriented, Interdisciplinary Research at Academic Institutions*. Hartford: Connecticut Renssalaer Hartford Graduate Center.

Farhar, Barbara C., Stanley A. Cangnon, Jr., Earl R. Swanson, Ray J. Davis, and J. Eugene Haas. (1977) *Hail Suppression and Society. Summary of Technology Assessment of Hail Suppression*. Urbana: Illinois State Water Survey.

. . . .

Guntermann, Karl, M.T. Lee, A.S. Narayanan, and E.R. Swanson. (1974) *Soil Loss From Illinois Farms: Economic Analysis of Productivity Loss and Sedimentation Damage*. Chicago: Illinois Institute for Environmental Quality Coducment No. 74-62, December.

. . . .

Johnson, Glenn L. (1971) "The Quest for Relevance in Agricultural Economics." *Amer. J. Agr. Econ.* 53:728-39.

Johnson, S.R., and Gordon C. Rausser. (1977) "Systems Analysis and Simulation" *A Survey of Agricultural Economics Literature, Vol. 2*, ed. George G. Judge et al. Minneapolis: University of Minnesota Press.

Koopmans, Tjaling C. (1979) "Economics among the Sciences." *Amer. Econ. Rev.* 69:1-13.

Kuhn, Thomas S. (1970) *The Structure of Scientific Revolutions*, 2nd ed. Chicago: University of Chicago Press.

Maruyama, Magoroh. (1974) "Paradigms and Communication." *Technological Forecasting and Social Change* 6:3-32.

Mitroff, Ian and Louis R. Pondy. (1974) "On the Organization of Inquiry: A Comparison of Some Radically Different Approaches to Policy Analysis." *Public Admin. Rev.* 34:471-79.

Mitroff, Ian I., Frederick Betz, Louis R. Pondy, and Francisco Sagasti. (1974) "On Managing Science in the Systems Age: Two Schemas for the Study of Science as a Whole Systems Phenomenon." *INTERFACES* 4:46-58.

. . . .

Nielson, James. (1974) "Accountability and Innovation: Challenges for Agricultural Economists." *Amer. J. Agr. Econ.* 56:865-77.

. . . .

Petrie, Hugh G. (1976) "Do You See What I See? The Epistemology of Interdisciplinary Inquiry." *J. Aesthetic Educ.* 10:29-43.
. . . .

Rossini, F.A., Porter, A.L., Kelly, P., and Chubin, D.E. (1978) *Frameworks and Factors Affecting Integration Within Technology Assessments*, Dept. Soc. Sci. Tech. Rep. NSF Grant ERS 76-04474, Atlanta, GA, Georgia Institute of Technology.
. . . .

Swanson, E.R., C.R. Taylor, and P.J. Von Blokland. (1978) *Economic Effects of Controls on Nitrogen Fertilizer.* Illinois State University Agr. Exp. Sta. Bull. 757, April.

. . . .

van Es, J.C., and A.J. Sofranko. (1977) *Environmental Decision Making: The Role of Community Leaders.* Illinois State University Agr. Exp. Sta. Bull. 756, September.

Weather Modification Advisory Board. (1978) *The Management of Weather Resources,* vol. 1. Washington, D.C.: Department of Commerce, Report to the Secretary.

Welch, L. Fred. (1979) *Nitrogen Use and Behavior in Crop Production.* Illinois State University Agr. Exp. Sta. Bull. 761, February.
. . . .

20

INTERDISCIPLINARY RESEARCH AND INTEGRATION: THE CASE OF CO$_2$ AND CLIMATE*

Robert S. Chen†

Introduction

The possibility of significant climate changes due to increasing carbon dioxide (CO$_2$) in the atmosphere presents an unprecedented challenge to modern society. The challenge is to respond effectively to the 'CO$_2$ problem' in advance, despite many remaining uncertainties. Possible responses range from a 'wait-and-see' policy to immediate actions to curb CO$_2$ emissions. To put decisionmaking on a firmer basis will require substantial natural and social science input. One key task for social scientists is to examine: (1) how and with what success people and their societies have responded to environmental stress in the past and present; (2) how they might respond to the prospect or advent of CO$_2$-induced changes in the future; and (3) what policy options are available or can be developed to prevent or mitigate potentially adverse impacts of CO$_2$ increases. Given the wide variety of possible environmental stresses, societal responses, and policy options and in view of the complexity of interactions among these, research to deal with CO$_2$ increases must involve extensive collaboration among scientists from many different academic disciplines. Considerable effort will also be needed to combine and translate individual research results into realistic, useful policy information. How *interdisciplinary* research can be fostered and *integration* of research results achieved is the focus of this paper.

---

* Reprinted by permission of D. Reidel Publishing Company from *Social Science Research and Climate Change*, edited by R.S. Chen, E. Boulding, and S.H. Schneider, pp. 230-248. Copyright 1983 by D. Reidel Publishing Company, Dordrecht, Holland.

† The views expressed in this paper are those of the author and do not necessarily represent the views of the Climate Board, the National Academy of Sciences, or the University of North Carolina.

Critical Research Considerations in the CO_2 Context

Several unusual aspects of the CO_2 problem and society's possible responses to it raise important issues that need to be considered in planning and conducting research.

First, the problem is *unique* in both scale and complexity. Increasing carbon dioxide in the atmosphere is generally believed to result from over a century of past fossil-fuel use, and possibly some land uses, on which modern industrial and agricultural development depends (Geophysics Study Committee, 1977). Present-day populations rely heavily on fossil-fuel energies for their survival and, in light of continuing population growth, are likely to continue to do so for at least several decades (OECD, 1979a: 39; WAES, 1977: 242-255). CO_2 increases may lead to potentially major global changes to the environment, with attendant effects—both beneficial and adverse—on human activities and welfare. Responses to the advent or prospect of CO_2-induced changes also could be global, and, in turn, could have widespread feedbacks to the environment and society (Climate Board, 1980).

Second, the CO_2 problem is inescapably *normative*. Climate changes will affect different people in different ways at different times. Even the interpretation of some specific effect as either beneficial or adverse is likely to vary greatly among individuals, depending on their own perceptions, values, and priorities (Chen, 1980). A drought-induced rise in food prices, for example, may help farmers but hurt consumers. Moreover, many value-laden issues arise quickly in responses to the CO_2 problem, as, for example, in making explicit tradeoffs between reducing CO_2 emissions and providing needed energy. Such issues include equity in the distribution of impacts and in the distribution of benefits from CO_2-producing activities, responsibility for adverse changes, the rights of future versus present generations, and the 'proper' relationship between humanity and the global environment. These normative aspects extend the bounds of the CO_2 problem well beyond the 'factual', technical realms of the natural sciences into consideration of social and ethical factors.

Finally, the challenge to society posed by the CO_2 problem is, as has been mentioned, *unprecedented*. Unlike many past situations, society has the opportunity to deal with the problem explicitly and in advance—not by default (e.g., see Brown, 1980; WMO, 1979: 61).

Many different policy options exist, ranging from 'doing nothing different' or 'more study' to active measures to 'build resilience' and even 'reduce the CO_2 insult' by altering energy, agricultural, or land-use policies (Schneider and Chen, 1980). Choosing among these options will be difficult, in part because of the unique and normative facets of the CO_2 problem and the great uncertainties that exist at present in the likelihood, magnitude, and timing of CO_2-induced climate changes, and in part because of the many different parties that are likely to be involved in any globally effective responses.

These unique, normative, and unprecedented aspects of the CO_2 problem have important implications for research. Obviously, no single academic discipline, nor several working by themselves, can provide all the answers needed. Many different disciplines must be called upon, and their expertise blended into an interdisciplinary effort. Some barriers to and requirements for effective interdisciplinary research are discussed in the next several sections. A second implication is that research must specifically address the decisions society may have to or may be able to make and the choices or policy options available to it. The role of various decision makers and their perceptions, evaluations, and choices thus becomes important. Moreover, it is notable that research is itself part of our response to the prospect of CO_2-induced climate change. We therefore need to understand what the benefits and limitations of research are, in terms of how research could materially change our understanding and perception of the problem and our ability to develop and implement timely, effective responses to it. These issues are discussed in more detail in Sections 7 and 8.

Another implication is that research on the CO_2 problem must be 'tied in' with research on other environmental and social issues. Given limited resources of time, money, and scientific talent, we must take advantage of past and present research on similar problems such as the societal impact of present-day climate fluctuations or non-climatic, slowly evolving environmental stresses on society, e.g., soil erosion. Indeed, an important by-product of research on the CO_2 problem may be the new knowledge gained that can be applied to these other problems—regardless of how critical the CO_2 problem itself becomes. In particular, we must look for new knowledge concerning societal adaptability to environmental stress. This subject is treated more extensively in Section 9.

Societal Response to Increasing CO_2: An Interdisciplinary Research Problem

Many different social-science disciplines can make important contributions to the understanding of potential responses to CO_2-induced climate changes or policies implemented to prevent or mitigate them. As is true of many other important human problems, the possibility of CO_2-induced changes is primarily of concern because of its potential stresses on society with consequent adverse impacts on human welfare. Human experience in responding to such stress and impacts is obviously immense and much of it could be directly applied to the CO_2 problem. In the fields of history and geography, the effects of climatic variability and change on various aspects of society have been extensively, if not consistently, examined through detailed case studies and comparisons among cases from different regions, cultures, and time periods (e.g., Rabb, 1983; Warrick and Riebsame, 1981). Economics provides a number of tools capable of analyzing some of the stresses on local, regional, national, and international economies that might arise; economics methods also help to quantify the potential monetary costs and benefits for different groups of people (e.g., Smith, 1980). Political science and law can help us to predict the ability of local, national, and international institutions to assess and respond to the CO_2 problem based on past experience with other environmental and social problems (e.g., Mann, 1983; Weiss, 1983). Anthropology and sociology can relate economic and institutional changes to their likely implication for people and various kinds of social organization (e.g., Torry, 1983; Panel IV, 1980). Psychology is important because of the key role of perception, evaluation, and choice in individual and group responses to actual or perceived stress (e.g., Fischoff and Furby, 1983). The humanities (e.g., philosophy) are needed to help clarify some of the difficult normative issues raised with regard to such fundamental questions as humanity's relationship to nature and the rights of present versus future generations (Schneider and Morton, 1981).

Research undertaken solely within each isolated discipline would be of relatively little value to understanding the CO_2 problem as a whole. The 'net' effect of climate changes, or of actions taken to adjust to them, will emerge from the interaction of many different processes. Changes in climate or in energy and agricultural policies will have diverse consequences for, and result in diverse responses by, different groups in society. These responses will in turn cause their own impacts and might lead to responses, which will in turn produce further repercussions, and so on. Influencing these responses will be the various perceptions of CO_2 issues held by individuals within a hierarchy of different decision units, including households, corporate bodies, governments, and international and non-governmental organizations. Furthermore, trends or changes in social and environmental factors, such as growing populations, increasing worldwide industrialization, altered economic interdependence, and resource depletion, are certain to affect the patterns of societal responses.

A research task is thus to explore the extremely complex and dynamic *system of interactions* among climate, other aspects of the environment, and society (e.g., see Butzer, 1980; SCOPE, 1978). Research efforts should not be restricted entirely to present divisions of scientific methods and knowledge represented by traditional academic disciplines. Rather, research should draw from diverse disciplinary expertise and combine and integrate available capabilities in ways that directly address the interactions among environmental and societal factors. Such an *interdisciplinary* approach will help match our evolving analytic abilities with the complexity of various aspects of the CO_2 problem.

Interdisciplinary research on the CO_2 problem could take different forms. Fischhoff (1980), for example, identifies four modes of interdisciplinary work:
  (1) clarification of assumptions and paradigms used in traditional disciplinary research to generalize results;
  (2) inclusion of factors other than those normally considered in disciplinary research;
  (3) 'borrowing' of methods and approaches developed in other disciplines; and
  (4) collaboration among scientists from different disciplines.

Interdisciplinary research may thus involve one scientist or many, one-way or two-way communication between disciplines, and different degrees of interaction among scientists. A higher degree of interaction is often encouraged by forming a research 'team' of scientists from different disciplines in one location to enable them to learn to work together effectively over an extended period (a year or more) (Fischhoff, 1980; Mar *et al.*, 1976). Alternatively, a 'pool' model is sometimes employed in which a center or institute serves as a locus and source of talent for a variety of interdisciplinary (or multi-disciplinary) activities (Mar *et al.*, 1976). With regard to the CO_2 problem, although the first

three of Fischhoff's modes of interdisciplinary work will be important
in some instances, extensive collaboration and interaction among
people of diverse backgrounds will be indispensable to effective
research on the CO_2 problem (Panel IV, 1980; DOE, 1980). . . .

Management of Interdisciplinary Research on the CO_2 Problem

How can interdisciplinary research on the CO_2 problem be encouraged
and managed effectively? Several interrelated needs are evident from
the previous discussion of difficulties. Although specifically cast in the
context of CO_2 research, these needs also apply to interdisciplinary
research in general.

First, new or modified institutional arrangements are clearly needed
to deal with the special problems posed by the interdisciplinary nature
of the CO_2 problem. For example, interdisciplinary experience and
publications should be given explicit credit in hiring and promotional
policies. Considerable attention should be devoted to finding
interdisciplinary thinkers and workers, and to developing disciplinary
balance within compatible teams of researchers. New internal and
external quality-control mechanisms should be established that are
capable of generating constructive criticism and ensuring the high
quality of the interdisciplinary, as well as disciplinary, aspects of
research. This should include the development of clearcut standards for
the peer review of interdisciplinary research, such as those purposed by
Schneider (1977: 41) and used as a basis for peer reviews in the
interdisciplinary journal, *Climatic Change:* '(a) disciplinary accuracy,
(b) clarity of cross-disciplinary communications, and (c) utilization and
combination of existing knowledge from many fields to help solve a
problem or to raise or advance knowledge about a new issue'.

Second, continuing high-level managerial commitment to
interdisciplinary research on the CO_2 problem is needed. Management
should help overcome problems caused by traditional,
discipline-oriented attitudes and institutions, and try to increase
support for interdisciplinary CO_2 research among researchers, their
scientific colleagues, and funding organizations (Horvitz and Evans,
1977). In particular, management of interdisciplinary CO_2 research
should itself be interdisciplinary, at least in the sense of having an
appreciation for and a working knowledge of the breadth and
complexity of the problem, including its implications for policy and the
approaches necessary to analyze it. Often, effective management

depends on the vigorous leadership of an interdisciplinary individual. Another way to ensure interdisciplinary management is to establish advisory or steering groups consisting of individuals experienced in interdisciplinary research, familiar with the broad aspects of the CO_2 problem, and willing to commit adequate time to keeping up with—and criticizing—research developments.

Third, stable financial support for interdisciplinary CO_2 research is a prerequisite. It must be recognized that the development of effective interdisciplinary research efforts may take large investments of time and resources—for a small group of three researchers, at least one year and many tens of thousands of dollars each, according to Mar et al. (1976). Individuals and groups may undergo an 'incubation period' of at least a year, and perhaps several, during which they may produce little in the way of interdisciplinary products. In some instances, money alone may not suffice. Many universities, for example, limit the time that their faculty members can spend on outside projects. Resources and services such as office space, laboratory facilities, travel funds, support staff, and financial assistance for students (e.g., assistantships, scholarships, and grants)* may be important incentives (Mar et al., 1976). Support should also extend to continuing quality control, interaction with users, and dissemination of results both inside and outside of the scientific community.

Fourth, the 'infrastructure' of interdisciplinary research on the CO_2 problem needs increasing support. Included in this infrastructure are networks of scientists engaged in interdisciplinary efforts such as environmental and social impact assessment and technology assessment; interdisciplinary and multi-disciplinary journals, newsletters, and other publications; and assorted workshops, symposia, courses, grants, and other educational activities supported by various public and private organizations. This infrastructure will be important to fostering communication and reducing institutional and methodological barriers among scientists from different disciplines. Such infrastructure could form the basis for careful, conscientious peer review of interdisciplinary work on the CO_2 problem, and help to improve overall scientific credibility and acceptance. Moreover, it could help attract the talent needed for interdisciplinary research on the CO_2 problem and begin the process of building a solid community of scientists involved in and supportive of such research.

---

* The author's own involvement in interdisciplinary research on the CO_2 problem was made possible in part by an unrestrictive graduate fellowship.

Finally, improvements in the 'science' of interdisciplinary research as applied to the CO_2 problem are needed (UNEP, 1980; Kates, 1980). Past examples of related research, such as that for the stratospheric ozone issue, should be closely examined and publicized (e.g., Glantz *et al.*, 1981). The advantages and disadvantages of various possible modes of interdisciplinary research such as those identified by Fischhoff (1980) and various ways of organizing interdisciplinary collaborative efforts should be assessed critically (Mar *et al.*, 1976; Scribner and Chalk, 1977; see also, Jones, 1979). Basic assumptions and methods within disciplines should be continually reviewed and reassessed (e.g., Dunlap, 1980; Bohrnstedt, 1980; Torry, 1979). Techniques such as scenario analysis that can help integrate diverse knowledge should be reviewed and documented (e.g., Ericksen, 1975; Lave, 1981). A variety of workshops, conferences, commissioned studies, and other activities should contribute greatly to such efforts (e.g., DOE, 1980).

Satisfaction of the five needs listed above cannot of course guarantee the success of interdisciplinary research on the CO_2 problem. However, unless steps to encourage such research are taken, the collaboration and interaction critical to useful results will be difficult to achieve. Indeed, for the CO_2 question and perhaps other issues, a major problem may be to gain sufficient scientific interest, especially among social scientists, to attract competent workers to the problem. Clearly, a long-term commitment to the funding of interdisciplinary research will be a principal stimulus of such interest. This issue is discussed further in Section IX.

Integration of Research Results in the CO_2 Context

An interdisciplinary approach to the CO_2 problem will help to ensure that research on important questions is analyzed from a broad perspective using a variety of techniques when necessary. Some means is also needed to formulate research questions and integrate the "answers" that are obtained into useful policy information.

A useful starting point is the analytic framework suggested by geographers Warrick and Riebsame (1981). Their conceptualization attempts to isolate explicitly many interactions among climate, other aspects of the environment, and society. It gives explicit recognition to the role of information, evaluation, and choice at many points in the model. Associated with this framework is a corresponding set of key research questions which divide the broad problem into (hopefully) more researchable parts. The framework and associated questions are designed to permit a consistent and systematic integration of knowledge about the CO_2 problem in several ways. Even though contemporary society as a whole has never before experienced the sort of massive climate change projected as possible from increasing carbon dioxide, past cultures have been subjected to major changes in climate. Additionally, some parts of modern society have experienced other kinds of environmental stress and shorter-term, more severe climatic variations which could provide useful analogues. With such experience as a 'laboratory', it may be possible to develop and test various physical, environmental, economic, and social models of society/environment/climate interactions. One approach, for example, would be to study particular past or present situations in which significant climate/society linkages are more easily discernible, for instance, marginal agricultural systems in arid lands or habitation in Arctic regions (Panel IV, 1980). If reasonable hypotheses of human/climate interactions can be developed from these case studies and applied to the more general research questions, they can then be incorporated into the overall framework. The proposed framework and associated questions thus provide one possible mechanism for helping individual researchers to keep their efforts focused on the most important issues and to combine diverse research findings into an integrated understanding of possible societal responses and their likely consequences. Other mechanisms should also be explored.

It is also important to note that the study of climate-society interaction can itself be approached at different levels of abstraction and complexity. Kates (1980), for example, postulates a hierarchy of models of the interaction between climate and society (see Figure 1): the input-output model, the interactive model, the interactive model with feedback, and the interactive model with feedback and underlying process. As in the natural sciences (e.g., climatology), there are clearly tradeoffs among such models between their tractability, verifiability, and realism. Ideally, one would want a highly realistic model which could generate highly accurate predictions of societal/environmental interactions efficiently. In practice, this is, of course, difficult in all but a few simple examples. While it may be possible to quantify partially the direct effects of some change in a climatic parameter on a particular economic unit or sector, indirect impacts arising from

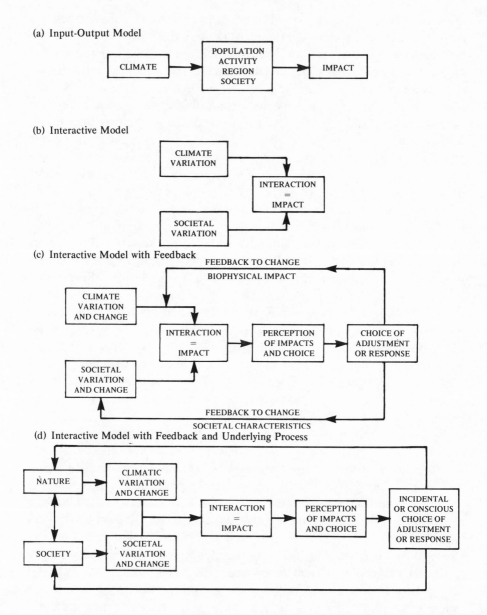

(a) Input-Output Model

(b) Interactive Model

(c) Interactive Model with Feedback

(d) Interactive Model with Feedback and Underlying Process

Fig. 1. A hierarchy of models of Climate-Society relationships
(from Kates, 1980)

intersectoral interactions or societal changes and responses are much more difficult to analyze quantitatively—or even qualitatively. Yet these indirect impacts could outweigh or mitigate the direct impacts. Models that fail to include important pathways or mechanisms for such impacts could yield extremely misleading results.

Research as a Response to the Prospect of CO_2 Impacts

The present disparity between disciplinary analytic abilities and the unprecedented number of interconnected dimensions of the CO_2 problem raise several important questions regarding the role of research. Research on the CO_2 problem is itself a response to the *perception* that CO_2-induced climate changes could adversely affect people and society in the future. It is essentially one way society can find out more about the implications of the CO_2 problem. We must therefore ask whether research by itself is an inadequate response—or perhaps even a harmful one. Will sufficient information of sufficient certainty be available in time for adequate actions to be taken to prevent, mitigate, or adapt to CO_2-induced changes? Is it likely that 'knowledge can probably be made to grow faster than the problem', as one report asserts (Climate Board, 1980:9)? To delay actions stronger than research (i.e., actions that could mitigate CO_2 increases or their impacts) merely commits posterity to a larger 'dose' of CO_2 than if those mitigating actions were taken now. Are the risks imposed by the delay of such more active responses worth taking in light of the present benefits from CO_2-emitting activities? Will the new knowledge that may be gained from research be likely to negate or increase the need for action or improve the effectiveness of future actions? Finally, are there actions which could be taken now that might allow society more options and choices in the future? These might include vigorous development of alternative energy systems or active efforts to make societal adaptation to environmental change easier (Schneider and Chen, 1980; Kellogg and Schware, 1981).

Obviously, inasmuch as words such as 'sufficient', 'adequate', or 'worth' are normative, these issues are value-laden policy questions. They cannot be answered by research alone. Nevertheless, research can certainly help to assess the options now available, their possible consequences, and the present areas of uncertainty. Research should be able to give a better idea of present and likely future levels of certainty and the usefulness of more knowledge and increased certainty in guiding future policy decisions. It could, by examining past cases, also identify the potential dangers and benefits of making decisions under uncertainty versus delaying them. Finally, and perhaps most importantly, research could help clarify the opportunities and constraints which condition society's decisions and could help begin the process of expanding the options available to it. Despite the cautions raised about unavoidable normative issues, research should nevertheless be able to help strengthen the scientific basis for present and future decisions about the CO_2 problem—provided the research results are disseminated in such a way as to allow non-specialists to easily separate issues of 'fact' from those of 'values'.

Research 'Tie-ins'

Not only must we be aware of the role of research in societal responses to the CO_2 problem, we must also recognize the links between research on the CO_2 problem and research on other social issues. Limitations in time, money, and scientific talent may restrict the amount of effort that can be expended on the CO_2 problem alone. However, the CO_2 problem is itself inextricably connected with such important social issues as future economic development in the developing and developed nations and population pressures on the environment and society. On the one hand, economic development and population growth, if made possible by increasing fossil-fuel use, wood burning, and massive clearing of land, are likely to be key factors in how fast CO_2-induced climate changes develop and how serious they become—if they occur at all. Developments such as breakthroughs in renewable energy technologies, resource depletion, or restrictions on fossil-fuel trade could also be important. On the other hand, the most serious impacts of CO_2-induced climate changes may well be the intensification of existing social problems such as hunger, poverty, poor health and sanitation, mass migration, environmental degradation, social unrest, and political tension. For example, greater climate variability, including more severe weather and seasonal extremes such as droughts, heat waves, cold spells, and persistent rains, could severely reduce food production, increase energy requirements, and aggravate water-related problems (e.g., shortages, floods, and contamination of drinking water). Such impacts are now visible at present levels of climate variability (e.g., Center for Environmental Assessment Services, 1980). Non-climatic events or episodes such as volcanic eruptions, earthquakes, trade embargoes, and wars also cause stresses on society, and engender responses, similar to those that might result from climate changes.

These two-way connections between CO_2 and other problems suggest that research efforts should be closely linked, or 'tied-in', with each other (Panel IV, 1980). Research on the CO_2 problem should be able to proceed more quickly and effectively by taking advantage of past and present research on these other problems and the policies used to deal with them. Conversely, society may well benefit from the new knowledge obtained from research on the CO_2 problem, and policies to prevent or ameliorate it, that can be applied to other problems. We might, for example, learn how to modify existing social institutions to make society more "resilient" to environmental stress or learn what social indicators are good precursors of social change. Research on policies such as the development of non-fossil fuel alternatives or food reserves would be applicable to other important social issues as well as to the CO_2 problem. Thus, even if the CO_2 problem proves moot, whether because of some new information or some breakthrough in energy-supply systems that reverses the trend of increasing fossil-fuel use, research on the CO_2 problem should itself have wide-reaching uses outside of the CO_2 context. This possibility may be one of the most important factors in generating interest in the CO_2 problem among scientists, who are likely to have other demands competing for their time, and particularly among those in control of research resources, who may feel that other social problems like poverty and nuclear proliferation are more important and deserving of research resources. Indeed, a major payoff of research on the CO_2 problem may in fact be the interdisciplinary and international linkages among scientists and others that it generates, which could provide a basis—and hopefully a successful precedent—for international cooperation on global, short- or long-term environmental and social problems.

Conclusion

The great variety of potential societal responses to the prospect or advent of CO_2-induced climate changes poses an unprecedented research problem of extraordinary breadth and complexity in the physical, biological, and social sciences and also in the humanities. Experience in integrating inputs from the many disciplines of relevance is limited, and the analytic techniques available are often crude. A comprehensive, interdisciplinary research approach will therefore be crucial to obtaining realistic, credible research results that can help society respond to the problem effectively. Development of such a research approach will require innovations, especially in the organization, nurture, and management of interdisciplinary research efforts. Many of these innovations may fail. Thus, interdisciplinary research should be viewed as a flexible, 'trial-and-error' type of evolutionary process. Indeed, enough of such endeavors may, at best, lead eventually to the development of a comprehensive theory of climate and society interactions; at the least, they should help put CO_2-related decisionmaking on a firmer scientific basis.

As a starting point, some key needs can be identified which any coordinated program of research on the CO_2 problem should attempt to meet. These are:

— the need to define, and continually refine, conceptual frameworks of climate/society interactions;

— the need to split the overall problem into a set of focused, disciplinary and interdisciplinary research questions which divide the problem into more tractable parts and explicitly address the role of information, evaluation, and choice at various levels;

— the need to develop a variety of approaches and techniques that may transcend traditional disciplinary boundaries and are able to address the climate/society system at different levels of organization and complexity; and

— the need to develop flexible, innovative approaches to research management, with special emphasis on quality control, stable funding, professional opportunities, and interdisciplinary supervision.

Ways of meeting these needs, though likely to be based initially on disciplinary methods and perspectives, will require ongoing refinements, largely and perhaps unavoidable through 'learning by doing'. Efforts must especially be made to ensure that research questions are relevant to the overall climate/society system and that they are posed so as to be intelligible to a variety of disciplines. Research should be flexible enough to direct a wide range of human experience toward the unique, unprecedented, and normative aspects of the CO_2 problem. It must stress the identification of mechanisms that can help us to respond to the prospect or advent of CO_2-induced changes, including consideration of the potential impact of the research itself. Such research should produce results that are directly applicable to many other problems involving interactions between society and the environment. Similarly, it is important that experience gained from research on such other problems be utilized in CO_2 research. These 'tie-ins' call for research efforts that are particularly sensitive to advances and retreats in the progress of other research across the physical, biological, and social sciences. Such efforts will require the disciplinary and interdisciplinary skills of scientists of extraordinary tolerance and creativity and the managerial talents of research sponsors of extraordinary breadth and judgment.

Acknowledgements

The author gratefully acknowledges the many comments and suggestions provided by the members of the Social and Institutional Responses Working Group, AAAS Climate Project, and the prompt and efficient typing of Doris Bouadjemi.

References

. . . .

Bohrnstedt, G.W.: 1980, 'Social Science Methodology: The Past Twenty-Five Years', *Am. Behav. Sci.* 23, 781.

. . . .

Brown, Jr., Hon. G.E.: 1980, 'The CO_2 Problem: Unprecedented Challenges and Opportunities', in *Workshop on Environmental and Societal Consequences of a Possible CO2-Induced Climate Change*, CONF-7904143, Carbon Dioxide Effects Research and Assessment Program, Rept. No. 009, U.S. Department of Energy, Washington, D.C., pp. 122-5.

Butzer, K.W.: 1980, 'Civilizations: Organisms or Systems?', *Am. Sci.* 68, 517.

. . . .

Center for Environmental Assessment Services: 1980, 'Climate Impact Assessment: United States', Annual Summary 1980, National Oceanic and Atmospheric Administration, Washington, D.C. 66 pp.

Chen, R.S.: 1980, 'Impacts of Carbon Dioxide Induced Climate Change', in *Proceedings, Bio-Energy '80: World Congress and Exposition*, Bio-Energy Council, Washington, D.C. pp. 544-7.

. . . .

Climate Board: 1980, Letter Report of the *Ad Hoc* Study Panel on Economic and Social Aspects of Carbon Dioxide Increase, National Academy of Sciences, Washington, D.C., 11 pp.

Climate Board: 1981, *Managing Climatic Resources and Risks*, Report of the Panel on the Effective Use of Climate Information in Decision Making, National Academy Press, Washington, D.C., 151 pp.

. . . .

DOE: 1980, *Environmental and Societal Consequences of a CO_2-Induced Climate Change: A Research Agency*, Vol. 1, DOE/EV/10019-01, Carbon Dioxide Effects Research and Assessment Program, Rept. No. 013, U.S. Department of Energy, Washington, D.C., 125 pp.

Dunlap, R.E.: 1980, 'Paradigmatic Change in Social Science: From Human Exemptions to an Ecological Paradigm', *Am. Behav. Sci.* 24, 5.

Ericksen, N.J.: 1975, *Scenario Methodology in Natural Hazards Research*, University of Colorado Institute of Behavioral Science, Boulder, CO.

. . . .

Fischhoff, B.: 1980, 'No Man is a Discipline', in Harvey, J.H. (ed.), *Cognition, Social Behavior, and the Environment*, Eribaum, Hillsdale, N.J., pp. 579-583.

Fischhoff, B. and Furby, L.: 1983, 'Psychological Dimensions of Climatic Change', in Chen, R.S., Boulding, E.M., and Schneider, S.H. (eds), *Social Science Research and Climate Change: An Interdisciplinary Appraisal*, D. Reidel, Dordrecht, Holland, 177-204 (this volume).

Geophysics Study Committee: 1977, *Energy and Climate*, National Academy of Sciences, Washington, D.C., 158 pp.

. . . .

Glantz, M.H., Robinson, J., and Krenz, M.E.: 1981, 'Report of a Workshop on Improving the Science of Climate Impact Study: An Assessment of Five Major Climate Impact Studies of the 1970's', 30 June - 2 July 1981, Institute for Energy Analysis, Oak Ridge, TN.

. . . .

Horvitz, D. and Evans, N.: 1977, 'Recommendations for Creating Effective Management Styles for Interdisciplinary Research', in Scribner, R.A. and Chalk, R.A. (eds.), *Adapting Science to Social Needs: Conference Proceedings*, American Association for the Advancement of Science, Rept. No. 78-R-6, pp. 239-42.

. . . .

Jones, C.O.: 1979, 'If I Knew Then . . . (A Personal Essay on Committees and Public Policy)', *Policy Analysis* 5, 473.

Kates, R.W.: 1980, 'Improving the Science of Impact Study', Project Summary for the Scientific Committee on Problems of the Environment, International Council of Scientific Unions, Paris, France, 19 pp.

Kellogg, W.W. and Schware, R.: 1981, *Climate Change and Society: Consequences of Increasing Atmospheric Carbon Dioxide*, Aspen Institute for Humanistic Studies and Westview Press, Boulder, CO, 178 pp.

. . . .

Lave, L.B.: 1981, 'Mitigating Strategies for CO_2 Problems', Collaborative Paper CP-81-14, International Institute for Applied Systems Analysis, Laxenburg, Austria, 10 pp.

. . . .

Mar, B.W., Newell, W.T., and Saxberg, B.O.: 1976, 'Interdisciplinary Research in the University Setting', *Env. Sci. Tech.* 10, 650.

. . . .

OECD: 1979a, *Interfutures: Facing the Future*, Organization for Economic Co-Operation and Development, Paris, France, 425 pp.

. . . .

Panel IV: 1980, 'Social and Institutional Responses', in *Workshop on Environmental and Societal Consequences of a Possible CO_2-Induced Climate Change*, CONF-7904143, Carbon Dioxide Effects Research and Assessment Program, Rept. No. 009, U.S. Department of Energy, Washington, D.C., pp. 79-103.

Rabb, T.K.: 1983, 'Climate and Society in History: A Research Agenda', in Chen, R.S., Boulding, E.M., and Schneider, S.H. (eds.), *Social Science Research and Climate Change: An Interdisciplinary Appraisal*, D. Reidel, Dordrecht, Holland, 61-70 (this volume).
. . . .

Schneider, S.H.: 1977a, 'Quality Review Standards for Interdisciplinary Research', paper presented at 'Can Research Institutions Accommodate Interdisciplinary Researchers?', Symposium at 143rd Annual Meeting of the American Association for the Advancement of Science, Denver, CO, 20-25 February 1977 (taped transcript available from AAAS).

Schneider, S.H.: 1977b, 'Climate Change and the World Predicament: A Case Study for Interdisciplinary Research', *Climate Change* 1, 21.

Schneider, S.H., and Chen, R.S.: 1981, 'Carbon Dioxide Warming and Coastline Flooding: Physical Factors and Climatic Impact', *Ann. Rev. Energy* 5, 107.
. . . .

Schneider, S.H. and Morton, L.: 1981, *The Primordial Bond: Exploring Connections Between Man and Nature through the Humanities and Sciences*, Plenum, New York, 324 pp.

SCOPE: 1978, 'SCOPE Workshop on Climate/Society Interface', December 10-14, 1978, Scientific Committee on Problems of the Environment, International Council of Scientific Unions, Paris, France, 37 pp.

Scribner, R.A. and Chalk, R.A. (eds.): 1977, *Adapting Science to Social Needs: Conference Proceedings*, American Association for the Advancement of Science, Rept. No. 78-R-8, Washington, D.C., 312 pp.
. . . .

Smith, V.K.: 1980, 'Economic Impact Analysis and Climate Change: An Overview and Proposed Research Agenda', Final Report to the National Climate Program Office, National Oceanic and Atmospheric Administration, Contract NA-79-SAC-00754, U.S. Dept. of Commerce, Washington, D.C., 55 pp.

Torry, W.I.: 1979, 'Anthropological Studies in Hazardous Environments: Past Trends and New Horizons', *Current Anthropology* 20, 517.

Torry, W.I.: 1983, 'Anthropological Perspectives on Climate Change', in Chen, R.S., Boulding, E.M., and Schneider, S.H. (eds.), *Social Science Research and Climate Change: An Interdisciplinary Appraisal*, D. Reidel, Dordrecht Holland, 205-228 (this volume).
. . . .

UNEP: 1980, 'Report of the UNEP Expert Group Meeting on Climate Impact Studies', United Nations Environment Programme, UNEP/WG 38/4, Nairobi, Kenya, 27 pp.

WAES: 1977, *Energy: Global Prospects* 1985-2000, Report of the Workshop on Alternative Energy Strategies, McGraw-Hill, New York, 291 pp.

Warrick, R.A. and Riebsame, W.E.: 1981, 'Societal Responses to CO_2-Induced Climate Change: Opportunities for Research', *Climatic Change* 3, 387.
. . . .

WMO:1980, *Outline Plan and Basis for the World Climate Programme* 1980-1983, Rept. No. 540, World Meteorological Organization, Geneva, Switzerland, 64 pp.

WMO: 1981, 'Report of the Joint WMO/ICSU/UNEP Meeting of Experts on the Assessment of the Role of CO_2 on Climate Variations and Their Impact', World Meteorological Organization, Geneva, Switzerland, 35 pp.

21

INTERDISCIPLINARY
PROBLEM-ORIENTED RESEARCH
IN THE UNIVERSITY*

F. A. Long

The societal problems that face us today are thorny ones. Even though most of them have large scientific and technological components, their solutions more often than not demand the *simultaneous and interactive* efforts of a wide spectrum of talented professionals: scientists, engineers, social scientists, political scientists, lawyers, and doctors, to name only the most obvious. These are the efforts that we have in mind when we speak of interdisciplinary research.

Neither the concept nor the practice of interdisciplinary research is new. Government laboratories, industrial laboratories, and nonprofit research groups like the Rand Corporation have been engaging in interdisciplinary research for years—often, however, oriented toward defense problems. What is new is the realization that a similar but vastly expanded approach must be directed toward society's problems. This realization has resulted in urgent calls for new research institutions: National Environmental Laboratories, Institutes for Health and Medicine, reoriented National Laboratories, and so on. In such rosters of needed organizations, the universities are often missing. Apparently, there is a common conviction that universities are not the place to obtain effective interdisciplinary research on societal problems. In my judgment this belief is both wrong and dangerous.

The reasons that are given for counting the universities out are well known. The universities, it is said, are discipline-oriented (physics, agronomy, sociology), an orientation inimical to interdisciplinary research. Furthermore, universities are oriented toward basic research, while the current need is for applied research. Finally, the pace of

---

* From *Science*, Vol. 171, March 12, 1971, pp. 961. Copyright 1971 by the American Association for the Advancement of Science.

university research is too slow to be effective. There is a germ of truth in each of these points, but they do not encompass the whole truth and, in sum, are grossly misleading. Try, for example, to persuade a College of Agriculture or Engineering that it is not interested in applied research!

Why should one turn to the universities for interdisciplinary research? First, the universities are repositories of much of the necessary brain-power and knowledge. The ecologists, political scientists, and sociologists who are essential to these interdisciplinary studies are, in large measure, to be found in the universities.

Second, the universities have a deep concern. Faculty, and especially students, are sensitive to social problems, are eager to work on them, and are often prepared to change their previous ways of life to do so. The pressures of discipline orientation and the tradition of individual scholarship are strong among faculty members, but not strong enough to counter the pressures of social concern. Universities are changing rapidly and will change much more.

But the most important reason why the universities must become involved in interdisciplinary research—and the central reason why society must *insist* on their participation—is their obligation to youth. Coming generations must be taught about society's problems and about the best ways to solve them. College students must learn a genuinely interdisciplinary approach; this can only happen when their professors have personal knowledge of and commitment to interdisciplinary research and when there are programs wherein students can learn by doing—in short, when an interdisciplinary approach permeates the universities.

Pressure the universities if you will; castigate their occasionally overly narrow behavior; insist on changed structures and reward mechanisms. But for earth's sake, don't count them out. Without their active involvement, the future will be a good deal dimmer than it might otherwise appear.

PART V

WHAT IS IT ALL ABOUT?

22

ON THE COMPATIBILITY OF APPLIED AND BASIC SOCIOLOGICAL RESEARCH: AN EFFORT IN MARRIAGE COUNSELING†*

Richard A. Berk

For the past ten years, I have found myself among the very small minority of sociologists who make applied social science their major professional commitment. By and large, the experience has been enormously satisfying. However, these satisfactions have derived from the challenging nature of the work, the prospect of doing something useful, contact with individuals trying to make the world a bit better place, and interactions with social scientists from other disciplines; the sociological community typically has been unsupportive and often downright hostile. Moreover, my experience certainly is not unique. One hardly needs to launch a major study to observe that applied research does not appear in the "major" sociological journals, plays almost no role in the training of our graduate students, and only counts in the academic hiring and promotion process if the candidate already has been certified as a "proper" scholar.

I will not consider here the many reasons why applied research retains a second-class status within the sociological community.[1] Rather, I will assume that simple ignorance within the broader profession is partly to blame. That is, too many sociologists have little understanding of applied research and do not fully grasp how applied research is systematically dismissed by the profession's gatekeepers. Consequently, my primary aim is to undertake a bit of consciousness raising.

† The research reported in this paper was generously supported by the U.S. Department of Housing and Urban Development (Grant No. H-2908-RG).

* From The *American Sociologist*, Vol. 16, November 1981, pp. 204-211. Copyright 1981 by the American Sociological Association.

What is Applied Research?

Perhaps the best place to start is with a definition of what all the fuss is about. What is applied social science research? As one might expect, there is a large number of definitions, and there is even no agreement among applied researchers about what distinguishes their enterprise from basic research (e.g., Berk and Rossi, 1976; Berk, 1977; Rossi, 1980). Of late, I have come to believe that applied research is best characterized by the stance it takes with respect to its subjects of inquiry. In particular, the substantive questions come first, and then a range of theoretical and methodological tools are brought to bear. In other words, a substantive problem motivates the research effort, and past studies, extant theory, and research technology are introduced solely in service of that effort. There is no concern with demonstrating whether, for example, differential association (Cressey, 1952), control theory (Hirschi, 1969), or biosocial explanations of criminal behavior (Mednick and Christiansen, 1977) in general are more useful perspectives, but rather with unraveling the cause (and perhaps cures) of specific instances of illegal activities. Thus, one might help a given community address apparent increases in teenage vandalism, for instance, and apply whatever tools seem best suited to solve *that* problem. Any implications for larger social science questions are of secondary concern.

In contrast, basic research focuses first on some larger sociological question and then goes out into the world (or into the laboratory) to find an appropriate site in which to undertake the research. Any fallout for particular applications is, at best, a fringe benefit. In other words, the primary aim is to advance the current level of discourse *within the discipline*.

To summarize, applied research uses sociology or other social science disciplines in a supportive role when empirical questions are addressed. Basic research makes the state of the discipline the primary focus. For applied research, sociology becomes a means to some end, while for basic research, sociology is itself the end.

If we take this initial distinction seriously, it allows us to organize a large number of attributes that previously have been associated with applied research. Moreover, it then becomes useful to think of these attributes not as essential in the definition of applied research, but as derivative properties. Consider the following example that I will use to illustrate this observation.

Over the past two years I have been involved in an evaluation of the effectiveness of water conservation programs undertaken in communities throughout California during the recent drought. For about 24 months between 1976 and 1977, California experienced its worst drought in this century, and many areas were faced with the prospect of severe water shortages. Some communities initiated a wide variety of conservation efforts: educational campaigns, surcharges for excess water use, moratoriums on new service accounts, city ordinances prohibiting watering lawns during the heat of the day, and the like. Other communities launched more modest acitivities, sometimes limited to a single conservation message enclosed in consumers' water bills. Among the many questions involved was whether conservation programs "worked," (i.e., whether water consumption declined), and whether some worked better than others (Berk et al., 1981).

In our evaluation of local water conservation efforts, we were addressing a particular set of substantive questions and were not especially concerned with advancing current thinking in sociology or any other social science discipline. Note that we could have turned our priorities upsidedown. For example, one of the useful ways to examine conservation programs is as a solution to the "dilemma of the commons" (e.g., Schelling, 1971), or what some have called the "prisoner's dilemma" (Luce and Raiffa, 1957) or "social traps" (Platt, 1973). Recall that the dilemma of the commons comes about "when some publicly provided good is scarce. Each individual has no incentive to reduce his/her consumption, but in the aggregate the good is rapidly depleted, and no one's self-interest is served" (Berk et al., 1980). There is a long tradition in basic social science research that treats the dilemma of the commons as a fundamental problem (e.g., Olson, 1971; Marwell and Ames, 1979), and other researchers could have used the California experience as a laboratory to study alternative perspectives on commons dilemmas. In contrast, we exploited theoretical notions and empirical generalizations from the commons dilemma literature only to the degree they helped us understand how conservation programs worked. More general contributions to broader social science concerns were of no immediate interest.

One of the important attributes of the evaluation study was that it was necessary to draw on perspectives from hydrology, sociology, economics, and social psychology. Thus, a combination of hydrology and microeconomics was used to characterize the social consequences of shortfalls in precipitation associated with droughts. On close inspection, it was not at all obvious what a water shortage really entailed, and insights from hydrology and microeconomics were critical in defining the problem to which communities were responding. Microeconomics also played a fundamental role in developing causal models for water consumption since water is an economic good (i.e., it is sold at a price). Finally, research from social psychology and sociology was used to explain how various kinds of conservation appeals might shift the location of the demand curve and hence lead to less water consumption. It cannot be overemphasized that without this interdisciplinary approach, we would have been lost. No single discipline had anything approaching the whole story, and sociology was certainly no exception. In short, the evaluation of California's water conservation efforts was like most applied research in its reliance on an interdisciplinary approach.

Second, it was apparent from the start that the evaluation could not be undertaken with a single research method. Data on what communities actually did in response to the drought, for instance, required qualitative research methods coupled with survey research techniques. Assessments of the impact of local conservation programs, in contrast, relied heavily on archival material coded from official records. In particular, it was necessary to transform data from customers' bills into aggregate, monthly summaries subject to analysis through an interrupted time-series design. Finally, we applied statistical procedures used by economists and operations researchers. Thus, our second observation about applied research is that it is likely to be multimethod.

In general, we found that water conservation programs reduced water consumption but that there was enormous variation in the effectiveness of these programs in different communities. This variation in turn was a function of several variables. For example, we found that conservation programs produced greater water savings among residential consumers in communities characterized by higher educational levels. However, while the impact of a community's median education was large, it was in one sense irrelevant. Whatever the level of education, a community's schooling is not subject to manipulation by the public officials trying to reduce local water consumption (at least in the short run). Therefore, public officials quite properly could respond with "so what?" when told that education mattered. In contrast, we also found that, for residential consumers, a greater number of conservation programs was more effective than a smaller number, and that there was no evidence of declining marginal returns. In other words, communities had the option of introducing a large number of different kinds of conservation programs with the likelihood that each would contribute to water savings. This was a finding that had real implications for public policy, since policymakers could (and did) manipulate the number of local conservation programs launched. We also found that residential consumers reduced their consumption with increases in the real marginal price of water, and that the savings did not compete with savings from other conservation programs. That is, policymakers had the option of shifting either the supply curve or the demand curve (or both). Again, the importance of this finding was that manipulable variables were involved. This leads to a third observation: applied research will typically focus on mutable variables although, of course, other causal variables not subject to manipulation must be considered to avoid specification errors.

We also were interested in which communities were more likely to invest heavily in water conservation programs during the drought. Among other things, we found that cities with larger populations were more likely, ceteris paribus, to make a major conservation effort. However, while the regression coefficient was statistically significant at conventional levels, the substantive significance was quite small. That is, the impact of population was not likely to result from chance but at the same time, cities would have to differ by plus or minus several million before anything approaching important changes would be found in the intensity of local conservation activities. Thus a fourth observation: applied research will emphasize the distinction between statistical significance and substantive significance.

The fact that both conservation programs and increases in price could be used to induce water savings was certainly of interest. But in addition, it was important to gauge the tradeoffs between the two water reduction strategies. After all, applied researchers usually live in the real world of practical constraints where questions of feasibility naturally follow from the initial substantive issues. For us, therefore, an answer to the question of "what works?" also required an answer to the question "compared to what?" In the case of residential water users, we found that on the average, the impact of a community's conservation programs yielded about the same reductions as doubling the real marginal price of water. A number of implications followed.

For example, while there are several reasons why it is more efficient to use price as a vehicle for inducing water conservation (e.g., it can be done within existing administrative procedures), doubling the price of water has unfortunate distributional consequences and would in addition face stiff political opposition. This leads to a fifth observation: applied research almost inevitably will be drawn into assessments of various tradeoffs which in turn typically will need to be addressed in quantitative terms.

It should be apparent that the water conservation study required a wide range of skills and many kinds of labor intensive activities. For example, the study was conducted in over 50 communities across the state and field workers had to be sent to each. Similarly, the interdisciplinary approach drew on at least four kinds of theoretical expertise while the statistical analyses went well beyond what one typically finds in sociology journals. Therefore, the research was necessarily a team effort. Thus a sixth observation: applied research usually will be beyond the skills and energies of a single individual, and a team approach often is required.

Finally, the research was supported by the U.S. Department of Housing and Urban Development and could not have been undertaken without the full (and even enthusiastic) cooperation of state and local public officials. That is, there was clearly a particular audience having few connections to academic settings. However, this followed from the initial questions addressed: we became interested in how well water conservation programs worked and then shopped for support. The search led us to the HUD and the California Department of Water Resources. Had we focused on solutions to commons dilemmas, in contrast, we would have shopped elsewhere and perhaps would have found support within the National Science Foundation. Of course, it is more often the case that clients initiate the search (commonly through a "request for proposal"), but it still seems to me that the client-researcher relationship is not essential to the definition of applied research. Rather, the client-researcher relationship follows from the ways in which applied efforts initially are phrased and undertaken. In any case, the final observation is that applied research often will have a well defined client outside of academe.

In summary, applied research treats sociology (or any of the social sciences) as a means to an end, not as an end in itself. Given this emphasis, a number of attributes typically follow:

1. an interdisciplinary approach;
2. the use of multiple methods;
3. an emphasis on mutable variables;
4. a clear distinction between statistical and substantive
   significance;
5. an emphasis on quantitative tradeoffs;
6. a team research effort; and
7. a greater likelihood of specific clients.

Given these characteristics, it is clear that many of the criticisms of
applied research heard within academic sociology departments are far
off the mark. Applied research *is* intellectually demanding; indeed, I
believe that it is at least as demanding as basic research. Applied
research is *not* narrow; indeed, I believe that it requires a much wider
range of abilities than basic research. Applied research is *not*
atheoretical; indeed, I believe that strong theoretical foundations are
absolutely essential. In short, if there are grounds for discriminating
against applied research, they stem from the conscious decision not to
build a piece of research primarily around issues *within* the discipline.
However, it also is important to stress that applied research frequently
plays a central role in the ways in which sociology evolves (Rossi, 1980),
although such feedback effects are often serendipitous and the product
of individuals who are not heavily involved in applied concerns.

What if Applied Researchers were the Gatekeepers?

... There are a number of ways one might set about demystifying basic
research, but I thought it might be instructive to imagine a world in
which applied researchers were the profession's gatekeepers. In other
words, suppose that sociology was built around applied concerns:
training in applied research was central to graduate training, the
mainstream journals were interested primarily in publishing applied
studies, and the basic research divisions of the NSF were disbanded.
What then would life be like for sociologists trying to do basic
research?

Consider a paper submitted to the *ASR* in which differential
association was the primary vehicle for explaining participation in
illegal activities. Suppose also that the differential association approach
was presented with conceptual clarity, was effectively operationalized,

and produced a sensible set of findings. However, our applied *American Sociological Review* summarily rejects the paper. The major problem is that by failing to take an interdisciplinary perspective, the underpinnings of differential association remain unexamined. In particular, differential association necessarily rests on a model of social learning, and our basic researcher sociologist has neglected an enormous literature from psychology directly addressing how learning occurs. (For a recent review, see Bugelski, 1973.) In short, the paper is rejected for an uninformed, parochial perspective, having failed to take an interdisciplinary approach. Indeed, one nasty reviewer claims that without the introduction of a formal model of social learning, differential association is nothing but a sloppy metaphor. Perhaps, therefore, the author should try his hand at writing poetry.

Consider a second paper submitted to the *ASR* addressing Marx's assertion that there is a tendency under capitalism for the rate of profit to fall. As one would expect, the discussion rests heavily on the labor theory of value formulated for capitalist societies as a whole. Thus, one of the paper's central concerns is with the importance of labor unions as a complicating factor. However, our reviewer is unimpressed. While it is apparent that the paper goes a long way toward clarifying a number of important conceptual issues, the paper is rejected because the author has provided no way to measure value without recourse to prices. And of course, there is no necessary correspondence between value in terms of labor inputs and prices that emerge from market processes. In other words, the paper is rejected as a masturbatory exercise. Indeed, the reviewer suggests that the real thing is a lot more fun and has the additional asset of no peer review.

A third paper focuses on the prisoner's dilemma and employs an experimental design in order to determine the role of subjects' feelings about making a "fair" contribution to group welfare. One finding is that subjects who enter the study with greater concerns for equity are more likely to bring about a better result for the group of which they are a member. However, it turns out that the experimental subjects were college students enrolled in an introductory sociology course. Despite a cogent theoretical perspective and a tight research design, therefore, the paper is rejected out of hand. Not only does there seem to be no way to confidently generalize from a laboratory setting to the "real world," but college students are not a particularly instructive population in which to study commons dilemmas. Why should anyone care whether college students with a more collective orientation perform better in the artificial setting of a social psychology laboratory? Indeed, one snotty reviewer closes with the suggestion that the study could have been undertaken as well with Rhesus monkeys, especially if SAT scores keep dropping.

A fourth paper addresses the severity of civil unrest in urban areas in the 1960s. After the introduction of a sophisticated model of unrest and some fancy statistical analyses, the author concludes that the best predictor of riot severity is the proportion of blacks in the city. The reviewers have a picnic with this one. They wonder at some length why anyone should care about the finding unless the author really is proposing to change the proportion of black residents in urban areas. One reviewer indicates that the only policy implication that he can find would involve busing large numbers of white suburbanites into the inner city on hot summer days. . . .

Whatever the validity of these examples, they provide, in reverse, a sense of the kind of reception that applied research receives from current sociological gatekeepers. Moreover, the narrow-mindedness that I have tried to describe is not overstated. In preparation for this paper, several of my colleagues and I submitted six manuscripts to mainstream sociological journals. All six had an applied focus and only one was accepted. The single success remains somewhat perplexing although in that paper a modest effort was made to take applied research results and use them to address several ongoing themes in the sociological literature. Four of the papers were rejected but were soon accepted for publication elsewhere in excellent applied or interdisciplinary journals, and one of these papers already has been reprinted in an annual review of outstanding applied studies. The final manuscript has been through two "revise and resubmits," and its status remains uncertain. Perhaps more instructive are the reasons why most of the papers were rejected by the mainstream. Here are a few reviewer comments, altered slightly to protect the review process.

This is an interesting and well-written paper, but it is not the kind of thing the majority of readers of this journal will bother to read. It belongs in a more applied journal.

This paper is technically sound but all we learn is that despite many obstacles, the social program worked as designed. This is not of general interest and links are never made to the organizational literature.

While the paper's overall conclusions seem correct, there is no need for all the fancy statistics. Have the authors reanalyze the data in the form of cross-tabulations. That way it will be accessible to a wider audience more interested in mainstream sociology.

While it is true that the authors have data on all of the 262 cases in which arrests were made, the N is too small to merit publication in a mainstream sociological journal. It's not an *ASR* N.

There are two features that militate against publication. First, the author's orientation to the subject of policy work seems to be practical rather than theoretical. . . .

This paper has some very good features and addresses a current hot topic. However, the paper should really be sent to a more specialized criminology journal since the variables are really more at an applied than a general theoretical level.

Toward Divorce or Reconciliation

I have tried to argue that applied social science has genuine intellectual merit, or at least measures up when compared to basic research. I also have argued, that, nevertheless, applied research is routinely discriminated against by the profession's gatekeepers. If I am reading current trends correctly, perhaps the most honest thing to do would be to make a clean break between basic and applied sociology. . . .

On the other hand, basic and applied social science need one another. Applied social science draws on a variety of ideas, and sociological ideas certainly are among them. In addition, applied research exploits innovations in research methods, and here sociologists have made a number of important contributions. Similarly, many of the most important advances within sociology have come from applied concerns (Rossi, 1980),[3] and sociology surely would benefit from exposure to perspectives from other academic disciplines. In short, perhaps a reconciliation of sorts is in order. It may well be possible to accept a number of important differences between applied and basic research and at the same time house them productively (if not blissfully) under one roof.

First, just as we allow graduate students to specialize in particular substantive and methodological concerns, we also should allow concentrations in applied areas. For example, a specialty in evaluation research might be coupled with a traditional Ph.D. in sociology.

Second, if we permit concentrations in applied concerns, students interested in such matters should be required to take courses outside sociology departments. While I believe that even basic sociological research should be leavened with interdisciplinary perspectives, it simply is impossible to undertake sound applied research solely from a sociological point of view. Moreover, communication with one's applied colleagues demands some familiarity with microeconomics, social psychology, quasi-experimental designs, psychometrics, and the like.

Third, if we allow students to do dissertations in applied areas, we routinely should solicit the active participation of economists, psychologists, political scientists, anthropologists, and even faculty outside of the social sciences when thesis committees are formed. The interdisciplinary training obtained in course work would be enhanced significantly.

Fourth, just as we advertise for individuals specializing in criminology, stratification, and sex roles, we should create positions in applied areas such as evaluation research, policy analysis, and risk assessment. While the precise boundaries of such activities often are unclear, they are not more unclear than between the usual sociological subspecies.

Fifth, when time comes for promotion, a candidate's work should be judged with its intellectual merit as the primary criterion. Whether it is applied or basic should be immaterial. Indeed, one could well imagine seeking letters from professionals outside academe. In economics, for example, it is common to seek assessments from economists working in industry and government.

Finally, we might follow the example of a number of disciplines, such as statistics, and include applied and basic sections in the *American Sociological Review*. And with this division, it might well make sense to have a special editor in charge and have some additional associate editors to handle submissions to the applied section.

These suggestions are hardly exhaustive but provide a sample of the kinds of reforms necessary if we are to have a reconciliation between basic and applied research. Of course, even these modest reforms imply changes in usual practice and in some instances introduce additional competition for scarce resources. Thus, it is entirely conceivable that the majority of sociologists will find divorce to be a better solution. I would be saddened by such a development.

FOOTNOTES

[1]One reviewer suggested that it was important to remind readers that when sociologists were members of the American Social Science Association (before the formation of the American

Sociological Association in 1906), basic and applied types across a variety of the social sciences shared the same organization. It was only with the desire to take on the trappings of a "science" that concerted efforts were made to distinguish basic from applied practioners.

. . . .

[3]For example, as Rossi (1980) explains, the original work on occupational prestige in 1948 was an applied effort to determine why scientists were leaving government jobs for employment in universities and businesses. The lower occupational prestige of government positions was thought to be a factor. Similarly, the "Coleman Report" was a congressionally mandated study to determine whether black and white students were enjoying the same level of support from local school districts.

REFERENCES

Berk, Richard A.
  1977 "Discretionary methodological decisions in applied research." *Sociological Methods and Research* 5(3):317-334.
Berk, Richard A., T.F. Cooley, C.J. LaCivita, S. Parker, K. Sredl, and M. Brewer
  1980 "Reducing consumption in periods of acute scarcity: The case of water." *Social Science Research* 9(2):99-120.
Berk, Richard A., T.F. Cooley, C.J. LaCivita, and K. Sredl
  1981 *Water Shortage: Some Lessons in Water Conservation from the Great California Drought: 1976-1977.* Cambridge, MA: Abt Books.
Berk, Richard A. and Peter H. Rossi
  1976 "Doing good or worse: Evaluation research politically reexamined." *Social Problems* 23(3):337-349.
Bugelski, B.R.
  1973 "Human learning." Pp. 515-529 in B.B. Wolman (ed), *Handbook of General Psychology,* New York: Prentice Hall.
Cressey, Donald R.
  1952 "Application and verification of differential association theory." *Criminal Law and Criminology, and Police Science* 43(1):27-41.
Hirschi, Travis
  1960 *Causes of Delinquency.* Berkeley: U. of California Press.
Luce, R.D. and H. Raiffa
  1957 *Games and Decisions.* New York: John Wiley.
Marwell, Gerald and Ruth E. Ames
  1979 "Experiments on the provision of public goods: I. Resources, interest, group size and the free-rider problem." *American Journal of Sociology* 84(6):1335-1360.
Mednick, S. and K. O. Christiansen
  1977 *Biosocial Bases of Criminal Behavior.* New York: Gardiner Press.
Olson, M.
  1971 *The Logic of Collective Action.* New York: Shocken.
Platt, J.
  1973 "Social traps." *American Psychologist* 28(3):204-221.
Rossi, Peter H.
  1980 "The challenge and opportunities of applied social research." *American Sociological Review* 45(6):889-904.
Schelling, T.
  1971 "On the ecology of micromotives." *The Public Interest* 25(1):1-14.

23

ON MIXING APPLES AND ORANGES: THE SOCIOLOGIST DOES IMPACT ASSESSMENT WITH BIOLOGISTS AND ECONOMISTS *

Rabel J. Burdge and Paul Opryszek

FOREWORD

Lake Shelbyville, located in Eastern Illinois, is a typical Corps of Engineers flood-control reservoir. It was planned in the early 1930's and completed in 1970. This chapter details the administrative problems of an interdisciplinary university research effort to examine the "real" environmental impacts of the reservoir ten years after it had begun operation. The project titled "Ex Post Reservoir Study: The Case of Lake Shelbyville" was housed in the Institute for Environmental Studies at the University of Illinois, and headed by Rabel J. Burdge, a rural sociologist (Burdge et al. 1980). Our experience in project administration illustrates some of the problems in doing interdisciplinary team assessment, which are here shared. While not implying that Apples and Oranges don't mix, problems do result when we try to bring together a group of disciplinary researchers. We write this chapter in the hope that environmental impact assessment will remain interdisciplinary. Indeed, one of the reasons we are in this "environmental fix" is the singleness of our disciplinary perspectives.

INTRODUCTION

Measuring and understanding the intricate impacts of a flood-control reservoir on the natural and human environment requires the combined expertise of many people from varied disciplines. A truly interdisciplinary effort is demanded to arrive at a comprehensive view

* Reprinted by permission of Westview Press from *Integrated Impact Assessment*, edited by *F.A. Rossini and A.L. Porter*, (Boulder, CO: Westview Press, 1983), pp. 107-117.

of the impacted physical and social environments, yet "interdisciplinary" can easily become a false label. If the principal investigator and researchers are not attentive to project administration on a day-to-day basis, the end product reflects the old saw about integrating findings "with a staple." Among the obstacles to true interdisciplinary work discussed herein are:

1. Establishment of budget sub-allocations;
2. Data compatibility;
3. Developing an effective decision-making structure;
4. Working at the interfaces between discipline and project segments; and
5. Enforcement of understandings between participants.

Failure to successfully meet these challenges is likely to produce a series of miniature discipline-based projects and a final report which dittos the list of university departments.

Although the lure of funding produces comfortable platitudes to the contrary, the realities of day-to-day research soon demonstrate that academic communities have not proven successful in producing truly interdisciplinary research. With the continuing contraction of many university budgets has come a hardening of the already formidable barriers to interdisciplinary work.

Among useful insights gained from the Ex-Post Facto Reservoir Project were an acid test for some organizational theories, and gradual awareness of realistic procedures for interdisciplinary project management. Problem areas in this type of work can, and for us did, occur in data collection, personnel retention, and budget management. Some intriguing, but impractical, approaches tried at Lake Shelbyville were:

1. Survey-based, local level input-output analysis (Suwanamalik 1977; Tuan and Scott 1978);
2. Collective project decision making;
3. The use of graduate students in supervisory roles;
4. The "shotgun" approach to social inventories; and
5. The assumption that "altruism," while rarely found in the real world, might be present in academia.

PROJECT ADMINISTRATION

Proposal Formulation

As in all research, interdisciplinary work begins with the proposal. Commonly, one person writes a proposal and then seeks other inputs. In such an approach the author's discipline is presented in a very sophisticated and knowledgable manner, while less familiar disciplines are treated in a very general way. The Shelbyville project did not permit total formulation of the final interdisciplinary proposal by one individual or from the orientation of one discipline. An effective alternative to the use of a single writer evolved during proposal development.

The leadership of the Shelbyville project circulated a call for ideas and interested researchers, based on the general problem to be studied. Disciplinary specialists were then urged to identify their point of entry. Two types of responses were received from among a target audience of university researchers. First, there was the identification of persons interested in the project, and second, a list of research topical areas. Collectively, these diverse responses produced a much wider assortment of approaches and insights than any one researcher could have devised. Diverse input is important in the formulation of an environmental impact assessment research program, because what is included under the rubric of impact is only now being established within the literature (Finsterbusch and Wolf 1977).

Not all persons expressing an interest in the project will want to become directly involved in the actual research. However, these persons may be willing (from personal curiosity or a sense of collegial responsibility) to lend their expertise in a non-paid consultant role. The informal evolution of such a process did in fact benefit the Shelbyville project, leading to a formalization of the position of these "advisory board" members. One outcome of crystalizing this role was that graduate research assistants could have access to an advisor, even though the student, and not the advisor, was paid from the project.

Multidisciplinary Versus Interdisciplinary Funding

Alternatives for funding the Shelbyville research ranged from total centralization of expenditures in a task force concept to subcontracting with investigators for a specific task. The disaggregation of funding into individual grants constitutes a fragmentation of the effort into a multidisciplinary rather than interdisciplinary study of reservoir impacts.

It was eventually decided that four teams would be set up—social, economic, biological, and integrative. Faculty members and their students from several disciplines would make up each team. One person was designated to lead each team, with the Principal Investigator assuming overall project responsibility. Initially, funds were allocated by the collective body of project designates.

After the total project was funded, and suballocations began to be passed to each research team, the hidden agendas of each discipline and the attendant researchers began to surface. We found that hidden objectives constantly threatened to subvert those portions of the project that were permitted to be excessively independent. Hidden agendas took various forms. Researchers covertly sought funding for work they wanted to do even before the project. If these private goals were close enough to project objectives, there was no conflict. The most common problem was that distant goals were quietly pursued, gradually sidetracking important areas of the project. One result of this problem for us was that one team acquired data it wanted, but failed to submit the analysis that was the end product and in turn needed by other teams.

The distribution of research funds from a central source can minimize the tendency of a project to fragment, and through the use of funding supervision to hold the various teams to a set of research objectives. Jealously independent researchers clearly dislike any administrative structure whose demands become capricious and needlessly intrusive. Such individual traits are reinforced by the traditionally decentralized university structure which houses faculty by discipline. Based on the Shelbyville experience, we suggest that the more centralized the administrative control, the more likely the project is to remain interdisciplinary.

DISCIPLINARY CHAUVINISM

Any effort to combine the resources of academic disciplines must always remember that professional careers advance by touching the chords of their specialty. Specialists, by very definition, are people who found one area so fascinating that they studied it to the depth of being expert. Interdisciplinary projects would benefit by screening out those researchers so narrowly specialized that they are incapable of collaborating with others.

Data Collection Costs

Outside of the need to take the time to find out what another person does, the most basic obstacle to integrated research is that one discipline does not understand what it costs another to do research. For example, the collection of quality ethnographic data by a trained anthropologist takes months simply to get to know the people. Salary costs are high. The collection of water quality data requires little human labor, but much equipment. The biologists could not see spending $6,000 for an anthropologist to live in Shelbyville, but would quickly spend four times that for a piece of equipment. Busy researchers do not want to take the time to become familiar with data collection costs for other disciplines. After the Shelbyville project budgeted a large amount for one team, the implied question from the others was, "What is it that you guys in x-ology really do to use all that money?" Such was the predominant attitude of the biological sciences toward the social sciences. The biologists were reliant on expensive technology to gather data. Assaying, analyzing, and measuring were seen as technical problems. For the social scientist, the quality of the data depended to a large extent upon the relationship with the local population (Burch 1971). What it boils down to is that each of the major teams (biophysical, economic, and sociology-anthropology-geography-planning) wanted two-thirds of the total funding for data collection, with an unwillingness to understand the data collection procedures of other areas. There seems no simple remedy for this.

Of course, the principal investigator or project coordinator must make a decision on the division of funding. Perhaps this would be easier if group budget proposals were submitted for ranges of data acquisition with corresponding levels of funding.

DATA COMPATIBILITY

Aside from an unwillingness to learn about data collection costs, the divergent nature of the data bases used by economists, biologists, and sociologists complicates earnest efforts at cooperation.

Economists

National level annual statistics are the strongest of the economic data bases. While economic analysis has blossomed out in a multitude of directions from this national starting point, local data bases are frequently incomplete or nonexistent. Monthly, even quarterly, statistics are unobtainable for some series; even when regularly available, they are often subject to later revision. For example, in Shelby County there was only one major manufacturer that produced farm implements. To protect the proprietary rights of that firm, its gross sales could not be reported unless there were three other manufacturers present in Shelby County for that category of information.

While regional data such as sales, regional imports, and regional exports are available (with the present common usage of regional input-output models), these models frequently are for overlapping geographical areas. Each study may adopt different numbers and content of categories, and studies are not compiled for identical points in time. They rarely reach down to the nonmetropolitan county level and are also expensive. "A survey based table may cost ten times as much and take eight to ten times as long to prepare as a secondary data table" (Richardson 1972). Local level economic data are therefore often limited to the bare essentials of employment figures by occupation (or type of employer) and sales tax receipts (perhaps broken down into broad categories for type of business). In the Shelbyville study we tried to interview small businessmen in the two county area to obtain figures on type and amount of expenditures, income, and employment, etc. However, these questionnaires that were to be the basis of an input-output table were lengthy and cumbersome. What little information we got was incomplete. Such an approach is therefore useless for small rural counties. Finally we found that graduate students in economics were not trained to collect reliable and valid primary interview data from respondents.

Biologists

The biologists did an excellent job of compiling a myriad of detailed measures for air and water quality as well as type and distribution of fauna and flora. The problem in relating to other disciplines stems from the extremely local nature of their findings. Descriptions vary drastically even for sites located side by side. Furthermore, interpretation was needed before nontechnicians could interpret their results as normal or abnormal. The experience at Shelbyville was that the biologists spent too much of the allocated funds in the collection of data that was of local interest and had little generalizability. A particular excess was raw data on chemical concentrations and fish counts.

The ability of biochemical scientists to make ecological generalizations is growing, but this capacity is still formative. The importance of ecological generalization and analysis came to light in an Illinois controversy over the proposed Oakley Springer Reservoir (Harris 1978). The decision not to build the project revolved almost exclusively around conflicting biological analyses of the effects of the impoundment on the ecosystem near the proposed reservoir's headwaters. Ecological generalizations concerning national level problems like pesticide accumulation are, however, of limited utility for a project studying a wide range of problems on a vastly smaller ecosystem. Our experience indicates that impact work needs scientifically derived biological statements at the project and county level.

Sociologists

The social scientists in the Shelbyville study collected data on the daytime recreation users, overnight campers, census data on control and comparison counties, historical records, life histories, and observational as well as available demographic information. Like the biologist, we found the applied sociologist was so deep in data that the level of analytical sophistication never exceeded tabular and descriptive analysis. In the case of the social impact portions of the project, the theory for analyzing and integrating the vast amount of information was weak. Lacking theoretical justification or guidance for targeting in on important impact variables, the sociologists dissipated much effort in a "shotgun" approach to impact assessment. Laundry lists of potentially impacted variables have been developed that would put even a descriptive biologist to shame (Burdge and Johnson 1977).

The identification of relevant impact variables was a particular problem when interfacing the biophysical and social scientists. Lack of familiarity with the other researchers' data needs made it difficult for one specialist to prepare data in such a form that made it useful for another specialist doing different but related work. The true mechanics of disciplinary interdependence take place through exchange of data and analysis. For example, one economist needed soil productivity information from the inventory of physical land use changes prepared at the beginning of the project. While the data obtained were quite successfully used by the economists, there would have been room for more formal understanding of what variations in form and further analysis would have been useful when reporting land use information. The only resolution to this problem is for team members to take the time to understand the basic unit of analysis for each discipline and how impacts in one might affect the other. Such issues as the effects of different types of recreational use on water quality were never addressed.

COMBATTING DISCIPLINARY CHAUVINISMS

Role of Principal Investigator

Disciplinary specialists need to be grouped together for most day-to-day work, yet the project must be governed and coordinated effectively. The allocation of resources and adherence to the research plan required that decision and direction be provided. Four alternatives for administration of the Lake Shelbyville project were originally discussed:

1. The principal investigator makes decisions based on advice from all participants.
2. A committee of participants makes decisions based on a majority opinion.
3. Each participant would have a veto on changes in direction or budget affecting their research; and
4. Unanimous consent of project participants would be required for changes in budget and research direction.

Although total harmony was sought, the fourth alternative requires too much time, even when attainable. The problem with the second approach became apparent when one large team with a big budget was represented by only a team leader at project meetings, while other teams, with less budget and less responsibility, were equally or even more heavily represented by faculty. The problem of allocating votes could not be resolved. The third alternative represents a valuable safeguard for the problem of disparity in the size of the budget and responsibility, but nobody wanted to give up part of their program for others. Therefore, it was difficult to shift resources from team to team even though it was necessary.

We found that if the principal investigator made a point to be sensitive to the needs of the research teams, as well as remain conscious of the research objectives, the first alternative was most practical. The more communication among participants and with the principal investigator concerning research direction and overlapping data needs, the better.

Our experience, in short, indicated a simple organizational scheme, plenty of communication, and a strong but sensitive principal investigator. That person was held responsible for overall coordination of the research effort, monitoring the budget and preparation of reports. The principal investigator must, therefore, set the general policy for the research teams and make the necessary budget "subgrants" after a thorough discussion with the participants. Placing both final obligations and final authority in one spot apparently is the only realistic way to ensure that interdisciplinary research achieves its goal.

Interfaces Between Disciplines

Working on an interdisciplinary project means a willingness to negotiate and to be held to specific performance targets, especially in providing data that can be used by other research teams. In the case of Shelbyville the centrifugal forces tugging at research teams created the need for written agreements concerning what data would be exchanged between disciplines. The enforceability of these subcontracts means coming up with the agreed product others need by the agreed time. When one team lets down another, frustrated expectations become a major cause of persons leaving the project and retreating to the disciplinary department.

Data Manager

Environmental impact assessment needs high quality valid data from a variety of disciplines that can be scientifically defended and justified before nontechnical funding agencies. Detailing the procedures for collecting quality data represents the crucial item in the decision on whether or not a project is funded. We found it necessary to have someone supervise data management to insure the collection of data in near-parallel form by the different research teams. Only then is it possible for the information to be used by more than one group. The data manager can assure that the agreed products are in on time, and then routinely distributed to project users.

The attempt to develop the position of data manager on the Shelbyville project was only partially successful, in that only graduate students were available for the position. As suggested in the case with the principal investigator, the data manager must possess adequate persuasive ability to deal with a variety of personalities and disciplines.

The ideal data manager is a full-time, nonfaculty person with at least masters level training. Besides an effective work personality and interpersonal skills, data managers must have a technical background. The ideal person also needs a flexible mind and the ability to intuitively grasp technical methods and results produced by biological scientists, economists, and sociologists. The institution of such a position worked quite well on another Institute for Environmental Studies project, *Illinois, Today and Tomorrow* (Burdge and Kelly 1978). The data manager of that project was able to keep faculty to agreed-upon deadlines by unobtrusive prodding.

A data inventory form was distributed to all Shelbyville project participants. Whenever a data set was acquired, a form was to be completed and returned to the data manager. Our return rate was too low to be effective, but in a successful application completed forms would be photocopied and periodically distributed as a "directory" of data availability. In this way everyone would know what was available and whom to contact. Redundancy would be eliminated and gaps in desired information become more readily apparent.

Finally, even the best administrative arrangements can be frustrated by team participants unsuited for cooperating in a working environment. Individuals making up each team must have the ability and willingness to collect and interpret data that can be understood by other teams. Conversely, they must be willing to recognize how data from others teams fit their projects.

Role of Graduate Students

We found that the graduate students were among the most dedicated members of the project teams. The successful completion of the project likely meant the successful completion of their thesis. However, their effectiveness as project participants depends upon:

1. Carving out a well-defined portion of the project for their participation, which ideally can also serve as a thesis.
2. Their not being given supervisory responsibility. Students must not be put in a position of having to remind a truant faculty member that a contribution is behind schedule.
3. Developing a written agreement between the research team and the student as to exactly what is expected and for how long.
4. Minimizing the use of graduate students as a stand-in for faculty members. It is a good idea to have them observe and take notes on the project meetings—but that is all. At a future date they must perform, and eventually direct, interdisciplinary research.

SUMMARY

Interdisciplinary research within the university creates its own set of operational necessities. Informal communication and decentralized decision-making may represent a comfortable work climate for the isolated scholar. Such tendencies here will defeat the goal of integrated impact assessment. An uncommon spirit of cooperation is demanded of all participants, along with an acceptance of the need to make explicit agreements with colleagues. The Lake Shelbyville project was only marginally successful in meeting the recommendations outlined in this chapter. Data management represented our biggest failure. Most of these recommendations evolved during the course of the project and are presented here to reduce some of the error in other interdisciplinary impact studies. The experiences shared here are offered not to endorse the authoritarian nature of the principal investigator, but to underscore the central characteristic of interdisciplinary research—the need to fit disciplinary parts together in such a manner that a complete scientific recommendation can be presented.

REFERENCES

Burch, William R., Jr. *Daydreams and Nightmares: A Sociological Essay on the American Environment.* New York: Harper and Row, 1971.

Burdge, Rabel and Johnson, Sue. "The Socio-Cultural Aspects of the Effects of Resource Development." In McEvoy, James, III and Dietz, Thomas, eds., *Handbook for Environmental Planning: The Social Consequences of Environmental Change.* New York: John Wiley, pp. 241-279, 1977.

Burdge, Rabel J., and Kelly, Ruth M. "Citizen and State Agency Response to University Research on Public Policy: The Case of *Illinois: Today and Tomorrow.*" In Grove, Samuel K. and Follinger, Richard A., eds., *State Policy Research at the University of Illinois.* Urbana, Illinois: Institute of Government and Public Affairs, University of Illinois, pp. 65-75, 1978.

Burdge, Rabel, et al. *Ten Years After: The Social, Economic, and Biophysical Impacts of Lake Shelbyville.* Urbana, Illinois: Institute for Environmental Studies, University of Illinois, 1980.

Finsterbusch, Kurt and Wolf, C.P., eds. *Methodology of Social Impact Assessment.* Stroudsburg, Pennsylvania: Dowden, Hutchinson, and Ross, 1977.

Harris, Britta B. *The Oakley Reservoir Mirage: A Case Study in Water Resource Decision Making.* Urbana, Illinois: Institute of Government and Public Affairs and the Institute for Environmental Studies, University of Illinois, 1978.

Richardson, Harry W. *Input-Output and Regional Economics.* New York: Wiley, p. 85, 1977.

Suwanamalik, Nuntana. *Economic Impact of Lake Shelbyville on Moultrie and Shelby Counties, Illinois.* Urbana, Illinois: University of Illinois, Urbana, 1977.

Tuan, Francis C., and Scott, John T., Jr. *Impact of the Shelbyville Reservoir on the Agricultural Sector.* Illinois Agricultural Economics Staff Paper, No. 78 E-45. Urbana, Illinois: Department of Agricultural Economics, University of Illinois, 1978.

24

INTEGRATED CIRCUITS*

Morton Jones

In the rapid development of integrated circuits, effective coupling was achieved principally through cross-licensing of patents among competitive industrial organizations.

Whereas the transistor required important new scientific understanding, the creation of the sophisticated integrated circuits resulted principally from inventiveness and engineering ingenuity, particularly in processing technology. At the same time, the small dimensions and extreme material purity needed for integrated circuits could not be achieved without a wide array of diagnostic tools and instrumentation provided by earlier unrelated scientific programs.

The development of the transistor had led to a number of basic techniques required for integrated circuits, such as semiconductor purification, crystal growth, alloying, diffusion, oxide masking and epitaxial growth. The semiconductor industry had reached the point in 1958, when the integrated circuit was born, where it worked daily with crystals of chemical, physical and structural perfection many orders of magnitude higher than in any other industry and produced novel discrete electronic devices, often with superior performance to that of vacuum tubes.

Silicon was beginning to become important, though germanium was the predominant semiconductor material. Silicon looked particularly promising in military applications where its superior high temperature performance was necessary. Transistors were being designed into circuits for which small size and weight and low power drain were critical, though the cost was still not competitive with vacuum tubes. The first commercial products to use significant quantities of transistors were miniature hearing aids and portable radios. Computers and communications were obvious candidates in the industrial area,

---

* Excerpted by permission of Elsevier Sequoia from "Materials Science and Engineering: Its Evolution, Practice and Prospect," Special Issue of *Materials Science and Engineering*, Vol. 37, No. 1, January 1979, edited by M. Cohen, pp. 61-64.

and IBM and Bell Laboratories had large semiconductor programs. Another was the development of military equipment such as the Polaris and Minuteman missile programs. All of these large-system applications of semiconductor devices spurred the push to miniaturization. This then was the status of semiconductors in 1958 when Kilby at Texas Instruments Inc. first conceived of and constructed an integrated circuit. Though the practical use of transistors was relatively new, the needs for even further reduction in size, weight, and power were already in sight.

Kilby, an electrical engineer, joined Texas Instruments from Centralab Electronics where he had been working on miniaturization of electronic circuits by the silk screening of conductive inks on a ceramic substrate to form resistance and capacitance. Hence, he had experience and a strong interest in miniaturization. In 1958, he conceived of processing the elements of a complete circuit, such as resistors, capacitors and diodes in a monolithic bar of semiconductor. The technology for accomplishing this already existed, having been developed for fabricating discrete devices. Diffusion and alloying were used for introducing controlled amounts of desired impurities to create localized p and n regions. Metal evaporation and thermocompression bonding were available for making electrical contacts to and between such regions. Kilby's first working semiconductor circuit was a simple phase-shift oscillator with components connected either through the bulk semiconductor when resistance was desired, or by bonding wires between them. This technology permitted fabrication of only simple circuits involving a few tens of devices, and several subsequent advances were necessary before the complex, reliable, and inexpensive integrated circuits of today became a reality. Some of the more important of these advances were made in the continuing effort to improve discrete transistors as mentioned earlier; however, their application to integrated circuits was rapidly recognized and exploited.

The key developments were (a) the application of photoresistant oxide etches to determine the regions into which impurities were to be diffused, (b) the planar process using the above techniques for diffusion but leaving the silicon oxide layer on the surface to protect the ambient-sensitive p-n junctions, (c) the use of evaporated and photoresist-patterned metal films on the oxide to interconnect the devices, and (d) the application of chemical vapor deposition for growing thin epitaxial layers of silicon on silicon substrates containing different impurity doping. Each of these developments, and their application to integrated circuit improvement, will be briefly described.

The ability of an SiO_2 layer to mask against the diffusion of many of the group III and V doping impurities was described by Frosch, a chemist at Bell Laboratories, in 1957. A wax pattern was applied to the oxide, the unprotected regions chemically etched away to expose the silicon, the wax removed, and impurities diffused into the exposed regions to form p- and n-doped material. Though this technique was useful, it was limited to formation of relatively large regions, several hundred microns in size. Photosensitive materials, known as photoresists, had been developed at Eastman Kodak for the patterned etching of metal on printing plates and on printed circuit boards. These were solutions containing organic compounds which polymerized upon exposure to ultraviolet light. The unexposed resist could be dissolved by appropriate solvents leaving an etch-resistant mask on the metal. Lathrop, a physicist, and Nall, a chemist, working on miniaturization of components at Diamond Ordnance Fuse Laboratory, realized in 1957 that photoresist might be applicable to patterning the SiO_2 for silicon-diffused transistors. This allowed windows of the order of 200 μm in size to be etched. Continued improvements in photoresists, with emphasis on their use with semiconductors, increased their definition capabilities to about 25 μm by 1960 and to less than 1 μm today. A major advantage in these photoresist techniques is the ability to pattern all of the areas on a 2 in diameter silicon slice simultaneously, with consequent reduction in processing cost.

The next major technological advance was the planar process, developed by Hoerni, a physicist at Fairchild Semiconductor Division. This process applies the oxide-masking and photoresist technologies already described; however, SiO_2 is regrown into the windows during the diffusion steps and the oxide is left over all of the device or circuit surface except the contact areas. This has two major advantages. The oxide, as had been shown by Atalla at Bell Laboratories, eliminates slow surface states and protects the sensitive regions (where p-n junctions intercept the silicon surface) from the effect of ambients, thereby leading to improved device characteristics and greater reliability. Also the oxide is a good insulator and allows evaporated metallization patterns connecting the devices to be formed directly on the oxide surface. Again, photoresist techniques are used to define these metal interconnections patterns. It is also possible, by depositing another SiO_2 layer over the first metallization, to form a second set of interconnections allowing even more complex circuits to be fabricated.

Still another significant development necessary for the success of integrated circuits was the application of chemical vapor deposition to grow epitaxial silicon layers. Circuits made with planar technology, but on bulk silicon slices, had severe limitations. Many circuits required significantly better electrical isolation between individual regions or devices than was afforded by the bulk silicon resistance alone. Hence, such circuits could not be integrated. Epitaxial growth, as will be described, allowed suitable isolation to be achieved.

Chemical vapor deposition for growing single crystals of silicon and germanium was demonstrated in the early 1950's by Sangster, a chemist at Hughes Aircraft Company, and by Teal and Christensen, chemists at Bell Laboratories. The conductivity type and resistivity of the deposited semiconductors could be controlled by introducing appropriate impurity gases during the deposition. Several investigators attempted to use this technique for growing successive multiple n- and p-type layers to form diodes and transistors directly, rather than by starting with uniform material and altering regions by impurity diffusion. However, these attempts gave poor results. The characteristics of the resulting p-n junctions were poor, probably due to imperfections or contamination at the interfaces between the layers. Whereas diffusion could be patterned into localized areas, there was no comparable way of patterning the epitaxial regions. However, an interdisciplinary team at Bell Laboratories, Loar (physicist), Christensen (chemist), Kleimack (physicist) and Theurer (metallurgist), realized and demonstrated that a more limited use of epitaxial deposition could significantly improve planar transistor performance.

The diffused base and emitter regions in planar transistors are quite shallow, extending only a few, or at most a few tens, of microns in from the silicon surface. Yet, in order to be handled during processing without excessive breakage, the silicon slices must be several times that thickness. Since the resistivity in the collector region adjacent to the base needs to be of the order of 1 Ω cm, the extra thickness adds additional collector series resistance which is detrimental to transistor performance. By starting with a heavily doped, hence low resistivity, silicon slice of sufficient thickness to provide the necessary mechanical strength, and growing a lightly doped epitaxial layer only thick enough to contain the active regions of the transistor, a significant reduction was obtained in collector series resistance.

This same technique was subsequently applied to silicon integrated circuits to achieve electrical isolation between components. A thin n-type epitaxial layer suitable for fabrication of the desired devices was grown on a p-type silicon substrate. During processing, a group III impurity was diffused through the thin n-layer to the p-type substrate in a pattern that surrounded those devices requiring isolation with p-type material. The high resistance of the reversed bias p-n junction provided the isolation.

Based on the technologies which have been described, integrated circuits containing bipolar transistors as the active devices were developed to perform a variety of electronic functions and a major commercial business resulted. Meanwhile, back in the laboratories, a new active semiconductor device was being studied, the metal-oxide-semiconductor (MOS) transistor. It is interesting to note that the MOS transistor is in essence the field-effect device that Shockley had originally sought, but only more recently made possible through advances in materials technology. This device had significant advantages over bipolar transistors for some applications. The electrical power requirements were lower. High packing densities on integrated circuits were possible and fewer processing operations were required during manufacturing, resulting in higher yields and lower costs. However, the device also brought new technical problems which had to be solved before its usefulness could be realized.

Inasmuch as the critical, active region of the MOS transistor lies very close to the silicon-SiO_2 interface, the instabilities in the SiO_2 and near the interface strongly influence the transistor properties. Such instabilities can be caused by many things, a common one being the presence of sodium ion contamination in the SiO_2. The high electronic field present across the oxide during operation of the device causes the sodium to migrate, and transistor characteristics shift accordingly. Many man-years of effort in several laboratories by chemists, physicists and electrical engineers were required before the causes of, and cures for, these instabilities reached a point where reliable MOS integrated circuits became practical. This area is now growing rapidly in importance, with integrated circuits containing as many as 10,000 individual components being manufactured in high volume and incorporated into equipment such as electronic desk and hand calculators.

So the integrated circuit has evolved, in a little over a decade, from Kilby's first phase-shift oscillator with a few components to the large-scale manufacturing of circuits with over 10,000 components, and these at much lower cost and higher reliability than the sum of the individual components.

The critical steps in the integrated-circuit story are shown in Fig. 1. The overall effort was both multidisciplinary and interdisciplinary. Chemists and metallurgists developed epitaxial growth techniques with the scope of the studies ranging from basic investigations of the kinetics and thermodynamics of the vapor-solid reactions to the design of production reactors capable of handling several slices at a time. A chemist discovered the diffusion-masking ability of SiO_2. A physicist, who had previously spent several years in a university chemistry department, conceived of the planar process. A physicist and chemist first applied photoresist methods to semiconductors. Metallurgists perfected the metal systems evaporated onto the surface for interconnecting the components. Electrical engineers designed the devices and circuits, and laid out the diffusion-masking and interconnection patterns so that circuits would perform the desired functions. Today, because of the extreme complexity of circuits containing in excess of 10,000 components, layout and interconnection patterns are performed on computers, requiring programmers and software specialists, and they must interact closely with the chemists, physicists and process engineers to ensure compatibility between the design and the process capabilities. Finally, metallurgists and ceramic engineers developed the hermetically sealed packages to protect the silicon circuits.

Interaction between science and engineering certainly existed to a high degree. While investigators were busy writing up their work for publication in scientific journals, they were simultaneously phasing their developments into the production lines. The time between scientific advance and production was extremely short.

The technological advances described here borrowed very heavily from developments in other areas. Nearly all were motivated by attempts to improve the performance of discrete transistors rather than integrated circuits. Diffusion of impurities had been studied for years in other materials, such as metals. Photoresist was developed for the printing and circuit-board industries. But those concerned with the perfection of the integrated circuit quickly recognized the applicability of such techniques.

There were certainly many individuals and institutions involved, both in the initial discoveries and even more in the subsequent development into useful processes. Few of the significant contributions to process technology involved basic research. Most grew out of applied research and engineering, with the latter predominating.

The development of integrated circuits, in fact the entire development of modern electronic devices, was not only a case where the MSE approach was followed, but one where this approach was essential for success to be achieved so effectively. . . .

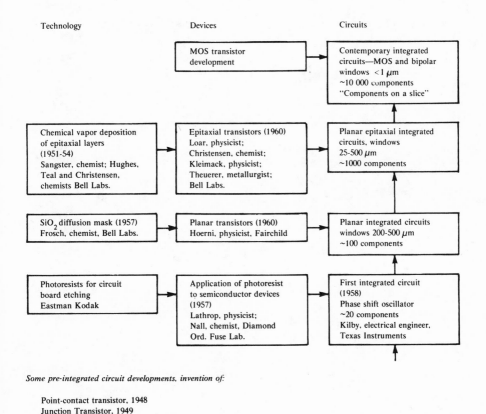

Some pre-integrated circuit developments, invention of:

Point-contact transistor, 1948
Junction Transistor, 1949

WORK BY

Chemists and metallurgists on growing, purifying and doping crystals. Grown junction, alloying and diffusion processes.	Physicists on recombination mechanisms, carrier transport, band structure, surface states.	Electrical engineers on transistor design, power and frequency improvement, circuit design.

Fig. 1. Key integrated-circuit developments, 1958-1971.

25

INTERFIELD THEORIES*

Lindley Darden† and Nancy Maull

1. Introduction. Interactions between different areas or branches or fields of science have often been obscured by current emphasis on the relations between different scientific theories. Although some philosophers have indicated that different branches may be related, the actual focus has been on the relations between theories within the branches. For example, Ernest Nagel has discussed the reduction of one branch of science to another ([27], ch. 11). But the relation that Nagel describes is really nothing more than the derivational reduction of the *theory* or *experimental law* of one branch of science to the theory of another branch.

We, in contrast to Nagel, are interested in the interrelations between the areas of science that we call *fields*. For example, cytology, genetics, and biochemistry are more naturally called fields than theories. Fields may have theories within them, such as the classical theory of the gene in genetics; such theories we call *intra*field theories. In addition, and more important for our purposes here, interrelations between fields may be established via *interfield theories*. For example, the fields of genetics and cytology are related via the chromosome theory of Mendelian heredity. The existence of such interfield theories has been obscured by analyses such as Nagel's that erroneously conflate theories and fields and see interrelations as derivational reductions.

The purpose of this paper is, first, to draw the distinction between field and *intra*field theory, and, then, more importantly, to discuss the generation of heretofore unrecognized *inter*field theories and their functions in relating two fields. Finally we wish to mention the implications of this analysis for reduction accounts and for unity and progress in science.

* From *Philosophy of Science*, Vol. 44, 1977, pp. 43-64. Copyright 1977 by the Philosophy of Science Association.

† Lindley Darden gratefully acknowledges the support of a faculty research award from the General Research Board of the Graduate School of the University of Maryland.

By analysis of a number of examples we will show that a field is an area of science consisting of the following elements: a central problem, a domain consisting of items taken to be facts related to that problem, general explanatory factors and goals providing expectations as to how the problem is to be solved, techniques and methods, and, sometimes, but not always, concepts, laws and theories which are related to the problem and which attempt to realize the explanatory goals. A special vocabulary is often associated with the characteristic elements of a field. Of course, we could attempt to associate institutional and sociological factors with the elements of a field, but such an attempt would fail to serve the purpose of our discussion. We are interested in conceptual, not sociological or institutional, change. Thus, the elements of a field are conceptual, not sociological, of primary interest to the philosopher, not the sociologist.

The elements are also historical. Fields emerge in science, evolve, sometimes even cease to be. (We have not yet explored the latter phenomenon of decline.) Although any or all of the elements of the field may have existed separately in science, they must be brought together in a fruitful way for the field to emerge. Such an emergence is marked by the recognition of a promising way to solve an important problem and the initiation of a line of research in that direction. For instance, what comes to be the central problem of a field may have been a long-unsolved puzzle and the techniques may have been used elsewhere, but the field emerges when someone sees that those techniques yield information relevant to the problem. Or, perhaps, a new concept is proposed, giving new insight into an old puzzling problem and generating a line of research. . . .

Examples of fields will now be examined in more detail. Cytology in its early days had the central problem—what are the basic units of organisms? This problem was solved by the postulation of the cell theory and its subsequent elaboration and confirmation in the nineteenth century. Afterwards, the problem for cytologists (or cell biologists as they have come to be called) became the characterization of different types of cells, of organelles within cells, and of their various functions. The problem is tackled primarily with the technique of microscopic analysis.

The field of genetics, on the other hand, has as its central problem the explanation of patterns of inheritance of characteristics. The characteristics may be either gross phenotypic differences, such as eye color in the fly *Drosophila*, as investigated in classical genetics, or molecular differences, such as loss of enzyme activity, as investigated in modern transmission genetics. The patterns of inheritance are investigated with the technique of artificial breeding. The laws of segregation and independent assortment (Mendel's Laws), once their scope was known and they were well-confirmed, became part of the domain to be explained. For many of the early geneticists, though not all, the goal was to solve the central problem by the formulation of a theory involving material units of heredity (genes) as explanatory factors. In attempting to realize the goal, T.H. Morgan and his associates formulated the theory of the gene of classical genetics. Extension of the theory and techniques from *Drosophila*, Morgan's model organism, to microorganisms marked the modern phase of the field of genetics, a phase which may be called modern transmission genetics.

The central problem of biochemistry is the determination of a network of interactions between the molecules of cellular systems and their molecular environment; these molecules and their interrelations are the items of the domain. As was the case with genetics in which laws became part of the domain, here too, the solution to a problem may contribute new domain items. For example, the Krebs cycle was part of the solution to the problem of determining the interactions between molecules and became, in turn, part of the domain of biochemistry; its relation to other complex pathways then posed a new problem. Many techniques of biochemistry are aimed at the reproduction of *in vivo* systems *in vitro*, that is, the "test tube" simulation of the chemical reactions that occur in living things.

The determination of the structure and three-dimensional configuration of molecules has become the concern of physical chemistry. Thus, the central problem of physical chemistry is the determination of the interactions of all parts of a molecule relative to one another, under varying conditions. The domain of physical chemistry is the parts of molecules and their interactions. Physical chemistry has evolved complex techniques for the determination of the structure and conformation of molecules: x-ray diffraction, mass spectrometry, electron microscopy, and the measurement of optical rotation.

With these examples of fields in mind we may contrast fields and *intra*field theories. A field at one point in time may not contain a theory, or may consist of several competing theories, or may have one rather successful theory. Well-confirmed laws and theories may become part of the domain and a more encompassing theory be sought to explain them. Although theories within a field may compete with one another, in general, fields do not compete, nor do theories in different fields compete. Furthermore, one field does not reduce another field; reduction in the sense of derivation would be impossible between such elements of a field as techniques and explanatory goals.

Even though fields do not bear the relations formerly thought to exist between theories, fields may be related to one another. Indeed, our main concern here is with the relations between fields which serve to generate a different type of theory, the *interfield theory*, which sets out and explains the relations between fields. Our task now is to discuss the conditions which lead to the generation of interfield theories. The discussion of general features of generation will be followed by examples of interfield theories: the chromosome theory of Mendelian heredity bridging the fields of cytology and genetics; the operon theory relating the fields of genetics and biochemistry; and the theory of allosteric regulation connecting the fields of biochemistry and physical chemistry. The examples will then serve as a basis for characterizing the general functions of interfield theories.

2. The generation of interfield theories. An interfield theory functions to make explicit and explain relations between fields. Relations between fields may be of several types; among them are the following:

(1) A field may provide a *specification of the physical location* of an entity or process postulated in another field. For example, in its earliest formulation, the chromosome theory of Mendelian heredity postulated that the Mendelian genes were *in* or *on* the chromosomes; cytology provided the physical location of the genes. With more specific knowledge, the theory explained the relation in more detail: the genes are part of (in) the chromosomes. Thus, the relation became more specific, a *part-whole* relation.

(2) A field may provide the *physical nature* of an entity or process postulated in another field. Thus, for example, biochemistry provided the physical nature of the repressor, an entity postulated in the operon theory.

(3) A field may investigate the *structure* of entities or processes, the *function* of which is investigated in another field. Physical chemistry provides the structure of molecules whose function is described biochemically.

(4) Fields may be linked *causally*, the entities postulated in one field providing the causes of effects investigated in the other. For example, the theory of allosteric regulation provides a causal explanation of the interaction between the physicochemical structure of certain enzymes and a characteristic biochemical pattern of their activity.

These types of relations are not necessarily mutually exclusive; as the examples indicate, structure-function relations may also be causal.

Several different types of reasons may exist for generating an interfield theory to make explicit such relations between fields. First, relationships between two fields may already be known to exist prior to the formulation of the interfield theory. We shall refer to such pre-established relationships as *background knowledge*. For example, prior to the proposal of the operon theory, the fields of genetics and biochemistry were known to be related; to cite one of many instances, the physical nature of the gene was specified biochemically as DNA. Thus, further relations could be expected between the fields and might lead to the generation of an interfield theory.

Secondly, a stronger reason for proposing an interfield theory exists when two fields *share an interest in explaining different aspects of the same phenomenon*. For example, genetics and cytology shared an interest in explaining the phenomenon of heredity, but genetics did so by breeding organisms and explaining the patterns of inheritance of characters with postulated genes. Cytology, on the other hand, investigated the location of the heredity material within the cell using microscopic techniques. Since they were both working on the problem of explaining the phenomenon of hereditary, a relation between them was expected to exist.

Furthermore, *questions arise in each field which are not answerable using the concepts and techniques of that field*. These questions direct the search for an interfield theory. For example, in genetics the question arose: where are the genes located? But no means of solving that question within genetics were present since the field did not have the techniques or concepts for determining physical location. Cytology did have such means.

In brief, an interfield theory is likely to be generated when background knowledge indicates that relations already exist between the fields, when the fields share an interest in explaining different aspects of the same phenomenon, and when questions arise about that phenomenon within a field which cannot be answered with the techniques and concepts of that field. . . .

We will now turn to the examination of detailed examples of interfield theories in order to illustrate the general features of their generation just discussed and to analyze their functions in more detail.

3. The chromosome theory of Mendelian heredity. Cytology emerged as a field in the 1820s and 30s with improvements in the microscope and the proposal of the cell theory. By the late 1800s, as a result of their investigations of the structures within cells, cytologists asked the following question: where within the germ cells is the hereditary material located? A widely accepted answer by 1900 proposed the chromosomes (darkly staining bodies within the nuclei of cells) as the likely location. (For further discussion see [40], [6], and [15].)

On the other hand, theories of heredity had been proposed in the late nineteenth century, but none had the necessary ties to experimental data to give rise to a field of heredity until the discovery of (what have come to be called) Mendel's laws in 1900. Although Mendel had worked with garden peas, noted their hereditary characteristics, crossed them artificially and proposed a law—he formulated only one—characterizing the patterns of inheritance, he did not found a field. Genetics emerged between 1900 and 1905 with the independent discovery of Mendel's law by Hugo de Vries and Carl Correns and with the promulgation of Mendel's experimental approach by William Bateson. Although Bateson did not (for reasons too complex to examine here), other geneticists postulated (what have come to be called) genes as the causes of hereditary characteristics. (For further discussion see [7], [8], and [10].)

Thus, by 1903 cytology and genetics had both investigated hereditary phenomena but asked different questions about it. At least some geneticists postulated Mendelian units to account for the patterns of inheritance of observed characteristics. Cytologists, on the other hand, proposed the chromosomes as the location of the hereditary material in the germ cells. Genes were, thus, hypothetical entities with known functions; chromosomes were entities visible with the light microscope with a postulated function. . . .

. . . The theory did more than explain properties of genes and chromosomes already known. It also functioned to predict new items for the domains of each field on the basis of knowledge of the other. For example, item 4 of Table 1 is a prediction Sutton made about the behavior of chromosomes on the basis of the behavior of genes. This prediction corrected a misconception of cytologists. Mistakenly, Sutton said ([37], p. 29), cytologists prior to the formation of the chromosome theory of Mendelian heredity had thought that the sets of chromosomes from the mother and father remained intact in their offspring and separated as units in the formation of gametes (sexual cells; in animals, eggs and sperm) in offspring. However, the independent assortment of hereditary characteristics, and therefore the genes which cause them, led to a reexamination of the behavior of the chromosomes, with the subsequent finding that the maternal and paternal chromosomes are distributed randomly in the formation of gametes ([37], [5]). The prediction for cytology of random segregation of chromosomes as a result of independent assortment of genes was thus substantiated.

Table 1. Relations Between Chromosomes and Genes

CHROMOSOMES

GENES

1. Pure individuals (remain distinct, do not join)

1. Pure individuals (remain distinct, no hybrids)

2. Found in pairs (in diploid organisms prior to gametogenesis and after fertilization)

2. Found in pairs (in diploid organisms prior to segregation and after fertilization)

3. The reducing division results in one-half to gametes

3. Segregation results in one-half to gametes

4. *Prediction*:
   Random distribution of maternal and paternal chromosomes in formation of gametes

4. Characters from maternal and paternal lines found mixed in one individual offspring; independent assortment (often) of genes

5. Chromosome number smaller than gene number

5. *Prediction*:
   Some genes do not assort independently in inheritance; instead are linked on the same chromosome

6. Some chromosomes form chiasmata, areas of intertwining
   Prediction:
   An exchange of parts of chromosomes at chiasmata

6. More combinations of linked genes than number of chromosomes; "crossing-over occurs

Predictions went both ways. The knowledge from cytology of the small number of chromosomes compared to larger numbers of genes led both Boveri and Sutton to the prediction that some genes would be linked in inheritance, in other words, that exceptions to independent assortment would occur. The finding of linked genes substantiated this prediction. (See item 5 of Table 1.) The finding of predictions made on the basis of the theory served to provide support for the theory. As a result, both genetic and cytological evidence provided confirmation. . . .

، In summary, the chromosome theory of Mendelian heredity is an interfield theory bridging the fields of genetics and cytology. It was generated to unify the knowledge of heredity found in both fields and thereby to explain the similar properties of chromosomes and genes. It functioned to focus attention on previously neglected items of the domains and to predict new items for the domains of each field. It further served to generate a new line of research coordinating the fields of cytology and genetics. Success in finding the predictions of the theory and in developing the common line of research resulted in the confirmation of the theory and the fruitful bridging of two fields of science.

4. The operon theory and theory of allosteric regulation. The chromosome theory was an important first step, eventually leading to the development of an explanation of how the genetic material acts as a carrier of information in biological systems. Once the DNA component of the chromosome was shown to carry the genetic information, then the problem of the *control* of such information emerged. The regulation of gene expression was seen to be of particular significance for an understanding of the development of organisms from embryo to adult. All cells of a multicellular organism have an identical complement of genes, but in different cells, different genes are expressed at different times. In short, differentiation occurs and must be explained. Even in unicellular organisms, gene expression varies with stages in the life cycle and, as we shall see in discussing the operon theory, with changes in the surrounding medium that affect the intracellular environment. The operon theory and the Monod-Wyman-Changeux theory of allosteric regulation are both theories of the control of gene expression: the operon theory of the control of protein *levels* (the quantity of a protein in a cell) and the theory of allosteric regulation of the control of protein *activity*.

Biochemists became interested in one aspect of the control of protein levels, *enzyme adaptation* (later called *enzyme induction*), some fifty years after its discovery in 1900 by Dienert ([9]). Dienert had described a process by which cells adjust the availability of an enzyme in response to the presence of specific metabolites (substances required for growth). This finding was later thought to suggest that gene expression is reversibly controlled by biochemical changes in the environment. For example, the bacterium *Escherichia coli* produces higher levels of the lactose-metabolizing enzymes when lactose precursors, the galactosides, are available. However, these enzyme levels are radically reduced in the absence of galactosides.

Further, transmission studies (artificial breeding and recording of characters transmitted to offspring) showed that the capacity to regulate enzyme levels in response to metabolites could be altered by mutation (heritable changes in the genes). Certain mutants in the lactose-metabolizing system within the bacterium were discovered; the mutants produce the enzymes required for the metabolism of lactose whether or not the lactose precursors are available. This mutation (i-, or inducer-negative) was found to be located at a site on the bacterial chromosome distinct from the sites of the genes for the lactose-metabolizing enzymes. This suggested that changes at a site somewhat distant from the genes for the lactose-metabolizing enzymes could affect the expression of those genes. Further investigation of mutants of this i gene and the critical experiment of Pardee, Jacob, and Monod in 1959 ([29]) implicated an i gene *product* as the controlling substance responsible for the repression of the lactose-metabolizing enzymes.

The control of these enzymes by an i gene product was incorporated into the proposal, in 1961, by Jacob and Monod ([16]) of a theory of the operon, a causal theory of biochemical changes that effect specific, heritable patterns of gene expression. Two kinds of genes were postulated: *structural genes*, like the genes for the lactose-metabolizing enzymes, carry the information that determines the molecular structure of enzymes, or carry the information for some proteins other than enzymes (for example, hormones); *regulatory genes*, of which the i gene represents only one type, are involved in the control of structural genes. Further, the operon theory postulates that the *lac* (lactose-metabolizing) system of *E. coli* is an *inducible* system; enzyme synthesis is induced by the presence of metabolites. Induction, that is, transcription of the lactose-metabolizing genes into a *cytoplasmic messenger* (mRNA) for protein synthesis, depends on the state of another regulatory gene called the *operator*. The structural genes whose activity is coordinately controlled, as are the lactose-metabolizing genes, form a unit of control, the *operon*. Transcription of the operon begins at the operator if the operator is not blocked by the i gene product, called the *repressor*. However, the repressor is not always in complex with the

operator; the repressor itself is controlled by its interaction with
inducer, in the case of the *lac* system, the galactosides. When inducer is
available, the repressor binds the inducer and cannot bind the
operator. And transcription of the operon proceeds. On the other hand,
when inducer is absent, the repressor binds the operator and
transcription is blocked. (See Figure 1.)

Questions about the physical nature of the repressor, whether a
polynucleotide like mRNA or a protein, were raised in the 1961
proposal. However, the *genetic* studies upon which the proposal was
based could not provide an answer to questions about the physical
nature of the repressor. Subsequent to the 1961 proposal, *biochemical*
findings implicated a protein repressor. Yet the *lac* repressor was not
isolated until 1966; the biochemical test used to isolate the protein was
its affinity for galactosides, a property predicted by the operon theory
on the basis of genetic findings. As the theory also predicted, the
protein was shown to be absent or functionally impaired in the *i* mutant
strains of bacteria. Finally the repressor protein was shown to bind an
operator, as the theory predicted.

Significantly, the protracted failure to isolate the repressor in the
five years after the 1961 proposal led to questions about the mode of
interaction between repressor, inducer, and operator. It was thought
that a better understanding of the inducer-repressor interaction would
facilitate isolation of the repressor. The characteristic biochemical
pattern of activity of the repressor (a sigmoid activity curve) was seen by

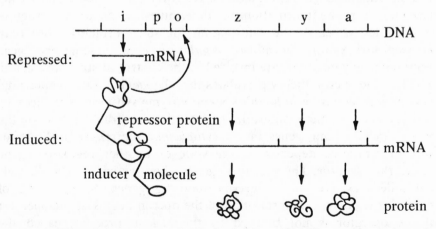

Figure 1. The *lac* operon of *Escherichia coli*. The repressed and
induced states are illustrated.

Monod and his colleagues to be similar to that of a class of "regulatory enzymes" and to hemoglobin, the "honorary enzyme." Thus, the operon theory served to direct new attention to an area of investigation in biochemistry, the functional similarities of a group of proteins. In addition to questions about the shared pattern of activity, questions about the possibility of shared structural features among such proteins were raised, thereby involving an area of investigation within physical chemistry, the structure or conformation of molecules.

Protein function (as revealed by a characteristic pattern of activity) was thought to be associated with protein structure as early as 1894; in that year Fischer ([11]) proposed his "lock-and-key" model of enzyme catalysis. In 1965, Monod, Wyman, and Changeux ([23]) proposed a causal theory to relate changes in protein structure to changes in protein activity. According to this theory of allosteric regulation, the alteration of protein activity (in the case of the repressor, its affinity for operator) is due to a reversible change in the conformation of the protein when it binds its regulatory metabolite (inducer). The theory predicts that the regulatory protein (repressor) will have two nonoverlapping sites: one, the *active site*, has a structure complementary to the substrate (operator) and therefore binds it; another, the *allosteric site*, has a structure complementary to the regulatory metabolite (inducer) and binds it. (See Figure 2.) The conformational change brought about by the formation of a protein-metabolite complex is called an *allosteric transition*, "which modifies the properties of the active site, changing one or several of the kinetic parameters which characterize the biological activity of the protein" ([22]. p. 307).

In both theories, the operon theory and the theory of allosteric regulation, two fields (genetics and biochemistry on the one hand and biochemistry and physical chemistry on the other) share a concern with the investigation of aspects of a phenomenon (with the operon theory, regulated gene expression and with the theory of allosteric regulation, regulated protein activity). Both theories are posed against a considerable body of background knowledge; extensive relationships between genetics, biochemistry, and physical chemistry had already been established. As a result, good reasons could be advanced for entertaining the hypotheses that patterns of gene expression are related to certain biochemical entities and processes and that the activity of proteins is related to their physicochemical conformation.

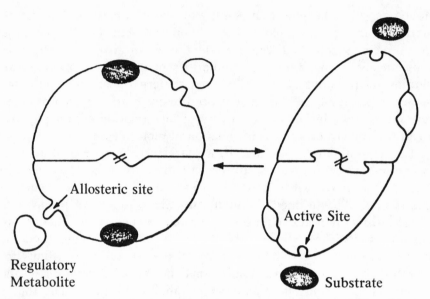

Figure 2: An allosteric transition in a symmetrical protein with two subunits.

In both cases, no one field had all the concepts and techniques to answer all the questions that arose concerning the phenomenon. Genetics provided the transmission studies of the *i* mutant and characterized the active *i* gene product as a cytoplasmic substance. The physical nature of the *i* gene product was determined by a biochemical test. And the structural features of the repressor required to explain its characteristic pattern of biochemical activity could only be supplied by physicochemical techniques.

Both the operon theory and the theory of allosteric regulation are causal theories. The operon theory is an account of biochemical causes and genetic effects; specific biochemical interactions explain the patterns of inheritance characteristic of the regulated system of genes. The theory of allosteric regulation explains the characteristic pattern of activity (the function) of certain proteins by a specific and reversible sequence of structural change. Both theories supply answers to theoretical problems by introducing new ideas about the relationship among items of different domains.

5. The function of interfield theories. In summary, an interfield theory functions in some or all of the following ways:

(a) To solve (perhaps "correctly") the theoretical problem which led to its generation, that is, to introduce a new idea as to the nature of the relations between fields;

(b) To answer questions which, although they arise within a field, cannot be answered using the concepts and techniques of that field alone;

(c) To focus attention on previously neglected items of the domains of one or both fields;

(d) To predict new items for the domains of one or both fields;

(e) To generate new lines of research which may, in turn, lead to another interfield theory.

. . . Our analysis suggests and provides a foundation for the further development of a conceptual apparatus for understanding the generation and function of theories. The advantage of paying attention to the developmental and functional characteristics of theories is shown by the fact that we have discovered similarities among theories that might not have been noticed otherwise. Although the relationships between genetics and biochemistry and between biochemistry and physical chemistry may be seen, at first glance, as in some way reductive, it is unlikely that anyone would claim that cytology is reduced to genetics (or vice versa) by the chromosome theory. In other words, our analysis shows important similarities between the generation and function of relationships which, on the older analysis, are in the different categories of "reductive" and "nonreductive" and would not have been seen as similar. It also indicates that there are important relations in science which are not reductive at all.

One is led to ask: what accounted, on the older analysis, for the different ways of categorizing these two types of cases? Again, our analysis proves illuminating. Although all three cases are examples of interfield theories, the relationships between fields which they establish are not identical. The operon theory and the theory of allosteric regulation primarily establish *causal* links; the chromosome theory, on the other hand, establishes a *part-whole* relation between genes and chromosomes. We suspect that causal relations are more likely to appear reductive than part-whole relations. Of course, this speculation is only a starting point for further investigation of these and other cases.

Not only does our analysis call attention to similarities and differences overlooked in reductive analyses, it also casts doubt on the view that the unity of science is to be analyzed merely as a series of reductions, realized or potential. Provided with a new analysis of the relations between fields, it becomes natural to view the unity of science, not as a hierarchical succession of reductions between theories, but rather as the bridging of fields by interfield theories. The unity of science analyzed as a hierarchical classification scheme of scientific theories, graded according to generality, is precisely the picture provided by Oppenheim and Putnam ([28]) as a "working hypothesis." Our preliminary analysis suggests another, new working hypothesis: unity in science is a complex network of relationships between fields effected by interfield theories.

Progress, too, receives a different analysis. Much of the progress of modern biology results from the development of interfield theories and the progressive unification (bridging) of the biological and physical sciences. With the chromosome theory, genes were associated with intracellular organelles; subsequently, with the development of the Watson-Crick model, the genes were identified with segments of DNA molecules with a specific type of structure. The operon theory provided further links between genetics and biochemistry, and the theory of allosteric regulation served as a bridge between biochemistry and physical chemistry. In sum, the chromosome theory was the first of a series of interfield theories, the operon theory and theory of allosteric regulation among them, that advanced our understanding of the relationship between the biological and physical sciences and resulted in progress in modern biology.

We have used a methodology here which ties philosophy of science, not to formal logic, but to the history of science, the proper subject matter of philosophy of science. But we must be clear about what our analysis has produced. We are not proposing a general analysis applicable to all varieties of theory, progress or unity in science. Indeed, we have no reason to prejudge the still open question as to whether there is *one* analysis applicable to all theories or instances of unification and progress. We have found *a* type of theory prevalent in modern biology which helps us understand one way in which unity and progress occurs. Further examination of other cases from the history of biology and the history of other sciences will reveal the extent to which this analysis may be generalized.

REFERENCES

. . . .

Darden, L. "Reasoning in Scientific Change: The Field of Genetics at Its Beginnings." Unpublished Ph.D. Dissertation. University of Chicago, 1974.

Dienert, F. "Sur la Fermentation du Galactose et sur l'Accoutamance des levures à ce Sucre." *Annales de l'Institute Pasteur* 14 (1900): 138-189.

. . . .

Fischer, E. "Einfluss der Konfiguration auf die Wirkung der Enzyme." *Berichte der deutschen chemische Gesellschaft* 27 (1894): 2985-2993.

. . . .

Jacob, F., and Monod, J. *"Genetic Regulatory Mechanisms in the Synthesis of Proteins."* Journal *of Molecular Biology* 3 (1961): 318-356.

. . . .

Monod, J., Changeux, J.P., and Jacob, F. "Allosteric Proteins and Cellular Control Systems." *Journal of Molecular Biology* 6 (1963): 306-329.

Monod, J., Wyman, J., and Changeux, J.P., "On the Nature of Allosteric Transitions: A Plausible Model." *Journal of Molecular Biology* 12 (1965): 88-118.

. . . .

Nagel, E. *The Structure of Science.* New York: Harcourt, Brace and World, Inc., 1961.

. . . .

Pardee, A., Jacob, F., and Monod, J. The Genetic Control and Cytoplasmic Expression of 'Inducibility' in the Synthesis of β galactosidase by *E. coli.*" *Journal of Molecular Biology* 1 (1959): 165-178.

. . . .

Sutton, W. "The Chromosomes in Heredity." *Biological Bulletin* 4 (1903): 231-251. Reprinted in *Classic Papers in Genetics.* Edited by J.A. Peters. Englewood Cliffs, N.J.: Prentice-Hall, 1959. Pages 27-41.

. . . .

26

A GOAL-ORIENTED PHARMACEUTICAL RESEARCH AND DEVELOPMENT ORGANIZATION: AN ELEVEN YEAR EXPERIENCE*

Jacob C. Stucki

DISCUSSION

The intended result of at least some of the pharmaceutical research and development effort put forth by a pharmaceutical company is the approval for marketing of new drugs by government drug regulatory agencies, the Food and Drug Administration in the U.S., or its equivalent in other countries. This R&D effort and the subsequent production and marketing efforts are always multidisciplinary in character. R&D success requires interactive contributions of people with scientific backgrounds and experience in such fields as organic chemistry, pharmacology, toxicology, pathology, clinical chemistry, analytical chemistry, physical chemistry, biochemistry, pharmacy, medicine, clinical pharmacology, biostatistics, chemical engineering, computer engineering, microbiology, immunology, bioengineering, and molecular biology. Full commercialization of new product requires people with training and experience in production, marketing, sales, finance, law, and business.

The drug discovery and development process can also be described as being pluralistic. Pluralism here refers to the dependence of success upon the involvement of organizations and people outside of the corporation undertaking the drug discovery and development effort. Drug development requires the active participation of physicians in clinics and hospitals outside of the immediate control of the

---

* From *Interdisciplinary Research Groups: Their Management and Organization*, edited by R.T. Barth and R. Steck, 1979, pp. 77-96. Proceedings of the First International Conference on Interdisciplinary Research Groups, Schloss Reisensburg, Federal Republic of Germany, April 22-28, 1979.

pharmaceutical company. Clinical evaluation of new drugs in patients of the type for whom such drugs are intended is, of course, the ultimate test of the benefit and the risk values which can be ascribed to these new drugs. The large number of patients required to demonstrate safety and efficacy and the diversity of approach to the application of drug therapy in illness can be found only through clinical studies with large numbers of private and institutional physicians. Typically, clinical studies supporting the successful drug regulatory agency approval of one new drug will require the services of as many as a hundred physicians.

The pluralism of drug discovery is also evidenced in the acquisition of the basic knowledge upon which drug discovery is built. Such knowledge derives from the whole scientific community, not only from the scientists employed by the sponsoring pharmaceutical company. Not infrequently, drug substances that are developed by pharmaceutical companies are actually discovered and patented by scientists working in academic institutions. In these instances the drug is developed and sold under a license agreement. Such agreements also involve government agencies when the discovery effort was government funded or when the discovery was made in a government laboratory. . . .

Time and cost are other dimensions which characterize the drug discovery and development process. The president of Merck Sharp and Dohme Laboratories, Dr. Lewis H. Sarett (1974), estimated identifiable development costs between the time a new drug is selected for study and the time it is approved for marketing to average 1.2 million dollars in 1962 rising to 11.5 million dollars in 1972. Schwartzman (1976) estimated that in 1973 the cost of discovering and developing each new drug was 24.4 million dollars if the cost of failures is prorated to the successful candidates.

Typical development times reported by Clymer in 1969 range from 5 to 7 years following a 3 to 4 year discovery research effort. Increasing regulatory pressures have greatly extended development times. Our own experience, which we believe is typical, includes a development time in excess of 17 years for one radically new therapeutic agent now nearing the point of marketing approval by several drug regulatory agencies. . . .

For some time it has been the opinion of Upjohn R&D management that drug discovery and development is of a complexity and nature such that it cannot be accomplished by functional departments that simply pass discovery and development information and problems along from one department to the next, but rather that the success of pharmaceutical research and development depends upon structured planning and people interactions and upon the utilization of project leaders, matrix organizations and matrix management.

Study of the environmental conditions which cause organizations to adopt a matrix organization and a matrix management approach have led Davis and Lawrence (1977) to postulate that the matrix is a preferred structural choice only when all of three basic conditions exist. The first condition is outside pressure for dual focus. This condition is characteristic of pharmaceutical R&D. Both a high level of technical knowledge and meticulous attention to the completeness and accuracy of information and knowledge about the candidate product are required by modern governmental drug regulatory agencies. Systems of government approval for marketing are such that the regulatory agencies have captured almost absolute control over the approval process leaving little room for compromise, negotiation or alternative approaches. Successful pharmaceutical companies, like successful aerospace companies, must focus intensive attention not only on complex technical issues, but also on the project requirements of the outside regulatory agency (or customer in the case of aerospace companies). The matrix approach allows the necessary balance of power to be maintained between the project manager and the functional managers contributing to the development project.

The second basic condition of Davis and Lawrence is the requirement for high information processing capacity. The hierarchical pyramid of a typical functional organization is considered inadequate to process and channel large amounts of information. This condition is also characteristic of the drug discovery and development process. Uncertainty, complexity, and interdependence, all generators of information, require the development and opening of new information and decision making networks. Matrix designs are seen as increasing organizations' information processing and decision making capacities by providing lateral channels.

The third basic condition seen as necessary for the adoption of a matrix organization is pressure to achieve high performance from expensive resources which are in high demand and in short supply and which must be shared. Technical specialists, as well as capital facilities, are examples of such resources. Few, if any, pharmaceutical R&D organizations can afford to staff for peak loads. R&D expenditures in the pharmaceutical industry are among the highest of high technology industries. Concern has been expressed that even this funding level may be insufficient to satisfy escalating regulatory agency demands for additional data.

Changing regulatory requirements have also created immediate shortages of certain technical specialists which must be shared by competing projects. Lag times in the training of additional members of these specialty groups are significant. The most recent example of an instant shortage created by regulation is in the field of veterinary pathology. This shortage was created by regulations subserving the Toxic Substances Control Act of 1976, and the U.S. Food and Drug Administration's Good Laboratory Practices Regulations (Kennedy, 1978).

The three Davis and Lawrence conditions are seen as necessary and sufficient to cause the adoption of a matrix. A matrix or multiple command system is seen by these authors as a stressful solution to complex problems and not one which should be lightly adopted. On the other hand, Sayles (1976) sees the matrix as the current dominant form of structure both in contemporary government and contemporary business.

An assessment of pharmaceutical R&D in contemporary, large corporations leads to the conclusion that all three of the Davis-Lawrence conditions are invariably present. It also leads to the conclusions that all pharmaceutical R&D organizations, to some degree, are matrix in form.

The term matrix, however, encompasses a wide range of organizational structures, management systems, decision making techniques, information management systems and communication networks. Before the particular matrices employed by The Upjohn Company's Pharmaceutical division are detailed, some general dimensions of the entire range of matrices will be described.

Gunz and Pearson (1977) have identified two basic models of R&D organizations classifiable as being matrix in form. These models reflect assumptions about how people and effort should be managed and have been called the "leadership matrix" and the "coordination matrix" (Table 1), with the project manager being a leader or coordinator, respectively. Characteristics Gunz and Pearson ascribe to each model

TWO MODELS OF MATRIX ORGANIZATION

	LEADERSHIP MATRIX	CO-ORDINATION MATRIX

THE MODEL ASSUMES PEOPLE	- TEND TO PURSUE THEIR OWN GOALS:
	  - PROFESSIONAL
	  - SPECIALIST
	 - NEED GALVANISING INTO WORKING TO PROJECT GOALS
		- ARE RATIONAL, OBJECTIVE
		 - ACT PREDICTABLY ON ADEQUATE INFORMATION

ROLE OF PROJECT LEADER IS TO:	- MOTIVATE TEAM TO WORK TO PROJECT GOALS	- KEEP EVERYONE INFORMED ABOUT:
		  - PROJECT STATUS
		  - WHEN THEIR CONTRIBUTIONS WILL BE NEEDED

CONSEQUENCES FOR PROJECT LEADER:	- NEEDS STATUS, AUTHORITY - GETS ACTION BY PERSONAL AUTHORITY, INFLUENCE, NEGOTIATING SKILLS	- IS CO-ORDINATOR, WITH MOST COMPLETE INFORMATION ON STATUS AND FUTURE NEEDS OF PROJECT - GETS ACTION BY SIGNALLING DEVIATIONS FROM PLAN
CONSEQUENCES FOR FUNCTIONAL MANAGER	- SCOPE OF AUTHORITY, RESPONSIBILITY LIMITED BY PROJECT NEEDS	- MUST CONSIDER PROJECT NEEDS IN CONJUNCTION WITH NEEDS OF FUNCTIONAL ACTIVITIES
CONSEQUENCES FOR PROJECT TEAM	- MUST BE COHESIVE GROUP - FUNCTIONAL ACTIVITIES INTERFERE WITH PROJECT WORK	- MEETINGS OF NOMINATED INDIVIDUALS - PROJECT WORK INTERFERES WITH FUNCTIONAL ACTIVITIES

from H. P. Gunz and A. W. Pearson, 'Matrix Organization in Research and Development', in 'Matrix Management', by K. Knight, 1977

may be found in any matrix organization, since to some extent an organization's characteristics are reflections of how its component individuals view their positions and their relations with their colleagues (McKelvey, 1975). Organizational characteristics are only in part a consequence of what organizational designers and top management believe the organization should be. The more people there are in an organization, the greater the diversity of opinion about how the organization actually works. It is appropriate at this point to acknowledge that the description of the past and present Upjohn organizations appearing in this paper represent my personal perceptions. They probably differ from those of some others in the organization.

The three conditions (problems) that Davis and Lawrence consider necessary and sufficient to adopt a matrix are confronted with differing results in leadership and coordination matrices. Conflicts over scarce resources are resolved better with a leadership matrix than with a coordination matrix. The coordinator must place his needs before the functional managers with whom rest the entire responsibility for balancing the claims of each of the competing projects. A coordinator is by definition precluded from adopting the negotiating stance that is the hallmark of the leader in a leadership matrix. Responses to outside pressures for focus on both the project and on functional excellence may appear to some to be met with both leadership and coordination matrices, but my personal belief is that such needs are better met by the leadership matrix. Information processing and information disseminating objectives are probably best served by the coordination matrix since information is the chief resource of the project coordinator.

Gunz and Pearson, in describing leadership and coordination matrics, acknowledge the fluid boundaries between the two types and the tendency for structural change and altered assumptions to occur as project work progresses and the needs of the project change.

Another description of matrix organization and management was offered by Galbraith (1971) in a diagram (Figure 2) showing a continuum of influence on output by the functional organization and the product organization. Galbraith considers matrix organization to be confined to a small band in the center of the diagram where the balance between functional and product influence is approximately equal. In this context, the shift from a coordination matrix to a leadership matrix could be thought of as a movement along the abscissa from relatively high functional influence to relatively high product influence. Such movement would occur within the band defining matrix organization.

Prior to 1968, Upjohn Pharmaceutical R&D was organized according to traditional disciplines into functional units. The drug discovery and development process was conducted by functional specialists assigned to project teams, mostly on a part-time basis. The

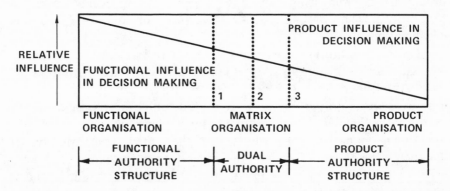

from J. R. Galbraith 'Matrix Organisation Designs', in 'Business Horizons', February, 1971

system operated as a coordination matrix with project management shifting from one functional specialist to another as the stages of development of a candidate drug changed. The functional departments involved in the drug development process included, but were not limited to, departments of Organic Chemistry, Microbiology (antibiotic isolation and identification), Pharmacology, Biochemistry, Endocrinology, Immunology, Infectious Diseases (antibiotic testing), Virology, Clinical Pharmacology, Medical Development, Pathology and Toxicology, Physical and Analytical Chemistry and Biostatistics. Steering committees at operating levels and at higher management levels provided oversight and an opportunity for reporting project status. The higher level steering committees made those project decisions which moved candidates from one state of development to the next. The very highest level of steering committee was chaired by the Vice President for Research and Development.

Product goals had been established for the company through the cooperative effort of representatives of all functional departments in R&D and the marketing organization. These goals were translated into functional activities by the respective functional specialists and their managers. Because the functional departments were relatively independent in the translation of goals to activities, the total organization experienced the problem of developing and maintaining concurrence on whether or not a given chemical compound was indeed a legitimate development candidate. Lack of consensus often led to delays in the creation and execution of development plans. Resolution of this type of conflict was often achievable only at the level of the R&D Vice President. This was the lowest level of common leadership of the critical functional departments which made, identified and proved therapeutic utility of the candidate drugs, *viz*, the chemistry, biology and medical departments.

Project managers in the coordination matrix which existed before 1968 frequently were unable to negotiate solutions to truly serious project problems or to negotiate consensus for full commitment to potential development candidates. As a consequence, conflict resolution required an inordinate investment of top executive energy and time. Decisions were often inappropriately delayed or were made on what can be regarded to be an inappropriate basis, for example, on the basis of disciplinary or functional prerogative rather than scientific evidence.

In 1968 the functional departments of Organic Chemistry, Pharmacology, Biochemistry, Microbiology, Endocrinology,

Immunology, Infectious Diseases, Virology, Clinical Pharmacology, and Medical Development were abolished and a large part of their memberships were re-organized around programmatic commitments of that time into seven departments or units, each responsible for drug discovery and development in separate disease or product area. Some of the members of the former functional departments were separated from R&D and moved to Marketing to provide technical support for marketed projects. The Product Research departments, or units as they are called, became responsible for the following product or disease areas:

Central Nervous System Diseases
Infectious Diseases
Cardiovascular Diseases
Hypersensitivity Diseases
Diabetes and Atherosclerosis
Cancer
Fertility Control Products

Each Product Research Unit consisted of all the chemists, biologists, and physicians required to make, identify and prove therapeutic utility of new drugs in their product or disease areas. Supportive research departments such as Pathology & Toxicology, Pharmacy, Biostatistics, Analytical Chemistry, etc., which are required to support all drug finding and development projects, continued to be organized functionally as they had been in the pre-1968 organization. These are the departments where resources are always in short supply and where project competition for resources is always manifested.

Individuals chosen to manage each of the new Product Research Units and to assume project management over the development projects in their disease areas were generally former functional managers who had had project management experience in the pre-1968 organization. The essential difference in the roles they played pre-1968 and post-1968 was that post-1968 the Product Research Unit managers assumed line management responsibility over a much larger part of the team required to complete the project task. Their positions post-1968 could be defined as those of relatively strong project managers in a leadership matrix. As previously noted, pre-1968 project managers were largely coordinators. Post-1968 project managers were in a somewhat better position to compete with each other and to negotiate for scarce resources in the supportive research departments than were the pre-1968 coordinators. Of greatest importance was that post-1968 managers were better able to resolve conflicts surrounding candidates under development and conflicts over the identification of development candidates. They were also able to assure the rapid preparation and execution of a development plan.

The organizational actions which were taken and which are described above can be regarded as having moved a part of the pharmaceutical R&D organization from approximately position 1 in the Galbraith diagram to approximately position 3, reflecting a significant shift in the decision making process from functional dominance to product dominance and a change from a coordination matrix to a leadership matrix. . . .

Upjohn continued to organize a portion of its chemical, biological and medical effort along traditional disciplinary or functional lines. In the 1968 re-organization it created departments of Experimental Chemistry, Experimental Biology and Experimental Medicine. The Product Research Units described above are largely independent of the Experimental Chemistry, Biology, and Medical Departments and vice versa. Exceptions occur when technology generated by either Product Research Units or by the Experimental Science Departments becomes specifically applicable to the other. Experimental Science Departments are also responsible for maintaining a discipline-oriented community for the continuing education and professional renewal of all chemists, biologists, and physicians. Each Product Research Unit, each of the Experimental Science Departments, and each of the supportive research units, e.g., Pathology & Toxicology, is responsible for conducting basic research in its own area of interest. The Experimental Sciences Departments can be regarded as constituting a coordination matrix not unlike that which existed in the entire R&D division prior to 1968. Synonyms for the two organization types which existed previously or now exist at Upjohn are shown in Table 2.

Both a discipline-oriented organization or coordination matrix and a goal-oriented organization or leadership matrix have been in existence simultaneously for eleven years in the same company. Some internal comparisons are possible, but it must be stressed that by no means can our experience be considered to constitute a valid experiment in comparative organizational effectiveness. Rather,

R & D ORGANIZATIONAL TYPES AT UPJOHN

PRE - 1968
- FUNCTIONAL UNITS
  DISCIPLINE ORIENTED ORGANIZATION
  FUNCTIONAL ORGANIZATION
  COORDINATION MATRIX

POST- 1968
- PRODUCT RESEARCH UNITS
  GOAL ORIENTED ORGANIZATION
  PRODUCT ORGANIZATION
  LEADERSHIP MATRIX

- EXPERIMENTAL SCIENCES UNITS
  DISCIPLINE ORIENTED ORGANIZATION
  FUNCTIONAL ORGANIZATION
  COORDINATION MATRIX

attention should be directed toward the interactions and influences each organization type has on the other, the synergism produced by their coexistence and their common top management and by the transfers of personnel, information, and projects that occurred between the two organizations. . . .

In 1974 we (Weisblat and Stucki) described Upjohn's goal-oriented pharmaceutical R&D organization and drew certain conclusions about performance of this organization and the behavior of its members. An additional period of observation and experience allows expansion and, in some cases, a modification of these conclusions.

In 1974 we concluded that there was a greater tendency for members of the post-1968 goal-oriented Product Research Units (leadership matrix) to share concern for the entire development process and for product success than for the members of the pre-1968 functional organization (coordination matrix). We noted an increased tendency of people of differing discipline to communicate with each other and to regard each other with respect. We attributed this to the existence of identifiable common goals and common immediate supervision. These conclusions continue to be valid. . . .

In 1974 we expressed concern about possible loss of functional professionalism which could lead to obsolescence and a possible tendency for goal-oriented units to concentrate on short term gains at the expense of longer term gains. In the period between our first report and 1979, there has been no evidence that our concerns had foundation. Strategies maintained to counter these tendencies include a strong pro-publication policy, an exploratory and methodology or basic research component in each Product Research Unit, and the designation of the Experimental Sciences Departments as responsible for maintenance of scientific functional communities for continuing education.

In 1974 we did not compare the performance and characteristics of our post-1968 Product Research Units with our Experimental Science Departments. Some comparisons are now possible but the previously mentioned caveat regarding lack of experimental validity must be emphasized.

During our 11 years of post-1968 experience, all but one Product Research Unit was successful in bringing one or more new products to commercialization. Three of the Units commercialized one product each, one commercialized two products, and two commercialized four products each. The Experimental Sciences brought three products to the market. The total time required to develop new discoveries in the pharmaceutical industry is long and growing so only two innovations were brought through all stages of the process during this 11-year period. The remaining 14 products brought to commercialization during this period had already been identified as leads prior to 1968. All units currently have a full complement of candidates under development. . . .

The performances of individual scientists in the two types of post-1968 organization did not differ in any discernible fashion. Publication patterns were similar for individuals in both goal-oriented and functional units. At Upjohn, scientists have an opportunity to progress along a professional career path (analogous to academic rank). Promotions on the path are a result of individual performance as judged by a top level oversight committee. Progress of individuals along the career path level are similar for the goal-oriented and the functional units. In both types of organization, at Upjohn and elsewhere, confusion does exist over the sources of reward. Some scientists perceive rewards to be highest for goal achievement. Others believe rewards are highest for excellence in discipline. The oversight committee attempts to reward both kinds of contributions. Beliefs of this type appear to be more a character of individuals than of organization.

A common criticism of goal-oriented organizations is that they lack ability to respond to new goals and opportunities that emerge over time. The simultaneous existence of a functional organization at Upjohn blunts this criticism. Our Experimental Sciences Units have responded well to new opportunities that presented themselves within their broad program areas. Another measure of flexibility, however, is the willingness of individuals to depart significantly from their current research activity or assignment. This kind of individual flexibility or inflexibility appears to be identical in both our goal-oriented and our functional organizations.

Our post-1968 goal-oriented departments appear to be less hierarchical in approach to technical decision making than our post-1968 discipline oriented departments, but department type alone does not satisfactorily explain differences in approach. Some individuals are more comfortable with a career in a hierarchical, discipline-oriented department, perhaps because such departments are similar to academic departments experienced in graduate school. Such individuals will gravitate toward a discipline-oriented department when the opportunity to move arises. However, the original hope that individuals would frequently move between the functional Experimental Science Departments and the goal-oriented Product Research Units, as technical problems changed, has not been completely realized. This is partly due to the long time required to complete any given project primarily because of regulatory demands.

Our post-1968 leadership matrix organization was created to correct communication and decision making defects that existed in our pre-1968 functional coordination matrix organization. This experience with goal-oriented research management or leadership matrix management can be regarded as highly successful. Problems of consensus and commitment on candidate products largely disappeared as did the problems of delay in preparation and execution of development plans insofar as they involved the members of the goal-oriented units. It must be concluded, however, that not all problems are amenable to solution by organizational shifts to leadership matrices. It is perhaps trite, but nonetheless necessary to note that both discipline and goal-oriented organizations have attributes and problems. . . .

A strategy that was successful for Upjohn involved deliberately shifting part of the organization from a coordination to a leadership matrix, the conferring of additional power on project leaders by making them line managers over key project resources, the maintenance of a competing and synergistic coordination matrix, a strong publication and basic research policy and a "Troika" approach to candidate selection and development in the functional organization. A final and perhaps obvious caveat presented at the conclusion of our 1974 report must be repeated here. A perfect organization, if there be one, will fail if not composed of capable, dedicated individuals. Our successes must be credited to the people, both technical and managerial, who make up our organizations.

REFERENCES

. . . .

Committee on Chemistry and Public Affairs (1977) 'Chemistry in Medicine: The Legacy and the Responsibility', Washington: American Chemical Society.

Davis, S.M. & Lawrence, P.R. (1977) *Matrix*, Reading, Mass.: Addison-Wesley Publishing Company.

Galbraith, J.R. (1971) 'Matrix Organization Designs: How to Combine Functional and Project Forms', *Business Horizons*, Vol. 14, No. 1, 29-40.

Gunz, H.P. & Pearson, A.W. (1977) 'Matrix Organisation in Research and Development' in *Matrix Management: A Cross-functional Approach to Organisation*, Knight, K.

Kennedy, D. (1978) 'Nonclinical Laboratory Studies: Good Laboratory Practice Regulations', *Federal Register*, December 22, Part II, 59986-60025.

. . . .

McKelvey, B. (1975) 'Guidelines for the Empirical Classification of Organizations', *Administrative Science Quarterly*, Vol. 20, No. 4, 509-25.

. . . .

Sarett, L.H. (1974) 'FDA Regulations and Their Influence on Future R&D', *Research Management*, Vol. 17, No. 2, 18-20.

Sayle, L.R. (1976) 'Matrix Management: The Structure with a Future', *Organizational Dynamics*, Autumn, Vol. 5, No. 2, 2-17.

Schwartzman, D. (1976) *Innovation in the Pharmaceutical Industry*, Baltimore and London: The Johns Hopkins University Press.

Weisblat, D.I. & Stucki, J.C. (1974) 'Goal-Oriented Organization at Upjohn', *Research Management*, Vol. 17, No. 1, 34-37.

PART VI

HOW IS IDR PERFORMED?

27

HOW DOES INTERDISCIPLINARY WORK GET DONE?*

Eric J. Cassell

INTERDISCIPLINARY WORK CAN GET DONE AND very well too—witness the work of this group. From my experience with this and other efforts at the Institute, I would like to make some observations on how it happens. I feel that the personal reference is justified because I believe that successful interdisciplinary work is based primarily on the participants undergoing personal change. Since none of us is all that willing to change beliefs and viewpoints, perhaps we should look at what softens people up enough to allow them to change.

The first essential is a healthy respect for the problem at hand. As a physician, I am quite accustomed to working with experts from other disciplines. Only I call it asking for a consultation, not interdisciplinary work. I do not do this out of largeness of character, but because I am scared of error and afraid of doing harm to a patient. That fear usually overrides pride because doctors soon learn how much damage can follow the failure to admit ignorance. If the first requirement is a healthy respect for the problem at hand, then the problems of ethics in the life sciences lend themselves naturally to interdisciplinary work. One must simply stand in awe of any set of issues which have withstood solution since the beginning of recorded time. Before working in these interdisciplinary groups, I thought that the difficulty was merely that well-established ethical systems or philosophical understandings had not been applied to the issues raised by modern biomedical science and technology. While that may be partly true, to a larger degree it is basic understanding that is lacking. As in other fields, exposure to new challenges has revealed gaps in previous knowledge, insight, and methods of analysis. In other words, it is not merely that we are seeing situations in medicine and the life sciences that are new and

---

* Reprinted by permission of The Hastings Center, Hastings-on-Hudson, New York from "Knowledge, Value and Belief," *The Foundations of Ethics and Relationship to Science*, edited by H.T. Engelhardt, Jr., and D. Callahan, 1977, pp. 355-361.

unique—to which, for example, Aristotle's *Ethics* have never been applied. Rather, these new things would pose exciting challenges to Aristotle (as only one example) if he were around today. Indeed, I am distressed with my own tradition, Judaism, because I believe Jewish ethicists have not by and large yet understood that we are dealing with situations that are new and unique in the experience of mankind.

If the first requirement for interdisciplinary work is respect for the problem, then I think that the second requirement is a belief that the problem demands solutions. When I call a consultant to see a patient with a puzzling illness, I do not do so solely out of intellectual curiosity. I ask for help because I know that decisions must be made and actions taken. Here again, the similarity to the problem of ethics in medicine and the life sciences is clear. Discovery, invention, and change proceed with consequences good, bad, and who knows what in between. Our disquiet with medicine and science, which for some reason continue to see themselves as "value free," is deepening. There is an urgency here that is pressing despite the fact that the work may go on at this pace for many decades.

These two basic requirements, respect for the problem and an urgency for answers, are necessary, I believe, because of the effect they have on the people who must participate across disciplines. They create a community of interest that, at least for a time, directs the interests and attention of the participants toward the outer need and not so much toward each other and each other's discipline. I know well that attention falters and that side issues may obscure common interest in the challenges, but I also know that the fundamental issues are so compelling that it is necessary only to raise them again to return common direction to the work.

What is being asked of those who do interdisciplinary research is that they leave the fixed intellectual navigating platforms from which each discipline or specialty views the world. For all its importance, I find that no easy thing. A person is defined, in part, by his conceptions, by the paradigmatic structure of values and beliefs about the world that relates each conception to the other. To ask of someone that he be prepared to call that conceptual structure into question is to ask that he be prepared to give up a piece of himself. People do not hold white-knuckle tight to their frames of reference out of pure reason but because to give up a frame of reference is extremely unsettling. The design of settings in which we do interdisciplinary work and the methods by which it is accomplished must take that potential for anxiety into account. It takes time for people to change their views; they are not changing something external to themselves, rather, they are changing themselves. Personal support is also required, and the best support is the sense that one is among friends and equals.

Therefore, to the requirements of respect for the problem and awareness of its urgency I must add more personal necessities for interdisciplinary research. I cannot emphasize strongly enough my belief that in successful interdisciplinary research, those things that promote change in individuals promote the work.

First among these is, I think, respect for the other participants. I lay aside a bit of myself out of the belief, derived from respect, that the view of the other person will support me even though I have not yet had time to test it myself. It is respect for the physician that enables a patient to do something for his health that he does not want to do, or that threatens injury or discomfort. In the setting of transdisciplinary work, respect arises from several diverse (and sometimes related) characteristics. One is sheer intellectual power: I do not see the problem as that man or woman does, but if someone as intelligent as that believes it to be so, I am forced to re-examine my own belief. Another characteristic often related, although not necessarily so, is depth and breadth of scholarship. Someone who knows his field and its literature so completely that it has become a part of him also commands my respect for I love learning itself. The personal integrity of a participant may make us accept what he or she says as something not idly come to or lightly held.

At the first meeting I ever attended at the Institute, when I wanted to play tapes of patients' conversations I found myself in direct conflict with the late Henry K. Beecher, M.D., over the lack of written permission for the recordings.[1] The patients had known their conversations were being recorded, and I did not see the necessity for formal permission. Some sharp words ensued, and I left the session angry. At the meeting the next morning, I apologized somewhat reluctantly, as much out of respect for Beecher as from agreement with his point of view. However, I did start getting written permission after that, and by now, I have taken Dr. Beecher's position on a number of occasions. Change is gradual, but the first willingness really to listen may come out of respect.

I may appreciate what another person has to say but I may not respect his discipline. Interdisciplinary efforts do not go well when the participants do not respect each other's disciplines or their methods. Most of us have prejudices against this or that branch of science, against all physicians or some specialties, against all philosophers or some philosophical schools, or against all theologians or some professed beliefs. No seminar, working group, or conference can survive too many participants with such feelings. On the other hand, there is no such group that does not carry some burden of simple prejudice. The solution for the problem of prejudice is, once again, personal respect and the appreciation of the importance of the goals of the work.

Having discussed these personal issues in transdisciplinary research, it seems necessary to mention some specific things that either promote or hold back the work. The first and foremost specific is language: social and professional communities are communities of language. The extent that any of us share the same conceptions or world view, or can come to know that we do, is the extent to which we share a common language. By language, I mean, of course, not merely the same words, but the same meanings and usage.

The problem of jargon is well known, but the meaning of the use of jargon is not as obvious. Jargon is often used as a short cut to pack wide meaning into few words. But, similarly, jargon is often used to cover up an absence of precise meaning. By convention, we all agree to use the word to denote the thing. However, we all also agree not to examine further the issue so denoted, knowing we might drown in any attempt at true explication. Perhaps for ordinary conversations we are better off to look no further, but interdisciplinary research is not ordinary conversation.

The use of jargon also symbolizes the fact that the user belongs to a special group. I believe the reason medical students and young physicians, for example, use more jargon than older physicians is the need the young have to feel a part of the group. Nonetheless, for any successful interdisciplinary work, the jargon has to go. When it goes, it is rather like pulling off a wart; it leaves bleeding. Daniel Callahan's dictum seems the best advice: you should always talk to others in the language you use to talk to yourself. (I wonder why we do not talk jargon to our inner selves?)

Problems of language usage, however, go deeper than jargon or technical terms. Both jargon and technical terminology can be translated into ordinary language. Further, people know and request clarification when they hear a word whose meaning they do not understand. The diverse meanings of everyday words may provide an even greater stumbling block. I suspect that the word "pain" has a different meaning to physicians than to non-physicians. Seeing a movie of a woman delivering a child by Cesarian section, under hypnosis and without anesthesia, had a profound effect upon me. I remember thinking that I had to revise my entire understanding of the meaning of pain. But both before and after that movie, I used the same word, pain, to label what had become different understandings. Difficulties in ordinary language are much harder to clarify precisely because we often do not know that the problem exists. Certain concepts can illustrate this confusion. It is quite common still to hear some philosophers talk of the difference between man and the animals. The distinction is most often made in discussing man as a rational being. To most biologists, such dichotomous distinctions seem unnatural since we see life much more in terms of similarities than of differences, as a continuum rather than as a step-like progression. This difference between life scientists and philosophers or theologians is absolutely fundamental. It is not merely something life scientists know, but it is a part of their being that underlies everything they learn and the way they approach the world. And, of course, the reverse is true. Kant is just a name to me, albeit an important one, but it is clear to me that for philosophers, Kant stands for something very much larger than I am able to comprehend.

These last two examples, difficulties arising from diverse meanings of everyday language and differences in a fundamental world view, would seem to deny the possibility of successful interdisciplinary research. And yet, success is achieved. How does it occur? Given the conditions of respect I noted above, respect for the problem and its urgency, for the other participants and their disciplines, personal change does take place. This change seems to me to have one fundamental characteristic to which all others are subservient: the change in one's frame of reference. Previously, I saw my work, the knowledge of my profession—its problems, goals, methods, ideas, and ways of thought—as being self-contained and existing alongside other similarly self-contained systems of greater or lesser interest to me. To be sure, these self-contained systems were seen by me as impinging on one another or of having importance one for another, but their distinctness was preserved within me.

Slowly dawning but then suddenly clear, the frame of reference enlarges. For me, it was coming to see medicine as existing within the much larger system of the moral life of mankind. I do not mean merely the realization that there is a world outside of medicine (although that, too, could be a first and vital change in a frame of reference). Rather, I realized that understanding in moral philosophy is fundamental to understanding medicine. With that change, what other participants had to say became not merely something I would have liked to understand in order to broaden my knowledge of the world, but rather something I realize that I *must* understand so that I can bring order back into my comprehension of medicine. The point is, of course, that with the enlargement of the frame of reference, the previous structure of my comprehension of medicine has become uncertain and the new knowledge from other disciplines is not merely useful but necessary to restore stability to the conceptual structure.

For a philosopher or a theologian, a similar change in reference frame might be the developed awareness that the biology of man is an overriding force. I cannot know what it feels like suddenly to become aware of biology, of its ineluctable operation of nature's finitude. I cannot know this because it is a part of me that developed as I developed. But I can guess that the change is as exciting for the philosopher as the reverse is for me.

The process I have described—and above all it is a process—is one of personal change. I know of no other terms that can adequately describe the nature of successful interdisciplinary efforts. Like all personal change, it takes place over time. The process is not smooth, but moves in fits and starts. For an outsider, watching it may prove exasperatingly slow and inefficient. Verbose and argumentative interchange may be more apparent than consensus. But appearances can be misleading because things are happening. Certain circumstances promote the process: obviously, judging from these meetings good food is not necessary, while alcohol seems quite useful. The idea of having papers and commentary read at one meeting and then presented again at a subsequent meeting has proved excellent. At first that seemed to me to be redundant. Why say the same thing a second time? Often, however, the discussion only comes alive at the second presentation, as the other participants begin to understand fully what the writer is saying. Problems of language and point of view are clarified over time.

As in every circus, good ringmasters are essential. Keeping all the tigers in the cage and sitting on their pedestals (each just the proper height) is no easy task. For any success we may enjoy, we are indebted to our trainers, the editors of this volume.

NOTE

[1]Dr. Beecher was the author of *Research and the Individual: Human Studies* (Boston: Little, Brown and Co., 1970), a seminal work on the ethical problems of human experimentation.

28

CONFLICTS IN INTERDISCIPLINARY RESEARCH†*

D. A. Bella
K. J. Williamson

INTRODUCTION

This study resulted primarily from the examination of our experiences and frustrations as members of an interdisciplinary research team. The team's research was concerned with the impacts of dredging on estuaries and involved seven principal investigators.

We began by reviewing the philosophy of science. Those concepts which helped to explain our experiences within this research team were selected and discussed. As systematic descriptions were developed, they were presented in workshops and seminars to members of other interdisciplinary teams. Several draft copies of this paper were circulated for review for more than two years. All comments and criticisms were carefully reviewed and appropriate changes were made.

Our descriptions of the conflicts in interdisciplinary research produced a range of emotional responses. At times, reviewers became angry because the descriptions were too personal. The most common response, however, was supportive humor that acknowledged the human frustrations, insecurities, conflicts and power struggles. These humanistic aspects which bear heavily on the potential success of interdisciplinary research are rarely acknowledged or discussed.

We have examined the nature of interdisciplinary research from the perspective of participants rather than as detached observers. Our descriptions are validated not from objective data, but from honest

† This work was supported by NSF-Rann Grant Number 34346 administered through the Ocean Engineering Program, Oregon State University and a research grant by the Office of Water Research and Technology, United States Department of the Interior, administered through the Water Resources Research Institute, Oregon State University.

* From *Journal of Environmental Systems*, Vol. 6, No. 2, 1976-77, pp. 105-124. Copyright 1976 by Baywood Publishing, Co., Inc.

experiences of actual participants. As such, our methods departed from the classical scientific approach. However, these methods proved to be successful in identifying subtle aspects of research organization not shown in typical organizational charts.

Our experiences are confined to a university setting; as such, we have not attempted to examine the more task-oriented research within large research organizations. However, important similarities, particularly with respect to the personal needs of participants, likely exist. . . .

Disciplinary Conflicts

THE PERSPECTIVE SPECTRUM

Social and ecological systems can be viewed from a spectrum of vantage points. One end of the spectrum is characterized by high perspective and low detail, while the other end, by high detail and low perspective. Movement towards a higher detail vantage point results in detailed images becoming clearer, while assemblages, patterns, and relationships formed by these images become less discernible. Movement in the opposite direction, towards a higher perspective region, results in the opposite effect; assemblages, patterns and relationships emerge while the detailed images that form them become more obscure. Components appearing in higher perspective views disperse into systems of sub-components with a more detailed view. Views from several vantage points over the entire spectrum provide complementary understandings of real-world systems whose complete nature is beyond our perception. Such a one-dimensional spectrum, even though highly simplified, is useful in comparing different disciplinary domains and paradigms.

A traditional discipline will encompass a portion of the detail-perspective spectrum. The domain will be closed in the higher-perspective direction, but open in the higher-detail direction. Increased detail will almost always fall within the disciplinary domain; however, expanded perspective can exceed the domain boundary. As a result, disciplinary outlooks will tend toward higher-detailed views and disciplinary paradigms will reflect this outlook. This "reductionist" orientation, however, can lead to the avoidance of questions and problems which become apparent only from an expanded perspective view that is broader than the disciplinary domain.

THE ROLE OF INTERDISCIPLINARY RESEARCH

Disciplinary domains are not static but rather evolve often in response to societal demands. Such evolution can lead to overlap of domains. Controversy and conflict between members of different disciplines may result due to their paradigm differences, yet such conflicts can provide creative and innovative changes. Paradigms of disciplines involved in such interdisciplinary conflict may be expanded and altered or new disciplines may evolve; thus, contact between disciplines provides a means of introducing challenges to creativity and innovation [8, 9].

Interdisciplinary environmental research is a directed effort toward such interdisciplinary contact and can provide unique opportunities for innovation. However, its potential is more than a means of promoting disciplinary innovation. Understandings of systems and problems may occur which are more than a collection of disciplinary results. Socio-ecological systems are best examined from a broad range on the perspective-detail spectrum. Such wide spectrum views are required because systems exhibit properties, activities and responses which are not only dependent on component parts, but also on the organization of these parts. The organization, behavior, and response to human activities of socio-ecological systems cannot be examined from within the boundaries of individual disciplinary domains. Both perspective and detail are needed to improve understandings of socio-ecological systems and an urgency exists for such understanding due to the expansive scope of human activities. . . .

INFLUENCE OF ASSERTIVENESS

Within early stages of interdisciplinary research, some doubt about the future success of the project probably exists. This skepticism reflects an understanding of the magnitude of the research problem and the potential inappropriateness of existing methodologies. As such, this skepticism is both healthy and realistic.

The opposite image of complete confidence, however, tends to provide a competitive advantage with respect to the control of research resources. Individuals who are willing to promise specific results by specific times tend to establish a sizeable control over research funds, personnel and equipment. However, such individuals may prove to be disruptive to interdisciplinary work because such overconfidence in providing specific answers to complex problems often reflects a shallow understanding of the important questions. Thus, an attitude of healthy skepticism is useful in both the planning and execution of interdisciplinary research, but may prove to be a hindrance in the process of obtaining resources for conducting such research.

We believe that this problem can be reduced by matching an individual's research funding to his or her personal time commitment. In this manner, the research can be closely managed by the co-principal investigators and integrated with the group's interdisciplinary approach. In addition, we believe that the tendency of granting agencies to insist on "no risk" interdisciplinary research is unrealistic due to the complexity of the environmental problems that need to be addressed. . . .

RESEARCH ACTIVITIES

The activities necessary for effective team research cannot be differentiated solely on a disciplinary basis. Thus, it is important to further identify research activities and the nature of the recognitions and risks associated with them. Four general categories of research activities common to a wide range of research teams are:

1. administration,
2. data collection,
3. development of unifying concepts within established paradigms, and
4. development of unifying concepts outside of established paradigms.

Hereafter these activities will be identified by the above numbers.

Activity 1 often leads to institutional titles and positions. The title "director" or "principal investigator" is frequently given to the administrator, often at the insistence of granting agencies. Identity is largely established through the size, sophistication and prestige of staff and facilities. Institutional demands are usually directed to administrators. Numerous necessary tasks are performed on a day-to-day basis and recognition for successful accomplishment, when it does occur, is typically of short duration. The use of disciplinary paradigms is seldom required; thus, recognitions and risks of a disciplinary nature are relatively low. A low-risk, broad professional recognition, however, is provided largely because of title and position.

Activity 2 generally is associated with a low level of recognition through institutional titles and positions. Individuals establish some identity and recognition through the size and sophistication of facilities and support personnel. The research team itself is often the primary source of recognition. Work generally is conducted safely within established paradigms and a moderate disciplinary recognition of short to moderate duration with a low risk of rejection typically can be expected. Scheduling and coordinated supplies, equipment and personnel can at times be a demanding task. Long periods of consistent, repetitive and sometimes boring activities are common. Progress is readily identified by measurable results.

Activity 3 can lead to moderate institutional titles and positions; however, higher advances usually require a shift to administrative activity. New applications of the general paradigms are often needed; cautious expansion and refinement of paradigms may be required. Disciplinary risk and recognition is generally moderate; nevertheless, success can occasionally bring about substantial recognition of a long duration. Cautious collaboration and overlap with Activity 2 are common. Individuals in Activity 3, however, are often required to "save" a project by making some sense of data previously collected.

Activity 4 is generally considered to be the most radical by disciplinary communities and institutions; consequently, high institutional positions and titles are not easily obtained. The risk of disciplinary rejection is high; however, if new concepts become accepted, the extent and duration of recognition are most significant. To offset the high risk of disciplinary rejection, individuals tend to ignore the risks of departing from institutional procedures, a reaction which removes them still further from the upper levels of institutional hierarchies. Individuals establish strong identities with concepts rather than with facilities and the size of projects.

PERSONAL CONFLICTS FROM UNREALISTIC EXPECTATIONS

A major difficulty in team research results from individuals not realistically dealing with the recognitions and risks associated with their activities (see Table 1). Individuals who identify with Activity 1 or Activity 4 are most vulnerable. Activity 1 individuals may aspire to

Table 1. Nature of Recognition and Risks for
Different Research Activities

	Activity			
Risk or Recognition	1	2	3	4
A. Title and Salary	H	L	M	M
B. Size of Staff, Facilities Equipment and Project	H	H	M	L
C. Duration of Recognition or Rejection	L	M	H-M	H
D. Risk of Rejection by Professional Discipline	L	L	M	H
E. Risk of Rejection by Institution	H	M	M	L

Note: H = high, M = moderate, L = low; ratings give importance or duration.

long term recognition for disciplinary contributions and they may feel frustrated by the difficulties of attaining this goal from their present position. Activity 4 individuals may be frustrated by the lack of day-to-day measurable progress and recognition; they may become bitter because "lesser" individuals have risen to higher and more prestigious institutional positions.

Failure to realistically deal with individual recognition needs and risks can be destructive to research efforts, especially interdisciplinary ones. Most commonly, individuals tend to drift back to the relative safety of their sub-domains. They also may attempt to compensate by identifying simultaneously with several of the four activities which results in conflicting recognition requirements and risks. Such individuals feel constant pressure; they attempt to compensate by leading hectic schedules and working long hours. Some may be able to gain an acceptable identity from such conflicting activities. Frequently, however, they do not achieve satisfaction and compensate by accepting more tasks. The resulting work overloads typically are detrimental because individuals often do not have time to examine new concepts or creatively interact with other team members.

CONFLICTS BETWEEN INDIVIDUALS FROM
ACTIVITY DIFFERENCES

Individuals tend to establish their primary identity with one of the four activities, although their actual responsibilities and interests may span more than one activity. This identity choice belongs primarily to the individual and reflects the individual's personality and ambitions. In a reasonably balanced research team, the personality and ambitions of individuals will differ considerably. The activities within the group will often conflict because individuals are responding to different frameworks of perceived recognitions and risks. The relative differences of these recognitions and risks are identified in Table 1. We believe that these differences are major factors in establishing conflicts. . . .

APPENDIX A

An Approach to Interdisciplinary Collaboration

In our study on the environmental impacts of estuarine dredging, the research team developed a shared conception of a typical temperate estuary. Estuarine features of interest to different disciplines were meshed in this conception such that disciplinary bias was discouraged. This conception itself did not provide specific answers, but served to identify a high perspective-low detail corporate domain within which more detailed collaborative study could proceed.

This shared conception of a typical estaury was formed by considering all regions within a typical estuary as points on a plot of two parameters (e.g., temperature and salinity). Such a plot would have texture since regions of common characteristics could be spatially congregated on the plot and appear darker than less common combinations of parameters. The precise dimensions and texture of the plot are not necessary to the success of this approach; only an agreement of a conceptual existence of such a plot is required. Additional dimensions now are added to form an nth-dimensional conceptual object which contains the geographical, geological, hydraulic, chemical and biological features of a typical temperate estuary. Spatial dimensions applicable to a broad class of estuaries (e.g., water depth, sediment slope) would be included.

It is not necessary to specify, describe or define each of these n dimensions, but only to imagine that such an nth-dimensional conception could exist. Its shape and texture will change with time in response to the temporal changes typical of estuaries. Changes in given parameters will cause deflections or distortions throughout the conception. The effects of dredging or other activities can be envisioned as alterations of the shape and texture of this shared conception.

Collaborative team dialogue must focus on more identifiable features of this conception to obtain useful information. This is accomplished by "dissecting" it with a kth-dimensional dissection space where $k < n$ and usually equal to 2. For $k=2$, dissection spaces become planes and the purpose of the dissection process is to locate relevant images and textures from the nth-dimensional conception onto such planes. This process is not a formal mathematical procedure, but rather describes the interdisciplinary dialogue which seeks to identify those images and textures which can be located on particular dissection planes. Such images and textures will usually lack precision and detail; complementary views from other dissection planes or higher dimensioned dissection objects may be needed. . . .

Summary

Interdisciplinary research has the potential to produce results that exceed the sum of disciplinary contributions. More holistic understandings can emerge from such research. These understandings are becoming increasingly necessary due to the potential magnitude and complexity of environmental alterations made possible through expanding technological capabilities. Typically, however, interdisciplinary research efforts rapidly decompose into loosely related disciplinary studies. A number of factors which contribute to this decomposition were examined. Methods of overcoming these factors in a manner which encourages collaborative and creative research were discussed.

ACKNOWLEDGMENT

We acknowledge the contributions to the ideas presented by the other members of our research team; D.R. Hancock, R.T. Hudspeth, J.E. McCauley, L.S. Slotta, C.K. Sollitt, and J.M. Stander. We also acknowledge the importance of many lively discussions on this material with colleagues from other research projects.

REFERENCES

. . . .

G. Bugliarello, Technological Innovation and Hydraulic Engineering, *J. of Hydraulics Div. ASCE*, *98*, p. 751, 1972.

K.E. Boulding, *Beyond Economics*, The University of Michigan Press, Ann Arbor, Michigan, 1970.

. . . .

29

INTERDISCIPLINARY INTEGRATION WITHIN TECHNOLOGY ASSESSMENTS*

Frederick A. Rossini
Alan L. Porter
Patrick Kelly
Daryl E. Chubin

1. Introduction

Technology Assessment (TA) and interdisciplinary research are related topics that have generated considerable interest in the research community. TA has attracted attention through such developments as the creation of the Office of Technology Assessment. Interdisciplinary research has been widely discussed as a fruitful approach to studying problems of social importance which cut across disciplinary boundaries. This article presents the complete research findings of a two-year study of the process of integrating the disciplinary components of TAs (Rossini et al., 1978).

Technology Assessment

Technology assessment is the study of the full range of consequences resulting from the introduction into society of a new technology or the modification of an existing technology, and of the policy alternatives for dealing with these consequences. Figure 1 schematically illustrates the process of change associated with a

*˙From *Knowledge: Creation, Diffusion, Utilization*, Vol. 2, No. 4, June 1981, pp. 503-528. Copyright 1981 by Sage Publications, Inc.

Authors' Note: This research was supported in part by the National Science Foundation under Grant ERS76-04474. Any opinions, findings, conclusions, or recommendations expressed herein are those of the authors alone and do not necessarily reflect the views of the National Science Foundation. Portions of this research have been reported elsewhere (Rossini et al., 1977, 1978, 1979; Rossini, 1977; Rossini and Porter, 1978, 1979; Chubin et al., 1979).

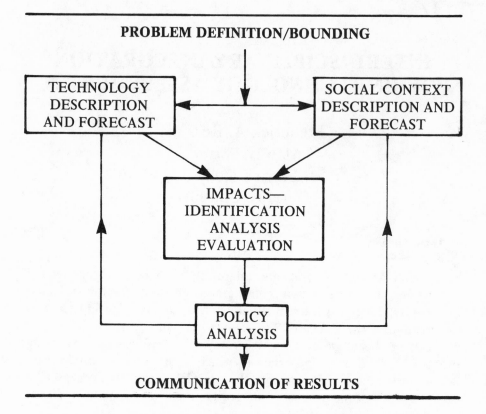

PROBLEM DEFINITION/BOUNDING

TECHNOLOGY DESCRIPTION AND FORECAST

SOCIAL CONTEXT DESCRIPTION AND FORECAST

IMPACTS— IDENTIFICATION ANALYSIS EVALUATION

POLICY ANALYSIS

COMMUNICATION OF RESULTS

Figure 1: A Basic Structure for Technology Assessment

technological innovation. At the same time, it presents a structure for assessing that technology.

The first concern of an assessment is to bound the study. Next the technology should be carefully described and its development forecast. Then its context—taken broadly to include social, institutional, and economic components—should be described and its development predicted. After this come the identification, analysis, and evaluation of the impacts—the results of the interaction between the technology and its context. Then policy alternatives for dealing with the impacts are identified and their effects on the technology and its context analyzed. This multifaceted analysis represented by the flow pattern of Figure 1 is to be repeated (iterated) as many times as necessary to complete the assessment satisfactorily. Finally, the TA results should be communicated to the user communities. For more detailed discussions of the TA process, see Porter et al. (1980: ch. 4 and 5) and Armstrong and Harman (1977).

Integration

TA has many properties which make it a complex form of research. However, most importantly for the purposes of this study, it involves contributions from a variety of academic and professional disciplines. A major premise of this study is that the disciplinary components of a TA should be put together, or integrated, so that the result both reflects interconnections existing among these components and is useful for decision-making. Integration is viewed as a product of the research process, and can most appropriately be determined by studying its output. In addition to being important to users (Berg et al., 1978), integration strengthens an analysis by exhibiting relationships and weighing their importance.

A threefold distinction, suggested in the literature, among multidisciplinary, interdisciplinary, and transdisciplinary integration is conceptually useful (Rossini and Porter, 1979).

(1) *Multidisciplinary* integration occurs when the component disciplinary analyses are sensibly ordered, with an introduction prefixed, and conclusions appended. In addition to editorial integration, terms and concepts are used consistently throughout the work (conceptual/terminological integration). The component analyses stand side by side, coupled externally. Causal explanations are likely to be limited within disciplinary boundaries. Separate authorship of individual components is typical.

(2) *Interdisciplinary* integration occurs when, in addition to editorial and conceptual/terminological integration, disciplinary analyses serve as substantive, rather than heuristic, inputs to other disciplinary analyses (systemic integration). For instance, an environmental analysis informs an economic analysis in depth, and vice versa; policy options are developed and analyzed across the relevant disciplines. Joint authorship of the study output is the norm.

(3) *Transdisciplinary* integration adds the presence of an overarching theoretical framework that serves to bind conceptually the various component analyses. Interfield theories (Darden and Maull, 1977) may be a first step towards such transdisciplinary theoretical frameworks. However, in the present state of the art of TA, and indeed of most crossdisciplinary efforts, this type of integration remains unattained.

Since transdisciplinary integration is not yet a realistic option, the choice is between multidisciplinary and interdisciplinary integration. Most TAs lie somewhere in between. The case for seeking only multidisciplinary integration incorporates several sound arguments. Academic training and professional experience typically reside in a discipline; therefore, division of labor along disciplinary lines is quite sensible. Depth of analysis is likely to reside in disciplinary analysis, and researchers typically prefer working on familiar grounds. On the other hand, it is arguable that the case is even stronger for interdisciplinary integration. Real world cause and effect relationships are likely to cross disciplinary boundaries. Separating impact analyses by disciplines, for example, is likely to miss critical linkages. Furthermore, this approach results in restricting the study of higher order consequences (i.e., the impacts of the impacts) to those within a particular disciplinary area. Such fragmentation makes it difficult to study political changes due to economic consequences. From the user's perspective, although it may be convenient for an economist to find all economic analyses in one place, it appears more important that impact or policy analyses be presented in an integrated fashion (Berg et al., 1978).

Having presented an argument in favor of interdisciplinary integration as an appropriate objective for TAs, the factors and frameworks which can facilitate such integration can be discussed. The account begins with an exposition of research strategy.

II. Study Strategy

A search of the literature on interdisciplinary research revealed, with few exceptions, tales of personal experience with little theoretical foundation to justify a strict hypothesis-testing study design (e.g., DeWachter, 1976; Petrie, 1976; Walsh et al., 1975; Weingart, 1977). Consequently this study was exploratory in nature. Despite the paucity of a serious research literature (e.g., Birnbaum, 1977), some insights directly applicable to the TA situation appeared (Arnstein and Christakis, 1975). Table 1 highlights the research strategy employed. The general approach consisted of identifying potentially significant features of the TA process, and analyzing how those features related to the integration of the project output. The preliminary analysis divided these features into three classes: management, social-psychological, and epistemological. A number of possible factors were identified and included in the first round interview instrument. To allow both exploration and some systematic examination of hypotheses, the sample of TAs was divided into two groups of 12. These groups were roughly comparable with respect to performing organization, type of

TABLE 1
Research Strategy and Chronology

1. **Initial Phase—Research Formulation**
   —study team reviewed the literature, established study design, generated preliminary hypotheses, and selected the sample of TAs to be studied; it also developed an instrument for first round interviews.

2. **First Round Interviews**
   —"focused" interviews conducted on-site with participants in 12 TAs.

3. **Model Construction**
   —based upon the first round interviews, study team formulated more precise hypotheses that combined to offer a model of what affects TA integration; second round interview instrument prepared to probe this model.

4. **Second Round Interviews**
   —combined structured and open-ended interviews conducted on-site with participants in 12 other TAs.

5. **Product Integration Rating**
   —two independent readers scored the TA products on various component and overall types of integration, comprehensiveness, and depth of analysis; neither reader had interviewed any member of the project team; (interrater reliability, p=.64).

6. **Small Group Experiments**
   —experimental interdisciplinary groups formed on basis of attributes of the 24 TAs were assigned structured "micro-TA" tasks and studied in execution of those tasks; another group session was devoted to the ranking of a set of academic disciplines.

7. **Analysis**
   —interviews analyzed with product ratings as 24 qualitative case studies, as a quantitative multivariate correlational study, and as a basis for causal modeling; findings combined with small group results and literature reports.

technology, emphasis on technology or policy, and projected study duration. From the first round of interviews, fairly precise hypotheses were formulated to be probed in the second round interviews (some of these putative linkages are discussed by Rossini, 1977). Major generic factors considered included the organizational environment of the study, management style adopted by the team leader, number of core team members (project participants who played major roles in the study through most of its duration), experience of the core team members in interdisciplinary and group research, bounding of the study, communication patterns, iteration, and epistemological factors. Independent of the interviewing, project reports were rated by study team members. Rating on a 1 to 5 scale was performed for comprehensiveness, depth of analysis, and the various forms of integration.

To supplement information gained through interviews of some 58 participants in the 24 TAs, a series of exploratory small group experiments (Chubin et al., 1979) was conducted. Groups were constituted to simulate the typical disciplinary composition of TA core teams. Two groups composed of faculty, researchers, and graduate students each met for four hours on three occasions. They worked on TA-like problems concerning a physical, a biological, and a social technology. In each session, group members were instructed to follow a design to implement one of three distinct approaches to integration that had emerged from the interviews (see section IV). In addition, a third group ranked and debated the intellectual stature of various academic disciplines. This provided a vehicle for expressing some epistemological differences that the interviews had suggested might be important barriers to integration.

The accumulated evidence thus consisted of the literature analysis, interviews with TA participants, TA report evaluations, and the small group experiments. The interviews were considered first as 24 case studies from which a variety of insights emerged. Second, interview responses were coded to test hypotheses advanced from the first round interviews, and then analyzed quantitatively. Second round projects were analyzed separately at first. Only those hypotheses confirmed from the second 12 studies were analyzed in all 24 projects. The latter results were used to capitalize upon the greater number of cases. Descriptive tabulations, correlations, and factor analysis afforded insight into the factors influencing integration. These factors were further explored by a path analysis. In sum, the results are:

—a general framework for understanding the process of integration in TA;

—identification of factors important in TA integration and an analysis of their interrelationships;

—a preliminary causal model of the factors affecting integration;

—identification and analysis of four idealized approaches to the social and intellectual organization of a TA within which integration can take place; and

—recommendations to practitioners for achieving integration within TAs and some consideration of appropriate extension to other types of interdisciplinary projects.

III. Factors Affecting Integration

Factors initially hypothesized as important influences on integration were winnowed through the two interview rounds and subsequent analyses. The resultant factors can be grouped as boundary conditions, or as structural and process factors.

Boundary Conditions

Boundary conditions refer to the characteristics of the TA project environment that may influence integration. Factors of interest include the character of the performing organization and the involvement of consultants and subcontractors in the study itself.

Organizational characteristics that support an integrated TA include organizational commitment to interdisciplinary research, capability of attracting and rewarding participants from various disciplines to work on the study, and flexibility in committing time and resources as the study unfolds. In the cases studied, a combination of small size and flexible structure seemed to provide a desirable environment. These were associated with small (i.e., 30 or fewer professionals) contract research organizations or close-knit institutes in academic institutions. Divisional barriers and strict time accounting practices in some larger contract research organizations caused problems in the conduct of some TAs. Corresponding rigidities due to narrow disciplinary perspectives and reward structures were sometimes a problem in academic units (see also Dressel et al., 1970). In one case, four participants in a TA failed to get tenure and thus lost their jobs, despite more than satisfactory performances in the TA. This is not to say, however, that effective TA integration could not take place in less hospitable organizational environments if the TAs were blessed with particularly able project leadership or other highly favorable conditions.

A number of the projects studied used *subcontractors, consultants,* or *major participants* affiliated with other organizations. Problems due to different organizational goals, interests, and structures can emerge. For instance, academic and contract research norms can clash in an area such as publication objectives. Likewise, a subcontractor who prefers qualitative methods may have difficulty interacting with a quantitatively-oriented primary research organization. It was observed that senior level consultants often functioned as critics rather than as substantive contributors due to heavy demands on their time. Physical separation, per se, posed another barrier to communication. But difficulties in subcontractor and consultant relationships could be overcome through able project management.

Structural and Process Factors

Structural and process factors refer to properties of the project that are more subject to project management control than are the previously mentioned organizational factors. Six general factors emerged from the analysis: leadership characteristics, team characteristics, iteration, bounding, communication patterns, and epistemological factors.

Leadership characteristics are critical in the conduct of a TA because of the influence of the project leader. Hill's (1970) categorization of three leadership styles appears useful in studying TA projects. The *laissez-faire* style is nondirective; the leader allows the group to set goals. In contrast, the *authoritarian* style leader allows the group little or no influence in setting goals and choosing procedures. The *democratic* style is participatory and group-centered; the project leader encourages mutual relationships with and among the team members. We were able to classify 20 of the 24 project leaders according to style. As Table 2 indicates, projects with a democratic leadership show a greater degree of interdisciplinary integration than those characterized by other styles.

Figure 2 suggests possible causal relationships of the structural and process factors with integration. The correlation analysis among various independent variables and integration focuses on the existence and the strength of the relationships. Causal relations among independent variables were hypothesized from interview data, i.e., the consistent perceptions of the participants. The details of this figure will be developed as we proceed. For now, note that leadership appears to exert both direct and indirect influences on project integration.

One might hypothesize (as was done) that persons with broad-ranging backgrounds associated with a "systems" or cross-disciplinary perspective would be preferable as project leaders if one were striving for an integrated study. The results shown in Table 2 run counter to this—in fact, these persons appear to be associated with the least well-integrated TAs. However, small sample size, difficulties in

TABLE 2
Factors Relating to Project Integration

Factor	Number of Studies	Report Integration[a]	Significance[b]
Leadership Style			p=.065
Democratic	10	3.27	
Authoritarian	7	2.14	
Laissez-Faire	3	1.93	
Disciplinary Background of Leader			p=.17
Social Scientists and Economists	3	4.00	
Engineers	2	3.25	
Natural Scientists	7	2.57	
"Systems," Professional, and Mixed	11	2.32	
Core Team Size			p=.20
1	2	1.00	
2	1	2.00	
3	3	3.50	
4	4	2.63	
5	7	2.63	
6	5	2.40	
8	1	4.50	
Communication Pattern—Body of Project			p=.36
All-channel	2	3.50	
Intermediate	12	2.96	
Hub and Spokes	7	2.29	
Communication Pattern—Final Phase			p=.007
All-channel	4	3.80	
Intermediate	8	3.25	
Hub and Spokes	9	1.92	

a. Overall rated interdisciplinary integration (1 to 5 scale) of the final report.
b. Based on analysis of variance (F-test). These values give the relative variance between categories and its statistical significance. Statistical significance should be considered cautiously here as we are dealing with a population, not a sample. However, we are interested in generalizing beyond that population, but do not have a representative sample.

measuring these concepts, and the likelihood of idiosyncrasies related to personalities and assessment tasks suggest these results be viewed with considerable caution. A possible explanation is discussed later in relation to intellectual distance among core team members.

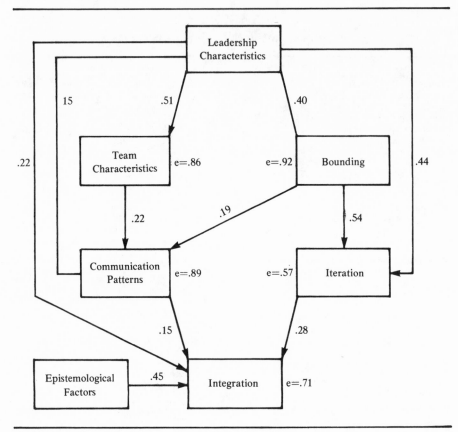

Figure 2: A Causal Model for TA Integration

The numbers along arrows represent the path coefficients, $e=\sqrt{1-R^2}$, where R is the multiple correlation coefficient. (For treatments of path analysis, see Nie et al., 1975; Duncan, 1975.)

Team characteristics of interest include the number of core team members, their prior experience in multi- or interdisciplinary projects similar to TAs, and the stability of project leadership and team membership over the course of the study.

Table 2 suggests that core teams of three to five members typically produce the best integrated projects. A core team of one or two members is usually insufficient to effect integration of a complex project. A team larger than five members begins to become too large for the intense communication required for effective integration (yet the only team studied with more than six core members did a fine job of integration by explicitly attending to this problem). The effects of overall project size may be important. This issue is discussed in the treatment of communication patterns below.

Evidence from the 24 TAs did not confirm the hypothesis of the importance of **prior** interdisciplinary experience in achieving integration. In small group experiments, such experience seemed helpful. It may be that over the life of a typical TA, much learning is possible and the lack of such experience can be overcome.

Changes in project leadership and core team membership had a negative effect, particularly on study bounding and iteration. One remedy to turnovers in project personnel is an infusion of additional time and money, either from the performing organization or from the sponsor, to enable satisfactory completion of the work.

Bounding the assessment (i.e., setting the limits and the form of the study) is a process which should continue throughout the project. Some openendedness appears desirable to accommodate important new developments and insights over the course of the assessment. Satisfactoriness of study bounding, as perceived by the participants, correlated with integration (see Table 3) and with many factors affecting integration.

Iteration is the process of redoing all or part of a study. It is reasonable that substantive interlinking of component analyses requires their reworking. Indeed, data from the 24 TAs support this (see Table 3). This finding reinforces the bit of TA folk wisdom: "First you write the final report and then you do the assessment." The Environmental Protection Agency has specifically required iteration in such studies as the National Coal Technology Assessment. Three iterations appear typical—the first a quick and simple assessment to establish the proper

TABLE 3
Examples of Spearman Correlations of Overall Substantive Integration with Selected Important Variables

	r_s	p (significance)
Leadership Style	.51	.01
Satisfactoriness of Study Bounding	.43	.02
Number of Times While Study Iterated	.50	.02
Character of Communication Pattern During Report Writing	.45	.02
Epistemological Distances Among Team Members (normalized)	.50	.01

study scope (see Rossini et al., 1976), the second the major assessment work, the third interlinking and supplementing the component analysis to yield an integrated study.

There are two ideal types of *communication patterns* in TAs. The "all channel" pattern involves substantial communication between all pairs of core team members. The "hub and spokes" pattern consists of communication links only between the team leader and each team member without links between pairs of members (see Figure 3).

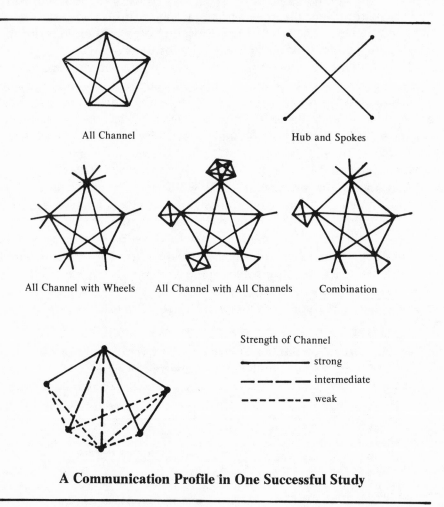

A **Communication Profile in One Successful Study**

Figure 3: Communication Patterns

Table 2 indicates how the characterization of project communication patterns corresponded with the rating of project integration. The desirability of "all channel" communication is especially striking in the crucial final phase of the project. It appears that the "hub and spokes" pattern overloads the person at the hub, placing the burden for integration there. In addition, individuals who had worked as "spokes" expressed dissatisfaction with such an arrangement as treating them unprofessionally by discouraging professional interchange with their colleagues. The "all channel" pattern suggests a limitation on core team size, for the number of linkages may become unwieldy as the number of participants increases. Consequently, on large projects one might wish to develop a hierarchy of groups (see Figure 3). On balance, a sensible approach appears to be what might be called "any channel"—a supportive environment that encourages all communications links among project participants. Figure 3 illustrates such a pattern with links of various strengths.

Epistemological differences among project team members present a potentially serious barrier to TA integration. These issues were specifically addressed in this research, but it was quite difficult to discuss epistemological problems with researchers (much more so than management or communications issues) since no common terminology or set of categories existed. However, in discussions with assessors, four specific problem areas were uncovered that proved particularly salient to TA integration: social impact assessment, data and the future, economists, and TA techniques.

Social Impact assessment is a serious problem area. Some "hard" science-oriented researchers saw no hope of significant social impact analysis beyond the level of common sense. One principal investigator referred to social impact assessment as "dreaming." Others turned to quasi-quantitative techniques to give the form and precision associated with a "harder" methodology. The social scientists involved in TAs tended to be data-oriented, and often sought to generate primary social data for the study. The subordinate position of the social sciences in the academic pecking order (which was observed in our small group experiments), compounded by the fact that social scientists on the teams were often junior in rank, created tension in several projects.

A related problem was the conflict between exclusive reliance on data in hand and the willingness to predict the future. Some professionals consider it improper to go beyond currently validated theory and data. One project leader related in vivid terms the difficulties in dealing with a data-oriented subcontractor unwilling to offer any extrapolations to the future. On the other hand, most TA practitioners viewed some form of prediction as necessary to conduct a TA.

Economists were singled out as frustration to noneconomist TA participants. Communication problems included excessive use of jargon, building and use of complex economic models that appeared to have little validity or applicability, and the demand for data that were often unobtainable. Perhaps the most significant problem was the inability of several economists to extend their analysis to areas where monetary values could not be assigned, and a corresponding disdain for the importance of such areas.

Finally, there was the question of the use of techniques designed for TA and other future studies, such as Delphi, KSIM, and relevance trees. The avowed purpose of these techniques is to make quantitative and precise what is qualitative and imprecise. Three reactions to these techniques were elicited. The first and most common reaction among our respondents was to ignore them since they recast what is already known and give a false impression of quantification. The second tack was to use selected TA techniques sparingly as devices for organizing the presentation and analysis of what is known. The final and least common reaction was to embrace the techniques as legitimating the study by making it quantitative and precise. When members of a TA project team differed on this issue, or on the previous three issues, serious difficulties in interrelating analyses typically resulted.

It was hypothesized that the greater the diversity in disciplinary background among team members, the greater the difficulty in integration. A simple index of intellectual distance among disciplines was constructed to explore this issue (see Table 4). Table 3 shows the unexpected finding—the greater the intellectual distance among the core team members, the more substantively integrated the study output. Further, the lower the proportion of "systems" (including multidisciplinary background) people on the core team, the more integrated was the study output. A possible explanation is that the presence of diversity may increase the awareness of the need for taking measures to achieve integration. The ability to interrelate a variety of perspectives in one's own work may not enhance one's ability to integrate it with the work of others. The relative effectiveness of

TABLE 4
Scale of "Intellectual Distances" Between Groups of Disciplines

	1	2	3	4	5	6
1) Social Sciences	0	1	2	2	2	2
2) Economics		0	2	1	0	2
3) Natural Science			0	1	1	2
4) Engineering				0	0	2
5) Systems Professional Mixed					0	2
6) Law						0

individuals with multidisciplinary backgrounds in the TAs merits further study.

A Causal Model of TA Integration

One must understand how various factors affect integration before effective action to improve TA integration can be taken. This section describes a causal path analysis of these factors (for treatment of path analysis, see Duncan, 1975; Nie et al., 1975).

A set of some 21 measured variables was associated with the nominal factor categories. Factor analysis, regression analysis, and judgment by the team members were used in constructing alternative sets of operational factors from the variables. The six factors of leadership, team characteristics, bounding, iteration, communication, and epistemological concerns were developed and related to integration (measured in terms of the rating of overall substantive integration of the project reports). Table 3 indicates selected correlations between integration and certain independent variables, while Table 5 shows the intercorrelation matrix of the factors involved in the final causal path analysis model.

The analysis suggests that the model shown in Figure 2 plausibly fits the empirical results. It is offered as a useful model that can serve as a basis for structuring projects and for studying the process of integration of interdisciplinary research. The model emphasizes the importance of the team leader who can affect integration both directly

TABLE 5
Intercorrelations of Factors in the Path Analysis Model

	Integration	Iteration	Epistemology	Bounding	Communication Patterns	Team Characteristics
ITER	.54					
EPIS	.44	.08				
BOUND	.32	.71	−.16			
COMM	.35	.52	−.06	.36		
TEAM	.22	.23	−.13	.52	.40	
LEAD	.40	.66	−.13	.40	.34	.51

NOTE: For degrees of freedom, p = .34 is significant at p = .05 for a one-tailed best. We have also computed the more conservative choice correlation coefficients for these ordinal data, Spearman's r_s, with quite similar results.

and indirectly. It also indicates separate and important status for the epistemological factors involved in the project. The model suggests that the project leader should attend to bounding and make provisions for iteration, and can and should encourage intrateam communication. While the present data could be found consistent with a number of alternative models, this particular model is consistent with the hypotheses and data of this study.

IV. Four Approaches to the Social and Intellectual Organization of a TA

The factors discussed in the preceding section affect integration. However, little has been said about the specific social structure within which the integration of the knowledge elements is effected. It became apparent from the interviews that whatever the abstract merits of analyzing knowledge and social organization separately, in discussing the question of integration they are best treated together. It proved possible to abstract four ideal types of approaches to the social and intellectual organization of a TA (Rossini and Porter, 1979). Although these approaches seldom appear singularly in a study, some combination of them appeared in each of the 24 studies. Each of the approaches has both advantages and disadvantages. They should be considered as potential elements in designing study strategy to attain integrated TAs.

Common Group Learning

The central feature of *common group learning* is that the research output reflects the common intellectual property of the entire research group (Kash, 1977; White, 1975). After a research problem is bounded, it is divided into areas based on the expertise and interest of the members of the research group. These individuals prepare preliminary analyses. The group criticizes the individual analyses. The pieces are then rewritten, almost always by a different individual—often by someone who is not an expert in that area. In addition, the group's productions are criticized by outsiders who are knowledgeable in some phase of the subject matter. This procedure is iterated until the group and its 'leader feel that the work is sufficiently complete. Figure 4 illustrates common group learning schematically. Note the deemphasis of individual expertise in the final project outcome. Because the status of expert belongs to the group as a whole, the project output is taken from the portion of each team member's knowledge that is common to all. This has the effect of limiting the technical sophistication of the study. Hence, it tends to decrease the depth of disciplinary analyses.

Modeling

A *model* is a simplified representation of part of the "real world" that contains its most important relationships so that its essential workings may be studied. Most commonly encountered in the 24 TAs were computerized models dealing largely with economic relationships for which quantitative data could, at least in principle, be obtained (see Enzer, 1974; Harvey and Menchen, 1974). Models addressing relationships among persons and institutions tended to take the form of influence diagrams. Figure 4B schematically illustrates the use of models as integrative frameworks.

The model may be constructed by the research team, or it may be imported from outside. Models narrow the focus of interest by considering a limited number of interacting factors. Data can be obtained to substantiate the working of the model. Thus, a model can link various forms of data from diverse sources. These data, however, must be compatible or be rendered so by the model. If data do not exist, they need to be invented by some suitable approximation. This usually precludes the use of quantitative and qualitative information in

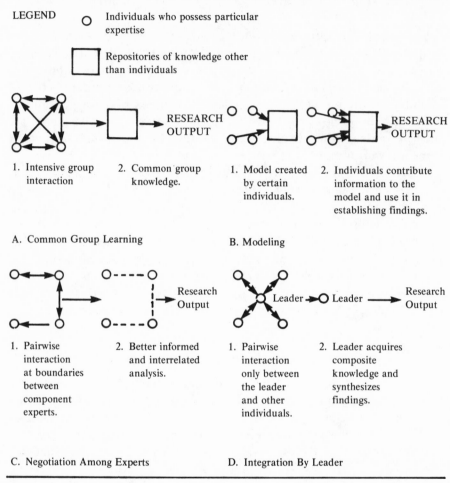

LEGEND ○ Individuals who possess particular
           expertise

        ▢ Repositories of knowledge other
           than individuals

1. Intensive group   2. Common group
   interaction   knowledge.

1. Model created   2. Individuals contribute
   by certain   information to the
   individuals.   model and use it in
                         establishing findings.

A. Common Group Learning   B. Modeling

1. Pairwise   2. Better informed
   interaction   and interrelated
   at boundaries   analysis.
   between
   component
   experts.

1. Pairwise   2. Leader acquires
   interaction   composite
   only between   knowledge and
   the leader   synthesizes
   and other   findings.
   individuals.

C. Negotiation Among Experts   D. Integration By Leader

Figure 4: Four Approaches to the Social and Intellectual Organization
          of a TA

the same model. In summary, models narrow the research focus by
excluding nonessential relationships (which is desirable), but also by
excluding relevant aspects of the world that do not fit within their
framework (which is not desirable). Modeling favors empirical analysis,
which is good, but sometimes goes to questionable lengths to invent the
required data.

Negotiation Among Experts

In the ideal case, *negotiation among experts* is a process where, after bounding, the study is divided among the members of the project team on the basis of their individual expertise and disciplinary background. Individual analyses reflect this expertise, incorporating any complex theories and approaches that seem germane. The integration of the various analyses then takes place by a process of negotiation.

The subject of the negotiation can be considered as the linkages between analyses in which their contents substantively affect the other analyses. Effective integration requires the initial analyses to be redone to reflect the inclusion of the findings of the other expert analyses. In negotiation among experts, depth and expertise are preserved. For example, in TA an economic analysis should be linked to the institutional analysis if it is to be realistic and thus useful. The risk in negotiation among experts is that it will lead to multidisciplinary, rather than interdisciplinary, integration. Figure 4C illustrates negotiation among experts schematically.

Integration by a Leader

Integration by a leader relies on the "hub and spokes" communication pattern. The problem is assigned by the leader on the basis of team members' expertise. The leader functions as the sole integrator, and interacts individually with each member of the team to understand and assimilate that member's contribution. The members *do not* interact significantly among themselves. See Figure 4D for a schematic representation.

A weakness of this procedure is the enormous demands it places on the leader-integrator (Taylor, 1975). Like common group learning, this framework tends to downplay depth. A single individual cannot be expected to grasp the details of highly specialized analyses outside that person's area of expertise.

Because of the risk of the nonexpert leader dominating expert nonleaders, the leader attempting integration may tend to downplay it in favor of perfunctory editorial revision. The result may lean more toward the multidisciplinary than the interdisciplinary.

V. Conclusions and Observations

This concluding section has two objectives. First, it presents the conclusions of the study, organized so as to offer guidance to practitioners of TA and persons involved in other, similar projects. Second, it discusses issues in extending those results to other forms of interdisciplinary research and notes important background considerations raised, but not addressed, in this study.

Clearly, achievement of a well-integrated TA is a complex undertaking. Factors that influence it include characteristics of the task itself, the context in which the assessment is performed, and structural and process features of its conduct. All these will be further colored by the values of participants and parties-at-interest and the need to address the interests of potential study users. Given this complexity, it would not be sensible to try to distill the relevant knowledge into any simple "how-to-do-it" rules. Thus a set of interrelated strategic considerations is used to communicate the conclusions of this study in a practical and usable form.

The first area of concern is the organizational environment of the study. Assuming a commitment to interdisciplinary research and TA, the major operational considerations are flexible unit boundaries which allow the assembly and efficient functioning of cross-disciplinary TA teams and the ability to reward participants in successful teams. Meeting those conditions means that it is both possible and desirable for an individual in the organization to manage or participate in a TA.

Within the study itself, leadership style is a most important causal factor in performing a well integrated assessment. The democratic style, in which the leader is supportive of the team members and allows them to participate in project decisions without ever relinquishing final authority or the responsibility of making hard, "bottom line" decisions, is most effective. The authoritarian style, in which the team leader totally controls the decision-making process, is less effective. Least effective is the laissez-faire leadership style in which the leader gives vague direction and lets the core team members do as they wish.

Core teams ideally should be composed of individuals from as broad a range of disciplines as is appropriate for the assessment without enlarging the team unnecessarily. Team members should be experienced in or at least favorably disposed toward cross-disciplinary work, and comfortable working in the "give and take" of team situations.

The team should bound the project effectively. A rough recipe for bounding is to allow an initial "wallowing" period in which the core team members immerse themselves in the subject being assessed. After this phase, the general scope and bounds of the study are set. Throughout the remainder of the study the final, low level bounding decisions are made. All the while, the study team should be prepared to cope with major developments which may force a significant change in the study's scope. Such a procedure avoids the extremes of a totally predetermined study and a rich, yet diffuse, intellectual effort which is unable to achieve closure.

Iteration is desirable, nay rather necessary, for TAs. One reasonable pattern where time and resources permit, consists of three rounds of iteration. A typical version follows.

(1) Bounding Round—A "micro assessment" which briefly runs through the entire assessment.
(2) Analyzing Round—Division of the major study elements for an analysis in depth. Each of the core team members takes the lead in part of each study component and draws upon other professional resources, parties-at-interest, and other potential users wherever possible. An informal conference will be scheduled involving both professionals and concerned parties to review the work of this assessment round, and to inform the next round.
(3) Interrelating and Polishing Round—This round will involve active interrelation of the component analyses and polishing the assessment into final form.

It is necessary to keep open all channels of communication within the core team. While these channels may be used unequally, their availability allows a maximal information exchange in the assessment. This "any channel" approach precludes the use of integration by leader as a framework for integration.

The four epistemological problem areas (social.impact assessment, data and the future, economists, and TA techniques) can conveniently be fused into three more general categories—permissible information, solution structure, and appropriate techniques. Core team members need to familiarize themselves with one another's views of these topics. The emphasis should be on the interrelations and complementarities among their differing inquiring systems.

There remains the social and intellectual organization of the TA in light of the factors discussed above—fitting the frameworks of Figure 4 to the TA components of Figure 1. Integration by leader has already been excluded as a viable framework. Because of the wide range of qualitative and quantitative factors dealt with in a typical assessment, modeling appears a poor overall framework. Yet various quantitative and qualitative models often play important roles in component parts of a TA.

For technology and societal context description and forecasting, common group learning seems the most appropriate framework. The core team, possessing varied and unequal expertise, needs to immerse itself in the subject matter and its context and to agree on a common core of information so that other components of the study may be consistently based. Treatment of impacts requires the analytic depth identified with expertise. Thus, it appears that negotiation among experts is the most appropriate framework here. Finally, policy analysis can be handled effectively by common group learning. The range and interconnectedness of policy alternatives is more important than depth of analysis. Table 6 summarizes these considerations.

Finally, this is a study of technology assessments. Yet by analogy, these results may be useful in other forms of interdisciplinary projects. Key properties of TAs, besides interdisciplinarity, are their typically wide range of discipline, future orientation, and the relatively small amount of new theory and new data generated in the study. Projects,

TABLE 6
Procedural Recommendations for Integration of Technology Assessments

Organizational Context:
  Commitment to interdisciplinary research and technology assessment
  Low organizational barriers to cross-disciplinary teams
  Rewards for successful TA performance

Structural and Process Factors:
  Democratic leadership style
  Wide range of disciplines on team
  Effective bounding of study
  Adequate iteration of assessment
  "Any channel" communication
  Understanding interrelationships and complementarities of permissible information, solution structure, and appropriate techniques of core team members

Frameworks for Performing TA Components:
  Technology and societal context description and forecasting—common group learning
  Impact identification, analysis, and evaluation—negotiation among experts
  Policy analysis—common group learning

such as environmental impact statements which are very close to TAs, surely approach the scope of this study. Indeed, of the three features noted above, only one, the amount of new data generated, may be more complex than in a TA. Generating new data alters a number of considerations affecting interdisciplinary organization. Simply put, the suggested changes are based on the uncertainty of original work. Thus, leadership moves slightly toward the laissez-faire, bounding contains greater uncertainty, and closure comes later in the study. Iteration is based on study developments rather than being planned. And, where depth of analysis is important, negotiation among experts becomes the dominant framework.

Not mentioned in this section are considerations of project size. In large projects the core team concept should remain; but, as discussed above, the core team members in this case are leaders of research efforts involving a number of other participants. Integration takes place within the core team. Figure 3 illustrates a two-level organizational hierarchy, but more complex structures are possible.

The dominant general finding, never explicitly hypothesized at the beginning of the project, is that in interdisciplinary research the social and intellectual elements involved are tightly coupled. Thus, the researchers' social and intellectual processes are inseparable. Yet researchers are not explicitly trained in the social development of knowledge. Thus, if interdisciplinary research is to become a major research form, alternatives to strictly individual and disciplinary graduate training need to be developed which incorporate the social and intellectual forms of interdisciplinarity. Indeed, this training should start from the beginning of the educational process. It is both exciting and frightening to contemplate this prospect.

References

ARMSTRONG, J.E. and W.W. HARMAN (1977) Strategies for Conducting Technology Assessments, Stanford, CA: Department of Engineering-Economic Systems, Stanford University.

ARNSTEIN, S.R. and A.N. CHRISTAKIS (1975) [eds.] *Perspectives on Technology Assessment,* Jerusalem: Science and Technology Publishers.

BERG, M.R. et al. (1978) Factors Affecting Utilization of Technology Assessment Studies in Policy Making. Final Report, Center for Research on Utilization of Scientific Knowledge, Institute of Social Research, University of Michigan (NSF Grant ERS 76-16805).

BIRNBAUM, P.H. (1977) "Assessment of alternative management forms in academic interdisciplinary research projects." *Management Sci.* 24: 272-284.

CHUBIN, D.E., F.A. ROSSINI, A.L. PORTER, and I.I. MITROFF (1979) "Experimental technology assessment: explorations in processes of interdisciplinary team research." *Technological Forecasting and Social Change* 15: 25-36.

DARDEN, L. and N. MAULL (1977) "Interfield theories." *Philosophy of Sci.* 44: 43-66.

DEWACHTER, M. (1976) "Interdisciplinary team work." *J. of Medical Ethics* 2: 52-57.

DRESSEL, P.L. et al. (1970) *The Confidence Crisis.* San Francisco: Jossey Bass.

DUNCAN, O.D. (1975) *Introduction to Structural Equation Models.* New York: Academic Press.

ENZER, S. (1974) Some Impacts of No Fault Automobile Insurance—A Technology Assessment. Report R30, Institute for the Future, Menlo Park, CA.

HARVEY, D.R. and W.R. MENCHEN (1974) A Technology Assessment of the Transition to Advanced Automotive Propulsion Systems. HIT 541, Hittman Associates, Columbia, MD.

HILL, S.C. (1970) "A Natural Experiment on the Influence of Leadership Behavioral Patterns on Scientific Productivity." *IEEE Transactions on Engineering Management*, EM-17, 10-20.

KASH, D.E. (1977) "Observations on interdisciplinary studies and government roles," pp. 147-167 in Scribner and Chalk (eds.) *Adapting Science to Social Needs.* Washington, DC: American Association for the Advancement of Science.

NIE, N.J. et al. (1975) *Statistical Package for the Social Sciences.* 2nd ed. New York: McGraw-Hill.

PETRIE, H.D. (1976) "Do you see what I see? The epistemology of interdisciplinary inquiry." *J. of Aesthetic Education* 10: 9-15.

PORTER, A.L. et al. (1980) *A Guidebook for Technology Assessment and Impact Analysis.* New York: Elsevier North-Holland.

ROSSINI, F.A. (1977) "How can we put it together: a first model of technology assessment integration," pp. 57-76 in J.T. Tarr (ed.) *Retrospective Technology Assessment.* San Francisco: The San Francisco Press.

——— and A.L. PORTER (1979) "Frameworks for integrating interdisciplinary research." *Research Policy* 8: 70-79.

———(1978) "The management of interdisciplinary policy-related research," pp. 302-333 in J.W. Sutherland (ed.) *Management Handbook for Public Administrators.* New York: Litton.

ROSSINI, F.A. et al. (1979) "On the integration of the disciplinary components in interdisciplinary research," pp. 136-158 in T. Barth and R. Steck (eds.) *Interdisciplinary Research Groups: Their Management and Organization.* International Research Group on Interdisciplinary Programs.

——— (1978) Frameworks and Factors Affecting Integration Within Technology Assessments. Report to the National Science Foundation, Grant ERS 76-04474, Georgia Institute of Technology, Atlanta, GA.

——— (1977) "The epistemology of interdisciplinary research; the case of technology assessment," pp. 451-498 in *The General Systems Paradigm: Science of Change and Change of Science.* Washington, DC: The Society for General Systems Research.

——— (1976) "Multiple technology assessments." *J. of Int. Society for Technology Assessment* 2: 21-28.

TAYLOR, J.B. (1975) "Building an interdisciplinary team," pp. 45-60 in Arnstein and Christakis (eds.) *Perspectives on Technology Assessment.* Jerusalem: Science and Technology Publishers.

WALSH, W.B. et al. (1975) "Developing an interface between engineering and the social sciences." *Amer. Psychologist* (November): 1067-1071.

WEINGART, J.M. (1977) "Transdisciplinary science—some recent experience with solar energy conversion research." Presented at the American Association for the Advancement of Science Annual Meeting, Denver.

WHITE, I.L. (1975) "Interdisciplinarity," pp. 87-96 in Arnstein and Christakis (eds.) *Perspectives on Technology Assessment.* Jerusalem: Science and Technology Publishers.

30

... AN INQUIRY INTO
SCIENTIFIC "PECKING ORDER"*

Daryl E. Chubin
Frederick A. Rossini
Alan L. Porter
Ian I. Mitroff

We have been perplexed by a reported difficulty in the performance of social-impact assessment due to project leaders who were not social scientists and had little knowledge of, or respect for, social-science methods. In a phrase, there seems to be a "pecking order," with social sciences on the bottom, impeding the conduct of TAs.

Prompted by this, we formulated an auxiliary experiment on a third group of four faculty members. Two senior participants represented chemistry and electrical engineering and two relatively junior ones, economics and political science. (In the 24 TAs only three of the principal investigators were economists or other social scientists; most social scientists were of junior status.)

This experiment consisted of a single 2-hr session devoted to an exercise called "rank ordering of the sciences." It was designed to elicit debate on the relative stature of academic disciplines. The members were instructed to rank 10 disciplines from 1 to 10 according to the criterion "intellectual stature." The term was left undefined to allow each member to attach his own meaning to it. To ensure that a rationale would be formulated, the second half of the exercise called for selection of a *different* criterion that would justify an *inversion* of the first rank ordering. After completion of the individual rankings, the team would discuss their respective rationales and decide on a *group*

* Experimental Technology Assessment: Explorations in Processes of Interdisciplinary Team Research, [Daryl E. Chubin, Frederick A. Rossini, Alan L. Porter & Ian I. Mitroff.) *Technological Forecasting and Social Change* 15, 87-94 (1979). Reprinted by permission, Elsevier Science Publishing Company.

rank-order according to at least one of the two criteria. The session involved an introduction (5 min), individual ranking (20), group discussion (40), and debriefing with the session leader (45 min).

Discussion addressed the bases for the ranking of intellectual stature—abstraction, vigor, predictive power, extent of mathematics involved, and distinction, as marked by awards such as the Nobel prize. "Usefulness to man" seemed to be the central feature of the second (reversal) ranking. The group agreed to a cluster, rather than an individual, discipline ranking on intellectual stature to achieve consensus: (1) physics, chemistry, and mathematics, and (2) economics, biology, and electrical engineering, and (3) anthropology, political science, psychology, and psychiatry.

In sum, the pecking order anticipated by the study of the 24 TAs was sustained in this experiment. The equation of "intellectual stature" with such factors as mathematization and rigor implicitly distorts the performance of interdisciplinary work.

Concluding Observations

Our experiments were designed as (1) an innovative methodological task in the study of TAs and similar studies and (2) a means of producing substantive insights about research processes in TA and related studies. These could be directly applied to sessions of short duration, such as those dealing with problem definition and bounding and, by analogy, to long-term studies.

Methodologically, we offer the experimental strategy described herein as advantageous by reason of (1) its limited resource requirements, enabling (2) multiple studies of phenomena of interest relative to TA performance, and thereby providing (3) comparisons/controls necessary for viable inferences. These sorts of laboratory simulations can augment (but certainly not replace) field observations that typically preclude controlled comparisons. Without research designs that incorporate such controls, one is left with a disconnected series of case studies that are unlikely to yield any substantial cumulation of knowledge about how to improve TA performance [6].

There are also notable compromises that could yield further insight by combining some elements of laboratory experiments with actual TAs [15]. We mention here only two design possibilities to extend the present investigation of what contributes to TA integration. The first is a monitoring of three separately funded assessments of the same topic in which iteration would be required and one of the three sociointellectual modes of operation would be assigned to each project. Within these constraints, leadership behavior, bounding, and communication within the team could be closely observed.

A different possibility is to pursue the process of negotiation among disciplinary experts, on their home turf, but perhaps with specially developed exercises to elicit psychological, value, and epistemological differences that represent potential barriers to interdisciplinary cooperation, communication, and problem solving. Graduate education has never addressed the need for such understanding as preliminary to fruitful collaborative research in a multidisciplinary team context, that is, three or more persons [3, 4]. This possibility, therefore, would serve to prepare for future TAs and related policy analyses. Moreover, it would act on the knowledge (anticipated by Bennis and Slater [2] a decade ago) that modern research organizations, like the creative people who comprise them, must adapt or be modified in response to the complexity of the problems they seek to investigate and solve [7].

Substantively, we can summarize our observations, noting again their exploratory nature. These results obtain from study of five-person groups dealing with TA-like problems in half-day sessions. They bear considerable similarity to specialized core-team meeting activities in a TA as mentioned above; nevertheless, they require considerable extrapolation to inform the performance of whole TAs:

1. The *leadership* role showed no variation across disciplines. Individuals playing this role assumed responsibility for completion of the task and coordinated the team's work on it. The leader's creativity suffered, however, until he resumed playing the role of team member during subsequent sessions.

2. An "all-channel" *communication pattern*, born of democratic leadership, characterized the interaction in these fruitful sessions. Only at the end of the sessions, when team members separated to summarize component sections of the final report, did the interaction assume a "hub-and-spokes" pattern of communication. The reports tended to reflect a lack of integration, despite the interdisciplinary process that preceded the actual writing. This suggests that the "all-channels"

approach should be used during the final-report preparations stage.

3. *Iteration*, that is, redoing analyses to reflect other contributions to the project, was a casualty of insufficient time in the sessions. Hence individual and provisional analyses were not internally interrelated. Iteration appears highly desirable, despite its high costs.

4. *Epistemological distances* were minimized in the experiments. However, the traditional pecking order that emerged from the auxiliary session was based on rigor and quantification, a finding that speaks loudly to the twin issues of team composition and disciplinary barriers in TA. These issues could be of acute importance in social-impact assessments. A sensitivity to social scientists may enhance the perspectives of TA practitioners from more quantitative disciplines.

5. In these short-term group exercises, the preferred *sociointellectual mode* of operation was common group learning. Modeling was only workable in a qualitative fashion, and negotiating from disciplinary bases was resisted (quite to our surprise). A fourth integration approach in which the leader is the integrator of the separate pieces prepared by TA participants was not included in the experiments. Based on the field observations, it appears largely ineffective for a task of the magnitude of a large-scale TA [14]. The experimental results thus suggest that group problem solving (e.g., in bounding the form of a TA) may reduce to a common-denominator mechanism. This may require careful consideration of its appropriateness, and unequivocal actions if it is deemed inappropriate (e.g., to force participants to reflect vigorously their expertise in "negotiations" and, indeed, throughout the TA process).

FOOTNOTES

. . . .

2Bennis, W.G., and Slater, P.E., *The Temporary Society*, Harper and Row, New York, 1968.
3Birnbaum, P.H., Assessment of Alternative Management Forms in Academic Interdisciplinary Research Projects, *Manage. Sci.* 24:272-284 (1977).

4Blau, P., *The Organization of Academic Life*, Wiley, New York, 1973.

. . . .

6Cook, T.D., and Campbell, D.T., The Design and Conduct of Quasi-experiments and True Experiments in Field Settings, *Handbook of Industrial and Organizational Psychology*, M.D. Dunnette, ed., Rand McNally, New York, 1976, pp. 223-326.

7Kamen, C.S., The Effect of a Social Problem Orientation on the Organization of Scientific Research, *J. Environ. Syst.*, 7:309-322 (1978).

. . . .

13Porter, A.L., Rossini, F.A., Carpenter, S.R., and Roper, A.T., *Guidebook to Technology Assessment and Impact Analysis*, Elsevier North Holland, New York, in press.

14Rossini, F.A., and Porter, A.L., Frameworks for Integrating Interdisciplinary Research, *Res. Pol.* 8:70-79 (1979).

15Rossini, F.A., Porter, A.L., and Zucker, E., Multiple Technology Assessments, *J. Internat. Soc. Technol. Assess.* 2:21-28 (1976).

16Rossini, F.A., Porter, A.L., Kelly, P., Lipscomb, A., Carpenter, S., and Havick, J., The Epistemology of Interdisciplinary Research, in *The General Systems Paradigm: Science of Change and Change of Science*. Washington, D.C.: Society for General Systems Research, 1977, pp. 451-498.

31

ENVIRONMENT AND BENEFITS OF INTERDISCIPLINARY TEAMS*

Lawrence W. Bass

. . . To achieve the proper interdisciplinary environment, two separate but complementary managerial systems must operate harmoniously in parallel: (1) the usual pyramidal structure to establish the framework within which the individual acts as a unit in the organization; and (2) the separate relationship which governs his participation in project teams under the guidance of individual project team leaders. They may be considered as the organizational and the activities systems, respectively.

The organizational system provides the policies and practices governing the place of the individual in the administrative structure. It defines the channels of general supervision of the way he conducts himself and applies his talents. It provides for appraisal of his performance and exerts managerial responsibility for rewarding his contributions. It serves as a resource for assisting with administrative problems which affect his project work.

The activities system, on the other hand, is the route through which he applies his skills to problem solving, as a member of groups of other specialists under the guidance of team leaders.

These two systems at first glance appear to be in direct conflict. That they can proceed smoothly side by side is proved by the experience of engineering groups over many decades. Gradually the scheme has been adopted for other types of activity. Those organizations which have used the principles would find a return to the formal structured pattern a source of frustration that would cause loss of morale and initiative.

The introduction of interdisciplinary teams into a cellular structure therefore requires basic alterations in managerial attitudes and

---

* Reprinted by permission of Lomond Publications, Inc. from *Management by Task Forces: A Manual on the Operation of Interdisciplinary Teams*, by Lawrence W. Bass, 1975, pp. 73-83. Copyright 1975 by Lomond Systems, Inc.

behavior. An abrupt change from one style of operation to the other is likely to produce a temporary condition of chaos. Adoption of task force principles may be selective, however, to be used only for certain types of work. To assist those who would like to try out the system in an experimental way, the appendix, which is based on personal experience in initiating the procedures in numerous situations, is devoted to a discussion of the steps I have found useful for this purpose.

A basic requirement is adequate recognition of both professional performance and administrative ability. In a rigid cellular organization, the route to promotion is chiefly through managerial rank in the hierarchy. This has the disadvantage that talented specialists are often seduced into positions in which they become reluctant and mediocre administrators. Unless the value judgments are based on impartial appraisal of contributions to the success of the organization, problem solving abilities do not achieve their proper measure of reward.

Contrasting Patterns of Responsibility and Authority

In the time-honored structured organization, each level of management has direct control of both administrative functions and the actual work of the members in its chain of command. The managers schedule the activities, supervise them directly, appraise performance, and pass on their interpretations and recommendations to another echelon. In theory, coordination of inputs from different specialized areas is effected at those levels which are cross-over junctions. In practice, the need for better integration of competent opinions is often met by some form of review panel, or particularly by informal discussions among different specialists at the working level.

The pattern of flow of authority and information in formal organizations is too well known to require detailed discussion here. In general, the findings from the working level, developed according to the assignments given them, pass upward through supervisory layers until they reach a level thought to be suitable for transmission to other groups or departments in the organization. The comments of the recipients are reviewed and passed down again to the working level for consideration. . . .

The contrasting relationships in a system of interdisciplinary teams are shown in Chart IV. Disciplines A, B, and C are assumed to have different fields of specialization, such as, for example, applied research,

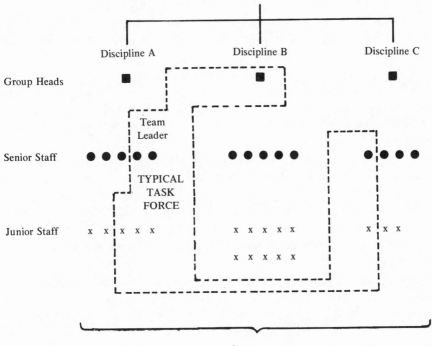

CHART IV
WORKING RELATIONSHIPS IN
AN INTERDISCIPLINARY ORGANIZATION

TASK FORCES

Direct Contacts with Users of Results

engineering, and market research. Here there is a built-in mechanism for obtaining collaboration among different groups of specialists acting as a team to reach a common objective. The leadership of the team does not depend on administrative rank. Participation is often on a part-time basis. Position in the formal managerial hierarchy does not determine the seniority of the individual in project work.

Included in this diagram is the composition of a typical task force, indicated by the dotted area. The team leader is a senior staff member from Discipline A. He does not have direct administrative authority over any of the team members, but he is given delegated authority over that part of their activities devoted to the project for which he is responsible. Because the brunt of the work falls within the skills of Discipline A, the team includes an additional senior specialist and three juniors from this administrative unit; he does not have administrative jurisdiction over them, but only control over their project work. To complete the interdisciplinary mix, he has enlisted the collaboration of the head of Discipline B and one senior and one junior specialist from Discipline C.

The respective titles of Group Head and Senior Staff Member do not have any significance for their roles as members of the team. Junior Staff Members, however, are considered to be still in process of developing their skills, and would not be considered ripe for team leadership. In the diagram they have the function of working with a senior associate, usually to carry out some of the detailed work necessary for the contribution from that particular section. On the other hand, if in spite of his lack of professional maturity he had developed some form of specialized expertise, he might be assigned to contribute this function without the need for a more senior supervisor, provided the team leader decides that this representation is adequate for the success of the project.

Finally, the presentation of the findings to the user of the information, including the preparation of reports, is the responsibility of the team leader, acting on behalf of and with the cooperation of the other members. This is a notable departure from the procedure in a structured organization in which this function would be carried out by someone at a higher administrative level. This provision in interdisciplinary systems adds greatly to the morale and professional satisfaction of those at the working level. In many organizations which use task force systems, very senior and experienced individuals often prefer to devote themselves to project work instead of assuming duties of an administrative nature. Further, even the senior administrators themselves take some part in project activities, thus permitting them to contribute their professional competence and to keep aware of the problems of those exclusively at the working level.

Interdisciplinary Teams and Management Theory

The advantages of interdisciplinary teams for problem solving can be attributed to the fact that they exemplify the basic principles of all modern schools of management analysis. Koontz and O'Donnell have provided a valuable concept for coordinating these theories (**Principles of Management**, 1968, pp. 34-42). They consider that the dominant doctrine is that of the operational school because "it attempts to analyze management in terms of what managers actually do." They regard the five other principal schools—empirical, human behavior, social system, decision theory, and mathematical—as specialized aspects of operational management theory.

In pointing out how interdisciplinary teams fulfill the teachings of these six doctrines, the definitions of Koontz and O'Donnell will be used. The reader who wishes to go more deeply into the subject should turn to their excellent book which is also a cornucopia of citations to the original literature.

> **The operational school**, regarded by them and also by this author as the unifying concept, "analyzes the management process, establishes a conceptual framework for it, identifies its principles, and builds a theory of management from them."
>
> **The empirical school** "analyzes management by a study of experience, sometimes with interest to draw generalizations, but usually merely as a means of transferring experience."
>
> **The human behavior school** "is based on the thesis that, since management involves getting things done with and through people, its study should be centered on interpersonal relations."
>
> **The social system school** "is closely related to the human behavior school. . . . It includes those who look upon management as a social system."
>
> **The decision theory school** "concentrates on rational decision—the selection, from among possible alternatives, of a course of action."
>
> **The mathematical school** "includes those theorists who see management as a system of mathematical models and processes."

Conformance with Operational Theory. An interdisciplinary team exemplifies the analysis of functional requirements and the logical programming of inputs and outputs of diverse specialized skills to achieve an objective. To make sure that all essential disciplines are included, the team leader must carry out some form of network analysis, either formal or informal, to determine the proposed level and timing of inputs from the array of specialists. When the assignment is one phase of a project involving a succession of major stages, undertaken by successive teams, the wise team leader will provide feed-back and feed-forward to insure continuity in development and application; this he can do by including key personnel from preceding functions and from those destined to become active later.

For large and complex projects, such as those in major defense or space programs, some type of Critical Path Method or Program Evaluation and Review Technique is required. For the more usual sort of R & D assignments or feasibility studies in industry, such elaborate procedures are not necessary, although the basic principles are used less formally by the skilled team leader. To promote efficiency in decision making, when the team consists of more than five or six members, it is advisable to select a small key team representing the dominant skills, and to use the others in a consulting capacity. This device avoids the inherent waste of time in large meetings when many of the participants are concerned with only parts of the subject matter, but the leader must make sure that each individual is kept informed of all pertinent activities on a need-to-know basis.

Empirical Expertise Is Effectively Utilized. When a team leader selects colleagues for a project, he puts a premium on expert knowledge and experience. Because the group is interdisciplinary, however, too much reliance on traditional know-how is counterbalanced by other members who will challenge stereotyped opinions. The pragmatic experience of experts from different disciplines is an essential ingredient to avoid impractical conclusions.

Individual Talents Are Put to Optimum Use. From the point of view of the human behavior school, it is hard to conceive of a procedure which provides a greater challenge to the individual to exert his abilities, with limitation only on the approach agreed to with the team leader for contribution to the common goal. He has joined the group as a volunteer in association with peers. He employs his creativity within his discipline to develop the details of his own attack, and he is free to express his opinion on the programs of the other members of the team.

Group Dynamics is an Essential Feature. The ideal team strives to perform as a unit. The give-and-take of informal team discussions leads to constructive criticism of individual ideas. The members are encouraged to test their concepts openly within the jury of the brotherhood. If the ideas are sound, but require adjustment for application to the problem, open discussion will lead to their modification to useful dimensions. Incidentally, differences of opinions among team members may at times be very deep-seated; reconciliation of diverging views requires a high order of ability on the part of the team leader to maintain a healthy climate in the group.

Decision Theory is Inherent in Team Procedures. The nature of the group activity leads to systematic testing of concepts and conclusions against alternatives. This provides a continuum of decision making, with close-coupled feed-back in broad perspective because of representation of varied disciplines. As an example, activities of successive teams carrying a new product concept to commercialization may need to make feasibility decisions at 100 or more distinct steps.

Mathematical Analysis is Often a Valuable Tool. In a well-rounded organization, many teams include members or are headed by specialists in operations research methodology. These are free to seek out and to apply mathematical analysis and model building wherever they can be shown to be useful. At the very least, they contribute to the systematic planning of investigations and to evaluation of the limits of accuracy in the conclusions.

Development of Managerial Capabilities. In addition to embracing the principles of the various theories of management, interdisciplinary teams provide the participants with on-the-job training in managerial practices. They afford concrete experience regarding those techniques which are effective in project leadership. The internal pressures on each individual to attain optimum contribution toward the goal lead him to better programming of his work to maintain planned performance.

Benefits of Interdisciplinary Systems

The scope of the foregoing material justifies a summary of the benefits which should result from the adoption of the principles of interdisciplinology. These are divided in this section into two parts: (1) those accruing to the organization and (2) those relating to the opportunities for the development of the individual. From my point of view, there are no real disadvantages except for the necessity for managers to conduct a thoroughgoing review of their policies and practices, which I consider to be an incentive to better administration and not a deterrent.

The examples given in earlier chapters will surely appear to some readers as too sophisticated for widespread use. I admit that the procedures described will not be carried out with entire success according to the models until the organization has gained enough experience to understand thoroughly the principles and their implications. This requires modifications in policies, practices, and administrative relationships. From personal experience in installing the system in a variety of groups, I have found that the changes are not hard to make provided the key managers approach the ideas in a constructive way rather than disputing their validity. The concepts are, in general, welcomed at the working level because they provide the individuals an opportunity to participate in projects in a way that gives them greater satisfaction in their roles. If appropriate activities are selected for a trial period, in the course of a few weeks or months performance reaches a satisfactory level and directions for improvement become evident. Then the system can be expanded to other activities which are judged to be susceptible to this approach.

Even when an organization adopts the procedures only in part, or merely on a token basis, the effect is often beneficial. The reconsideration of managerial principles, particularly the greater recognition to be accorded to the views of those at the working level, tends to stimulate a groundswell toward more open structures and communications.

Benefits to the Organization. The listing below gives my views of the advantages obtained by the use of interdisciplinary teams:

Greater effectiveness in the use of human resources through more critical control of expenditure of effort, which leads to better appreciation of the real value of expertise;

Stimulation of a sense of purpose throughout the staff as a result of more incisive selection, appraisal, and planning of programs through the direct involvement of all participants;

Speeding up of problem solving by effective and timely feed-in of information and opinion from competent sources;

Acceleration of implementation as a result of forewarning to new levels of participation by means of their earlier involvement in the collaborative endeavor;

Prompter recognition of major obstacles to feasibility in time to change direction of program or to curtail activity;

Continuity in the transfer of knowledge and expertise from one group to another;

Reduction of "empire-building" in groups by providing a smooth channel for using skills available elsewhere in the organization;

Elimination of redundant levels of supervision with resultant shorter lines of communication in a flatter organization;

Development among the staff of more versatile competence and improved managerial skills through interaction with co-workers on a wider range of problems;

Improvement in information retrieval through a network of specialists, each having familiarity with his own area of expertise;

Better personnel evaluation through a wider range of opinions from co-workers.

Benefits to the Individual. A well organized task force system places greater responsibilities upon the teams and their members and, at the same time, gives them more freedom in applying their skills. In smoothly running organizations, the team leader designs the work outline, subject to managerial approval, selects specialists to supply the required expertise, and invites them to serve in the group, usually on a part-time schedule, in the capacities which he has planned. He recognizes their competence, without being an expert himself in some of the disciplines represented, and is familiar enough with the nature and the techniques of these specialized areas in relation to the objective, so that he is able to inject their contributions effectively into the total effort. This really means that each team member is essentially a volunteer.

This participative role enhances each team member's sense of professional opportunity because of the following incentives:

Increased confidence in and loyalty to the organization as a whole;

Personal responsibility for planning and carrying out special functions which he has participated in defining;

Improved managerial ability for the use of his own expertise to accommodate it to the total program;

Greater sense of achievement through better knowledge about the advances of projects on which he has worked toward commercialization;

Increase in professional self-confidence through maintenance of status in a composite group of peers;

Increased skill in interpersonal relations through the experience of
close cooperation with other team members;

Enrichment of understanding of other areas of specialization;

Enhancement of ability to communicate with representatives of
other disciplines and functional groups;

Opportunity to evaluate his innovative ideas with a peer group
before submitting them to the more conservative managerial
hierarchy.

32

CHARACTERISTICS OF INTERDISCIPLINARY RESEARCH TEAMS*

William R. MacDonald

Drawing from the variety of accounts about IR we can identify a number of characteristics or variables associated with IR teams. Unfortunately there has been very little actual research into these teams, thus the data available have to be supplemented by the observations of administrators and the team scientists themselves. Additionally, because there isn't a lot of information concerning different organizations, care has to be exercised in inferring that characteristics of a team in a university setting will be the same as a government or industrial centre.

There are a considerable number of variables mentioned in the IR literature, although many of them receive only minor attention. As I am not aware of any system to select the important characteristics, I have had to rely on the frequency with which they are reported as an ·indication of their importance. Other variables are included since they receive some attention in the general group dynamics literature, but are mentioned infrequently in IR reports. Obviously the choice is very subjective.

The variables can be arranged in two general groupings: those which relate to the interactions of team members as a result of being a team and those more related to the research tasks. The former group includes: leadership, conflict, communication, size, age, co-ordination, and cohesiveness; the latter group includes: complexity, urgency, and predictability/certainty. . . .

* From The *Management of Interdisciplinary Research Teams: A Literature Review*, January 1982, pp. 15-29. A report prepared on behalf of the Department of the Environment and the Department of Agriculture, Government of Alberta, Edmonton, Alberta, Canada. Reprinted by permission of the author. Appendices and references in the text have been omitted from the reprint.

1. LEADERSHIP

The role of the leader in academic research teams is discussed by Birnbaum (1979a, 1979b) and Birnbaum *et al* (1979). Birnbaum's review of the previous literature on research teams (1979b) indicates that tasks tend to be unstructured and the leader's position power weak. Leadership effectiveness will, as a result, depend on the group atmosphere developed by the relationship between the leader and team members. The author divides leadership styles into two categories: those behaviours which involve initiating structure (emphasis is on tasks, authority, control and providing structure to team activities); and consideration behaviour (the leader is more concerned with the social needs of the team, relationships amongst team members, and involves the staff more frequently in decisions). Research results indicate that behaviours in effective projects change over time. In projects less than four years old, leaders who exhibit both behaviours (initiating and consideration) will encourage mutual trust and support while emphasizing organization within the team. In older projects, task oriented behaviour is more important to ensure co-ordination among researchers who become increasingly independent as they develop their expertise and a sense of security with their research abilities.

Birnbaum's model (1979a) includes only the initiating structure behaviour of leadership. According to this model, the leader's main relationship to performance is through monitoring the perceived sense of urgency of the project (deadlines, time demands, etc.) and ensuring that disagreements between team members are openly discussed. The importance of open discussion of disagreements (conflict resolution) is only made clear in Birnbaum *et al* (1980) where it is reported that group age and open discussion are the two most important variables in predicting research success.

Pearson *et al* (1979) have a somewhat different terminology in considering leader styles, emphasizing the relationship between the leader and the organization in which he/she works. These authors suggest there are two forms of organizational structure, one of which is based on the concept of co-ordination, the other stressing leadership. In the former the project leader acts more like a co-ordinator in the team and has less authority in the organization; in the latter the leader has authority in the team and organization, while his project role is to motivate team members to work to project goals. (For anyone familiar with organizational management theory, this is a curious mix of concepts from mechanistic and organic models, with matrix management thrown in.) For teams which work in organizations where competition for resources if frequent, the latter style will be the most successful. Some support for this is given by Stucki (1979) in suggesting that a leadership organizational structure in a pharmaceutical company has been more successful than the previous co-ordination structure. (It should be noted the emphasis of these authors is on the relationship between the team and the organization; obviously this will have a direct bearing on how the leader acts within the team).

A third approach to examining leadership, by Barth and Manners (1979), is to consider the IR leader's role as consisting of three major components in terms of managerial functions (planning, training, control, technical, administration), relational factors (evaluator, motivator, director) and the target scope (external, superiors, subordinates, peers, self). Different situations will then require different emphasis across these role functions, which in turn will influence the style of the manager. Thus, the authors indicate, there is a need for a manager to be flexible in performing his/her duties.

Stankiewicz (1979) looked at the interaction between size of an academic research group (size was determined as the average number of scientists in a group during the three years prior to his survey) and leadership. Productivity was determined from the output of published papers divided by the group size. Of particular note is the difference in productivity with leader experience: for leaders with about 14 or more years experience, productivity of a group will increase until there are four members, then it will level off; for leaders with less experience, productivity will start high in very small groups, but will rapidly fall when there are more than four team members. Maximum productivity is about the same for experienced or inexperienced leaders, but occurs with different group size. Stankiewicz believes that younger leaders strive for maximum individual productivity, which might result in neglect of the group as a whole, as it gets larger. Actual leadership styles are not discussed in this paper.

2. COMMUNICATION

There are two aspects of communication which are relevant to IR teams. One relates to the difficulties encountered by team members in communicating with each other, the other considers the communication networks (structural linkages) which are established in teams. Both aspects are considered here.

Communication can be defined as the process of exchanging information through the use of commonly understood symbols. The efficiency of communication (i.e. fidelity) between individuals can be affected by communication skill and perceptual, conceptual, social or environmental factors. There are also several barriers to communication: structural (the organization of a group); social-psychological (the individual's make-up and his relations within the group); and semantic (based on the use of language). Because the most obvious difference between IR teams and other research teams is the existence of scientists representing a variety of disciplines, many authors identify semantics as *the* barrier to communication. This in turn focuses attention only on the conceptual factors (i.e. knowledge of the subject matter), eliminating the other factors and barriers from consideration.

Comment in the literature about communication problems is based on observations by administrators and scientists themselves (McEvoy, 1972; Nilles, 1975; Bella and Williamson, 1976; Barmark, 1979). Their general comments can be briefly summarized in the following sentences. In an IR project the nature of the problem being studied requires the input of a number of different disciplines. Each discipline will have its own perception of the problem, paradigms, procedures, etc., which are considered the "best" to study the problem. Consequently, team members are faced with communicating their different perceptions, explaining their paradigms, and understanding the problem from the viewpoint of others, if the team is to undertake an interdisciplinary as contrasted to multidisciplinary project. It is in this context that communication can be extremely difficult; it will require time and acceptance of others before interdisciplinary understanding can occur. Unfortunately many scientists identify very strongly with their discipline and have difficulty accepting or communicating with scientists in other disciplines.

Interestingly, a major survey of university teams (Birnbaum, 1979c) found that about 80% of the scientists responding did not consider there were extreme communication problems due to differences in terminology. Also, a survey of seven interdisciplinary environmental projects at one university (Kendall and MacIntosh, 1978, p. 19) found that differences among disciplines explained few of the management problems encountered. This was explained on the basis of a common environmental attitude being possessed by team members.

Communication patterns are mentioned by only two authors. Rossini *et al.* (1979) found these patterns had a direct effect on the degree to which integration of technology assessments (TA) occurred. They found TA teams established patterns on a continuum from communication with all members (all channel) to a central person being the main contact with little communication occurring between other members (hub and spokes). Although there is no indication which patterns were most effective, they did change during the team's lifetime. Academic research teams changed communication pattern over time also, being mainly hub and spokes in young projects (3 years or less), but becoming all-channel in older projects (Birnbaum, 1979c). There does not appear to be any best way to reduce the problems of communication. The idea of a bridge scientist, one who acts as a translator between disciplines, has been suggested (Anbar, 1973). There are also formal techniques becoming available, such as cross-impact analysis (Allen, 1978), a method designed to force team members to carefully analyze their research problem prior to beginning actual research.

3. CONFLICT

Conflict is generally considered to be a disagreement between individuals. Within IR teams conflict can occur over technical issues such as definition of the problem, research methodologies, scheduling, etc., or it may occur over interpersonal issues, such as leadership style, ethnocentrism (perception that one discipline is not as good as another), or within an individual as he/she is confronted with views (paradigms) which challenge his/her own views (Anbar, 1973; Bella and Williamson, 1976; Birnbaum, 1979c; Luszki, 1958; Rossini *et al*, 1979). Most scientists trained in a mono-discipline approach to research come to identify with the beliefs held by that discipline and will tend to view a research problem from that narrow perspective. In actuality there will be many facets of a problem, which is why a multi-disciplinary investigation is needed; the scientists involved must recognize the legitimacy of the views of their team members and work to understand and incorporate them into the interdisciplinary approach. (Conflict can

- exist between scientists even within a discipline when each adheres to a different paradigm.) [1]

Conflict over technical operations can occur throughout the lifetime of a project. Both Wilpert (1979) and Barmark (1979) report conflict existed over definition of the problem, over experimental methodologies, over data analysis and in the final report writing. Bella and Williamson (1976) suggest scientists will have skills and abilities that are appropriate for different activities of the research process; conflicts may also occur when individuals identify strongly with one activity, and do not believe other project activities are as important.

There is a general impression in the IR literature that conflict is always negative, i.e., it is a "problem"; because of conflict many projects go through great difficulty and fail. Conflict, however, can be beneficial, when, as a form of communication between individuals with differing views, it is used to create a new understanding of the topic.

The IR literature is of little assistance in suggesting approaches to conflict resolution. Birnbaum *et al* (1979) report that open discussion of disagreements, or the confrontation mode of conflict resolution, is one of the major factors contributing to the success of academic research teams. This approach is also supported in a review paper by Baker and Wilemon (1977), where it is reported that successful project managers most frequently use a confrontation mode of conflict resolution.

4. TEAM SIZE

The number of participants on a team can be expected to affect the research activities in various ways: the topic areas to be covered, need for particular communication patterns, synthesis of data, management control, or interpersonal relations among members.

Stankiewicz (1979) found academic research teams reached an optimum size at 5-6 scientists; both productivity and quality of work increased to this size but decreased in larger groups. Stankiewicz identified three factors which helped to explain the changes occurring:

— the degree of coherence of the group's research project (how well the project was integrated)—performance began to fall at 5-6 members, but declined much more rapidly for poorly organized groups;

— the cohesion among group members (how well they were able to get along with each other)—productivity peaked at 5-6 members, remained high for highly cohesive groups, but decreased in groups with low cohesion;

— leaders with more than 14 years R & D experience maintained productivity in large groups whereas it fell for less experienced leaders as the group increased beyond 5-6 members.

In another analysis of academic research teams, Birnbaum (1977) reported the highest performance occurred when the teams were large (no specific number is given), consisting mostly of Ph.D.'s who stayed with the project, and where there was a clear division of labour. Interestingly, Birnbaum's model of research teams does not identify size as an important factor affecting performance.

Dailey (1980) studied groups in several private and public research organizations and found size only indirectly affected performance. His model indicates size has an effect on group cohesion and co-ordination, both of which have a direct positive effect on performance. Whereas groups became less cohesive as their size increased, co-ordination, (the formal or informal interaction of members to accomplish the project tasks) was found to increase with size. . . .

5. TEAM AGE

Team age can have an effect on performance in a number of ways, as will be seen in the following statements. Age should not be considered as an isolated variable, as other variables, such as team size or the relationships among members, may also change with time. Another factor to consider is the definition of age. Essentially there are two determinants: the actual age of a project or the average length of time members have been together. Both of these are used in the literature. Both will have different implications for understanding the team's dynamics; for example, the characteristics of a team with changing members are expected to be different than a stable one, even for projects of similar age.

A major study of groups in government and industry was reported by Pelz and Andrews (1966). Group age was defined as the average number of years each member had belonged.

There are two types of performance suggested by Pelz and Andrews. The scientific contribution (related strictly to scientific or technical advances) is highest in groups under two years of age, decreases, and then increases up to 4-5 years of age before falling off considerably. On the other hand, the overall usefulness to the organization (the ability of the group to work efficiently and on different problems) does not reach a maximum until 4-5 years of group age. In other words, groups will generally exhibit bimodal performance maxima, one very early and one at about 4-5 years of age.

Some characteristics which vary with group age and contribute to the performance were also suggested by Pelz and Andrews. As a group ages, communication frequency between members decreases continually; however, the cohesiveness of the group (association with each other) rises as members become better acquainted; cohesiveness reaches a maximum at 4-5 years. As scientists work together their competition between each other begins to decrease after 2-3 years, reaches a minimum at 6-7 years, then rises again. In addition, the interests of scientists change from a desire to engage in "broad mapping of new areas" to "probing deeply in narrow areas". At 4-5 years of age these two interests provide a strong balancing influence on the group.

Birnbaum et al. (1979) define group age as the length of time the group has been in existence. These authors report the two major factors relating to performance are open discussion of disagreements (conflict resolution) and group age. In other words, the longer a group stays together and discusses its disagreements, the better its chances of success. Age is considered to be important because of the time needed to overcome differences in terminology, for different levels of analysis or for different problem solving approaches.

Other characteristics also change over time. Communication patterns are found to vary from single-channel, leader centered in young teams (less than 3 years project age) to multi-channel in older teams (Birnbaum, 1979c). Furthermore, in young projects, team members are interested in working together, examining broad areas, etc., in contrast to older projects where specialization and independent writing is of greater interest (Birnbaum, 1979b).

Taking a different approach, Stone (1969) suggests some concepts of group psychology can be used to understand development in a research team. Over time successful teams appear to develop interpersonal relationships which support the integration of individual and group needs. In other words, a new group and an older group are different; Stone refers to the former as a secondary-group and the latter as a primary-group. A secondary-group pattern of relationships exists in a team during its early history. Members will have entered the team with their individual knowledge, expectations, and perceptions; the relationships initiated will be basically self-protective. The team members are not expected to have developed a sense of "teamness", and this is reflected in the use of "I" when talking about activities related to the project. As members become more comfortable with the team (which may take considerable time if individual differences, conflicts, etc:, can be worked out) a sense of "teamness" can develop. This is the formation of the primary-group, and with it individuals begin to identify with the team and refer to "We" when talking about the team. Stone states ". . . the degree in which a research team approaches primary-group relationship patterns determines the long-range effectiveness of that group."

This concept of primary and secondary groups is useful in two ways. First, it helps identify signs of change in the team's development, as evidenced by individuals relating to "We" rather than "I". Second, it emphasizes the importance of social issues that may affect a team's performance and goes beyond some of the variables previously discussed.

6. COHESIVENESS AND CO-ORDINATION

The following two parameters are directly related to the social interactions which occur in teams, although there is little attention paid to them in the IR literature.

Cohesiveness

Group cohesiveness has received considerable attention in research on group dynamics (Cartwright and Zander, 1970, p. 91). Group cohesiveness refers to the degree to which members desire to remain in the group; there is a concern with membership, motivation to contribute to the group's welfare, advance its objectives and participate in its activities. It may be considered as an emotional cement which contributes to the maintenance of stable group membership. Team cohesiveness was found to be the most significant variable in contributing to performance (Dailey, 1980). Cohesiveness was considered by Pelz and Andrews (1966) to be measured by the ratio of "significant colleagues" chosen within a group to the total possible within-group choices. They found cohesiveness within a group rose continually to a maximum at 4-5 years, but then declined to below its initial level after 8-9 years. This rise in cohesiveness also corresponded with the increased "usefulness" of a group to its organization.

Co-ordination

As used here, co-ordination will relate to interactive processes of team members in developing an understanding of the research problem. Dailey (1980) considers co-ordination as an integrating mechanism in teams, accomplished by unplanned communications or informal conferences between two or more group members. In an earlier paper, Dailey (1978) also used a similar concept; he defined collaborative problem solving as "the presence of mutual influence between team members, open direct communication and conflict resolution, and support for innovation and experimentation". The extent to which a team achieves co-ordination (or collaborative problem solving) has been found to be directly related to its productivity (performance), both in government/industry (Dailey, 1978, 1980) and universities (Gillespie and Birnbaum, 1980; Birnbaum, 1979).

7. RESEARCH TASK PARAMETERS

Variables associated with the research problem itself are mentioned in the literature; however, none of them are treated in any detail. Three of these are briefly discussed here: problem complexity, urgency, and task predictability or certainty.

Complexity

Complexity is not really defined, nor is any measurement scheme for it given in the literature. When it is referred to, the degree of complexity is a subjective judgement. We could consider complexity varying from project to project, but is a project requiring several related disciplines (e.g., the effect of sulphur dioxide on agricultural crops) less complex than one requiring disparate disciplines (e.g., watershed management)? The complexity may exist in the definition of the problem (see Section 2), in the research methodologies, or in the integration of research findings. McEvoy (1972) stresses the need to address problem complexity early by developing an integrated framework (model) for the various research thrusts. Without such a framework the individual disciplines will produce data that cannot be integrated during a project's final stages.

Birnbaum (1979a) developed a model which includes complexity. The model suggests complexity is related to team performance through its negative effect on a perceived sense of urgency: the more complex a problem the less a sense of urgency team members have about it. This relationship is not clearly explained by Birnbaum, and the negative outcome is not what one would intuitively expect. Avoidance of complexity may be attempted by scientists who participate in IR teams by restricting their investigations to their own discipline (Kendall and MacKintosh, 1978). Barmark and Wallen (1979) indicate the complexity of a large scale forestry research program was not realized when it was initiated, thereby contributing to the lack of success for the program.

Urgency

Urgency is the need for rapid research results. Pearson *et al.* (1979) suggest urgency and predictability are important parameters in IR and will require different organizational structures (such as communication, project authorization, or leadership styles) as they vary from project to project. An urgent project will require a leader who is decisive and has delegated authority; project resources will also need to be readily available. When urgency is less critical, leadership can be more supportive, time is available to develop an understanding of the research problem and resources can be planned for, or shared among, various teams.

Birnbaum's (1979a) model identifies urgency as a variable related to performance through its effect on conflict resolution and leadership style. An increased sense of urgency might lead team members to change from open discussion to forcing a resolution (using power or intimidation) or withdrawal. According to Birnbaum, a team leader who fails to recognize this effect of urgency and does not maintain open discussions will have difficulty in maintaining performance.[2]

Predictability/Certainty

As mentioned above, predictability, the extent to which steps necessary to achieve results are predeterminable, can have an impact on research performances (Pearson *et al.* 1979). Low predictability will require team members to be continually developing and analyzing their project and to take risks; high predictability may remove the challenge of a project, although this may be balanced if the work is urgent. The findings of Pelz and Andrews (1966) tend to support this idea. They suggest a certain amount of "stress" on teams will encourage performance. They describe an index of intellectual tension, which is a measure of the similarity of team members (implying diversity and uncertainty) and their secretiveness (hesitation to share ideas). When there was low tension (low secretiveness and similar members), overall usefulness of the group started high but decreased after three years. In contrast, high tension teams (high secretiveness plus dissimilarity, which one might expect in IR) began with a low performance which dramatically increased after 2-3 years and had a relatively high performance for the next four years. It appears the first period of this latter group is spent working through its internal conflicts.

Task certainty is defined by Dailey (1980) to consist of two dimensions: task difficulty—the analyzability of the work, and predictability of work methods; and task variability—the number of work exceptions encountered. Certainty was found to affect team cohesiveness negatively (teams are less cohesive as certainty increases), but to have a direct positive effect on performance.

FOOTNOTES

[1]One of the reviewers (M. O'Driscoll) has suggested his personal experience with teams indicates authoritarianism, dogmatism, interpersonal skills and personal motives of individuals are factors which severely limit group effectiveness and lead to conflict. The IR literature is, unfortunately, devoid of any good analysis of social and psychological factors which contribute to conflict or communication problems.

[2]The effect of urgency needs to receive more attention. Birnbaum suggests open discussion is always the most satisfactory approach to good performance. This may not always be so, for example, when "all hell breaks loose" and research must be done within very tight time constraints. Under these conditions a leader may have to dispense with long discussions and push the team to perform.

PART VII

POSTSCRIPT

33

THE BROAD SCOPE OF INTERDISCIPLINARITY

Julie Thompson Klein

The topic of interdisciplinary team research which dominates this book is just one part of a rich and rather broad set of interdisciplinary activities which have evolved in the twentieth century. Interdisciplinarity is an old concept, based as it is on such long-expressed values as integration, synthesis, the unity of knowledge and a community of scholars. Several scholars, in fact, are fond of extolling such "true interdisciplinary thinkers" as Plato, DaVinci, Leibniz, Comte and even Confucius, as well as the legions of researchers who pioneered modern disciplinary and professional study. However, despite these appeals to tradition, the overwhelming thrust of interdisciplinary discourse is centered upon the distinctly modern need for meaningful interactions across disciplinary boundaries which developed in the West during the nineteenth century.

The need for interaction is neither simple nor singular. Interdisciplinarity has emerged across a wide range of disciplinary, professional, social, political, cultural, and epistemological boundaries for three primary reasons. For some it facilitates the search for unity of knowledge, a quest which expresses both a classical and a more modern belief in knowledge as a unified whole. At the same time, interdisciplinarity is also part of the general evolution of knowledge. It emerges through the processes of both differentiation—a fissioning of subjects into new and smaller specialties and subspecialties, and integration—a fusion of separate perspectives into common and sometimes new relation. Finally, and especially for the authors represented in this book, it functions as a means of solving "practical" problems within a society. While some interdisciplinary activities may be quite different from others, all interdisciplinary work is rooted in a fundamental epistemology of convergence, an integrative synthesis which has tended to produce five major kinds of disciplinary interaction:

(1) the integration of disciplinary perspectives brought to bear on shared topics, questions or themes;

(2) the solution to intellectual or social, technological, medical problems with no necessary modification of original disciplinary perspectives, only a solution to the problem;

(3) the emergence of a new discipline, specialty, or subfield;

(4) enduring dependence on a borrowed method, concept or theory;

(5) increased consistency of subject matters, methods, and theories between fields.

Broadly-based search of disciplinary and professional literatures across the humanities, social sciences, and natural sciences reveals that interdisciplinary work appears in a considerable variety of contexts, beginning with four groups of educational activities:

(1) GENERAL, LIBERAL, AND INTERDISCIPLINARY UNDERGRADUATE PROGRAMS: core curricula, interdisciplinary colleges and programs, interdisciplinary seminars, interdepartmental majors, pre- and post-specialist courses

(2) UPPER-LEVEL AND GRADUATE TRAINING IN PARTICULAR INTERDISCIPLINARY APPROACHES, TOPICS, PROBLEMS AND RESEARCH QUESTIONS: interdisciplinary relationships in the social sciences, "applied" philosophy, the study of complex topics such as poverty and the city, systems theory and other synthetic/integrative concepts

(3) PRE-PROFESSIONAL AND PROFESSIONAL TRAINING IN INTEGRATIVE AND INTERDISCIPLINARY APPROACHES IN A VOCATIONAL CONTEXT: public health, social work, business, recreation, law, engineering, medicine

(4) ACADEMIC FIELDS ORGANIZED AS INTERDISCIPLINARY STUDIES: American Studies, Black Studies, Women's Studies, Area Studies, Environmental Studies, Gerontology

Within both applied and basic research, there are six identifiable interdisciplinary contexts ranging from formal institutes to invisible colleges, *ad hoc* teams, and lone scholars:

(5) FORMAL INTERDISCIPLINARY STUDIES, DEPARTMENTS WITHIN UNIVERSITIES: including examples listed above, particularly in categories 3 and 4

(6) INTERDISCIPLINES: converged fields such as social psychology, biochemistry

(7) RESEARCH CENTERS AND INSTITUTES BOTH EXOGENOUS AND ENDOGENOUS TO THE UNIVERSITY: The Center for Craniofacial Anamolies, Research School of Pacific Studies, Center for Asian Studies, various Centers for Interdisciplinary Studies which function as umbrella organizations for interdisciplinary activities

(8) SOCIAL, MEDICAL, AND TECHNOLOGICAL PROBLEM-SOLVING TEAMS AND "MISSIONS": projects and task forces assembled to handle problems of urban planning, environmental health, the space shuttle; social, psychological, and medical care

(9) DISCIPLINES CLAIMING TO BE SYNOPTIC, METADISCIPLINARY OR PLURALISTIC: older examples such as history, philosophy, and literature; newer examples such as anthropology, semiotics, rhetoric

(10) NEW SUBJECTS WHICH ATTRACT ENOUGH RESEARCHERS TO CONSTITUTE A NEW DISCIPLINE OR A PROMINENT SUBSPECIALTY: immunopharmacology, demography, oral history, family history, urban history, ecotoxiciology, interdisciplinary criminology, the study of written discourse

There is also a less formal, though nonetheless substantial interdisciplinary, presence which can be classified into four categories:

(11) BORROWING:
   * *instrumental tools and methods* such as mathematical, statistical, instrumental, polling, survey, interview and observation techniques for measuring and testing purposes
   * *concepts, theories, models and paradigms used for auxiliary problem solution or wide explanatory power*: ecological principles used in archaeology, theories of magnetism and economic flow, general systems theory, structuralism, Marxism, phenomenology, hermeneutics, etc.

(12) INTERFIELD THEORIES: the chromosome theory as it related to genetics and cytology, the theory of allosteric regulation as it connected biochemistry and physics; converging theory levels among biology, chemistry and physics

(13) PROBLEMS AND ISSUES OF SCOPE AND COMPLEXITY, PARTICULARLY THOSE AT THE "FRONTIERS" OF KNOWLEDGE:

   * *topics, problems and queries which cross disciplinary lines*: the problem of "human agency" in history and sociology, the study of culture, theories of development and modernization, climate change, the psychology and sociology of language use, oral testimony, the interdisciplinary connections between science and ethics, and the mind-body problem in the Middle Ages as advanced from a narrow religious interpretation through modern psychology and anthropological insights

   * *attempts to locate disciplinary material in time (an age) and in place (a national or cultural identity)*: cultural and material history of the "longue duree," archaeological excavations as holistic test beds for other fields

   * *synthetic scholarship by individuals*: Edward Said's *Orientalism*, Hannah Arendt's *The Human Condition*, Hayden White's *Metahistory*, Raymond Williams' *The Country and The City*

(14) THEORIES OF UNIFIED KNOWLEDGE:

   * attempts to define a unified science, a unified social science

   * *individuals' synthetic schemata*: Oliver Reiser's philosophical method, K. William Kapp's "science of man in society," Parsons/Shils general theory of action

Early Movements

The evolution of interdisciplinary movement may be classified roughly into three historical periods. The first, most prominent from the World War I era to World War II, was marked by initial debates. The second, dating from the World War II era through the late 60's, was characterized by a widening and more visible interdisciplinary presence. The third, extending from the late 60's through the present, saw the rise of a professional interdisciplinary movement. Since the early 20th century, there has been continuous discussion of the interdisciplinary concept in three areas: educational literature, social science literature, and a rather widely-dispersed debate on the relationship between specialized knowledge and interdisciplinary competence which cuts across all disciplinary and professional literatures. During the World War I era, interdisciplinarity was most visible as "interdisciplinary" education, itself part of a much wider "general" education movement. Both were reformative responses to a "liberal" education tradition which was being fragmented by a general scientification of knowledge, the emergence of new disciplines, the growth of specialization, and demands upon the university by its external communities. While a good many "general" education courses and even many allegedly "interdisciplinary" courses proved to be merely eclectic studies of selected themes and issues, a genuinely interdisciplinary course was one which dealt with particular issues, problems, or questions of knowledge by drawing on more than one relevant discipline. As a protest against specialization, the interdisciplinary movement during the World War I and II eras was in large part an attempt to reorganize and integrate knowledge along other than disciplinary lines, though there was also an implicit attempt to deal with the human problems created by specialization. In both periods, however, the momentum for both "interdisciplinary" and "general" education was undermined: after the World War I era by a depression and ever-increasing specialization; after World War II by a post-Sputnik wave of specialization, and emphasis on foreign languages and programs for the gifted. [1]

Between the Wars there was considerable debate on the nature of "integrative" versus "interdisciplinary" thought. Integration was a familiar topic in the social sciences. In the 1920's the Social Science Research Council was established to promote integration across disciplines increasingly isolated by specialization and later, in the 1930's and '40's, the Chicago school of social science worked toward integration of scientific inquiry. The Unity of Science movement which appeared in 1930 attempted to unify the rational and empirical domains through logical positivism. There was also a new attempt to achieve encyclopedic knowledge when Otto Neurath, Rudolf Carnap and Charles Morris envisioned the foundation for a philosophy of the natural and social sciences. Although both movements eventually dwindled, their influence was widespread at the time. Integration had a number of meanings in educational circles, though in the 1930's it was used specifically as a slogan for an educational movement associated with changing social conditions. In 1935, when the Department of Superintendence of the National Educational Association held a meeting on the concept of "integration," its participants concluded that complete unity was impossible. The fundamental distinction they drew between the notion of a comprehensive, "unified" experience and a more realistic, modern notion of "unifying" experiences prevails even today in the continuing tension between proponents of a single meta-language or a unified science, and proponents of more modified integrative concepts along specific problem spheres, narrowly defined research queries, and clusters of related disciplines.[2]

There were in effect two interdisciplinary movements in the social sciences. The first was primarily instrumental and empirical. Borrowing from other disciplines was done primarily for testing and measuring. Statistics and psychology, to use two prominent examples, were approached as *tools*. Because there was, as Landau et al. put it, "no direct challenge to the *status quo* of social science," existing categories remained for the most part intact, although occasional disciplinary "spillage" did lead to the evolution of hybrid disciplines such as social psychology, political sociology, physiological psychology and social anthropology.[3] At the same time, there was also a further and much broader kind of instrumentality in the pressure for an "applied social science" focused on such complex problems acknowledged to lie beyond the domain of one discipline: the war, labor, propaganda, population shifts and location, housing, social welfare, and crime.[4]

The second interdisciplinary movement in the social sciences was based on conceptual rather than instrumental integration of knowledge. A good example is the "area" approach, a much-heralded synthetic movement which emerged between the wars. Area Studies were to provide comprehensive knowledge of every area of the earth, based upon the methodological premise that disciplinary gaps can be bridged when teams of specialists work together. While clearly more difficult than the instrumental form of interdisciplinarity, this conceptual interdisciplinarity derives from the first stage of interdisciplinary contact and may lead logically to several efforts: restructuring fields in theoretic terms, transcending institutionalism by providing a theoretical coherence, or even producing a new system for the division of labor and the distribution of resources based upon a set of explicit ordering principles.[5] Despite its promise, the "area" approach did not live up to initial expectations. Many supposedly "interdisciplinary" team members fell back upon their disciplinary perspectives and there were, consequently, demands for new "integrative" categories which would go beyond existing categories. The older "interdisciplinary" approach in the social sciences has been likened to the "old Baconian belief that broader basic generalizations will almost automatically drop out of the vast accumulation of discrete fact," a naive conviction challenged by the "integrative" conviction that new and powerful concepts might be developed for treating the problems at hand in the most effective manner. If the new category were to have greater analytic power and therefore replace the older disciplines, Landau, et al. explain, "this—in the logic of scientific inquiry—is as should be." [6]

Subsequent to the "area" debates, a parallel interdisciplinary/ integrative distinction emerged in the work of a separate and rather remarkable group of integrative scholars. In 1947 such philosophers and scientists as Northrop, Margenau, Sinnot, Mather, Laslow, Laszlo, Sorokin, and Kluckhorn joined others in founding the Foundation for Integrative Education (later called the Center for Integrative Education). At conferences and in the pages of their journal, *Main Current in Modern Thought* (1945-1975), they worked to overcome the divisiveness of modern education by integrating new scientific knowledge into the educational system. They too tended to define "interdisciplinary" as a linking of existing categories, and "integrative" as a much higher, more powerful conceptual synthesis. On behalf of the Foundation, Alastair Taylor explained that "integrative" models were based on a fundamental distinction between integration as a synthesis of presently accepted postulates, "with their attendant corpus of knowledge, methodologies, and modes of behavior," and integration as a new conceptual model which pointed to no less than "a holistic educational philosophy capable of understanding and documenting the philosophical principles inherent in the natural and social sciences, together with the major humanistic systems of mankind." [7] While the interdisciplinary/integrative distinction is not so closely observed today, there are two generalized positions on interdisciplinarity in the present discourse which can be traced back to these more technical distinctions. In these early debates, the interdisciplinary concept tended to be conceived in terms of both a problem-solving theory and a unity theory. The first was more pragmatic and instrumental. Social, technological, and intellectual problems were to be solved by integrating relevant disciplinary concepts, methods, and principles. The second was more comprehensive and even "transdisciplinary" in its commitment to a larger synthesis. Proponents believed that it is still possible, if not telelogically correct, to unite separate perspectives in a partial or even a comprehensive synthesis, the kind of holistic scheme envisioned by the Foundation for Integrative Studies.

At mid-century, there was a significant widening of the interdisciplinary concept with the increased visibility of interdisciplinary team research, the growth of two particularly powerful synthetic movements known as general systems theory and structuralism, and a growing number of interactions across existing disciplines. Multidisciplinary- and interdisciplinary mission-oriented research projects were funded then as now in order to solve the technological and social problems of society. The most famous of these projects was, of course, the Manhattan Project to build an atom bomb. Graham Toft and F. Tomlinson Sparrow point out that interdisciplinary engineering centers during the Sputnik era emphasized the engineering sciences, while in the 70's the "driving force" shifted to non-market goods and social concerns such as product safety, environmental quality, mobility, technology assessment and so forth. Interdisciplinary engineering centers thus became "sociotechnical think tanks."[8] There were two major reasons, Rustum Roy concludes, why these mission-oriented projects became so numerous. There was and still is considerable financial incentive for universities to participate in the form of government and foundation grants. Moreover, there was the *"inexorable logic that the real problems of society do not come in disciplinary-shaped blocks."*[9]

General systems and structuralism proved to be such powerful interdisciplinary approaches because they both enhanced the search for interactions. Systems analysis is concerned with patterns and interrelationships in wholes, while structuralism is concerned with the deep structures which underlie human thought. Both appealed to a wide range of disciplinarians as explanatory models. At the same time general systems and structuralism were attracting wide attention, many once-isolated disciplines were reaching across their boundaries for both instrumental and conceptual purposes. "New" historians were moving in the direction of the social sciences, while literary scholars were moving in the direction of social explanation, psychology, anthropology and linguistics. Interdisciplinary research was also developing in other areas. The earliest report of interdisciplinary research studies in agriculture were studies of input-output relationships in milk during the 1940's. By the 1950's and 60's, Randolph Barker notes, there was even more research of this type being conducted between agricultural economists and biological scientists, especially at Iowa State and Michigan State, though the degree of collaboration varied from project to project.[10] Up to that time in the sciences the primary process of knowledge growth had been fission. However, scientific subgroups were now seeking fusion through grand simplifying conceptualizations such as the second law, the mass-energy equivalence, and quantum mechanics. These constituted, Rustum Roy emphasizes, "an intellectual impediment strangely at variance with the increasing administrative and pedagogic specialization."[11]

The Professional Interdisciplinary Movement

In the late 1960's, in response to increasing levels of interdisciplinary activity and a growing critique of educational structures in Europe and America, the Centre for Education Research and Innovation in Paris (CERI.OECD) conducted a pioneer survey on interdisciplinarity in universities, followed in 1970 by a seminar on interdisciplinarity in education and research, and then, in 1972, by a publication of a book containing their conclusions and key conference papers, *INTERDISCIPLINARITY: Problems of Teaching and Research in Universities* (Paris: Organisation for Economic Co-operation and Development, 1972). Dominated by the cybernetics, systems and structuralist thinking of its major theorists (among them Léo Apostel, Jean Piaget, and Erich Jantsch), the CERI.OECD book incorporated analyses of interdisciplinarity in the social and natural sciences, descriptions of the different levels of interdisciplinary activity, and definitions of the relationship between disciplinarity and interdisciplinarity. It was, as Guy Michaud correctly foresaw, a "preliminary balance sheet," a "working" tool which became not just the "starting point for new thought and action,"[12] but the seminal reference in the field.

Since the early 1970's, the professional interdisciplinary movement has advanced through both scholarly and financial support. Interdisciplinary education has been supported in the 1970's and 80's by such American agencies as the National Endowment for the Humanities, the Fund for the Improvement of Post-Secondary Education, and the Carnegie Corporation. Financial support for interdisciplinary team research has come from the National Aeronautics and Space Administration (NASA) and the National Science Foundation (NSF). The NSF, in particular, has been quite active, organizing a program in 1969 called Interdisciplinary Research Relevant to Problems of our Society (IRRPOS) which later, in 1971, evolved into the Research Application Directorate and the Research Applied to National Needs (RANN) program. Now, in 1984, the Office of Interdisciplinary Research of the NSF is publicizing new funding support for cross-disciplinary research in engineering, the Engineering Research Centers program. In Europe, the study of interdisciplinarity has received strong and continuing support from the London-based Society for Research into Higher Education (hosts for a symposium on interdisciplinary courses in European Education in 1975), the Paris-based CERI.OECD (hosts for 1970, 1980 and 1984 conferences and numerous smaller meetings), and UNESCO (hosts of a symposium on interdisciplinarity in higher education in Bucharest from 24-26 November 1981).

It was 1979, however, that proved to be a watershed year for the professional interdisciplinary movement. In that year a second major critical book emerged, *Interdisciplinarity in Higher Education*, edited by Joseph Kockelmans (University Park: The Pennsylvania State University Press, 1979). A collection of essays by participants in a postdoctoral seminar on interdisciplinarity held under the auspices of the Interdisciplinary Graduate Program in the Humanities at Pennsylvania State University in 1975-76, this book contains studies of the definitions of interdisciplinarity, problems of interdisciplinary methodology, research reports in the natural and social sciences and to an extent interdisciplinarity in the humanities, in addition to critiques of structuralism, general systems and the unity of science movements from an interdisciplinary perspective. It is also notable for bringing to wider attention three prior book-length studies in the American literature: Margaret Barron Luszki's *Interdisciplinary Team Research* (Washington, D.C.: The National Training Laboratories, printed by New York University Press, 1959), Muzafer and Carolyn Sherif's collection of essays on *Interdisciplinary Relationships in the Social*

Sciences (Chicago: Aldine, 1969) and Larry Mahan's dissertation, *Toward Transdisciplinary Inquiry in the Humane Sciences* (Unpublished Dissertation, United States International University, San Diego, 1970).

The year 1979 was of even greater significance, however, because of the groundwork laid for two interdisciplinary professional organizations which draw upon dramatically different constituencies. They are INTERSTUDY and the Association for Integrative Studies (AIS). In the early 1970's, NSF had come to play a prominent role in the study of IDR through its Research Management Improvement (RMI) program. RMI was designed to help improve the ability of nonprofit research organizations to manage federally-funded research projects. Before its funding was terminated by Congress, the Program distributed $3.88M among 35 projects, almost half of them interdisciplinary.[13] Much of our present knowledge about the management of interdisciplinary team research stems from the independent reports of RMI grant recipients and a growing scholarship prompted by more formal attempts to arrive at conclusions about the NSF/RMI efforts of the 70's. INTERSTUDY was founded in 1980 after the International Research Group on Interdisciplinary Programs (IRGIP) held the first International Conference on Interdisciplinary Research Groups from April 22-28, 1979, at Schloss Reisensburg in the Federal Republic of Germany. Scholars and various personnel from universities, government, and industry met at their first conference, again in 1981 (July 19-23 in Manchester, England), and then again in 1984 (August 1-3 in Seattle, Washington). Though largely an informal organization coping with the difficulties of being an international body, INTERSTUDY has accomplished a great deal, including three international conferences and about a dozen workshops, the sponsorship of articles in refereed journals (including special issues of the *Journal of the Society of Research Administrators* and *R & D Management*), a dozen issues of an INTERSTUDY bulletin, and the publication of books from the first two international conferences.[14] INTERSTUDY is now assembling papers for the publication of a book from the third international conference, making plans to hold a fourth international conference near Budapest, Hungary, and considering how to structure a future research agenda concerned with understanding the management of IDR. Participants at the Third meeting in Seattle expressed particular concern about exploring interorganizational and interpersonal problems in R & D management within industry as well as a greater understanding of the nature of disciplinarity and interdisciplinarity.

Whereas the membership of INTERSTUDY consists primarily of academic, governmental and industrial faculty and personnel concerned about the management of team research, with most of the academic faculty coming from Engineering and Business Schools, the membership of the other interdisciplinary professional organization is dramatically different and their exploration of the interdisciplinary concept is wider in scope. The bulk of the membership in the Association for Integrative Studies, which is an American national professional organization incorporated in the state of Ohio in 1979, consists primarily of teachers and scholars involved in both undergraduate and graduate interdisciplinary education. The AIS holds annual conferences and publishes both a quarterly newsletter and a monograph series on interdisciplinary and integrative issues in both education and research, *Issues in Integrative Studies*. The AIS has several goals: to articulate the nature of interdisciplinary and integrative studies, to maintain a communication network for the exchange of scholarly and pedagogical information, to establish standards of excellence for the conduct of integrative studies in research and teaching, and to promote the study and development of interdisciplinary theory and methodology. While members of the AIS tend to be centered strongly around the issues of interdisciplinary education, the AIS has been instrumental in promoting the epistemological study of interdisciplinarity as well as attempting to consolidate the dispersed literature and raise the level of collective dialogue on the interdisciplinary concept.

While the broad literature on interdisciplinarity is older than the specific literature on IDR, which Chubin, Porter, and Rossini date at a little over 30 years beginning in 1951,[15] there is an important correlation between them. The literature on interdisciplinarity in Periods 1 and 2 was significantly more limited in volume and in focus than the literature of Period 3, which corresponds to the second "emergent" era (1969-74) and the third "take-off" era (1975-82) of IDR literature. This means that the Chubin et al. finding of an exponential growth in IDR literature during the 1970's and 80's applies across the breadth of interdisciplinary literature, with the 1972 CERI.OECD book serving as a veritable foundation based on both the criteria of citation frequency and critical authority. Within this remarkably prolific period, there have been important shifts in the discourse upon interdisciplinarity. Whereas interdisciplinary discourse within the first half of the century tended to focus primarily on problems in the social sciences, overarching schemes for unification, and the goals as well as pedagogical and administrative issues of interdisciplinary education, discussions within the last fifteen years have widened and deepened.[16]

In both professional scholarship and across disciplinary forums, scholars are now paying more attention to the intricacies of designing, teaching and managing interdisciplinary curricula. In addition to closer scrutiny of interdisciplinary interactions between specific clusters of disciplines and analyses of the nature of interdisciplinarity in particular fields, there are more sophisticated deliberations on interdisciplinary health care, the practical and philosophical consequences of borrowing from other disciplines, the problems of interdisciplinary communication, the epistemology of interdisciplinarity, and the variety of interdisciplinary approaches. Within the literature which INTERSTUDY attempts to consolidate, there is a more exact deliberation and growing empirical investigation of management problems in interdisciplinary research. Within the literature which the AIS attempts to consolidate, there is a much more sophisticated inquiry into the logical foundations of interdisciplinary study and renewed reflection on the theory and methodology of the interdisciplinary concept at large.

Finally, there is in the 1980's a heightened awareness of the necessity for interdisciplinary solutions to local and global problems which lie outside academic communities. In fact, after a survey (1976-78) and a 1980 conference on "Higher Education and the Community: New Partnerships and Interactions," CERI.OECD arrived at a significant new formulation of the interdisciplinary concept. They concluded that the demand for interdisciplinarity had shifted from *endogenous university interdisciplinarity* to *interdisciplinarity exogenous to the university*. Endogenous interdisciplinarity is more concerned with the production of new knowledge with the implicit aim of realizing a unity of science. Exogenous interdisciplinarity, in contrast, interrogates the disciplines on the demarcations they apply to "real life" and demands that the university fulfill its full social mission.[17] The new CERI.OECD formulation appears at a time when members of the INTERSTUDY movement have heightened their study of interdisciplinarity in industry, when American educators are increasingly concerned about problem-based curricula, and when Europeans are forging new and vital links among industry, government, and society. Indeed, CERI joined the Swedish National Board of Universities and the University of Linköping in sponsoring a conference in October of 1984 at Linköping, Sweden, to reassess the concept of interdisciplinarity in light of activities since the pioneering CERI.OECD work on the early 1970's. Moreover, the Sweden conference took place the very same month that the Association for Integrative Studies and the Association for General and Liberal Studies co-hosted a conference in the United States on "Higher Education and the Citizenry: Reciprocal Responsibilities."

The evidence of exogenous interdisciplinarity is strong and pervasive. However, it should not obscure the importance of less exogenous interdisciplinary work which must be recognized when attempting to generalize about the nature of interdisciplinarity.[18] The Philadelphia Social History Project (PSHP), to give an outstanding example, has generated not only important interdisciplinary work in the area of urban history, but also valuable reflections on how the PSHP "interdisciplinary" computerized data base works and the disciplinary impediments to collaborative research. Both topics are of great relevance to those in the IDR literature. Scholars defining the nature of interdisciplinary work in such fields and subjects as African history, American studies, area studies, anthropology and archaeology, the behavioral sciences, biology, climate research, the family, geography, gerontology, health care, landscape, linguistics, oral testimony, peace research, rural Indian studies, and strategic planning have had much to say about problems shared by their counterparts in the IDR literature. And vice versa.

There is much in the IDR literature which is of direct value to the literally hundreds of teachers and administrators who are concerned about devising more effective interdisciplinary teaching teams as well as the most feasible bureaucratic structures for housing interdisciplinary courses within a predominantly disciplinary environment. Physicians using role negotiation to enhance communication in interdisciplinary treatment teams have much to offer both the IDR and non-IDR scholars who try to organize and maintain interdisciplinary teams. Asian scholars using a regional research center would profit from exploring parallels between their own methodological problems and the methodological challenges of working in such new areas as oral history, immunopharmacology and the study of written discourse. An historian with the Philadelphia Social History Project would benefit greatly from discussing the nature of integrative concepts with a biochemist, an engineer, a social psychologist, or an educator trying to establish science curricula in less-developed countries. However, at present, these people do not usually share each other's insights. In most cases, they are not even aware of each other's existence.

Scope of the Interdisciplinary Future

The ability to translate these heightened interdisciplinary energies into a more consolidated and sophisticated dialogue upon the interdisciplinary concept is complicated by the continuing dispersal of the interdisciplinary concept. Each year, there are new notices of "interdisciplinary" conferences across the humanities, social sciences, and natural sciences. Each month, there are journal articles on interdisciplinarity appearing in almost all disciplinary literatures and there is a growing "fugitive" literature of conference papers, grant reports, and university working papers which has always been undervalued. There are also several organizations such as the Institute for Renaissance Interdisciplinary Studies (IRIS), the Literature and Science Society, and the Society for Social Studies of Science which deal with interdisciplinary scholarship in their own areas. And, finally, across all epistemic communities there is a vigorous though generally uncoordinated discussion of such shared topics as the general critique of specialization, prospects for unifying theory and methodology among related disciplines, grounds for bridging the humanities, social and natural sciences, and connections among the university and its various communities.

Given the dominance of disciplinary socialization patterns and the obvious breadth of the interdisciplinary concept, it would be naive to assume that an ultimate *consolidation* of the discourse is possible in either the foreseeable or the distant future. What is possible, however, is more effective *coordination* of the dispersed dialogue and under-identified sub-literatures. That task is already being undertaken by the two major professional organizations which emerged in 1979. To the extent that they succeed in their efforts, and to the extent that they make their successes more widely known, the more productive will be the exploration of interdisciplinarity.

FOOTNOTES

1Ernest L. Boyer, "The Quest for Common Learning," *Common Learning, A Carnegie Colloquium on General Education* (Washington, D.C.: The Carnegie Foundation for the Advancement of Teaching, 1981), p. 4.

2Edward Ciccorico, "'Integration' in the Curriculum," *Main Currents in Modern Thought,* 27 (November-December 1970), 61.

3Martin Landau, Harold Proshansky and William H. Ittelson, "The Interdisciplinary Approach and the Concept of Behavioral Science," *Decisions, Values and Groups,* ed. Norman F. Washburne (New York: Pergamon Press, 1962), Volume II, pp. 13-14.

4Landau, Proshansky, and Ittelson, p. 12.

5Landau, Proshansky, and Ittelson, p. 15.

6Landau, Proshansky, and Ittelson, p. 16.

7Alastair Taylor, "Integrative Principles and the Educational Process," *Main Currents in Modern Thought,* 25 (May-June 1969), 130.

8Graham Toft and F. Tomlinson Sparrow, "University Interdisciplinary Engineering Centers: New Directions—Persistent Organizational Problems," Paper presented at the Third International Conference on Interdisciplinary Research. Seattle, Washington (1 August 1984).

9Rustum Roy, "Interdisciplinary Science on Campus, The Elusive Dream," in *Interdisciplinarity and Higher Education* (University Park: The Pennsylvania State University Press), p. 163.

10Randolph Barker, "Farming Systems Research: Interdisciplinary Response to Problems," *Enabling Interdisciplinary Research: Perspectives from Agriculture, Forestry, and Home Economics* (St. Paul: University of Minnesota Agricultural Experiment Station, 1982), p. 101. Miscellaneous Publication #19.

11Roy, p. 163.

12Guy Michaud, "General Conclusions," *Interdisciplinarity, Problems of Teaching and Research in Universities* (Paris: Organization for Economic Co-operation and Development, 1972), p. 281.

13Nancy Lindas, "Conclusions From the American Society for Public Administration's Assessment of Four Interdisciplinary Research Management Projects," *Interdisciplinary Research Groups: Their Management and Organization,* ed. Richard T. Barth and Rudy Steck (Vancouver: IRGIP, 1979), p. 279.

14I thank Brian Mar and Don Baldwin, both of whom have been active in the INTERSTUDY movement, for providing me with this historical information during the Third International Conference on Interdisciplinary Research Groups in Seattle, 1-3 August 1984.

15See their essay, "Interdisciplinarity: How Do We Know Thee? — A Bibliographic Essay" (in this book).

16For a bibliography of essential references on all the areas listed below, see Julie Thompson Klein, "Interdisciplinary Literature," Scheduled for the Fall 1984 issue of *Perspectives. The Journal of the Association for General and Liberal Studies*; available also as an early "reprint" in the Institute for Renaissance Interdisciplinary Newsletter 5 (March 1984), 1-11.

17"Communities Have Problems, Universities Have Departments," *The University and The Community, The Problems of Changing Relationships* (Paris: Organisation for Economic Co-operation and Development, 1982), pp. 127-138.

18References for all of these areas can be found in the Klein bibliography.

PART VIII

LITERATURE

34

INTERDISCIPLINARITY:
HOW DO WE KNOW THEE? —
A BIBLIOGRAPHIC ESSAY*

Daryl E. Chubin
Alan L. Porter
Frederick A. Rossini

This volume has sought to present a comprehensive introduction to interdisciplinarity as a subject, a process, and a mode of intellectual and social organization. From our opening essay advocating the so-called STRAP framework, through the excerpts collected and grouped thematically, we have captured the state of the art—or at least fashioned a retrospective on it.

The capstone of any introduction, however, should be a research agenda defined by the corpus of literature. This essay is an attempt to inventory that literature, quantitatively and qualitatively, to assist the reader in developing his/her own perspective on the diverse analyses and commentaries pertaining to the phenomenon of "interdisciplinary research" (IDR).

A Bibliometric Profile

The literature on interdisciplinary research (IDR) is over 30 years old—if one cites its origin as a paper containing the word "interdisciplinary" in its title—beginning with a paper published in 1951 about the problems of collaboration between an anthropologist

* This essay and the Annotated Bibliography that follows were supported in part by the National Science Foundation Award OIR-8209893 and issued as Final Report, Volume 2, of INTERDISCIPLINARY RESEARCH (PROBLEM-FOCUSED, MULTI-SKILLED RESEARCH) - NATIONAL SCIENCE FOUNDATION EXPERIENCES by A.L. Porter, F.A. Rossini, and D.E. Chubin, Georgia Institute of Technology, March 1984. The views expressed do not reflect those of either NSF or Georgia Tech.

and a psychiatrist [35]. (Numbers appearing in [ ] refer to items included in the annotated bibliography that follows.)

A more quantitative glimpse at the literature we have identified and retrieved as IDR requires what is known as "bibliometrics" [exemplified here by items 71 and 124]. Bibliometric analysis characterizes trends in literature growth by publication type, source scatter, and usage. Given the dearth of systematic study of IDR as a literature [but see 20, 74, 107, 125], we have some statistics to report, but an abundance of impressions to offer. (Recognize that our literature sample is not all-inclusive; it tends, for example, not to itemize chapters *within* books.) We invite the reader to sample the bibliography discreetly, pursuing what intrigues and ignoring the seemingly irrelevant. Because IDR encompasses a range of activity, and presumably motivation, a comparable range of utility to the reader is expected.

Figure 1 displays two curves. The broken line portrays a frequency distribution by year of the 136 items in the annotated bibliography; the solid line portrays the cumulative frequency distribution of those IDR items over the period from pre-1969 to 1982. What appears to be an irregular growth pattern is marked by a clear "take-off" in 1975. Thus, the literature divides into three segments or "eras": the first spans 1951-68 and features no more than a sprinkling of IDR, the second, "emergent" era, 1969-74, indicates a measurable flow averaging five items per year, and the third, take-off era, 1975-82 (the latter incomplete due to retrieval lag) signals a "leaping" step-function of IDR.

Another way of characterizing growth is through "doubling times": how many years does it take for the literature to increase its total size by 100 percent? The following spurts can be noted. The 1969 total nearly equalled the sum of the 1951-68 items; the literature doubled between 1969-72; the 1975 output increased the size of the literature preceding that year by 37 percent; two years later there was another 30 percent increase; from 1973-77, the literature grew by 120 percent; and from 1978-82, 95 percent growth occurred. The overall doubling time, then, approximates 4.5 years—a brisk pace, but a small population nonetheless.

Still another method of calculating literature spurt is to summarize the proportion of IDR by era. The significant figure is the nearly three-quarters of the literature sample that was produced during the

Figure 1
Frequency ($\cdots$) and Cumulative Frequency (———) Distributions
of 136 IDR Items

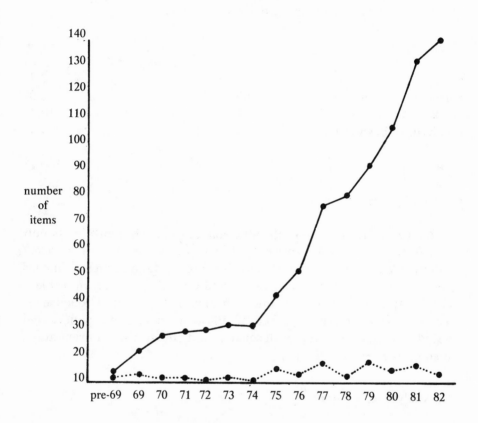

take-off era. More than half of this work, and 40 percent of the 136 items, was produced since 1979. This suggests that specialists in IDR now exist [19] and that a portion of the literature is coalescing around a core of journals and practitioners [20]. Such observations, however, move away from bibliometric data to an analysis of publication and source content.

As shown in Table 1, journal articles dominate as the publication type for IDR. Slightly more than one-fourth of IDR appears in books, book chapters, and reports/unpublished papers combined. This domination by the serial literature prompts a tally of the journals publishing IDR.

Table 1

Distribution by Publication Type
of 136 IDR Items, 1951-82

Type	n	%
book	10	7.4
journal	99	72.8
chapter	14	10.3
report/unpublished	13	9.6
total	136	100.1*

* rounding error

As seen in Table 2, 36 of the 99 serial items are concentrated in only 10 journals—and 9 of these published no more than 4 articles/ editorials each. Thus, the outlets for the remaining items in this category are 63 *different* journals. In addition, the journals in Table 2 dispel suspicion that there is much, if any, of a core of IDR journals. We would characterize the set of 10 as management, policy, and multidisciplinary science, social science, and engineering in orientation. In sum, dispersion is the norm.

An Analysis of Content

At this juncture, bibliometric analysis might profitably yield to a content analysis of titles and annotations. The dimensions of interest, in the case of the former, are keywords. Table 3 lists the most frequently-appearing keywords among the 136 items. (More than one of these keywords, of course, could be found in a single title.) Again, diversity reigns.

A major concern, it would seem, has been the conduct of IDR in academic settings, and particularly, in campus-wide research centers or ORUs ("organized research units") [4, 27, 36, 60, 68, 109, 120]. Some of these titles link other popular keywords in Table 3 to the academic setting. Some examples include "Assessment of Alternative *Management* Forms in Academic Interdisciplinary Research Projects"

Table 2

Major Source Journals for IDR Items

Journal	n
Journal of the Society of Research Administrators	9
R&D Management	4
Science	4
Daedalus	3
Engineering Education	3
International Social Science Journal	3
Policy Sciences	3
Technological Forecasting & Social Change	3
Academy of Management Journal	2
Management Science	2
total	36

Table 3

Most Frequently-Appearing Keywords
in Titles of IDR Items

Keyword	n
academic/university	25
management	16
team(work)	12
organization	9
discipline(s)	6
policy	4
communication	3
conflicts/pitfalls/barriers	3
funding	2
government	2
innovation	2
applied	2
effectiveness	2

(italics ours)[21], "Interdisciplinary Research *Management* in the University Environment" [85], "*Managing* Multidisciplinarity: Building and Bridging Epistemologies in Educational R&D" [108], and "Trends in the *Organization* of Academic Research: The Role of ORUs and Full Time Researchers" [120].

"Management," "teamwork," and "organization" also signal other, nonacademic IDR directions. To wit: *Management by Task Forces* [12], "Some Barriers to Teamwork in Social Research" [14], "Ethical Problems in Team Research: A Structural Analysis and an Agenda for Resolution" [30], "Interdisciplinary Team Work" [46], "Interdisciplinary Team Preproposal Management" [53], "The Effect of a 'Social Problem' Orientation on the Organization of Scientific Research" [62], "Group Dynamics of the Interdisciplinary Team" [86], "Problems in Interdisciplinary Policy Research and Management in Government" [94], "Phases Encountered by a Project Team" [98], and "Building an Interdisciplinary Team" [119].

On the basis of titles alone, several concepts and issues in IDR, such as "policy," "communication," "conflicts," "funding," and "innovation," appear to receive little attention. For this reason, we extend our analysis to the annotations themselves. An inspection of this content reveals that titles sometimes obscure what the IDR piece is all about. For example, categories of team research activities are developed in "Conflicts in Interdisciplinary Research" [13]; Birnbaum finds that IDR "is more appropriate for very difficult research questions and at early stages of the research process" in "Contingencies for Interdisciplinary Research" [23]; Boulding and Geertz, respectively, reflect on overcoming knowledge specialization [29, 51]; industry's IDR organization is extolled as a model of university-industry cooperation in "Science Futures: The Industrial Connection" [43]; the utility of a multidisciplinary approach to the study of "ill-structured" problems is discussed in "On the Methodology of the Holistic Experiment" [80]; and bibliometric indicators of IDR in biotechnology are offered in "Measuring European Scientific Capability in Biotechnology" [104].

A final approach to the classification of the IDR annotations focuses on the empirical content of the bibliography and the methods/techniques employed. Slightly more than one-third of the items [47/136] appear to be empirical studies, as opposed to editorial statements, essays, memoirs, or review articles. Listed in Table 4 are the methodological emphases within the empirical works. A

Table 4

Methodological Emphases in IDR Items*

Method/Technique	n of items
multiple/eclectic	19
modelling	10
technology assessment/impact assessment	6
questionnaires/interviews	4
(lab) observation	4

* based on annotations, not just title keywords

combination of methods characterizes 19 items. These include papers citing the inevitability of differing epistemologies operating within IDR teams [28, 90] to pronouncements of the virtues of multiple methods [17]. The other items within this category divide between *case studies* of single projects, departments, companies, or research units [11, 13, 26, 77, 92, 118, 130, 131] and items that detail *cross-project, -unit,* and/or *-cultural* findings. In most of these items, authors relate "what worked" in a context and conjecture as to the reasons for the success. Modelling is the single-most favored technique, especially computerized models of, e.g., "expert group consensus" [55], problem-solving "cultures" [105], and the relationship between interdisciplinary cooperation and group size [115]. Mathematical models that synthesize components of IDR processes have also been attempted [87, 127]. Conceptual or verbal model-building was occasionally noted, as in Campbell's classic "fish-scale" model [33]. Examples of other methodologies used in the study of IDR are technology assessment [e.g., 72, 103], questionnaires /interviews [e.g., 32, 44], and observation in both a lab setting [39] and at sites in the field [109].

The examination of methods appearing in the annotations prompted a similar survey of cited theories. We were surprised to find very few explicit references to theoretical perspectives (though one paper addresses the problem of "interfield theories" [42]). General systems theory appears four times [e.g., 61]. Role theory frames four other items which define types of IDR actors: the "bridge scientist" [5], "adaptors" and "innovators" [65], field "switchers" and "retainers"

[71], and the "primary-secondary group" hybrid [117]. Structuralism is prominent in Piaget's book [91], evolution theory in Toulmin's review article [12]; status concordance theory is tested in Gillespie and Birnbaum's analysis of academic IDR teams; dialectical inquiry as a theory of research practice is reviewed by Mitroff and Mason [81]; and a new theory, "paradigmatology," is formulated by Maruyama [76].

Overall, one might conclude that IDR is largely *atheoretical*, i.e., guided as much by pragmatic concerns and ad hoc perspectives as by systematic frameworks. Although such a conclusion overstates the lack of theory in the IDR literature, it does underscore the often implicit use of theory in specifying variables and relationships in the study of IDR.

A Research Agenda

With a bibliometric profile and content analysis of the IDR literature in hand, we can proceed to a research agenda that derives from it. Usually, such an agenda is tied to a community of IDR practitioners. What we outline here anticipates ways for building an interdisciplinary research knowledge base.

We begin with a three-dimensional conceptualization of IDR. All three dimensions were introduced above; they are merely reordered for presentation here. The first dimension encompasses *barriers* to the performance of IDR which reside in the individual researcher. These barriers have at least three components: epistemological, psychological, and disciplinary. Each of these reinforces the other—and militates against IDR cooperation.

Researchers are predisposed to view the world in certain ways. Part of their storehouse of what Polanyi calls "tacit knowledge" are axiomatic assumptions about science, inquiry, natural and social phenomena, etc. These assumptions constitute one's epistemology; they make some theories and methodologies more appealing than others. They also make certain research modes more intrinsically appealing than others, e.g., collaborative v. individual style, theoretical v. empirical study, lab v. field setting, quantitative v. qualitative analysis. Out of such deep epistemological stirrings springs the willingness to engage in multidisciplinary research. Psychologically, one's openmindedness, ability to listen, propensity to give support, and general security enables researchers trained in disparate disciplines and intellectual traditions to interact—perhaps over a lengthy period of time—on a mutually interesting research problem or topic. Since disciplines socialize researchers to communicate to fellow disciplinarians, indeed subdisciplinary specialists, the incentive to abandon esoteric jargon to promote *cross*-disciplinary exchange is not great. The psychological costs exacted on those who attempt such exchange is often too much to bear.

The upshot of the first dimension is that barriers exist within the individual—barriers that are transmitted institutionally—which discourage participation in IDR. Neither internal motivations nor external rewards prepare the researcher for the role of IDR team member. Only idiosyncratic needs and experiences draw the researcher to such collaboration. Representative evidence of barriers, and their origins, can be found in [25, 26, 32, 39, 50, 54, 65, 77, 90, 103, 126]. Perhaps the most apt description of the barrier problem is Rose's classic title, "Disciplined Research and Undisciplined Problems" [100].

The second dimension of IDR is implicated by the first, i.e., the *contexts* in which IDR is done. The two contextualizing components are cultural and organizational. Culture, of course, can refer to a country or a sector where research is performed, e.g., industry. Countries have sponsored week-long conferences as well as year-long experiments to assess the role that IDR might play in problem-solving and alternative university structure [e.g., UNESCO, 1, 47; OECD, 36; Canada, 37, 66, 83, 96; United Kingdom, 82, 99; Poland, 134]. Likewise, appraisals of R&D carried out in "independent research centers," e.g., Rand and SRI [9]; industrial labs [materials science, 7; pharmaceuticals, 118]; in U.S. government agencies [94]; or under the auspices of Federal agencies [NASA and NSF/RANN, 27, 77, 133] have highlighted sector-specific problems.

At the organizational level, the focus is those units within a sector which house research, e.g., programs, departments, centers, and laboratories. The literature subsumable under the dimension of context focuses on the impacts of motivations, pressures, structures, and rewards on individual research behavior. Although, as we have seen, the preoccupation has been with academic IDR, the portrait of the academic interdisciplinary research is ambivalent. On the other hand, the research is cast as a victim of the university—a "cultural outcast" [49] and erstwhile member of "the un-faculty" [67, 118]. On the other hand, the IDR worker is a savior—a "culture broker" [57], or euphorically, an "ideal polymath" [119]. We find such characterizations hyperbolic and rather wishful. Yet the IDR worker, at least in academe, does seem caught betwixt and between. Universities appear to be oppressive environments for IDR with little understanding or inclination to facilitate extra-departmental, multidisciplinary research [65, 66, 84]. University administrators are especially defensive, obdurate and parochial in coping with the organizational challenges which IDR typically entails, be they budgetary [10, 49, 53] or structural and evaluative [19, 22, 106, 109]. Careers are surely not "launched" by participation in IDR projects; rather, those careers may be stifled by pursuits occurring outside the mainstream of disciplines. It is the established researcher, e.g., the tenured professor, who can afford to contribute without excessive risk.

The third dimension of IDR links its practice and performance to *applications*. The two components we stress are policy-formulation and pedagogy. The first asks how IDR affects outcomes—does anything change? Are findings based on IDR inquiry any more useful than disciplinary research? Is the problem-solving rhetoric voiced by interdisciplinary researchers borne out by deeds? Precious little evidence speaks to these questions. Documented success stories are rare [e.g., the design of inventions [7]. More common are works promising IDR-inspired "reform-mongering" [8], task force effectiveness at A.D. Little [12], success of a graduate program to apply technology assessment to the fossil-fuel problem [64], and 15 kinds of creative achievements [113].

The most discernible consensus-laden folk wisdom on the application of IDR products concerns the "integration" of specialists' skills and knowledge [22]. Indeed, integration is what makes IDR interdisciplinary. As Meeth [78] puts it, the "attempt to integrate the contributions of several disciplines to a problem, issue, or theme from life" is what distinguishes *inter*disciplinary from cross-, multi-, and transdisciplinary. It is the integration of interdisciplinary contributions that is claimed as a solution, for example, to environmental issues [38]. Linstone [72] argues that integration should be left to the "decision-maker"; Rossini and Porter [102] advocate integration at the project level; Toulmin [122] suggests that such details may be inconsequential anyway since, in the evolution of disciplines and knowledge specialization, "problem-oriented" issues will gain hegemony over "discipline-oriented" research and "will need about thirty years to develop their own specialized theoretical ideas and techniques . . ."

To most, the site of this development of IDR will still be the university. Where pedagogy prevails, utopian visions proliferate. A decade ago, CERI [36] offered a "sample model of an interdisciplinary university." Jantsch [61], writing about the same time, proposed a "transdisciplinary university" in which "systems design laboratories" and "function-oriented departments" would coexist with "discipline-oriented departments." Long [73] made a similar plea in a *Science* editorial. More recently, Nelson [83] echoed the theme of initiating IDR training with *under*graduate instruction by urging consideration of "replenishing our academic gene pool" with "interdisciplinary-oriented colleagues."

Nowhere is the vision fuller than in Roy's [106] assertion that "interdisciplinarity is inherent in the nature of reality." For Roy and many others [96], the "elusive dream" *is* an interdisciplinary science campus. As Nilles [85] explains (writing in 1975), "The universities have the unique advantage of being able to maintain a large pool of expertise which is not dependent for survival on externally funded research." The optimism of this statement, eclipsed by the resource situation of most universities, sounds worse than an "elusive dream" in 1985—it rings of illusion. Research universities are utterly dependent on external funding from government and industry alike. Interdisciplinary "experiments," it seems, must be fiscally self-sufficient, while the entrenched disciplinary departments—staffed by tenured faculties—command some continuing resource allocation.

Yet the dream has been financed to some extent. If it were not, we could not talk about the barriers, contexts, and applications of IDR. There would be no such animal—no literature to retrieve and no research agenda to compile. Clearly, that is not the case. Researchers on IDR have gained a certain legitimacy and visibility. They have formed an International Association for the Study of Interdisciplinary Research, publish a newsletter (INTERSTUDY), held three conferences [see 88], and are planning another for 1986. All the social trappings of specialization, in other words, are present for IDR.

Here, then, is a contemporary example of a scientific specialty which emanates from no single discipline, is endemic to no single setting (if anything, IDR—under various rubrics—thrives in nonacademic settings), and is not formally transmitted via a graduate degree-granting curriculum. Specialists in interdisciplinarity are self-selected and -identified "converts." What remains clouded is whether a purpose of interdisciplinary researchers is to counter the trend toward knowledge fragmentation and over-specialization. If this is an objective, then IDR may become a victim of the very trend it seeks to buck. That is, if it is to develop and compete for the mechanisms that sustain modern science—its own journals, associations, meetings, funding programs, and doubtless its soon-to-be-heralded orthodoxies and heroes—it will succumb to the same parochialism that insulates other intellectually-myopic specialties. As a community of researchers, IDR will take on the coloring of its chief authors, their disciplinary origins, and preferences of theory, method, and problem. The saving grace of IDR will be diversity—its collective ability to tolerate differences of approach and application.

Individual and institutional efforts to foster multidisciplinary cooperation, i.e., interaction without "integration," have already resulted in the emergence of several "interdisciplines." As Porter et al. [95] wrote in 1980:

> The presumption that 'science' is conducted solely within disciplines dominates establishment practices in funding research, publishing findings, and advancing careers. Unfortunately, this not only occasions cracks between disciplines, it fails to provide adequate bridges across intellectual and societal chasms.

If problems do not conveniently distribute themselves into the niches traditionally defined by disciplines, then scientific specialization can be seen as a bureaucratic creation—reified in the university department, for instance—instead of a sensible intellectual stratification for conceptualizing, studying, and acting on reality. The paradox, of course, is that the deeper one delves into an esoteric problem, the less "disciplinary" its dimensions become.

Many interdisciplines today have a decided policy focus, e.g., technology assessment, social and science indicators, information science, science studies, and bibliometrics. The overlap between these research domains and the IDR literature is obvious. Nevertheless, training in these interdisciplines occurs via research experience, not through doctoral study per se. This absence of systematic pedagogy suggests the following hypothesis: the subject matter of interdisciplines consists of urgent but ephemeral problems which themselves resist institutional treatment. Therefore, they require an adaptable form of intellectual organization that can mobilize the personnel and resources appropriate to solution, or at least mediation, of the problem. The essence of *inter*disciplinary research is the integration of subdisciplinary contributions to a team product. The product itself is an innovative blend of perspectives and analyses that have immediate utility to a particular audience of users, i.e., policy-makers.

Included in our research agenda for the IDR-inclined, then, must be some so-called reflexive or self-examination of the enterprise in which we are engaged, indeed which expands with every title containing keywords such as those reviewed earlier. Thus, we would urge consideration of the following:

1. Intellectual migration: where do interdisciplinary researchers come from? Which disciplines? Which journals have they published in and do they now utilize?

2. Training for interdisciplinary problem-solving: which skills need to be imparted? Who might teach them?

3. Local organizational behavior and cosmopolitan rewards: how can researchers be induced to undertake IDR? What incentives and rewards can the employers of IDR workers provide?

4. Assessing interdisciplines: how do they differ from disciplines, specialties, invisible colleges, networks, etc.? Are their norms, communication patterns, modes of collaboration and publication any different from other scientific collectivities?

5. Cognitive styles: Is there a psychological profile or set of traits which sets IDR workers apart from mainstream disciplinarians? Are they more entrepreneurial, less indulgent of dull colleagues, more theoretically-inclined, etc.?

These five sets of queries are shared for their heuristic value. They are ingredients for future study—whether under the rubric "multi-skilled, problem-focused" research or the more familiar academic designation "interdisciplinary" research—to be seasoned by the annotations which immediately follow. They are intended to whet the appetite and, yes, to attract converts to the IDR table.

We therefore urge you to share with us the novel uses to which you apply both the annotated bibliography and this book as a whole. We'd like nothing better than to discover new colleagues whose own parochial tendencies converge somewhat with our own. That is how we know thee, interdisciplinarity—by the complementary perspectives on mutual research problems that ignite new approaches and collaborative efforts.

ANNOTATED BIBLIOGRAPHY*

1. Abestalo, Marja, "Interdisciplinarity in the light of the development of science and the actual research work." In J. Farkas (ed.), *Sociology of Science and Research*. Budapest: Akademiai Kiado, 1979.
A review of a cross-national UNESCO study of 219 research units. The emphasis is on different forms of interdisciplinarity, including "the interdisciplinarity of the research problem, the interdisciplinary diversity of R&D experience of scientists, the use of interdisciplinary theories and methods by members of research units, and the interdisciplinary contacts with other scientists."
2. Adler, L.L., "Plea for interdisciplinary cross-cultural research—some introductory remarks." *The Annals* (of the New York Academy of Sciences) 285 (March 1977): 1-2.
Expresses the hope that interdisciplinary cross-cultural interaction among psychologists, anthropologists, and sociologists will be achieved.
3. Allen, T. Harrell, "Cross-impact analysis: A technique for managing interdisciplinary research." *Journal of the Society of Research Administrators* 9 (Summer 1978): 11-18.
"The cross-impact method makes it possible to integrate the opinions of experts from different disciplines . . ." The cross-impact matrix "can serve as a testing ground for policies." General systems theory, and especially the interdependence of future events, guides the application of this method.
4. Alpert, D. *The Role Structure of Interdisciplinary and Multidisciplinary Research Centers*. Washington, D.C.: Council of Graduate Schools of the U.S., 1969.
An essay, circa 1969, which admonishes that "if the university wants to address itself to today's problems, it must establish interdisciplinary centers which are administered, staffed, and run very differently from those of the present."
5. Anbar, Michael, "The 'bridge scientist' and his role." *Research/Development* (July 1973).
Asserts that "bringing together professionals with different disciplinary affiliations generates profound problems of

---

* The base collection on which statistical compilations are based is numbered from 1-136. Those contributed by Julie Thompson Klein are designated [JTK].

interpersonal communication." Suggests that "the successful performance of a 'bridge role' in the management of such teams may mitigate these problems." Distinguishes four types of bridge scientist and discusses training for the role.

6. Andrews, Frank M., "Motivation, diversity, and the performance of research units." In F.M. Andrews, (ed.), *Scientific Productivity: The Effectiveness of Research Groups in Six Countries.* Cambridge University Press, 1979.

   A cross-national analysis of research units shows a significant diversity-performance relationship, where diversity refers to "R&D functions," "time allocations," "specializations," and "project commitments." Researcher motivation tends not to overlap with diversity in predicting the performance of research units.

7. Anonymous, *Materials Science and Engineering*, 37 (January 1979): 56-70.

   Several short case descriptions of important interdisciplinary developments in materials science and engineering—including integrated circuits, coated stainless steel razor blades, synthetic fibers, transistors, and TV phosphors—provide a unique glimpse at the individuals, disciplines, organizational settings, and problems that comprise this field.

8. Archibald, K.A., "Three views of the expert's role in policymaking: systems analysis, incrementalism, and the clinical approach." *Policy Sciences* 1 (1970): 73-86.

   Approaches to "reform-mongering" based on interdisciplinary inspirations.

9. Baers, W.S., "Interdisciplinary policy research in independent research centers." *IEEE Transactions on Engineering Management* 23 (May 1976): 76-78.

   Argues that "the major problems of managing interdisciplinary research projects include building a strong interdisciplinary team, selecting and motivating project leaders, maximizing institutional support selecting the right projects and clients, and linking research to policy-making." The focus is on "independent research centers," research institutions such as the Rand Corporation and the Stanford Research Institute not administered by universities, government agencies, or industrial firms.

10. Baldwin, Donald R. and Barbara J. Faubian, "Interdisciplinary research in the academic setting." *Journal of the Society of Research Administrators* 6 (Spring 1975): 3-8.

    An overview of obstacles and suggestions for improved-management of interdisciplinary research, including new budgeting and accounting methods, and better integration of the research and teaching functions.

11. Barmark, Jan and Goran Wallen, "The development of an interdisciplinary project." In K.D. Knorr, R. Krohn, and R. Whitley (eds.), *The Social Process of Scientific Investigation*, Sociology of the Sciences, Vol. 4. Dordrecht and Boston: D. Reidel, 1980: 221-235.

Case study of a forest project that examines "the different motives of the researchers for entering the project, the basic differences in outlook and personality between empirical and theoretical scientists, and the effects of the existing academic career structure" which threaten the solidarity of the research team. A major finding is that "integration of knowledge is dependent on integration at different stages of the research process."

Barth, Richard T. and Steck, Rudy (eds.), *Interdisciplinary Research Groups: Their Management and Organization*. First International Conference on Interdisciplinary Research Groups, Schloss Reisensburg, Federal Republic of Germany, 1979 (available from Donald Baldwin, University of Washington, Seattle.)

Twenty-two papers focused on the conduct of interdisciplinary research. These papers (some abstracted individually in this bibliography) provide a key basic source. They encompass self-reflection on how to study interdisciplinarity, conceptual frameworks, case studies, and comparative research on interdisciplinary groups, and consideration of specific issues in industrial, university, and international research efforts.

12. Bass, Lawrence W., *Management by Task Forces*, Mt. Airy, Maryland: Lomond Books, 1975.

Subtitled "A Manual on the Operation of Interdisciplinary Teams," this book summarizes the wisdom of a former Arthur D. Little vice-president. The chapters on "Categories of Interdisciplinary Activities" and "Environment and Benefits of Interdisciplinary Teams," plus an appendix on "How to Start Task Force Systems," make this worthwhile reading for the interdisciplinarian—researcher or manager.

Baum, Archie J., "Interdisciplinology: The Science of Interdisciplinary Research." *Nature and System* 2 (1980): 29-35.

Discussion of the difference between interdisciplinary research to solve a problem using knowledge already available and that which results in new theoretical knowledge. Reviews problems of "interdisciplinology" in three states: initial generalizations, systematic universalizations, and comprehensification [JTK].

13. Bella, D.A. and K.J. Williamson, "Conflicts in interdisciplinary research." *Journal of Environmental Systems* 6 (1976-77): 105-124. Case study of personnel conflicts developed in the course of an interdisciplinary project assessing the impacts of dredging on estuaries. Four categories of team research activities are identified with a risk or recognition factor attached to each. Methods of dealing with these factors are discussed.

14. Bennis, Warren G., "Some barriers to teamwork in social research." *Social Problems* 3 (April 1956): 223-235.
    Factors which impede interdisciplinary social science research in the university include the language of disciplines, changes in team personnel, the use and misuse of group "findings," and autonomy vs. reliance on team members' work.

15. Benton, Douglas A., "Management and effectiveness measures for interdisciplinary research." *Journal of the Society of Research Administrators* 6 (Spring 1975): 37-45.
    "The management characteristics most important to IDR effectiveness appear to be (1) Teamwork, (2) Competence of Professionals, (3) Morale, (4) Feedback and (5) Organizational Structure and Flexibility."

16. Benton, D.A., Meiman, J.R., Simons, D.B., Sjogren, D.D., Taylor, D.C., and McPhail, M. Organization and Personnel Management for Effective Interdisciplinary Research Projects, Colorado State University, Fort Collins, CO, Feb. 1977 (available through NTIS, PB 271 796), 349 pgs.
    This report develops management and effectiveness measures from theoretical bases in effective large scale interdisciplinary research projects. It examines the relationships for six projects at Colorado State University.

17. Berk, Richard A., "On the compatibility of applied and basic sociological research: An effort in marriage counseling." *The American Sociologist* 16 (November 19, 1981): 204-211.
    In a provocative essay that espouses reconciliation of basic and applied sociological research, the author advocates, among others, "an inter-disciplinary approach," the use of multiple methods, and "a team research effort." He argues that "applied research is routinely discriminated against by the profession's gatekeepers," and that "sociology surely would benefit from exposure to perspectives from other academic disciplines."

18. Birnbaum, Norman, "The arbitrary disciplines." *Change* (July-August 1969): 10-21.
    An historical examination of disciplines which "have become -

despite our volition - means of perpetuating the irrationalities inherent in contemporary society's use of knowledge."

19. Birnbaum, P.H., "Academic interdisciplinary research: Problems and practice." *R&D Management* 10 (October 1979): 17-37.

A profile of North American academic scientists engaged in interdisciplinary research includes the findings that they are younger (under 40) and either already tenured or not in tenure-track positions compared to their colleagues not engaged in interdisciplinary research. Interdisciplinary teams typically consist of five to six individuals and seldom for more than five years.

20. Birnbaum, P.H., "The organization and management of interdisciplinary research - a progress report." *Journal of the Society of Research Administrators* 13 (1982): 11-23.

Reviews the state-of-the-art of IDR across academia, government, and industry in 11 nations. Sections include definitions, issues, a framework for current research inputs, outputs, and a 62-item bibliography.

21. Birnbaum, P.H., "Assessment of alternative management forms in academic interdisciplinary research projects." *Management Science* 24 (1977): 272-284.

Large academic projects with a clear division of labor and centralized policy making were found to be associated with the highest performance levels. Planning time spent by the project leader was not significantly related to performance. A clear diagnosis of problems in administering interdisciplinary research projects does not emerge here.

22. Birnbaum, P.H., "Integration and specialization in academic research." *Academy of Management Journal* 24 (1981): 487-503.

Examines "integrating specialized experts from different disciplines in academic research projects." The hypothesis that "if academic research groups agree on the importance of research outputs as organizational goals, then higher performing groups will have fewer interdisciplinary characteristics and will be less integrated" is supported. Other findings indicate that interdisciplinary integration increases the difficulty in publishing the team's research and that interdisciplinary graduate training does not provide "readily marketable graduates for the scientific marketplace."

23. Birnbaum, P.H., "Contingencies for interdisciplinary research: Matching research questions with research organizations." *Management Science* 27 (November 1981): 1279-1293.

A study of the conditions under which interdisciplinary research helps to improve research performance in 67 ongoing academic interdisciplinary teams in the U.S. and Canada. The chief conclusion is that "interdisciplinary research is more appropriate for very difficult research questions and at early stages of the research process."

24. Birnbaum, P.H., Newell, W.T., and B.O. Saxberg, "Managing academic interdisciplinary research projects." *Decision Sciences* 10 (October 1979): 645-665.

Out of 40 variables suggested by the literature and experienced interdisciplinary research managers, two were found to predict high performance—"the longer an interdisciplinary research group stays together and encourages open discussion of disagreements."

25. Black, R.G., "The interdisciplinary communication problem - Its etiology and therapy." *The Trend in Engineering* 21 (January 1969): 10-18.

The problem exists between the engineer and the physician; course materials in biology and medicine are proposed to facilitate interdisciplinary relations.

26. Blackwell, G.W., "Multidisciplinary team research." *Social Forces* 4 (1955): 367-374.

Early reflections based on the author's experiences at the Institute for Research in Social Science at the University of North Carolina. Reviews "potential problems" and "adjustive mechanisms" in multidisciplinary team research.

27. Blankenship, L.V. and W.H. Lambright, "University research centers: A Comparison of NASA and RANN experiences." AAAS Conference Proceedings 76-R-8, American Association for the Advancement of Science, 1977.

An assessment of two programmatic strategies "to link portions of the scientific community into a research system whose output would be information and technology of applied relevance to problems of national concern."

28. Blunt, Peter, "Methodological developments in the social sciences: Some implications for interdisciplinary study." *New Zealand Psychologist* 10 (1981): 55-70.

A useful discussion, motivated by questions of epistemology and particularly Popper's falsificationist perspective, of methodology in psychology, social anthropology, and management theory. The author advocates the practice of a "methodological eclecticism" by social scientists in interdisciplinary fields such as organizational behavior. The eclecticism should begin at the epistemological level and extend to data analysis, informing the researcher of the "social engineering" potential of his/her methods.

29. Boulding, Kenneth E., "Science: Our common heritage." *Science* 207 (22 February 1980): 831-836.

An adaptation of the author's 1980 AAAS Presidential Lecture that traces knowledge specialization to a common scientific "heritage." Discusses images of science, including "the scientific method," and the relations between "secure" and "insecure" sciences. Concludes with a vision of the unity of human knowledge that is provocative as epistemological and cultural commentary.

30. Bradley, Raymond, T., "Ethical problems in team research: A structural analysis and an agenda for resolution." *The American Sociologist* 12 (May 1982): 87-94.

Discusses organizational needs and forms of team research "to guide prospective collaborators in the negotiation of a written agreement which will protect their individual rights and interests." Though narrowly sociological, the paper has direct relevance to interdisciplinary team composition and perhaps performance.

31. Burdge, R.J. and P. Opryszek, "Interdisciplinary problems in doing impact assessment." *Coping with Change: An Interdisciplinary Assessment of the Lake Shelbyville Reservoir*, University of Illinois at Urbana: Institute for Environmental Studies, (June 1981): 349-359.

Documents an "interdisciplinary effort to examine the 'real' environmental impacts of the Lake Shelbyville (IL) reservoir ten years after it had begun operation." Among the issues explored are project funding, combatting disciplinary chauvinism, and the role of graduate students as team members.

32. Busch, Lawrence, "Disciplinary worlds of agricultural scientists: Scientific and societal implications." Annual Meeting, Rural Sociological Society, Guelph, Ontario (1981).

Examines the extent and implications of disciplinary insularity using data derived from a mail questionnaire sent to agricultural scientists at American state agricultural experiment stations and USDA laboratories. Among the findings germane to interdisciplinarity are: (1) disciplinary problems are likely to receive more support than those that cross disciplinary lines, and (2) the stock of knowledge produced by each of the disciplines may be divorced from that of other disciplines.

33. Campbell, Donald T., "Ethnocentrism of disciplines and the fish-scale of omniscience." In M. Sherif and C.W. Sherif (eds.), *Interdisciplinary Relationships in the Social Sciences*, Chicago: Aldine, 1969.

A conceptual forerunner of much empirical work on

interdisciplinary problems and processes. Within the "fish-scale model," narrow intellectual specialties should overlap to form a comprehensive social science. Instead, due to the ethnocentrism of disciplines, we observe a redundancy among specialties that leaves interdisciplinary gaps. Campbell advocates the training of specialists in these interdisciplinary areas.

34. Cassell, Eric J., "How does interdisciplinary work get done?" In H.T. Engelhardt and D. Callahan (eds.), *Knowledge, Value, and Belief.* New York: The Hastings Center, (1977): 355-361.

A no-nonsense non-technical discussion of interdisciplinary group processes informed by observations made by an M.D. at The Hastings Center, New York.

35. Caudill, W., and B.H. Roberts, "Pitfalls in the organization of interdisciplinary research." *Human Organization* 10 (Winter 1951): 12-15.

An anthropologist and a psychiatrist discuss problems arising from their research collaboration, including "the pressure of publicity," "the common denominator of knowledge," and differences in "orientation to field work."

36. CERI, *Interdisciplinarity: Problems of Teaching and Research in Universities.* Paris: Organization for Economic Cooperation and Development, 1972.

A classic source of wisdom on interdisciplinarity based on a 1970 Seminar on Interdisciplinarity in Universities which was organized by OECD's Centre for Educational Research and Innovation in collaboration with the French Ministry of Education and the University of Nice, France. The report features three parts: Opinions and Facts, Terminology and Concepts, and Problems and Solutions. The latter includes a "sample model of an interdisciplinary university" and a plan for "a center for interdisciplinary synthesis."

37. Chapman, B. and C. Farmi, "The funding of interdisciplinary research in Canada." *Journal of Canadian Studies* 15 (Autumn 1980): 30-33.

Emphasizes "the need to bring about a change in perception - not just in the government but in the Councils and the university community - of the value of interdisciplinary research. There seems at present little encouragement for the development of teams of experts . . . to help tackle the urgent problems facing Canada today."

38. Chen, R.S., "Interdisciplinary research and integration - The case of CO_2 and climate." *Climatic Change* 3 (1981): 429-447.

An interdisciplinary research program on the atmospheric carbon dioxide problem that ties into research on other social and environmental issues is advocated. The steps in such a program include the need to define "conceptual frameworks of climate/society interactions," a division of the problem into tractable parts that allows addressing "the role of information, evaluation, and choice at various levels," and the need "to develop flexible, innovative approaches to research management, with special emphasis on quality control, stable funding, professional opportunities, and interdisciplinary supervision."

39. Chubin, D.E., Rossini, F.A., Porter, A.L., and I.I. Mitroff, "Experimental technology assessment: Explorations in processes of interdisciplinary team research." *Technological Forecasting and Social Change* 15 (1979): 87-94.

Presents the results derived from laboratory simulations of mini-technology assessments. Observations of the TA team interactions reveal a preference for "common-group learning" as the method of problem-solution and an intellectual pecking-order that favors the (stereotyped) insights of the quantitative sciences.

40. Compton, W.D., "Multidisciplinary research." *Physics Today* 24 (1971): 11.

A letter that cautions "that a multidisciplinary research program will fall short of what each discipline would hope for, if that discipline were to examine the problem in its own way."

41. Coyne, Dermot P., "Horticulture and interdisciplinary research." *Hortscience* 14 (December 1979): 686.

A pep talk to horticultural scientists in which the author reminds that "interdisciplinary research is not new in agricultural experiment stations" . . . [but] is also useful in basic research. For example in epidemiology, plant pathologists could cooperate with horticultural geneticists and microclimatologists."

42. Darden, L. and N. Maull, "Interfield theories." *Philosophy of Science* 44 (1977): 43-64.

Analyzes the generation and function of theories which bridge two fields of science. Examples from the history of modern biology are discussed, followed by their implications for understanding the unity and progress of science. Interdisciplinarity remains implicit throughout.

43. David, Edward E., Jr., "Science futures: The industrial connection." *Science* 203 (2 March 1979): 837-840.

Focuses on the need for industrial-academic collaboration in research to enhance both U.S. innovation and economy. Industry's interdisciplinary research organization is advocated as a model.

44. Davis, W.E., III, Interdisciplinary Research in Theory and Practice: A View from the University. Syracuse University, April 1970 (NASA project available through NTIS, N70-33934), 157 pgs.

This master's thesis evaluates the NASA sustaining university program as to its success in meeting a key goal—fostering interdisciplinary research in universities. Drawing on 56 interviews at 5 participating universities, it concludes that the program failed. The thesis explores the premises for interdisciplinary research and the essentials of university structuring. It blames several factors for the failure of the NASA program, including lack of university support for truly interdisciplinary research and that neither side seriously tried to attain that goal. Recommendations for organizational structuring and project managing are offered.

deBie, Pierre, "Introduction" to the special section on "Multidisciplinary problem-focused research." *International Social Science Journal*, 20 (1968): 192-210.

Definition and explanation of problem-focused research in relation to fundamental research and applied research, also a comparison of multidisciplinary to interdisciplinary research [JTK].

45. Delkeskamp, Corinna, "Interdisciplinarity: A critical appraisal." In H.T. Engelhardt and D. Callahan (eds.), *Knowledge, Value, and Belief.* New York: The Hastings Center, 1977.

Reviews the relation of interdisciplinarity to ethics, especially philosophical foundations of the dialogue that separates scholars who consider this very relation.

46. DeWachter, M., "Interdisciplinary team work." *Journal of Medical Ethics* 2 (1976): 52-57.

Five years of experience as a member of a medical ethics team studying "fertility and sterility problems" frames the author's observations on patient contributions to the team's work.

47. di Castri, Francesco, "International, interdisciplinary research in ecology: The case of the man and the biosphere (MAB) programme." *Human Ecology* 4 (1976): 235-246.

Implementing this UNESCO program illustrates "both the potential and the limitations of integrated, international ecological research programs." One imperative for success is that "research workers in various natural and social sciences disciplines and the administrative decision-makers must share responsibility for planning and execution."

48. Epton, S.R., R.L. Payne, and A.W. Pearson, editors, *Managing Interdisciplinary Research.* Chichester, U.K., John Wiley and Sons, 1983.

This volume contains a selection of papers from the Second International Conference on the Management of Interdisciplinary Research held at the Manchester Business School, Manchester, England, in July 1981. Five introductory chapters prepared by the editors on the difference between multidisciplinarity and interdisciplinarity, cross-disciplinarity in action, cross-disciplinarity and organizational forms, and implications for management begin the volume. This is followed by 20 papers and 8 abstracts representing the contributions to the Conference. The collection includes a number of case studies dealing with specific organizations and projects as well as some cross-sectional studies of various aspects of cross-disciplinary research.

49. Fenner, E.H., "A project accounting system that encourages multidisciplinary research." *Engineering Education* 71 (November 1980): 167-169.

   Describes the overcoming of budgetary and accounting obstacles to cross-department research projects at Texas A&M. A "dual accounting system" seems to provide "the proper climate and incentives for interdisciplinary research in educational institutions."

   Frey, Gerhard, "Methodological Problems of Interdisciplinary Discussions." *RATIO* 15 (December 1973): 161-182.

   A careful consideration of conditions which facilitate interdisciplinary discussion, with a survey of methods for achieving agreement and working with different structures of scientific languages [JTK].

   Friedman, Robert C. and Renee C. Friedman, "The Role of University Organized Research Units in Academic Science." Report to the National Science Foundation, Pennsylvania State University, 1982. Everything you wanted to know about organized research units (ORUs) based on interviews with and mail questionnaire responses from representatives of "78 leading research universities and their medical schools." Recommendations include: "Policy makers within the university should develop a system for governing, evaluating, and dismantling ORUs."

50. Gaff, Jerry, A. and Robert C. Wilson, "Faculty cultures and interdisciplinary studies." *Journal of Higher Education* 42 (1971): 186-201.

   A survey of university faculty reveals, among other things, that (1) "most interdisciplinary efforts must be staffed by 'cultural outcasts,' faculty who have resisted narrow cultural conditioning ... (and) are not easy to locate," and (2) "interdisciplinary programs typically pass through a period of adjustment" while faculty members choose to realize their commonly shared values in different ways.

51. Geertz, Clifford, "Blurred genres: The refiguration of social thought." *American Scholar* 56 (Spring 1980): 165-179.
A trenchant essay on the scope of disciplinary provinces, knowledge, and methods and how they might be connected to provide rich interpretations of social systems.

52. Gillespie, D. and P. Birnbaum, "Status concordance, coordination, and success in interdisciplinary research teams." *Human Relations* 33: (1980) 41-56.
Tests a theory on a sample of 67 ongoing interdisciplinary research teams in universities. The authors conclude that team success is not determined by status of participants alone, and that external status criteria are not important in the coordination of teamwork.

53. Gillespie, D.F. and B. Mar, "Interdisciplinary team preproposal management." *Journal of the Society of Research Administrators* 9 (Fall 1977): 33-40.
Focus on inchoative teams engaged in the development of large-scale research proposals. Success was defined as "gaining financial support for the project." Among the findings are: (1) "seed money" is a prerequisite for success, though increasing the amount does not increase team effectiveness; and (2) successful preproposal teams enjoy consensus on goals.

54. Goodwin, William M., and William K. LeBold, "Interdisciplinarity and team teaching." *Engineering Education* 66 (December 1975): 247-254.
A classroom study to evaluate and "improve the social dimensions of engineering practice." The most elusive objective remains development of an interdisciplinary approach to problem-solving.

55. Gumnick, J.L., Appan, S.G., and C.S. Dunn, "Computerized mind support to interdisciplinary consensus formation processes." *Journal of Energy and Environment* 1 (September 1982): 37-60.
How the modeling of "expert group consensus" can improve decision-making. Such "knowledge engineering" utilizes artificial intelligence capabilities.

56. Gusdorf, G., "Past, present and future in interdisciplinary research." *International Social Science Journal* 29 (1977): 580-599.
A French historian warns that "the appeal to interdisciplinarity is seen as a kind of epistemological panacea, designed to cure all the ills the scientific consciousness of our age is heir to." He goes on to show that the appeal is ancient.

57. Hegedus, David M., "The Novel Experiment." Sloan School of Management, M.I.T., Working Paper 1102-80 (February 1980).
Provocative case study of the academic department as "the arena where intellectual forces from several disciplines meet to locally define (and re-define) the academic discipline." Among the issues discussed are "domestic and imported modes" of integrating new content, loyalty, turf defense, and the department as culture broker.

58. Henshel, Richard L., "Effects of disciplinary prestige on predictive accuracy: Distortions from feedback loops." *Futures* (April 1975): 92-106.
Explores the relationship "between predictive power and disciplinary prestige," focusing on the social sciences. The implications of this relationship in multidisciplinary projects—for the interpretation and receptivity of findings—are intriguing.

59. Hopeman, Richard J., and David L. Wilemon, "Reflecting on interdisciplinary research." Syracuse University, occasional paper prepared for NASA and available as NASA document N70-18480, 1970.
This little think piece is notable for 14 recommendations to improve the performance of interdisciplinary research in academic settings. These should be of interest as practical guidance and as potentially testable hypotheses for those studying interdisciplinary research processes.

60. Ikenberry, Stanley O., and Renee C. Friedman, *Beyond Academic Departments: The Story of Institutes and Centers.* San Francisco: Jossey-Bass, 1972.
A study of 125 university institutes, centers, and other research units created to foster multi- and interdisciplinary collaboration and problem solving. As an alternative to academic departments, institutes multiplied in the 1970s but created new problems of organization and administration.

61. Jantsch, Erich, "Inter- and transdisciplinary university: A systems approach to education and innovation." *Policy Sciences* 1 (1970): 403-428.
A transdisciplinary structure for the university is briefly outlined; "its main elements are three types of organizational units - systems design laboratories, function-oriented departments, and discipline-oriented departments - which focus on the interdisciplinary coordination between . . . method and organization."

62. Kamen, Charles S., "The effect of a 'social problem' orientation on the organization of scientific research." *Journal of Environmental Systems* 7 (1977-78): 309-322.

A survey of Israeli scientists and engineers involved in research on environmental quality problems shows that those who define their topics as having social relevance are more likely to employ an interdisciplinary orientation than those who do not.

63. Kaplan, M.B., "The case of the artificial heart panel." *Hastings Center Report* 5 (October 1975): 41-48.

The case is presented as an example of "lay participation in medical policy-making." The paper poses two questions about the interdisciplinary panel and its deliberations: "In what capacity were its members acting, as professional experts applying the skills of their disciplines, or as citizens exercising personal wisdom or representing community values? . . . Could the task of *informing* NHLI (National Heart and Lung Institute) as to the non-medical consequences of the device be separated from the *evaluation* of those consequences?"

64. Kash, D.E., "Observations on interdisciplinary studies and government roles." In R. Scribner and R. Chalk (eds.), *Adapting Science to Social Needs.* Washington, D.C.: AAAS, 1977: 147-167.

Presents a summary of a study of off-shore oil and gas conducted by the Science and Public Policy Program at the University of Oklahoma, one of the first established to do technology assessment. It became noted for its successful interdisciplinary research. The second part of the paper discusses "the institutional levers necessary if a university is to have much chance of carrying out interdisciplinary problem-oriented research."

65. Kast, F.E., J.E. Rosenzweig, and J.W. Stockman, "Interdisciplinary programs in a university setting." *Academy of Management Journal* 13 (1970): 311-324.

A report on "organizational and administrative problems associated with interdisciplinary research programs," as illustrated by the Ceramic Materials Research Program at the University of Washington. A major conclusion: "interdisciplinary research often requires that a hybrid form of organization structure be developed to compensate for obstacles inherent in the university setting."

66. Kendall, Stephen and E.E. Mackintosh, *Management Problems of Polydisciplinary Environmental Research Projects in the University Setting,* Guelph, Ontario: University of Guelph, 1978. Centre for Resources Development Publication #86 (May 1978); also listed as

CANADA/Man and the Biosphere Committee Report #13 (November 1979).

A review of problems and solutions in management of polydisciplinary research focused on both environmental problems and group work in general with valuable summary tables [JTK].

67. Kirton, Michael J., "Adaptors and innovators." *Planned Innovation* (March/April 1980): 51-54.

Presents a theory of the way people approach problems—either as "adaptors" or "innovators." The paper includes a description of the behavior of each type in a group context.

Klein, Julie Thompson, "The Dialectic and Rhetoric of Disciplinarity and Interdisciplinarity." *Issues in Integrative Studies, An Occasional Publication of the Association for Integrative Studies*, 2 (1983): 35-74.

A lengthy critical essay on the relationship between disciplinarity and interdisciplinarity, the interdisciplinary critique of intellectual dichotomies, and the rhetoric of interdisciplinarity [JTK].

Kloza, Marian, Szutukowski, Czeslaw, and Wasniowski, Ryszard (eds.), *Management of Research, Development and Education*, IV International Conference Proceedings, Wroclaw, Poland: Futures Research Center of Wroclaw Technical University (No. 13), 1980.

Includes eleven papers relating to interdisciplinary research. Issues in the conduct of such research in planned economies, the CMEA nations, come forth as relevant to counterpart research in the market economies. International cooperation is explicitly addressed in one paper; papers consider the performance of team research in university (Poland) and industrial (Sweden) settings; and two papers offer conceptual frameworks to study interdisciplinary research.

68. Kockelmans, Joseph (ed.), *Interdisciplinarity, New Experience in Higher Education*. University Park, Penn.: Pennsylvania State University Press, 1979.

Eleven essays on disciplinarity and interdisciplinarity, including curricula, methodology, personal and institutional problems. A "selective listing of interdisciplinary (degree) programs" in Canada and Western Europe is appended. In all, a good source book for the serious interdisciplinarian.

69. Kruytbosch, C., and S.L. Messinger, "Unequal peers: The situation of research at Berkeley." *American Behavioral Scientist* 11 (1968): 33-43.

The second-class citizenship of "researchers" with non-faculty appointments emerges from this Berkeley survey. While not on interdisciplinarity per se, the paper recognizes that "the recent growth of researcher ranks at major universities represents the emergence of a new academic role," and anticipates problems of teamwork, evaluation, and reward entailed by this new role.

70. Lenk, Hans and Gunter Ropohl, "Toward an interdisciplinary and pragmatic philosophy of technology: Technology as a focus for interdisciplinary reflection and systems research." *Research in Philosophy & Technology* 2 (1979): 15-52.

A long review article that synthesizes "philosophical and technological efforts at description, explanation, and interpretation, which are devoted to basic problems of technology." A section is devoted to "Methodology, Interdisciplinary Cooperation, and 'Technocracy'."

71. LePair, C. "Switching between academic disciplines in universities in the Netherlands." *Scientometrics* 2 (May 1980): 177-191.

Field "switchers" and "retainers" in the Netherlands university system, and their implications for informing neighboring scientific disciplines and assessing interdisciplinary merit, are examined empirically.

72. Linstone, H.A. et al., "The multiple perspective concept: With applications to technology assessment and other decision areas." *Technological Forecasting and Social Change* 20 (1981): 275-325.

An empirically-based conceptual paper that concludes with useful "guidelines to assist assessors, forecasters, policy analysts, and other users." Among the most provocative are: "Form the team to assure an interparadigmatic mix rather than merely an interdisciplinary mix" (i.e., the team needs individuals who have been nurtured on different inquiring systems); "Understand the quasicontinuous range of perspectives from the personal to the large formal organization"; and "In most cases, leave the integration of the perspectives to the user or decision maker, but do point out cross-cuing links among them."

Lipton, Michael, "Interdisciplinary Studies in Less Developed Countries." *The Journal of Development Studies* 7 (October 1970): 5-18.

Consideration of why interdisciplinary studies are more strongly indicated in less-developed countries, why they are so sparse, and how they may be improved. See also the reply to Lipton by M.P. Moore, "The Logic of Interdisciplinary Studies," *The Journal of Development Studies* 11 (October 1974): 98-106 [JTK].

73. Long, F.A., "Interdisciplinary problem-oriented research in the university." *Science* 171 (12 March 1971):

Editorial that declares "the most important reason why the universities must become involved in interdisciplinary research . . . is their obligation to youth . . . . College students must learn a genuinely interdisciplinary approach . . ."

74. Luszki, Margaret Barron, *Interdisciplinary Team Research: Methods and Problems*. Washington, D.C. National Training Laboratories, National Education Association, 1958.

A classic analysis of interdisciplinary research successes and failures.

75. MacDonald, William R., "The management of interdisciplinary research teams: A literature review." Report of the Department of the Environment and the Department of Agriculture, Government of Alberta, Edmonton, Alberta, Canada (January 1982).

An attempted synthesis of findings on "factors influencing team performance," "problems with teams," and "problems with the literature." Among the latter, the author observes little attention paid to interdisciplinary teams in nonacademic organizations and "a lack of insight into social issues" such as the need for "new expertise" and the development of "team skills." A perceptive and well-written document.

76. Maruyama, Magorah, "Paradigmatology and its application to cross-disciplinary, cross-professional, and cross-cultural communication." *Cybernetica* (1974): 136-156, 237-281.

A treatise, in two parts, on the origins of "paradigmatology" as a "science of structures of reasoning which vary from discipline to discipline, from profession to profession, from culture to culture, and sometimes even from individual to individual." Part II relates paradigms to social organization and perception, extolling "non-disciplinary programs, decategorization of science and transspecialization." If one can tolerate the neologisms, this is an exemplary discussion by a polymath unchained.

77. McEvoy, James III, "Multi- and interdisciplinary research—Problems of initiation, control, integration and reward." *Policy Sciences* 3 (1972): 201-208.

Outlines the author's "experience as project director of a large interdisciplinary project concerned with man's effects on Lake Tahoe." The difficulties of conducting the project under the NSF-RANN definition of "national need" are described.

Meadows, A.J., "Diffusion of Information Across the Sciences," *Interdisciplinary Science Reviews* 1 (September 1976): 259-267.

Examination of the flow of information within and between scientific disciplines and technologies, including formal channels of communication and interdisciplinary contacts [JTK].

78. Meeth, L. Richard, "Interdisciplinary studies: A matter of definition."
    Change 7 (August 1978): 10.
    An editorial that describes an "interdisciplinary pyramid." *Intra*-
    disciplinarity forms the basis, with *cross*-disciplinary courses
    ("observing one discipline from the perspective of another") a level
    above, *multi*-disciplinary ("several disciplines focused on one
    problem or issue") one higher, *inter*disciplinary ("attempt to
    integrate the contributions of several disciplines to a problem,
    issue, or theme from life") at the next level, and *trans*disciplinary
    ("*beyond* the disciplines ... programs start with the issue or
    problem") at the highest level.

79. Milgram, Stanley, "Interdisciplinary thinking and the small world
    problem." In M. Sherif and C.W. Sherif (eds.), *Interdisciplinary
    Relationships in the Social Sciences*. Chicago: Aldine, 1969.
    Contains conjectures on which stages in the research process
    "interdisciplinary thinking" can be useful.

   Miller, Raymond C., "Varieties of Interdisciplinary Approaches in the
    Social Sciences," *Issues in Integrative Studies, An Occasional
    Publication of the Association for Integrative Studies* 1 (1982):
    1-37.
    A useful account of multidisciplinary, crossdisciplinary, and
    transdisciplinary approaches with a review of definitions, the
    concept of "world view," and many examples of different
    interdisciplinary approaches [JTK].

80. Mitroff, I.I. and L.V. Blankenship, "On the methodology of the holistic
    experiment: An approach to the conceptualization of large-scale
    social experiments." *Technological Forecasting & Social Change* 4
    (1973): 339-353.
    Proposes a multidisciplinary approach to "ill-structured"
    problems. The guidelines for a holistic methodology include "at
    least two 'radically distinct' disciplines of knowledge, . . . kinds of
    conceptualizers, . . . [and] philosophical inquiry models."

81. Mitroff, I.I. and R.O. Mason, "Dialectical pragmatism: A progress
    report on an interdisciplinary program of research on dialectical
    inquiring systems." *Synthese* 47 (1981): 29-42.
    The philosophy and methodology of the "dialectical inquirer" are
    reviewed as an interdisciplinary theory of social scientific practice.

82. Mooney, G.H. and A.H. Williams, "Economists in multidisciplinary
    teams: Some unresolved problems in the conduct of health services
    research." *Social Science and Medicine* 14 (1980): 217-221.
    Report of a meeting at the University of Aberdeen, U.K., that
    brought together five multidisciplinary research teams "to discuss
    the problems involved in integrating economics and economists

into multidisciplinary research teams in health care." Two notable findings: "The economists complained about the difficulty of getting statistical ideas across to doctors, and felt that there should be some obligation on 'the system' to improve its own receptivity to economic argument." Also, "it was unclear who was the 'client' for health services research with an economic component."

83. Nelson, Neil, "Issues in funding and evaluating interdisciplinary research." *Journal of Canadian Studies* 15 (Autum 1980): 25-29.
Argues that IDR contributes three things "to scholarship and to society": "gap-bridging," "synergy," and "problem-solving." This paper reports on two workshops convened in 1978 and 1979 by the Human Environment Committee of the Social Science Federation of Canada. Each workshop focused on the research team reward systems, and evaluating both proposals and outcomes. Considerations of "replenishing our academic gene pool" with "interdisciplinary-oriented colleagues" are raised.

84. Nilles, J.M., "Interdisciplinary research and American university." *Interdisciplinary Science Reviews* 1 (1976): 160-166.
Addresses the central question "Can interdisciplinary research be managed effectively at a university in the United States?" The perspectives of several actors at this site are considered: administrator, educator, faculty researcher, research manager, donor of external funding, and ultimate user of the research. A series of recommendations are included.

85. Nilles, J.M., "Interdisciplinary research management in the university environment." *Journal of the Society of Research Administrators* 6 (Spring 1975): 9-15.
After outlining the difficulties of managing interdisciplinary research at the university, the author waxes optimistic: "The universities can provide the detachment from the immediate pressures of certain short term first order applications and special interest goals . . . which is so necessary for effective IDR. The universities have the unique advantage of being able to maintain a large pool of expertise which is not dependent for survival on externally funded research. They are beginning to realize this strength and take effective measures to develop it." Unfounded optimism?

86. Odhner, Fred, "Group dynamics of the interdisciplinary team." *American Journal of Occupational Therapy* 24 (October 1970): 484-487.
Reviews T-group process and its application to interdisciplinary interaction and "the effectiveness of the health team," not research per se.

87. Paelinck, Jean H/P. (ed)., *Issues in Interdisciplinarity*, Proceedings of a Seminar, Rotterdam Institute for Multi- and Interdisciplinary Research (RIMIR), Erasmus University, Rotterdam, The Netherlands, 1982.

Features ten papers, four on "fundamental issues" and six "applications" to psycho-medicine, spatial analysis, statistical modelling, and medical care. An eleventh, purported synthesis afterward by the econometrician-editor fails to consolidate the diverse, largely quantitative contributions that precede it.

88. Payne, Roy and Alan Pearson, "International Conference on Management of international comparison of their organization and management." *R & D Management* (1979): 35-37.

A summary report on the first International Conference on Management of Interdisciplinary Research held in Schloss Reisensburg, West Germany, in April 1979. Thirty experts representing 10 countries participated. The importance of developing evaluation measures of interdisciplinary research was stressed.

89. Peston, Maurice, "Some thoughts on evaluating interdisciplinary research." *Higher Education Review* 10 (1978): 55-60.

"The key issue is a somewhat paradoxical one of preventing the interdisciplinary project from being destroyed by the competing claims of the individual disciplines while providing for it some appropriate foundation which, to put the point in its crudest terms, enables it to be 'academically respectable'." According to Peston, "the trouble is simply that . . . we have no subject called interdisciplinary science, and, therefore, no resting home for our results."

90. Petrie, H.D., "Do you see what I see? The epistemology of interdisciplinary inquiry." *Journal of Aesthetic Education* 10 (1976): 9-15.

Reports the experience of an interdisciplinary faculty group discussing "the interdisciplinary research and teaching process." Considers participants' psychological characteristics, institutional setting, and Polanyi's notion of "tacit knowledge." Suggests that metaphor may be a key to bridging the categories and concepts of different disciplines.

91. Piaget, Jean, *Main Trends in Interdisciplinary Research*. London: Allen and Unwin, 1973.

A structuralist approach to IDR. Locating responsibility for developing IDR in the "human sciences," the author declares that "to reshape or reorganize the fields of knowledge by means of exchanges which are in fact constructive recombinations" or hybridizations. Examples include psycholinguistics, social psychology, and ethology.

92. Pignataro, L.J. and W.R. McShane, "Interdisciplinary research - transcending departmental conflicts." *Engineering Education* 69 (January 1979): 349-351.

   A discussion based on the Transportation Training and Research Center at the Polytechnic Institute of New York.

93. Pilet, P.E., "The multidisciplinary aspects of biology - basic and applied research." *Scientia* 116 (1981): 629-636.

   Building on the "interdisciplinary nature" of biology, the author, (translated from the French) expounds on the need for "centers devoted especially on research into research," and on researchers' "dialectical reflection upon . . . the reasons underlying their intellectual activity."

94. Polishuk, Paul, "Problems in interdisciplinary policy research and management in government." *IEEE Transactions on Engineering Management* 23 (May 1976): 92-100.

   Interdisciplinary research is seen as appropriate for establishing "a telecommunications policy analysis function within the U.S. Department of Commerce." A detailed guide to managing interdisciplinary policy research is provided.

95. Porter, A.L., Rossini, F.A., Chubin, D.E., and T. Connolly, "Between disciplines." *Science* 209 (29 August 1980): 966.

   Letter lamenting the lack of NSF funding for research that studies interdisciplinary problems and processes.

96. Porter, Arthur, "Expansion of transdisciplinary studies." *Transactions of the Royal Society of Canada* 11 (1973): 11-20.

   After praising academic departments, the author considers the administration of transdisciplinary studies. He concludes that "faculty members . . . who undertake transdisciplinary teaching, research, and service to the community should be encouraged and rewarded appropriately," and "existing administrative arrangements . . . should be reassessed in the light of increasing interest in mission-directed activities. Perhaps an interdisciplinary division should be added to the traditional divisions of graduate faculties."

97. Rajagopal, R., "Interdisciplinary research and education for ecosystems management." *Urban Systems* 4 (1979): 43-52.

   Discusses the scope and limitation of systems analysis as a framework for integrating varied disciplinary efforts in resource and environmental management.

98. Riley, M.W., "Phases encountered by a project team." *IEEE Transactions on Education* 23 (November 1980): 212-213.

Seven phases of interdisciplinary study that "all engineers" will encounter "sometime during their career" are outlined. They are: initial enthusiasm, data gathering, group divergence, group convergence, group panic, group effort, and group accomplishment.

99. Robertson, Ivan T., "Some factors associated with successful interdisciplinary research." *Journal of the Society of Research Administrators* 13 (Fall 1981): 44-50.

A preliminary analysis of 150 interdisciplinary research projects conducted within manufacturing or service organizations in the U.K. Emphasis is on psychological and personal characteristics of the individual researchers.

100. Rose, Richard, "Disciplined research and undisciplined problems." *International Social Science Journal* 28 (1976): 99-121.

Examines "the organizational causes of the uneasy relationship between social scientists and government officials and the extent to which the intrinsic character of the 'undisciplined' problems of contemporary societies make this relationship both relevant and difficult." Multi- and interdisciplinary research approaches are proposed to relieve the difficulty.

101. Rossi, P.H., "Researchers, scholars, and policy makers: The politics of large-scale research." *Daedalus* 93 (1964): 1142-1161.

Considers "the organizational consequences of the development of research centers within the university environment." Much of this has been superseded by the creation of "organized research units" in the late 1960's and '70s, but this paper foreshadows such innovations without discussing interdisciplinarity per se.

102. Rossini, F.A. and A.L. Porter, "Frameworks for integrating interdisciplinary research." *Research Policy* 8 (1979): 70-79.

Summarizes the findings of a two-year, NSF-supported study of process of integrating the disciplinary components of technology assessment (TA) projects. Findings include factors affecting project integration, especially communication pattern, leadership style, and "intellectual distances" between team members. Recommendations for integrating TAs stress "organizational context," "structural and process factors," and "frameworks for performing TA components."

103. Rossini, F.A. and A.L. Porter, "Interdisciplinary research: Performance and policy issues." *Journal of the Society of Research Administrators* 13 (Fall 1981): 8-24.

A conceptualization of interdisciplinary research that argues for its growth and significance. Among the issues discussed here are approaches to the social and intellectual organization of a TA, a causal model of TA integration, and institutional arrangements that affect interdisciplinary research performance and proposed problem solutions.

Rossini, F.A., Porter, A.L., Kelly, P., and Chubin, D.E., "Interdisciplinary Integration Within Technology Assessments." *Knowledge: Creation, Diffusion, Utilization* 2 1981: 503-528.

An empirical study of factors affecting the degree of interdisciplinary integration achieved in 24 technology assessments supported by the National Science Foundation.

104. Rothman, Harry, "Measuring European scientific capability in biotechnology." Presented to the FAST Biosociety Meeting, Brussels (March 1982), mimeo: Technology Policy Unit, University of Aston, U.K.

Intriguing tidbits on interdisciplinary research based on various literature-based indicators, including journal and national citation patterns, in the area of biotechnology.

105. Rouse, William B., "On models and modelers: N cultures." *IEEE Transactions: Man, Systems, and Cybernetics* SMC-12 (September/October 1982): 605-610.

Multidisciplinary problem-solving is contrasted with disciplinary perspectives. Three dimensions are seen as barriers to disciplinary solutions: age of discipline, nature of the phenomena investigated, and "intellectual world within which the discipline operates." Systems engineering, the author concludes, spans the boundaries of problems, disciplines, and solution, rendering it the ideal interdiscipline.

106. Roy, Rustum, "Interdisciplinary science on campus—the elusive dream." *C&E News* (29 August 1977): 28-40.

Asserting that "interdisciplinarity is inherent in the nature of reality," especially that part of it dealing with the problems of society, the author proposes models for creating interdisciplinary units on campus, their relationship to departments, and resource needs.

107. Russell, Martha Garrett (ed.), *Enabling Interdisciplinary Research: Perspectives from Agriculture, Forestry, and Home Economics* Miscellaneous Publication - 19, Agricultural Experiment Station University of Minnesota, 1982.

A provocative four-part collection plus a 48-item annotated bibliography. The two dozen chapters are capped by the editor's thoughts on evaluating IDR: "It explores the need to employ multiple assessment criteria so as to maintain both disciplinary rigor and interdisciplinary relevance."

108. Salmon-Cox, Leslie and Burkart Holzner, "Managing Multidisciplinarity: Building and Bridging Epistemologies in Educational R&D." Presented to American Educational Research Association (April 1977): mimeo.
Building a multidisciplinary environment in an academic setting "requires both strategies of resocialization and organization." An application to a Learning Research and Development Center is offered.

109. Saxberg, B.O., Newell, W.T., and B.W. Mar, "Interdisciplinary research - A dilemma for university central administration." *Journal of the Society of Research Administrators* 13 (Fall 1981): 25-43.
Based on site visits to major research universities, the authors report on problems related to "organized research units," e.g., institutes and centers. In general, there is an absence of policies or procedures for recognizing interdisciplinary research efforts and rewarding them relative to "single discipline/single investigator" projects.

110. Schneider, Stephen H., "Climate change and the world predicament: A case study for interdisciplinary research." *Climatic Change* 1 (1977): 21-43.
Presents a rationale for an interdisciplinary treatment of climate change. Discusses obstacles to and opportunities for the performance of interdisciplinary research, including how to foster it in the university.

111. Sharp, James M. and James L. Gumnick, "A method for peer group appraisal and interpretation of data developed in interdisciplinary research programs." *Journal of the Society of Research Administrators* 13 (Fall 1981): 51-66.
Report of insights gained by Gulf Universities Research Consortium after 16 years of operation, and particularly, how "peer groups" are used to frame and perform interdisciplinary projects.

112. Sherif, Muzafer and Carolyn W. Sherif, "Interdisciplinary coordination as a validity check: Retrospect and prospects." In M. Sherif and C.W. Sherif (eds.), *Interdisciplinary Relationships in the Social Sciences.* Chicago: Aldine, 1969.
Reviews the utility of interdisciplinary work in the social sciences.

113. Simonton, Dean Keith, "Interdisciplinary creativity over historical time: A correlational analysis of generational fluctuations." *Social Behavior and Personality* 3 (1975): 181-188.

The interdisciplinary relationships among 15 kinds of creative achievements are examined "over 130 generations of European history." Three major interdisciplinary clusters are found: "(a) discursive (science, philosophy, literature, and music), (b) presentational (painting, sculpture, and architecture), and (c) rationalism - mysticism (physical science and general philosophy versus religion and painting)." Among the possible explanations given is that "because scientists, philosophers, poets, and even . . . musicians all employ 'discursive' writing as a communicative medium, creativity in any one discipline may encourage creative activity in others."

114. Sinaceur, M., "What is interdisciplinarity?" *International Social Science Journal* 29 (1977): 572-579.

An editorial statement hailing the study of interdisciplinarity as a problem in its own right.

115. Steck, R. and J. Sundermann, "The effects of group size and cooperation on the success of interdisciplinary groups in R&D." *R&D Management* 8 (1978): 59-64.

Tests a mathematical model of the "relationships between cooperation among researchers and the chances of success interdisciplinary groups may have." Team size and internal structure of research groups emerge as significant correlates of success.

116. Steck, R., "How can research on research contribute to a better management of university research?" *R&D Management* 6 (February 1976): 81-86.

Reports on the "*Sonderforschungsbereich* 79, a large interdisciplinary academic research unit concerned with 'water research in the coastal area'." The results of this experiment to involve "research on research" scientists with specialists in the subject under investigation appear worthwhile for informing participants about management problems in research organization.

Stoddard, Ellwyn R., "Multidisciplinary Research Funding: A 'Catch 22' Enigma," *The American Sociologist* 17 (November 1982): 210-216. Case study of problems in funding interdisciplinary research, based on U.S.—Mexico borderlands studies [JTK].

117. Stone, Anthony R., "The interdisciplinary research team." *Journal of Applied Behavioral Science* 5 (July 1969): 351-365.

A role analysis of the interdisciplinary team as an interacting task-oriented group. Groups are discussed as approximating, and often combining, the characteristics of primary - and secondary - group ideal types.

118. Stucki, J.C., "A goal oriented pharmaceutical research and development organization: An eleven year experience." In R.T. Barth and R. Steck (eds.), *Interdisciplinary Research Groups: Their Management and Organization*, (1979).

Upjohn Company's pharmaceutical R&D organization is compared "then and now." Multidisciplinary organization and decentralized leadership are seen as central for product discovery, development, and commercialization.

119. Taylor, James B., "Building an interdisciplinary team." In S.R. Arnstein and A.N. Christakis (eds.), *Perspectives on Technology Assessment*. Jerusalem: Science and Technology Publishers, 1975: 45-60.

Presents a profile of the "ideal polymath" and his/her role in interdisciplinary problem-solving.

120. Teich, A.H., "Trends in the organization of academic research: The role of ORUs and full time researchers." In R.T. Barth and R. Steck (eds.), *Interdisciplinary Research Groups: Their Management and Organization*, (1979).

A empirical study of the "organized research unit" within U.S. universities. ORUs operate outside of discipline-centered departments, usually have large-scale facilities, and are problem-oriented (in a multidisciplinary sense). Such campus-wide institutes, centers, or programs present challenges to traditional organizational structures, rewards, and personnel. Of particular interest is what Teich terms "the unfaculty."

121. Thomas, Dorothy Swaine, "Experiences in interdisciplinary research." *American Sociological Review* 17 (December 1952): 663-669.

The author's presidential address to the American Sociological Association stresses the connections, derived from 30 years of research experiences, between economics and sociology, theory and data.

122. Toulmin, Stephen, "From form to function: Philosophy and history of science in the 1950s and now." *Daedalus* 106 (Summer 1977): 143-162.

An intellectual history, partly autobiographical, in which the author traces the parallel developments of the history and philosophy of science in the 1950s and before to their convergence, if not interdisciplinary synthesis, beginning in the mid-1960s. The author, an evolutionary thinker, sees "problem-oriented" issues as gaining precedence over "discipline-oriented" research, and boldly predicts that "after a generation of concentration on interdisciplinary, concrete issues, new constellations of technical problems will be abstracted out to serve as the foci of new disciplines; and these will then need about thirty years to develop their own specialized theoretical ideas and techniques . . ."

123. Valaskakis, K., "Rewards and tribulations of interdisciplinary futures studies." *Industrialization Forum* 6 (1975): 41-46.

Within the context of "an interdisciplinary study of the problems and repercussions of conservation policies in a 'consumer' society," the author declares interdisciplinarity "virtually indispensable for futures studies." The avoidance of "discipline-imperialism" and the skills of the project leader are stressed.

124. Vlachy, Jan, "The measures of interdisciplinarity in research." Czechoslovak Academy of Sciences (June 1971).

Features a 92-item bibliography, including much Eastern European literature; grapples with the question "what is interdisciplinary research?".

125. Vlachy, Jan, "More data on interdisciplinarity." *Teorie a Metoda* 3 (1971): 63-79.

Presents a quantitative picture of interdisciplinary and multidisciplinary activities. A range of bibliometric data is displayed by specialty and author.

126. Walsh, W.B., G.L. Smith, and M. London, "Developing an interface between engineering and the social sciences." *American Psychologist* 30 (1975): 1067-1071.

Describes a first-hand experience with teaching an interdisciplinary course in societal problem-solving and the virtues of a student-centered approach.

127. Walters, C., "Interdisciplinary approach to development of watershed simulation models." *Journal of the Fisheries Research Board of Canada* 32 (1975): 177-195.

The key feature of the approach is "intimate involvement of resource specialists in the model building process, so that communication between resource disciplines is greatly enhanced." Two watershed models are discussed at length.

128. Weinberg, A.M., "Scientific teams and scientific laboratories." *Daedalus* 10 (January 1970): 1056-1075.

The author seeks "to trace the origins of big team science . . ., to estimate the capacity of this new scientific style to launch and carry off the scientific breakthroughs so necessary for the progress of science, and finally to speculate on the future of team research and its institutions." The author urges "trying an interdisciplinary team attack."

129. Weingart, Jerome M., "Transdisciplinary science - Some recent experience with solar energy conversion research." Annual Meeting, American Association for the Advancement of Science, Denver (February 1977).

An informal think-piece informed by the author's experiences at the Caltech Environmental Quality Laboratory in a solar energy research team.

130. White, I.L., "Interdisciplinarity." In S.R. Arnstein and A.N. Christakis (eds.), *Perspectives on Technology Assessment.* Jerusalem: Science and Technology Publishers, 1975: 87-96.

A review of the author's experiences in the University of Oklahoma Science and Public Policy Program. Four salient items in the conduct of interdisciplinary technology assessments are discussed: language problems, quality control, institutional barriers/ incentives, and personality characteristics associated with team success.

131. Wilbanks, Tom, "Communications between hard and soft sciences." *Oak Ridge National Laboratory Review*, (Spring 1979): 24-29.

Reflecting on his experiences in "an interdisciplinary technology assessment program" at the University of Oklahoma and as a senior planner at ORNL, the author describes ways to "build a first-rate social science research capability in a research institution that has always emphasized the physical sciences, life sciences, and engineering specialties." Wilbanks' prescription includes "joint responsibility for written reports," physical proximity of team members, and the presence of "exceptional gatekeepers."

132. Wilcox, Timothy J., "The Interpersonal Group As a Facilitative Structure for Grant Review Decision-Making." PhD Dissertation, University of Nebraska, Lincoln, 1982.

Notes that there is evidence that grant support depends on acceptance by most dominant members of the grant review group. Suggests possible utility of the "Interpersonal Transaction" approach wherein all interaction except voting on the proposal's merits takes place in dyads (every combination). Experiment with psychology undergraduates supports possible efficacy of IT in mock proposal review process.

133. Williams, Anne S., Nielsen, G.A., Shovic, H.F., Stuart, D.G., and J.W. Reuss. Guidelines for Conducting Interdisciplinary Applied Research in a University Setting. Montana State University, Institute of Applied Research Monograph No. 2, Bozeman, MT, April 1976, (available through NTIS PB 260 503), 22 pgs.

Researchers reflect on the experiences of a six-year sequence of interdisciplinary research projects on the proposed Big Sky resort development in Montana. This large scale, university-based effort began with 27 subprojects, experienced a shift in project goals as the sponsoring NSF unit changed from IRRPOS to RANN, and readjusted its research management strategy markedly. This report chronicles project activities in terms of interdisciplinary research issues.

134. Winnicki, T. and B. Glowiak, "Management of large-scale interdisciplinary environmental programs." *R&D Management* 8 (1978): 127-132.

Summarizes the experience of organizing and managing environmental research programs in Warsaw.

135. Wohl, R. Richard, "Some observations on the social organization of interdisciplinary social science research." *Social Forces* 33 (1955): 374-383.

The author observes, in 1955, that "interdisciplinary ventures abound" in the social sciences; that a 1952 survey at Harvard reveals that "the chief complaints against interdisciplinary research seemed less directed to its intrinsic characteristics than to the uncritical enthusiasm of some of its advocates"; and that "the occasion for interdisciplinary collaboration arises from the very fact of specialization." Finally, "the successful conduct of an interdisciplinary research enterprise imposes on its members and leadership the need to synchronize moods, feelings, and social relationship as well as their pattern of ideas and inquiry." Sobering words to read three decades later: how far has interdisciplinarity come? Wohl anticipates that, too: "Interdisciplinary social science research is essentially an act of faith continually renewed by the hopeful."

136. Wolfle, Dael L., "Interdisciplinary research as a form of research." *Journal of the Society of Research Administrators* 13 (Fall 1981): 5-7.

Lead article in a special issue devoted to interdisciplinary research. The author reminds us that consensus on the definition of interdisciplinary research is lacking, and that both management issues (related to people) and scientific issues (related to work) are involved in such research and must be analyzed accordingly.

Zaprielian, Z.A. and J.M. Nilles, "Background Material and Summary Report for a Workshop on the Management of Interdisciplinary Research, 9-10 July 1974," University of Southern California

Report to National Science Foundation on Grant No. NM-39528, 1974.
Appendix C contains findings and directives on issues such as tradeoffs in IDR, incentives, managerial control, maintaining flexibility, and planning, review and evaluation.

NAME INDEX

SUBJECT INDEX